Race, Taste and the Grape

With the introduction of wine to the Cape Colony, it became associated locally with social extremes: with the material trappings of privilege and taste, on the one side, and the stark realities of human bondage, on the other. By examining the history of Cape wine, Paul Nugent offers a detailed history of how, in South Africa, race has shaped patterns of consumption. The book takes us through the Liquor Act of 1928, which restricted access along racial lines, intervention to address overproduction from the 1960s, and then latterly, in the wake of the fall of the Apartheid regime, deregulation in the 1990s and South Africa's re-entry into global markets. We see how the industry struggled to embrace Black Economic Empowerment, environmental diversity and the consumer market. This book is an essential read for those interested in the history of wine, and how it intersects with both South African and global history.

PAUL NUGENT is Professor of Comparative African History at the University of Edinburgh. He specializes in borders and wine history, is the Founder/Chair of African Borderlands Research Network (ABORNE), a recipient of ERC Advanced Grant, a member of the American Association of Wine Economists, and teaches 'Wine and Global History' in Edinburgh. His most recent book is *Boundaries, Communities and State-Making in West Africa: The Centrality of the Margins* (Cambridge University Press, 2019).

Race, Taste and the Grape

South African Wine from a Global Perspective

Paul Nugent

University of Edinburgh

CAMBRIDGE
UNIVERSITY PRESS

CAMBRIDGE
UNIVERSITY PRESS

Shaftesbury Road, Cambridge CB2 8EA, United Kingdom

One Liberty Plaza, 20th Floor, New York, NY 10006, USA

477 Williamstown Road, Port Melbourne, VIC 3207, Australia

314–321, 3rd Floor, Plot 3, Splendor Forum, Jasola District Centre, New Delhi – 110025, India

103 Penang Road, #05–06/07, Visioncrest Commercial, Singapore 238467

Cambridge University Press is part of Cambridge University Press & Assessment, a department of the University of Cambridge.

We share the University's mission to contribute to society through the pursuit of education, learning and research at the highest international levels of excellence.

www.cambridge.org
Information on this title: www.cambridge.org/9781009184250

DOI: 10.1017/9781009184274

First published 2024
First paperback edition 2025

A catalogue record for this publication is available from the British Library

Library of Congress Cataloging-in-Publication data
Names: Nugent, Paul, 1962- author.
Title: Race, taste and the grape : South African wine from a global perspective / Paul Nugent.
Description: Cambridge ; New York, NY : Cambridge University Press, 2024. | Includes bibliographical references.
Identifiers: LCCN 2023026575 (print) | LCCN 2023026576 (ebook) | ISBN 9781009184267 (hardback) | ISBN 9781009184250 (paperback) | ISBN 9781009184274 (epub)
Subjects: LCSH: Wine industry–South Africa–History. | Wine and wine making–South Africa–History. | South Africa–Race relations–Economic aspects.
Classification: LCC HD9387.S72 N84 2024 (print) | LCC HD9387.S72 (ebook) | DDC 338.4/766320968–dc23/eng/20230705
LC record available at https://lccn.loc.gov/2023026575
LC ebook record available at https://lccn.loc.gov/2023026576

ISBN 978-1-009-18426-7 Hardback
ISBN 978-1-009-18425-0 Paperback

To all the Nugents, Skinners and Langfords scattered around Cape Town, Perth and the UK

to Kwally and Jasmine

and to the memory of Francis 'Duimpie' Bayly, a true legend of the Cape wine industry

Note on the Text

The term 'Coloured' is a heavily loaded term embodying a complex history in the South African context. It emerged over the course of the nineteenth century on the back of the ending of slavery. It was a composite category that included those who were of slave and Khoi ancestry. It became further entrenched under segregationism in the 1920s, and was inscribed in law under the Population Registration Act of 1950, but with the recognition of Cape Malays (Muslim and mostly urban) and other sub-categories. People categorized as Coloured occupied an intermediate social position between people legally designated as White and as Bantu/Black. Despite the attempt to guarantee racial purity, many Coloured people had White ancestry and many White people had ancestors who were actually Khoi or slave. In the twentieth century, most of the work on wine farms was carried out by those who were formally classified as Coloured (excluding the Cape Malays). Although many have objected to the term on political grounds, it continues to be used today - including by those to whom the name is attached. In this text I refer to 'White', 'Coloured' and 'Black' - categories that are rooted in segregationist and apartheid discourse, but which are impossible to avoid using because they have meaning for the actors themselves.

Contents

Figures

Tables

Acknowledgements

The seeds for this book were sown in the 1970s, when I was growing up in Fish Hoek in the southern suburbs of Cape Town. Fish Hoek was (in)famous for being a dry town, with local bylaws prohibiting bottle stores and even the sale of alcohol in restaurants and hotels. Putting it crudely, the intention was to keep the Coloured population from coming to the town and drinking in the streets.[1] Predictably, liquor outlets operating just beyond the border did a roaring trade in wine and beer that was ordered by telephone and shipped in by minibus. Fish Hoek was historically a bastion of temperance, but it was also a place where prodigious amounts of alcohol were consumed. I can still recall my first encounter with a product called *Paarl Perlé* that my brothers, Peter and Tony, had smuggled into the house. On weekends, when my father visited the bottle store in Glencairn, I would tag along with my sister, Diddy – captivated by the packaging and advertising images that were on display.

Having spent most of my academic career researching West Africa, I eventually began to reflect more on this period of my life. As my personal tastes shifted towards wine, I also began to read my way into the subject. A reconnaissance visit convinced me that while there was much that was written about South African wine, there was rather little of a historical nature. On my return, I applied successfully for a Leverhulme Trust Research Fellowship for a project entitled 'Race, Taste and the Grape: The Cape Wine Industry' (2009). This enabled me to spend a year located in Franschhoek, and to secure an attachment to the University of Stellenbosch with the assistance of Joachim Ewert. I am grateful to the Leverhulme Trust for the opportunity to engage in a sustained period of research, which has taken much longer to put in the bottle than I could possibly have imagined at the time.

When I embarked on this journey, I imagined that I would be able to negotiate access to the archives of the KWV, which had accumulated information on every wine farm. But despite the cooperation of the then chairman,

[1] The term 'Coloured' is rooted in segregationist and apartheid discourse. See the 'Note on the Text' on page vi for more detail about the history and use of this term in South Africa.

Danie de Wet, I was only able to access the photographic collection. I remain grateful for this, and a couple of examples grace the pages of this book. But when I enquired about all the other material that I knew must surely exist, I was variously told that there were no records or that they were confidential. A small group of files relating to quota regulations had been passed to the South African Wine Information and Systems (SAWIS), and I am most grateful to Yvette van der Merwe for granting access to these as well as to statistical data. At SAWIS, I also spent many weeks poring over copies of *Wynboer* and dissertations submitted to the Cape Wine Academy, with the friendly guidance of Joan Fortuin and Samantha Bennett. It was here that I was also able to meet one of the legends of the KWV, Kallie Hickman, who walked me through the quota regulations.

Having failed to secure access to the kind of documentary record that I had anticipated, I needed to find another way into my topic. Fortunately, two old hands in the industry, David Hughes and Francis 'Duimpie' Bayly (alas both recently deceased), alerted me to the fact that Distell maintained an archive of its own. This brought together the materials collected by the Stellenbosch Farmers Winery (SFW) and Distillers Corporation, and the records of the many companies they had absorbed over many decades. I secured permission to use this collection and spent a good part of my time delving into the ledgers that covered winemaking at specific farms and the Guard Books that detailed all the products that these companies marketed. I am most grateful to Distell for access and to Mareza Nel for giving me the run of the open shelves. My other way in was to ask particular producers if I could view their farm records. Simon Barlow very kindly permitted me to immerse myself in the diaries kept by successive winemakers at Rustenberg. In addition, Phillip Myburgh Jr invited me to look at the records of Joostenberg.

In the early stages of this project, I received invaluable assistance from a number of individuals. Gavin Williams showed me the documents he had collected. This exchange helped me to define certain lines of enquiry which I hoped would not overlap too much with his own. In Stellenbosch, Diko Van Zyl was overwhelmingly generous and shared the extended version of his official history of the KWV. Michael Fridjhon, who many regard as the doyen of South African wine critics, kindly helped me with a number of introductions to producers. I encountered the indefatigable Duimpie Bayly at an early point in the research, and he remained a sounding board until the end – with discussions often transacted, most enjoyably, over a glass of wine.

I have never ceased to be surprised by the generosity of farmers who have shared information and opinions freely. In the Hemel-en-Aarde valley, Tim Hamilton Russell agreed to be interviewed on successive occasions and granted me access to his papers, which enabled me to piece together the story of his own battles with the KWV and the Wine and Spirits Board. I also benefited from discussions with the late Spatz Sperling at Delheim, with the assistance of Nora Sperling. I am immensely grateful for all those who agreed to share their insights into some of the more contentious issues – especially Charles Back (Fairview/Spice Route), Paul Cluver Sr (Paul Cluver Wines), Jan 'Boland' Coetzee (Vriesenhof), Danie De Wet (De Wetshof), Lourens Jonker (Weltevrede and former chairman of KWV), Johan and François Malan (Simonsig), John Nel (Camberley) and Mark Solms (Solms-Delta).

I was extremely fortunate to be granted a fellowship at the Stellenbosch Institute for Advanced Study (STIAS), which I was allowed to stretch out over 2012, 2014 and 2015. I am thankful to the then director, Hendrik Geyer, and to all the staff, especially Nel-Mari Loock, Maria Mouton and Christoff Paauw, for their help in rendering my time there productive. I benefited from many discussions with other fellows over the legendary lunches. I would especially like to acknowledge Simon Bekker, Jane Carruthers and Eddie Webster. It turned out that Eddie was related to the prominent temperance activist Rev. A. J. Cook, and he helped put me in touch with Fiona McCutcheon. She, in turn, permitted me to view some of his papers that are in her possession. I am also grateful to Chris Venter for sharing some of his unpublished work. I would also like to acknowledge others who have shared information and experiences, especially Tim James, Mike Meadows, Jonathan Steyn, Karl Storchmann and Raphaela van Embden. Finally, I would also like to acknowledge the School of History, Classics and Archaeology in Edinburgh for the funding that enabled me to update the original research in 2019. I have benefited enormously from comments and critique by anonymous external reviewers, who went to extraordinary lengths to improve the manuscript and saved me from some egregious errors. At Cambridge University Press, Maria Marsh and Atifa Jiwa were as accommodating and helpful as ever.

As one might expect, a project such as this has been dissected with friends and colleagues over countless windswept *braais* in Cape Town, Stellenbosch, Princeton and Edinburgh. I would especially like to thank Tom Molony, José-María Muñoz, Elaine Peña, Hugh Lamarque, Rob Macdonald, Ellie Gambino, Sidy Cissokho, Jean-Benoît Falisse, Laavy Kathiravelu, Basile Ndjio, Ulf Engel, Jan-Bart Gewald, Preben Kaarsholm, Filippo Petrucci, Nicola Melis, Alessandro Pes, Valeria Deplano, Emma Hunter, Hazel Gray, Barbara Bompani, George Karekwaivanane, Ton Dietz, Manuel Ramos, Andreas Mehler, Davide Chinigò and the entire team at the Centre of African Studies, including the 'Mozzies'. As has become the custom, Isabella Soi read drafts of most chapters when they were in a less than elegant state, and in most cases, she even helped to make them better. In Cape Town, I have enjoyed sharing opinions with Margaret Howie and Dale Whitfield. Fiona De Beer and Rod Baker have helped me to keep up with what is hot in Constantia and have hosted numerous (faintly surreal) *braais* with family and the occasional winemaker in attendance.

This book is dedicated to all the Nugents in South Africa, Australia and the United Kingdom, and those they got hitched to. In Cape Town, my brother Tony, and Daniela Vignazi, have hung out and (helpfully) grilled me about when this book might ever see the light of day. I am grateful to them, to Diddy and Marc Skinner, to Mike Nugent and Mel Andrews, and to Colleen Nugent for keeping the pressure on. I would also like to acknowledge the Australian Nugents, especially Peter, Aoife (with whom I conducted a memorable road trip in the company of Frank Zappa and Osibisa), Medhbh, Fionnuala, Colin and Hilde Mooney. Finally, Eliane, Kwally and Jasmine shared much of this wine journey in Franschhoek and Stellenbosch. I am hoping that some of the interest in wine and history will eventually rub off on the last two, who are already displaying some impressive wine knowledge of their own.

Note on Measurements

In the text, conversions have been made to hectolitres (hl.) and hectares (ha) based on the following conversion factors:

1 hectolitre = 100 litres
1 leaguer = 578 litres or 5.78 hectolitres
1 imperial gallon = 4.55 litres or 0.0455 hectolitres
1 morgen = 0.86 hectares or 2.12 acres
1 acre = 0.405 hectares

Abbreviations

ANC	African National Congress
AOC	Appellation d'Origine Contrôlée
ARC	Agricultural Research Council
B-BBEE	Broad-Based Black Economic Empowerment
BAWSI	Black Association for the Wine and Spirits Industry
BEE	Black Economic Empowerment
BUSCO	Wine Industry Business Support Committee
BWI	Biodiversity and Wine Initiative
BWSA	Biodynamic and Organic Wines of South Africa
CCLC	Cape Coloured Liquor Commission
CEWPA	Cape Estate Wine Producers Association
COSATU	Confederation of South African Trade Unions
CWD	Cape Wine and Distillers
CWSI	Cape Wine and Spirits Institute
DA	Democratic Alliance
DEVCO	Wine Industry Development Company
DPSC	Directorate of Plant and Seed Control
DRC	Dutch Reformed Church
DTI	Department of Trade and Industry
EEC	European Economic Community
EFF	Economic Freedom Fighters
FAWU	Food and Allied Workers' Union
FLO	Fairtrade Labelling Organizations
HP	high-priced
HRW	Human Rights Watch
INAO	Institut National des Appellations d'Origine
IOGT	International Order of Good Templars
IOTT	International Order of True Templars
IPW	Integrated Production of Wine
KWV	Koöperatieve Wynbouwers Vereniging van Suid-Afrika
LFFT	Lebanon Fruit Farm Trust

LRAD	Land Reform and Agricultural Development
M&S	Marks & Spencer
MCC	Méthode Cap Classique
MP	Member of Parliament
MP	medium-priced
NAMC	National Agricultural Marketing Council
NGO	non-governmental organization
NP	National Party
NRF	National Research Foundation
NTU	natural terroir units
OIV	l'Office International du Vin at le Vigne
PIWOSA	Premium Independent Wineries of South Africa
RFF	Rhodes Fruit Farms
RMB	Rand Merchant Bank
RTD	Ready to Drink
SAB	South African Breweries
SABVA	South African Black Vintners Alliance
SACP	South African Communist Party
SAFCOL	South African Forestry Company Limited
SALBA	South African Liquor Brandowners' Association
SAP	South African Party
SATA	South African Temperance Alliance
SAWB	South African Wine and Brandy Company
SAWFA	South African Wine Farmers' Association
SAWIS	South African Wine Information and Systems
SAWIT	South African Wine Industry Trust
SFW	Stellenbosch Farmers' Winery
SIP	Swartland Independent Producers
SP	standard-priced
SWSA	Sustainable Wine South Africa
UD	United Distillers
UP	United Party
VDQ	Vin Delimité de Qualité Supérieur
VINPRO	acronym with no abbreviation
VOC	Dutch East India Company
VORI	Viticultural and Oenological Research Unit
WCTU	Women's Christian Temperance Union
WIETA	Wine and Agricultural Ethical Trade Association
WINETECH	Wine Industry Network for Expertise and Technology
WIP	Wine Industry Strategy Plan
WISE	Wine Industry Strategic Exercise

WLAA	World League Against Alcoholism
WO	Wine(s) of Origin
WOSA	Wines of South Africa
WSB	Wine and Spirits Board
WWF-SA	World Wide Fund-South Africa

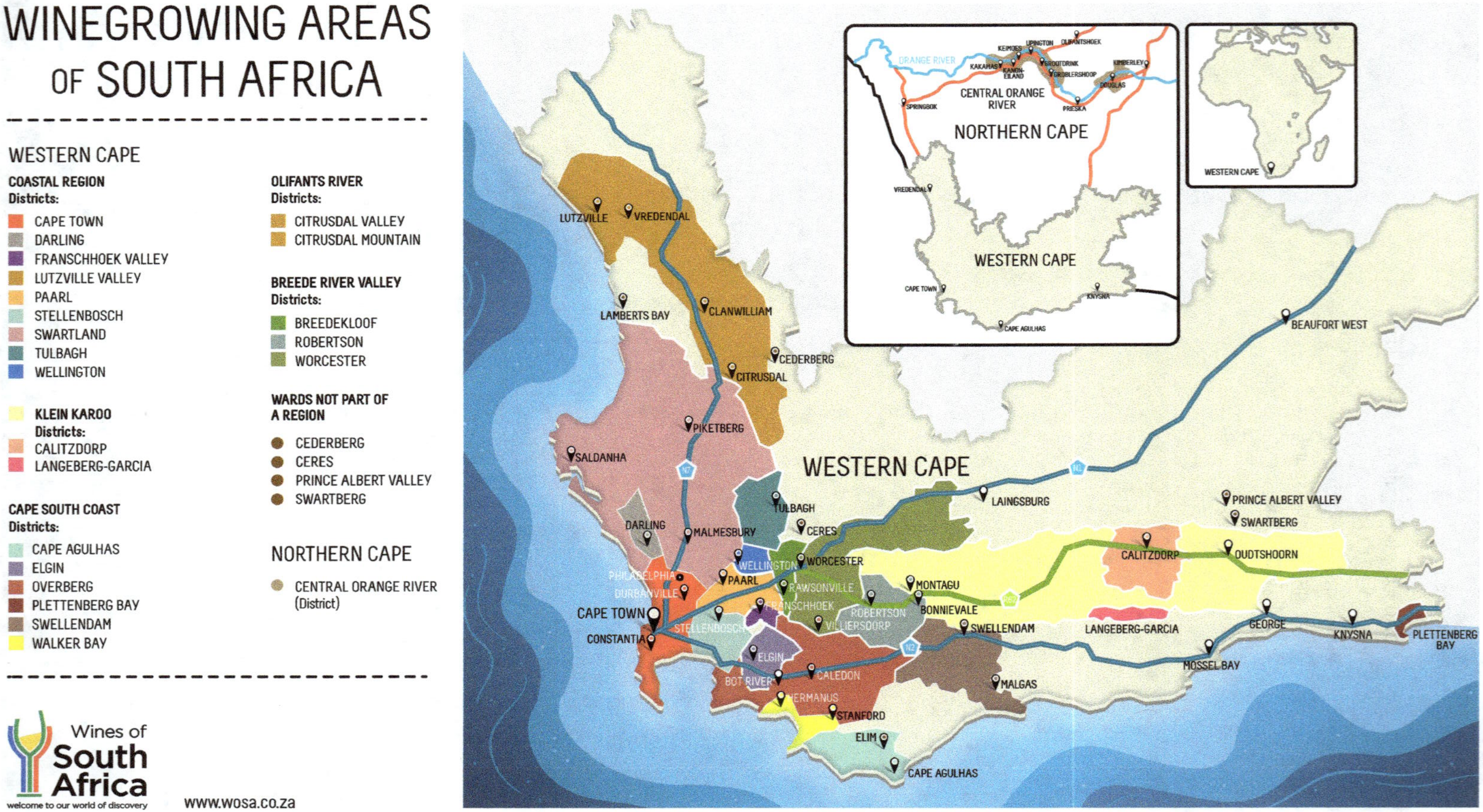

Map 1 “Winegrowing Areas of South Africa” (as of 2023), reproduced with kind permission of Wines of South Africa

Introduction

History through a Wine Glass – Empire, Slavery and Microbes

If the recent outpouring of wine histories has taught us anything, it is that wine has never been just a drink, even, and perhaps especially so, where the product has been unexceptional. Across the Old World, wine has been considered an everyday beverage consumed by the very people who have tended the vines, fermented the must and disposed of the finished product. But some wine has also been elevated to an iconic status, with prices to match those of expensive jewellery or works of art. In France, as Kolleen Guy and Marion Demossier have demonstrated, wine consumption came to define a sense of national identity,[1] at the same time as its production underpinned the assertion of distinct regional identities, from Burgundy to the Languedoc.[2] In Britain, the quintessential consuming country, Charles Ludington has written at length on how the choice of port as against claret inscribed a political dividing line between England and Scotland at the same time as it became associated with notions of refinement and gendered rules of social etiquette.[3] Wine was also exported from Europe to the colonies in large volumes – especially to the Americas, where it came to be associated with the affluent lifestyles of governing and commercial elites.

1 Kolleen M. Guy, "Wine, champagne and the making of French identity in the Belle Epoque", in Peter Scholliers (ed.), *Food Drink, and Identity: Eating and Drinking in Europe since the Middle Ages* (Oxford: Berg, 2001); Kolleen M. Guy, *When Champagne Became French: Wine and the Making of a National Identity* (Baltimore: Johns Hopkins University Press, 2003); and Marion Demossier, *Wine Drinking Culture in France: A National Myth or a Modern Passion?* (Cardiff: University of Wales Press, 2010).

2 For Burgundy, see Gilles Laferté, *La Bourgogne et ses vins: imagine d'origine controlée* (Paris: Belin, 2006); Philip Whalen, "'Insofar as the ruby wine seduces them': cultural strategies for selling wine in interwar Burgundy", *Contemporary European History* 18, 2009; Philip Whalen, "'A merciless source of happy memories': Gaston Roupnel and the folklore of Burgundian terroir", *Journal of Folklore Research* 44 (1) 2007; and Marion Demossier, *Burgundy: The Global Story of Terroir* (New York and Oxford: Berghahn Books, 2018). For the Langudeoc, see Andrew W. M. Smith, *Terror and Terroir: The Winegrowers of the Languedoc and Modern France* (Manchester: Manchester University Press, 2016). On the role of geographers in upholding distinct regional traditions in France, see Jacqueline Dutton, "Geographical turns and historical returns in narrating French wine culture", *Global Food History* 5 (1–2), 2019.

3 Charles Ludington, *The Politics of Wine in Britain: A New Cultural History* (Houndmills and London: Palgrave Macmillan, 2013).

European vines arrived with Dutch East India Company (VOC) ships in the years soon after the initial landing by Jan van Riebeeck at the Cape in 1652, and remarkably the first wine was announced by him as early as 1659.[4] Wine became central to the local economy, as well as to that of the Cape Colony when it entered the British imperial orbit after the Napoleonic Wars.[5] At the Cape, wine came to be particularly associated with social extremes: that is, with the material trappings of privilege and taste, on the one side, and the stark realities of human bondage, on the other. By the twentieth century, which is the main chronological focus of this book, the image of wine continued to be tainted with the image of chronic alcoholism and abject poverty amongst Coloured workers in the wine-farming districts.[6] The romance of the vine was therefore distinctly attenuated in the South African case. Here, there was no virtuous peasantry enjoying ancestral ties to the land and revelling in the fruits of its own labour. Rather, it was slaves and then landless farmworkers who provided the necessary labour, whilst consuming a large proportion of the cheap wine that resulted. The vicious circle, which is central to the concerns of this study, is one that the country is still struggling to extricate itself from.

In 2009, at the height of power struggles within the tripartite governing alliance,[7] the chairman of the African National Congress (ANC) Youth League, Julius Malema, took aim at his detractors in the South African Communist Party (SACP) who had accused him of using racially inflammatory language and of corruption:

> We don't care about fakes. There is a small group of elites in the alliance who present themselves as working-class leaders, while there is very little to show that in everything they do. They spend most of their time drinking red wine.[8]

The reference to red wine might seem like a throwaway comment, but it is a line that Malema repeatedly returned to. In 2015, by which time he had

[4] C. Louis Leipoldt, *300 Years of Cape Wine* (Cape Town: Stewart Publishers, 1952), pp. 4–6. The grapes were allegedly Muscadel and other white varietals.

[5] The VOC held the Cape from 1652 until Britain seized it in 1795. It was returned to Dutch government control for a short period from 1803 before it was seized for a second time in 1806. The Cape was formally annexed in 1814.

[6] The term 'Coloured' comes with a considerable political baggage. Because it was one of the apartheid racial categories, it was rejected by many activists during the apartheid years. However, it remains the term that is most in use today. In the Western Cape, it refers to people whose forebears would have been slaves as well as Khoi. On the shifting associations with the term before and after the end of apartheid, see Courtney Jung, *Then I Was Black: South African Political Identities in Transition* (New Haven and London: Yale University Press, 2000), chs. 6–7. See the 'Note on the Text' on page vi for more detail about the history and use of this term in South Africa.

[7] The alliance was forged between the African National Congress (ANC), the South African Community Party (SACP) and the Congress of South African Trade Unions (COSATU).

[8] Matuma Letsoalo, "Malema raps ANC leaders on race", *Mail and Guardian*, 28 August 2009, https://mg.co.za/article/2009-08-28-malema-raps-anc-leaders-on-race/ (accessed on 23 January 2022).

founded the Economic Freedom Fighters (EFF), Malema accused the SACP secretary-general, Blade Nzimande, of being an alcoholic and noted that while he was imbibing red wine the EFF was out distributing red tee-shirts to its supporters.[9] And in July 2020, Malema took his attack to the new president, Cyril Ramaphosa, when he remarked in even more colourful terms that, ‘Zuma was selling the country for a plate of curry and Ramaphosa is selling the country for a glass of wine from the Rupert family.’[10] Beneath the crude simplicity of the rhetoric, one can discern a number of layers of meaningful significance. At one level, Malema was tapping into a deep current of temperance sentiment in Black South Africa dating back to the nineteenth century. But Malema was no teetotaller, and reputedly had a taste for champagne. And while he criticized his detractors for talking the language of the left whilst living the good life, he was certainly no ascetic. On the contrary, he had a reputation for spending lavishly on expensive watches, designer clothes and smart cars. But this was precisely the point. While consuming foreign luxuries was the mark of having made it in the new South Africa, imbibing Cape wine was tantamount to having sold out to White moneyed interests. Black South Africans had traditionally consumed beer (both homebrewed and bottled) or spirits, whereas wine had generally been the preserve of White and Coloured people. In the new millennium, red wine typically fetched the highest prices and the most esteemed examples were hard to find, which meant that a certain cachet attached to possessing them. In this case, the focus was on the most coveted Cape wines rather than those of Burgundy, Bordeaux, Tuscany or Napa. For the newly rich, hoarding and imbibing the best wine was but a step away from acquiring stakes in a farm that had a reputation, or at least the unrealized potential, for producing the finest red wine. In Malema’s mind, the gated wine farm also represented an enclosed, secretive space where elite deals could easily be cut. Johann Rupert was a particular target not only because he was one of the country’s wealthiest business magnates, but also because his family owned a couple of wine estates where dignitaries were wined and dined. The Rupert family had always managed to sail close to power without being burned by it. Anton Rupert, arguably the founder of the first genuine Afrikaner business empire – based mostly on tobacco, but later also on spirits and wine – had cultivated an image of being a liberal during the apartheid era. However, he remained networked within the National Party (NP) and while he critiqued some of the most obtuse policies of the day, he never came over as

[9] www.enca.com/south-africa/malema-said-whaaat. The EFF adopted red, the symbolic colour of resistance, as its own. The red beret and red tee-shirts became the party uniform.

[10] The reference to curry was the close relationship between Zuma and the Gupta family that came to be seen as emblematic of state capture www.news24.com/news24/southafrica/news/zuma-sold-country-for-a-plate-of-curry-ramaphosa-selling-it-for-a-glass-of-wine-malema-20200726.

being overly condemnatory.[11] His eldest son, Johann, was clearly regarded by Malema as playing the ANC in a comparable way.

Scroll back a hundred years and one enters a very different world of wine and politics, but one that already bore the seeds of the present. The mid-1920s witnessed the height of the influence of the temperance movement, which claimed the 1928 Liquor Act as its handiwork. As we will see in detail, this piece of legislation permitted White and Coloured people in the Cape to purchase wine, but made it illegal to sell wine, beer and spirits to Black consumers right across the country. Black South Africans drank very little wine anyway, but then neither did Afrikaners. Rural Afrikaners preferred sweeter wines, typically made from Muscadel grapes, that were high in sugar and correspondingly low in alcohol content. Self-appointed spokesmen of the wine industry lobbied repeatedly for the right to develop the market for so-called 'light wines'. In the interwar years, the worry for Afrikaner nationalists was that 'poor whites' drifting to the cities would become mired in alcoholism, driven in part by the availability of cheap spirits. Part of the case for 'light wines' was that they represented a safer alternative to hard liquor for White working-class males. By the 1950s, the 'poor white' spectre had receded and a solid Afrikaner middle class, with disposable income to flaunt, had begun to coalesce. This was regarded by wine-industry leaders as the perfect opportunity to market table wines to the White population, including women. As we will see, significant production and marketing innovations drove an expansion in white wine sales to consumers of a whiter hue. The structural problem, however, was that substantially more wine was being produced than could be disposed of. A crucial amendment of the 1928 Liquor Act in 1962 opened wine consumption to all racial categories, and there were high hopes that Black consumers could be tempted to join the wine waggon. As it happened, the optimism proved misplaced and the industry was saddled with a large surplus that could only be distilled into brandy – which was, or course, the outcome that the temperance movement had most feared. A long-term solution potentially lay in improving the quality of table wines that might bring higher margins to producers. While leaders in the industry looked to German white-wine styles, farmers and consumers began to gravitate to the darker side of the spectrum. The mounting demand for red varietals in the 1970s created a problem, however, because there was precious little desirable planting material, partly because quarantine provisions created lengthy delays.

The upheavals that finally culminated in the end of the apartheid regime over 1990–1994 were mirrored in the equally rapid implosion of the regulatory

[11] At one point, Rupert had been seen as a possible leader of the country and was favoured by the Cape National Party as a liberal alternative to H. F. Verwoerd who won out. See Ebbe Dommisse, *Anton Rupert: A Biography* (Cape Town: Tafelberg, 2013).

regime that had locked wine production into certain fixed patterns. With the ending of sanctions, there was a desire to catch up with international trends and that largely meant embracing red cultivars. Existing vines were stripped out and replaced with varietals like Cabernet Sauvignon, Merlot and Shiraz. At the same time, there was an influx of capital into the vineyards, some of it emanating from overseas, but even more from those who had made their money in Johannesburg. For the country's wealthiest White businessmen, acquiring a wine farm became the ultimate status symbol. Hence, when members of an emergent Black elite began to display an interest in red wine after the millennium, they were only a decade or so behind their White counterparts. Wine was the great leveller, it seemed, but only at the summit of the social pyramid. For Malema, the lives of those who worked to make the wine had showed little sign of improvement. But even here there was a twist, in that while Malema insisted that the land should be returned to the people, he had in mind not the Coloured workers whose ancestors had worked on the farms since the days of slavery but the growing numbers of Black work-seekers who had been drawn to the winelands, mostly from the Eastern Cape, after the fall of apartheid.[12]

As should be apparent from this brief synopsis, the shifting contours of race, ethnicity and class were not only embedded in the realities of wine production, but also in everyday patterns of consumption. How different segments of the population related to drinking wine, or to temperance, became central to the framing of identities at many levels. And perhaps not surprisingly, tensions manifested themselves at the various intersectional boundaries, as reflected, for example, in fretting about whether encouraging Afrikaner women to drink white wine posed a danger to the integrity of the family and hence the *volk*, or in doubt as to whether Black middle-class men would emulate their White counterparts in making the transition from sweet white to dry red wine. Some tensions became apparent in the 1960s and 1970s, but a similar dynamic was also apparent in other periods as well, including the most recent past when Malema gave vent to his own fears about what drinking red wine *really* meant.

This brings me to the specific focus of this study. One of the three main signifiers on the title is race, which is intended to stand not for something that exists 'out there', but rather as a bundle of associations that most of the actors related to at some level, even when they were opposed to segregation and

[12] The Western Cape had been defined as a 'Coloured labour preference area' during the apartheid era and there had been a conscious effort to apply influx controls that blocked migration from the Eastern Cape. See Ian Goldin, *Making Race: The Politics and Economics of Coloured Identity in South Africa* (London and New York: Longman, 1988), pp. 86–91, 105–107, 137–144.

apartheid.[13] My interest is less in how racial categories were defined and instrumentalized than in how they became normalized in everyday thinking and drinking. However, race only really makes sense in its articulation with class, ethnicity and gender, to which one could add generation, religion and locality. The second signifier, that of taste, embraces both the physical act of consumption and the ways in which particular products were valorized, denigrated or simply passed over. Here I am interested in who drank what, how wine advertising and marketing strategies targeted specific groups of consumers and what impact drinking patterns had on shaping the next phase of vineyard plantings. The third signifier, namely the grape, is an allusion to the production process from vineyard to bottle or, just as often, the unadorned bag or *papsak*. Here, I am interested in how bursts of innovation that took place at different times in the vineyard and the cellars shaped what was marketed to consumers, and how they responded.

These three signifiers are, in turn, threaded through two themes that run through the book. The first is the structural tension between grape growers and wine farmers,[14] on the one side, and the merchant-manufacturing companies like Stellenbosch Farmers' Winery (henceforth SFW) and Distillers on the other. Their relationships were constantly recalibrated in light of the innovations that took place in the vineyards and cellars as well as the more glacial shifts in consumer preferences. The second theme is the way in which wine became a political subject, arising from the perceived need to regulate aspects of production and consumption alike. As we will see, extensive regulatory powers were devolved upon the Koöperatieve Wynbouwers Vereniging van Suid-Afrika (henceforth KWV) from 1924 and then ramped up further in 1940. On the production side, farmers from different districts were pitched against each other over the intertwined issues of quality and pricing. On the consumption side, farmers and merchants joined forces against the temperance onslaught, but parted company when it came to matters of distribution. Moreover, the wine companies engaged in ferocious competition for mastery of a limited market. This is not a study of the politics of race, and yet one finding is that legislation that related to consumption was broadly congruent with segregation in the 1920s and 1930s, whereas it was running in the opposite direction to most apartheid policies from the 1960s. This reinforces

[13] I refer to 'White', 'Coloured' and 'Black' as categories that are rooted in segregationist and apartheid discourse, but which it is impossible to avoid using because they have meaning for the actors themselves. See the 'Note on the Text' on page vi for more detail about the history and use of this term in South Africa.

[14] In the twentieth century, most were growers who sold their grapes to the local cooperative. However, they have tended to be called 'wine farmers' alongside those who have owned their own cellars. This wider usage will be adhered to in the pages of this book.

a broader observation that apartheid was, in practice, far from being monolithic, coherent or consistent.[15]

Wine farmers in South Africa have never exhibited an especially deep interest in history, being rather more concerned with where the next vintage is coming from. To be sure, the 300th and 350th anniversaries of the making of the first wine were celebrated, and key turning points like the onset of phylloxera, the foundation of the KWV in 1918 and the end of regulation became part of the collective folklore. The industry has also venerated the contribution of individual pioneers, many of whom grace the pages of this book. But the granularity of historical engagement is largely absent and there are large gaps in the collective memory that are apparent in the timelines that circulate almost as a substitute for history. For its part, the historical profession has displayed limited interest in wine as such. The most significant contributions relate to the eighteenth and early nineteenth centuries.[16] The one exception is a rich literature on labour that underlines how the wine industry was forged in the context of slavery and the ambiguous processes of emancipation from the 1830s.[17] Much academic interest in more recent times has been concerned with the so-called *dop stelsel*, or tot system, under which farm workers were administered rations of wine over the course of the working day.[18] There is much detailed sociological work that details the larger patterns of paternalism that continued to characterize the relationship between farmworkers and owners well into the twenty-first

[15] Saul Dubow, *Apartheid, 1948–1994* (Oxford: Oxford University Press, 2014).

[16] Diko Van Zyl, *Kaapse Wyn en Brandewyn, 1795–1860: Die Geskiedenis van Wynbou en Wynhandel in die Kaapkolonie* (Kaapstad: Hollandsch Afrikaansche Uitgevers, 1975); Robert Ross, "The Cape of Good Hope and the world economy, 1652–1835", in Richard Elphick and Hermann Giliomee (eds.), *The Shaping of South African Society, 1653–1840* (London: Longman, 1980) and Pieter van Duin and Robert Ross, *The Economy of the Cape Colony in the Eighteenth Century* (Leiden: Center for the History of European Expansion, 1987).

[17] Pamela Scully, *Liberating the Family? Gender and British Slave Emancipation in the Rural Western Cape, South Africa, 1823–1853* (Oxford: James Currey, 1998); Pamela Scully, "Liquor and labor in the Western Cape, 1870–1900", in Jonathan Crush and Charles Ambler (eds.), *Liquor and Labor in Southern Africa* (Athens: Ohio University Press, 1992); Mary Rayner, "Wine and slaves: the failure of an export economy and the ending of slavery in the Cape Colony, South Africa, 1806–1835", unpublished PhD thesis, Duke University, Durham, NC, 1986; and Wayne Dooling, *Slavery, Emancipation and Colonial Rule in South Africa* (Scottsville: University of KwaZulu-Natal Press, 2007). For the later period, see Lars Olsson, "Capital, market and labour in the Western Cape winelands c.1900: agricultural capitalism?", *International Review of Social History* 63 (1), 2018.

[18] Gavin Williams, "Slaves, workers and wine: the 'dop system' in the history of the Cape wine industry, 1658–1894", *Journal of Southern African Studies* 42 (5), 2016. The dop features prominently in Jeanne Viall, Wilmot James and Jakes Gerwel, *Grape: Stories of the Vineyards in South Africa* (Cape Town: Tafelberg, 2011), chs. 6–7. See also Fredrik Lilja, *Whip of the Vine: Labour Relations and the Role of Alcohol in Western Cape Wine Farming from the 1940s to the 2010s* (Malmö: Malmö University, 2019).

century.[19] But there is relatively little that is concerned with wine itself over the past century and a half.

Within the country, there is often an assumption that the Cape was somehow different from everywhere else, which may be understood as a variant on South African exceptionalism. But a similar case could be made for Georgia or Argentina. In each instance, there were distinctive elements in their historical trajectories that continue to shape the profiles of the industries today. However, one should also not lose sight of the many common threads, from diseases of the vine to the circulation of cultivars and consumption patterns. One of the critiques of the turn to global history is that while it may be acutely sensitive to multiple forms of connectivity, it risks flattening the landscape and privileging flows over other phenomena that remain stubbornly rooted in place.[20] The globalization of wine over recent decades has stimulated an interest in earlier moments of interconnectivity across the wine world. Arguably, this had the positive effect of nourishing rather than supplanting regional histories whose vinous contours are anything but flat. And if wine history is now 'a thing', that is also because the turn to global history has made it easier to draw together certain threads that are customarily divvied up between economic, environmental, cultural and political history. Moreover, the new wave of wine histories has pointed to the fruitfulness of comparative enquiry.[21] As things stand, however, South Africa remains somewhat at the margins of this historiography.[22] This book therefore takes up the challenge of positioning South Africa squarely within a larger story relating to viticulture, oenology, marketing, consumption and much else besides. It is driven as much by an ongoing interest in comparative history as it is informed by histories of wine and globalization.[23]

[19] See Andries du Toit, "The micro-politics of paternalism: the discourses of management and resistance on South African fruit and wine farms", *Journal of Southern African Studies* 19 (2) 1993; and Joachim Ewert and Andries du Toit, "A deepening divide in the countryside: restructuring and rural livelihoods in the South African wine industry", *Journal of Southern African Studies* 31 (2) 2005.

[20] Sebastian Conrad, *What Is Global History?* (Princeton, NJ and Oxford: Princeton University Press, 2016), pp. 224, 230–235.

[21] James Simpson, *Creating Wine: The Emergence of a World Industry, 1840–1914* (Princeton, NJ and Oxford: Princeton University Press, 2011); Gwynn Campbell and Nathalie Guibert (eds.), *Wine, Society and Globalization: Multidisciplinary Perspectives on the Wine Industry* (New York: Palgrave, 2017); Kym Anderson and Vicente Pinilla (eds.), *Wine Globalization: A New Comparative History* (Cambridge: Cambridge University Press, 2018); and David Inglis and Anna-Mari Almila (eds.), *The Globalization of Wine* (London: Bloomsbury Academic Press, 2019). An early marker was laid down by Leo Loubère, *The Red and the White: A History of Wine in France and Italy in the Nineteenth Century* (Albany: State University of New York Press, 1978).

[22] A recent exception is Nick Vink, Willem H. Boshoff, Gavin William, Johan Fourie and Lewis S. McLean, "South Africa", in Anderson and Pinilla, *Wine Globalization*.

[23] My own interest in comparative history is reflected in Paul Nugent, *Boundaries, Communities and State-Making in West Africa: The Centrality of the Margins* (Cambridge: Cambridge

Lineages of the Cape Wine Industry

Having broached the matter of comparison, I turn now to three domains where it is possible to gauge how exceptional the South African engagement with wine really was. These are the configuration of capital and labour in the context of empire; the balance between domestic and overseas markets; and the emergence of wine science. Performing this exercise will enable me to tease out certain patterns that were set by the late nineteenth century, which is where this book properly begins.

Empire, Capital and Labour

Wine may be considered as something of an outlier in relation to imperial commodities. Tropical goods, such as sugar, cotton or coffee, generally travelled in the direction of the imperial metropole, and revolutionized consumption patterns there. By contrast, *vitis vinifera* thrived in the temperate regions of Europe. In the Americas, there were indigenous wild vines – *vitis rupestris, vitis riparia* and *vitis labrusca* – but the wines that were made from these were generally considered unpalatable.[24] Not surprisingly, therefore, the colonies tended to import wine directly from Europe, at least to start with. According to the zero-sum logics inscribed in mercantilist thinking and practice, there were other reasons why that direction of flow needed to be maintained. While goods could be produced to satisfy local consumption requirements, the principle was that they should not compete with the products of the metropole.[25] As late as the 1840s, the official line in Algeria was that vines should not be planted on a significant scale in order to avoid competing with France itself.[26] In practice, the outcomes were shaped by the clashes of vested interests that clustered around the structures of power in the imperial centres as well as in the colonies, as the unlikely success of madeira in the Americas amply demonstrates.[27]

University Press, 2019), and "Do nations have stomachs? Food, drink and imagined community in Africa", *Africa Spectrum* 3, 2010.

24 Thomas Pinney, *A History of Wine in America, Volume I: From the Beginnings to Prohibition* (Berkeley, Los Angeles and London: University of California Press, 1989), chs. 1–7.

25 For a comparison of how this played out differently, see Elizabeth Heath, *Wine, Sugar and the Making of Modern France: Global Economic Crisis and the Racialization of French Citizenship, 1870–1910* (Cambridge: Cambridge University Press, 2014).

26 Owen White notes that the objection to wine production was dropped from around 1860, and seven years later Algerian wine was permitted to enter France free of duty. This exception was only conceivable because Algeria came to be defined as an integral part of France. Owen White, *The Blood of the Colony: Wine and the Rise and Fall of French Algeria* (Cambridge, MA and London: Harvard University Press, 2021), pp. 29, 37.

27 David Hancock, *Oceans of Wine: Madeira and the Emergence of American Trade and Taste* (New Haven, CT: Yale University Press, 2009), p. 113.

Many efforts to establish *vitis vinifera* in the Americas failed, whether for reasons of disease, soil or climate.[28] The fragility of the European vine meant that it was certainly never destined to become one of the great invasive species.[29] But where the domesticated vine was aggressively pushed, and especially so as a form of monoculture, it could serve as the handmaiden for colonizing projects of one kind or another. Indeed, Erica Hannickel goes as far as to maintain that 'a potent wine culture acted as both a civilizing practice and one that strengthened Americans' grip on the continent'.[30] As is well known, Catholic religious orders in Europe played a foundational role in establishing vineyards and achieving a modicum of consistency in winemaking techniques. It is hardly surprising, therefore, that French and Spanish colonists in the Americas chose to transplant the European vine to some of the lands they aspired to dominate. From Quebec to Mexico, the cultivation of *vitis vinifera* was regarded as an exercise in taming nature and native populations alike. It was closely associated with mission stations, one legacy of which was the 'mission grape' that derived from the European vine and came to widely grown across the Americas.[31] Plantings were promoted in the Australian colonies in the nineteenth century on the familiar basis that *vitis vinifera* would tame nature and sustain livelihoods, but also on the more pragmatic grounds that wine consumption was infinitely preferable to the mass consumption of spirits.[32] Again, in nineteenth-century Algeria, some of the earliest vineyards were planted by the Trappists and the White Fathers, whose founder, Cardinal Lavigerie, repeated a familiar mantra about the civilizing properties of the vine.[33]

The trajectory of wine at the Cape stands apart from these other cases in three respects. Firstly, the Cape revolved within the Indian Ocean rather than the Atlantic trading system. The VOC was primarily interested in commerce with the East Indies and conceived of the Cape as a refreshment station located roughly half-way between the Europe and Asia. The principle was that ships rounding the Cape would be able to break the journey and be provisioned with

[28] Pinney, *History, Volume I*, chs. 1–7.

[29] On the issue of the ways in which alien fauna and flora assisted imperial conquest, the reference point remains Alfred W. Crosby, *Ecological Imperialism: The Biological Expansion of Europe, 900–1900* (Cambridge: Cambridge University Press, 2004).

[30] Erica Hannickel, *Empire of Vines: Wine Culture in America* (Philadelphia: University of Pennsylvania Press, 2013), p. 5.

[31] The mission varietal has now been identified as Listan Prieto, whose origins (not surprisingly) reside in Spain where it was almost extinguished by phylloxera. Jancis Robinson, Julia Harding and José Vouillamoz, *Wine Grapes: A Complete Guide to 1,368 Wine Varieties, Including Their Origins and Flavours* (London: Allen Lane, 2012), pp. 550–551.

[32] J. A. McIntyre, "A 'civilised' drink and a 'civilising' industry: wine growing and cultural imagining on colonial New South Wales", unpublished PhD thesis, University of Sydney, 2008.

[33] White, *Blood*, p. 96.

foodstuffs and wine that was locally produced. In a context where water on board quickly became contaminated, wine inoculated with spirit was a considerably safer option. Although wine seems to have been envisaged as a staple industry from the start, the VOC never intended to invest directly in its production. Instead, creating vineyards and making wine was initially left to its employees, notably those in senior positions, and increasingly to free burghers who took to farming once they left company service. The individual most associated with the active promotion of the vine was Simon van der Stel, who served as the first substantive Governor between 1691 and 1699. Surprisingly, he came with some first-hand experience. Although the Netherlands lies well to the north, Van der Stel had been contracted to tend vines and make wine in North Holland in the 1670s.[34] At the Cape, he established the largest estate of all, namely Groot Constantia.[35] His son and successor, Willem Adriaan van der Stel, followed in his footsteps and founded Vergelegen in what is now Somerset West. After local protests over land-grabbing and corruption, he was recalled and VOC employees were debarred from wine production after 1705, leaving the field open to the burghers.[36]

What the VOC did have at its disposal was the grant of land-use rights. After jumping the sandy stretches of the Cape Flats, a second wave of plantings took place in Stellenbosch where land was allocated to burghers on generous terms around 1680.[37] The VOC did not encourage migration outside of company service, a principle that was made explicit after 1708,[38] but the Huguenots were an early exception. Most arrived from the Netherlands in the 1680s and were allocated land in the Drakenstein Valley. The town of Franschhoek at the eastern corner of the valley is the most obvious reminder of these French origins. The VOC did, however, seek to profit from wine in various ways. When Constantia wines began to generate some interest in Europe, the company asserted its right to a commercial monopoly. The two main Constantia farms were required to sell wine to the VOC at a fixed price that was set well below what the wine would sell for in Europe. One owner of Groot Constantia,

[34] David Van Stappen, "Simon van der Stel en die uitbreiding van de Kaapkolonie, 1679–1699", unpublished PhD thesis, University of Ghent, 2007, pp. 12–13.

[35] The farm returned to the VOC on his death and was divided in three. Groot Constantia remained the name for the part including the original homestead, while Klein Constantia (later renamed Hoop de Constantia) and Bergvliet were hived off as separate farms. G. J. Schutte (ed.), *Hendrik Cloete, Groot Constantia en die/and the VOC, 1778–1799* (Cape Town: Van Riebeeck Society, 2003), p. 13. Bergvliet underwent further subdivision. Stefan K. Estreicher, "A brief history of wine in South Africa", *European Review* 22 (3), 2014, pp. 515–516.

[36] Leonard Guelke and Robert Shell, "An early colonial landed gentry: land and wealth in the Cape Colony 1682–1731", *Journal of Historical Geography* 9 (3) 1983, p. 280.

[37] Guelke and Shell, "Early colonial", p. 266.

[38] Johan Fourie and Dieter von Fintel, "The dynamics of inequality in a newly settled, pre-industrial society: the case of the Cape Colony", *Cliometrica* 4, 2010, p. 235.

Hendrik Cloete, petitioned against what he regarded as an unjust arrangement, and eventually a compromise was struck.[39] Because Cape wines were never competing with a Dutch product, exports to Europe were never considered problematic, and yet Pieter Van Duin and Robert Ross insist that the VOC never pushed them very hard.[40] Indeed, they note that wine exports actually dropped from a range of between and 15 and 22 per cent of production in the 1750s to between 5 and 10 per cent in the 10 years, leading up to the termination of VOC rule in 1795.[41] The VOC concentrated much more on wine that was sold locally. By making wine sales at the Cape subject to franchises (called the *pacht*) which merchants competed for, the VOC accrued money from wine that was sold in local taverns and to passing ships. Indeed, Van Duin and Ross indicate that these franchises accounted for no less than 38 per cent of government income in the last decade of company rule.[42] However, this revenue was essential to cover the hefty administrative expenses of the Cape. The core business of the VOC remained the trade with the East Indies.

A second key difference is that wine was scarcely bound up with some grand conception of a civilizing mission. The indigenous Khoi population were pastoralists, and their allotted role was originally to supply meat to the VOC rather than to work on vineyards. The burghers themselves were not just made up of the Dutch but included many whose origins lay in what is now northern Germany and Scandinavia. Very few of these came with any knowledge of viticulture or with significant financial resources. French wine had been sold to northern Europe in significant volumes since medieval times, and the Dutch perfected a trade in sweet wines in the seventeenth century.[43] But these wines were intended for the upper echelons of society, and wine was not the drink of the labouring sort who were recruited by the VOC. Again, the Huguenots are a partial exception. Although they mostly originated in France, that did not necessarily mean they had substantial knowledge of wine.[44] As Protestants, they shared little of the imagery that linked wine to Catholic religious observance. Nevertheless, Johan Fourie and Dieter von Fintel make a credible case, based on the regional origin of surnames, that a good proportion of the Huguenots came from wine-producing regions of France, and that they

[39] In 1793, the VOC formally conceded a free trade in wine. In 1794, it was agreed that the VOC would purchase a quantity of wine from Groot Constantia at a fixed price with the farm then being free to sell the remainder as it wished. Schutte, *Hendrik Cloete*, pp. 43–45.

[40] Van Duin and Ross, *Economy*, p. 19.

[41] Van Duin and Ross, *Economy*, p. 50.

[42] Van Duin and Ross, *Economy*, p. 51.

[43] Marcel Lachiver, *Vins, vignes et vignerons: histoire du vignoble français* (Paris: Fayard, 1988), pp. 254–260.

[44] A number seem to have come at an earlier point from northern Italy where they were followers of the Waldensians. I am grateful to Isabella Soi for pointing this out.

were more likely to go on to produce wine at the Cape.[45] They also maintain that their relevant skills made them more successful winemakers than the burghers who preceded them. But, as later leaders of the industry would lament, the Cape nevertheless failed to produce a wine culture in the European sense. The consumption of wine does not seem to have been invested with any deep cultural significance, and there is a striking absence of religious festivals marking the annual cycle of renewal that was characteristic of Europe. More fundamentally, the farmers, including those of Huguenot origins, imbibed precious little wine.

A third crucial difference was that the trajectory of the Cape wine industry hinged on an institutionalized form of slavery.[46] While slaves were used occasionally in the Americas, the Cape is unique in the modern wine world for its dependence on a mode of slavery that was fully institutionalized and embedded with a larger Indian Ocean complex. At an early point, the VOC had ruled that the Khoi should not be enslaved. The latter did sell their labour, but after the demographic damage wrought by the 1713 smallpox epidemic, it became clear that they would never provide a lasting labour solution.[47] Since assisted European migration was discouraged, that left an alternative form of unfree labour as the most feasible option. The number of slaves climbed from 891 to 4,709 between 1701 and 1733 and reached 6,045 20 years later, at a time when the number of burghers stood at 5,419. By 1793, on the eve of the British takeover of the Cape, there were 14,747 slaves and 18,830 burghers.[48] The slaves originated largely from South and Southeast Asia and were supplied by trading ships returning to the Netherlands rather than by dedicated slaving vessels. However, in the later decades of the nineteenth century, slaves were also drawn from across East Africa or born into servitude. The inventory of the estate of Sibella Passman in 1778 reveals that most of her slaves bore the name 'Van den Caab' (or 'from the Cape'), indicating that they had been born locally.[49] The testament of Hendrik Cloete in 1799 mentioned two slaves that

[45] Johann Fourie and Dieter von Vintel, "Settler skills and colonial development: the Huguenot wine-makers in eighteenth-century Dutch South Africa", *Economic History Review* 67 (4) 2014.

[46] There is a very large literature on Cape slavery. Some of the foundational contributions are Robert Ross, *Cape of Torments: Slavery and Resistance in South Africa* (London: Routledge & Kegan Paul, 1983); Nigel Worden, *Slavery in Dutch South Africa* (Cambridge: Cambridge University Press, 1985); and Robert Shell, *Children of Bondage: A Social History of the Slave Society at the Cape of Good Hope, 1652–1838* (Hannover, NH and London: Wesleyan University Press, 1994).

[47] Guelke and Shell, "Early colonial", p. 276. Van Duin and Ross, *Economy*, pp. 47–48.

[48] Worden, *Slavery*, table 2.1, p. 11.

[49] Two slaves bore the name 'Van Mallabaar'. Inventory of goods in estate of Sibella Passman, widow of Jacob Cloete (and father of Hendrik Cloete), dated 25 April 1778, copy of document from Stellenbosch District Archives.

were bequeathed to his son, whose names of 'Aurora von Mosambicque' and 'Amor van Madagascar' indicate their African regional origins.[50]

In place of a wine culture, one could say that the Cape developed a slave culture of a very specific kind. Most VOC servants and Huguenot settlers were initially poor and lived cheek by jowl with their slaves when they could afford them. However, slaveholding gained wider currency over time. In 1705, 39.1 per cent of farmers in Drakenstein owned at least one slave, but by 1752 this rose to 81.3 per cent. The comparable shift in Stellenbosch over the same period was from 59.3 to 67.5 per cent. In the Cape district, closest to Cape Town, 98.5 per cent of farmers owned slaves by 1705.[51] Wayne Dooling notes that the mean number of adult male slaves between 1752 and 1773 stood at around 11 in the Cape District (as against between 5 and 6 in Stellenbosch) but by the turn of the century, this had risen to 15.75.[52] Van Duin and Ross indicate that the number of vines planted and the amount of wine produced per head of slave population increased substantially between 1739 and 1773. Given that the number of slaves did not increase as rapidly, they conclude that the labour of slaves was exploited more intensively, and this was especially so around Stellenbosch and Drakenstein.[53] In a nutshell, slavery became more integral to the production of wine with the passage of time.

At the same, there was evidence of greater social differentiation within the ranks of wine farmers over the course of eighteenth century. A minority were able to accumulate significant assets in the shape of multiple farms and larger numbers of slaves, whilst constructing the impressive manor houses that emblazon the Cape winelands today. The striking differences of wealth were manifested in the manner in which the ownership of slaves was concentrated. Hendrik Cloete was reputedly one of the colony's largest slaveholders in the 1770s. He doubled the number of slaves on Groot Constantia to 50 at a time when more than half of farmers in the Cape district, and 83.3 per cent in Stellenbosch, owned fewer than 10 male slaves.[54] On a grander scale, Martin Melck, who acquired Elsenburg in Stellenbosch through marriage, owned

50 Schutte, *Hendrik Cloete*, p. 305. Other slaves bore the name 'Van de Caab', or from the Cape, signalling that they were born into slavery. The name Malgas, which remains a surname today, is clearly a reference to Madagascar.

51 These figures are taken from Worden, *Slavery*, table 2.2, p. 13. See also Gavin Williams, "Who, where and when were the Cape gentry?" *Economic History of Developing Regions* 28 (2) 2013, figure 6, p. 90.

52 Dooling, *Slavery*, p. 30.

53 The number of vines in the Cape District on 'pure wine farms' increased from 25,000 to 32,000. The expansion was more striking in Stellenbosch, where the numbers increased from 6,000 to 30,000, and in Drakenstein where they increased from 9,000 to 31,000. Van Duin and Ross, *Economy*, table 4.3, pp. 47–48.

54 Worden, *Slavery*, table 3.3, p. 32.

more than 200 slaves and was reputedly the wealthiest man in the colony.[55] The most successful also invested in the outward markers of respectability and achievement in the form of luxury goods for consumption and social ostentation.[56] By 1783, one visitor was struck by 'nothing except signs of affluence and prosperity, to the extent that, in addition to splendors and magnificence in clothes and carriages, the houses are filled with elegant furniture and the tables decked with silverware and served by tidily clothed slaves'.[57] Indeed, the spiral of conspicuous consumption prompted Governor Ryk Tulbagh to introduce restrictive sumptuary laws in 1755.[58]

This has prompted some discussion as to whether, and for what period, it is appropriate to refer to the consolidation of a Cape gentry.[59] In the most systematic analysis to date, Fourie and Von Vintel indicate that inequalities amongst the White population increased initially as poor burghers and Huguenots weighed heavily in the overall numbers, but then with the imposition of restrictions on immigration the tail diminished and inequality declined until around 1738, after which it rose again as those at the top of the social pile pulled away.[60] This raises some interesting questions about the dynamics underpinning accumulation. The institution of marriage was clearly central to a generational game of snakes and ladders. On the one hand, the principle of marriage in community of property meant that assets were united at the point of marriage.[61] On the other, the Roman Dutch legal principle of partible inheritance meant that estates were divided at the point of death, with between a half to a third going to the surviving spouse and the remainder being divided amongst the children. The first principle made it possible for elite families to forge alliances and thereby to pool their assets, including landed property and slaves. The second principle potentially led to a fragmentation of family assets at the moment of death. Evidently, marriage served as a means for some to accumulate great wealth, in the context of low rates of life expectancy. Melck

55 Wayne Dooling, "The making of a colonial elite: property, family and landed stability in the Cape Colony, c.1750–1834", *Journal of Southern African Studies* 31 (1) 2005, p. 158.

56 For a detailed treatment see Robert Ross, *Status and Respectability in the Cape Colony, 1750–1870: A Tragedy of Manners* (Cambridge: Cambridge University Press, 1999).

57 Hermann Giliomee, *The Afrikaners: Biography of a People* (London: C. Hurst, 2011), p. 30, quoting S. D. Naudé on Willem Cornelius Boers.

58 These laws were imported from Batavia. Stan du Plessis, "Pearls worth Rds 4000 or less: reinterpreting eighteenth-century sumptuary laws at the Cape", Economic Research Southern Africa (ERSA) Working Paper 336, 2013.

59 Guelke and Shell, "Early colonial"; Robert Ross, "The rise of the Cape gentry", *Journal of Southern African Studies* 9 (2) 1983; Wayne Dooling, "The decline of the Cape gentry, 1838–1900", *Journal of African History* 40, 1999; Dooling, "Making of a colonial elite"; and Williams, "Who, where".

60 Fourie and Von Fintel, "Dynamics", pp. 252–258.

61 Dooling, "Making of a colonial elite", pp. 154–155; Williams, "Who, where", p. 103.

Table I.1. *Vineyards planted, 1808–1825 (triennial averages)*

Years	Triennial Average for Vines	Triennial Average for Production
1808–1810	14,890,487	9,445 leaguers
1811–1813	19,776,254	9,671 leaguers
1814–1816	22,384,623	12,820 leaguers
1817–1819	25,737,27	12,213 leaguers
1820–1822	29,177,730	15,604 leaguers
1823–1825	31,365,439	17,324 leaguers

Source: Rayner, "Wine and slaves", data consolidated from tables 1.2 and 1.3, pp. 14a and 16a.

himself rose from humble origins in the service of the VOC and did so by marrying a succession of propertied widows.[62]

Regardless of whether the term 'Cape gentry' is worth preserving,[63] there is a serious question about the impact of the ending of the slave trade and slavery upon the continued upward mobility of wine producers. In the first decades of the nineteenth century, Cape farmers invested heavily in the planting of new vines in anticipation of greater external demand, as Mary Rayner's calculations in Table I.1 demonstrates.[64] This required a corresponding deployment of labour, but new slaves ceased to arrive after Britain withdrew from the trade in 1807. This meant than any increase in the number of slaves needed to come from biological reproduction. In 1808, there were 29,569 slaves (across the entire colony) and by 1928 there were 33,198, which was but a modest increase. Some of the slack was taken up by drawing more on free Khoi workers, which blurred the boundaries with the (ex-)slaves and eventually helped to constitute the 'Coloured' category itself. Worden indicates that of 956 farms in Stellenbosch and Drakenstein districts in 1806, only 381 relied on slaves exclusively, whereas 518 deployed slaves and Khoi together and 57 were reliant on Khoi workers exclusively.[65] The financial outlays on labour and other investments designed to maximize production came to be reflected in high levels of indebtedness. In 1823, Rayner estimates that mortgages on 374 wine farms in the Cape and Stellenbosch districts accounted for an average of 47 per cent of the declared value of the farms. Of the 13 large-scale farms,

[62] Guelke and Shell, "Early colonial", p. 280; Williams, "Who, where", p. 100; Dooling, "Making of a colonial elite", p. 158. In the early days, some women of slave descent married men of means and thereby became property owners and slaveholders in their own right. A case in point is Angela van Bengalen (or 'Maai Ansela') whose daughter, Anna de Koning, married Oloff Bergh. They acquired the part of the original farm thar remained Groot Constantia. Another example is Ansela van de Caab, who married Lourens Campher of Muratie in Stellenbosch.

[63] Williams advocates abandoning a term that has outlived its usefulness. Williams, "Who, where", p. 108.

[64] See also Van Zyl, *Kaapse Wyn*, tables, pp. 10–11.

[65] Worden, *Slavery*, table 3.4, p. 35.

the average was 36 per cent, but this rose to 49 per cent for the 162 small-scale farmers and 44 per cent for the 125 medium-scale farmers.[66]

The ending of slavery in 1838 compounded the difficulties confronting ordinary farmers. Although the apprenticeship system had avoided a sudden rupture, many former slaves moved away from the farms they had hitherto lived on, often travelling in the direction of mission stations. Although this posed a problem for wine farmers, Stellenbosch itself seems to have attracted former slaves from other locations,[67] presumably drawn from the outlying districts more commonly associated with grain and stock-farming. The role of the mission stations was a source of annoyance to the farmers, who lobbied for government action. Pniël was a case in point because it was located adjacent to the farms of the Drakenstein valley. Ex-slaves who established themselves there fought a sustained campaign to protect their autonomy.[68] However, limited access to land generally meant that there was no realistic possibility that most former slaves could convert themselves into free peasants. The majority ultimately had few options than to enter into new five-year labour contracts under the Masters and Servant Legislation Act of 1856, which were skewed in favour of the farmers.[69] At the same time, farmers needed to provide basic housing and to extend advances to attract workers, while the promise of the dop alongside a cash wage became part of the quasi-formal labour arrangements.[70] Labour costs were generally higher than before and the possibilities for mechanization was limited. Wine farmers needed labour at peak times and rather than risk a shortage at critical moments, notably the harvest, many found it preferable to retain access to labour across the year. This implied a greater commitment to the relationship, but it also meant that workers could be employed on a range of more general tasks. In this way, the peculiar mix of domination and intimacy between farmers and workers resident on the farms – which came to be sedimented in the language of paternalism – was born out of the recalibration of power relations in the decades following the ending of slavery.

Dooling indicates that the compensation payments to former slave owners created a temporary glut of easy credit that led farmers to over-extend themselves.[71] In the 1840s, heavily indebted farmers were squeezed between low prices for wine that resulted from a conjuncture between rising production and falling exports (see Table I.2), high interest payments on their debts and the

[66] Rayner, "Wine and slaves", table 1.9, p. 35a.

[67] Pamela Scully, *The Bouquet of Freedom: Social and Economic Relations in the Stellenbosch District, South Africa, c1870–1900* (Cape Town: Centre for African Studies, University of Cape Town, 1990), p. 8.

[68] Pniël has a very strong sense of its collective identity today, as is reflected in its monuments invoking slavery and liberation. It is also reflected in local history writing. See Lot Cyster, Matthew Cyster, Eleanor Damon and Freddie Simpson, *Pniël en sy Mense* (Pniël: authors, 2008).

[69] Scully, *Bouquet*, pp. 5–6. [70] Scully, *Bouquet*, pp. 54–55.

[71] Dooling, "Decline", p. 225.

Table I.2. *Production and exports of Cape wine, 1824–1860 (leaguers)*

Year	Total Wine Produced	Total Wine Exported	Total Exported to Britain
1820	15,210	4,338	3,169
1821	16,254	5,005	3,736
1822	15,348	7,257	5,448
1823	21,147	7,013	6,176
1824	16,183	8,013	6,672
1825	14,641	6,814	5,052
1826	unknown	6,026	4,236
1827	unknown	9,433	7,169
1828	20,404	9,572	6,462
1829	15,539	10,305	5,857
1830	14,977	7,660	5,471
1831	18,467	4,537	2,272
1832	unknown	unknown	2,728
1833	14,501	8,235	4,222
1834	12,005	6,780	4,244
1835	15,548	7,986	4,401
1836	16,693	6,134	3,944
1837	18,103	7,324	4,754
1838	17,915	7,137	3,166
1839	18,899	7,328	5,458
1840	15,829	6,381	3,518
1841	23,312	5,739	2,056
1842	18,299	3,606	1,774
1843	13,426	3,504	1,188
1844	16,412	4,000	3,292
1845	17,156	3,582	2,629
1846	19,528	3,347	1,711
1847	19,528	2,653	1,626
1848	10,799	3,376	2,270
1849	20,892	2,905	1,915
1850	20,892	2,455	1,667
1851	20,892	3,071	2,485
1852	17,692	1,647	991
1853	28,834	1,788	860
1854	24,187	2,377	1,918
1855	24,765	3,237	2,264
1856	24,765	4,739	3,653
1857	24,765	6,226	5,268
1858	24,765	5,281	4,576
1859	24,765	7,201	6,576
1860	24,736	3,630	2,653

Source: D. J. Van Zyl, *Kaapse Wyn*, pp. 106, 169.

declining value of their properties, forcing many into insolvency. Dooling indicates that farmers had typically lent to each other rather than from banks and insisted on the principle that interest rates should not be permitted to rise above 6 per cent. But banks increasingly held the farmers' debt, and from 1860 they were empowered to increase the interest rates.[72] In the 1880s, prices for wine fell sharply at the precise moment when phylloxera struck, compounding the disaster for many marginal producers and threatening several banks with financial insolvency. By then, the logic was less one of accumulation than of a fragmentation as owners sold off parts of their farms in an effort to keep afloat, often by resorting to the production of fruit and vegetables. Although farms were released onto the market by insolvency, few had the financial means to scoop them up. This brings me to some of the vagaries of the market for wine.

Domestic and Overseas Markets

The fact that the Cape was strategically located on a major international shipping route meant that there was always some potential for its wines to find an external market. Van Duin and Ross observe that Europeans communities across South and Southeast Asia preferred wine from the Cape to drinking local forms of alcohol.[73] However, there were two fundamental constraints on selling wine to Europe. Wine that was sent on a sea voyage through the tropics needed to be inoculated against harmful bacteria through the addition of spirit. But this contributed to a reputation for being harsh on the palate. The exception was the best Constantia wines, which were made from desiccated grapes of the Muscat Blanc à Petits Grains (Muscat de Frontignan) and/or Pontac varietals.[74] These wines came to be highly esteemed across Europe in the eighteenth and nineteenth centuries. The second constraint is that Cape wines faced high levels of competition in wine-producing countries as

[72] Dooling, "Decline", pp. 239–241.

[73] Van Duin and Ross, *Economy*, p. 16. In 1788, the First Fleet to Australia carried both vines from the Cape as well as a supply of its wine. McIntyre, "A 'civilised' drink", p. 22.

[74] Muscat Blanc à Petits Grains/Muscat de Frontignan has also been a minor component of Hungarian Tokaji, which was the main rival of Constantia at its height. Robinson, Harding and Vouillamoz, *Wine Grapes*, p. 686. Klein Constantia and Groot Constantia both produced white and red 'Constantia wine'. Cloete apparently produced a blend from the Muscat de Frontignan and Pontac grapes. By the 1830s, the notional red wine from Groot Constantia also included Pontac, Hanepoot (Muscat d'Alexandrie) and Chenin Blanc, while the white included the latter two varietals. Schutte, *Hendrik Cloete*, p. 79; Estreicher, "Brief history", pp. 512, 515, 522. A red wine called Frontignac was also produced in Constantia. It is likely that this was a red mutation of the Muscat de Frontignan grape. Tim James, *Wines of the New South Africa: Tradition and Revolution* (Berkeley, Los Angeles and London: University of California Press, 2013), p. 68. Henry Vizetelly, a judge at the 1873 Vienna Expedition, distinguished 'so-called Frontignac' from 'celebrated Constantia'. Leipoldt, *300 Years*, p. 127.

well as high rates of duty outside of the Netherlands. In the all-important British market, the tariffs were designed to favour Portuguese and Spanish wines. Any increase in overall production had therefore to be absorbed by the domestic market. Clearly, much of the wine ended up being drunk in the wine districts themselves, largely in the form of the dop. But more important was the demand for wine in Cape Town. The key here was the sale of wine to the crew of passing ships. Boshoff and Fourie note that whereas the free burgher population of the Cape stood at around 8,000 in 1770, an average of between 9,700 and 11,600 people rounded the Cape per year on VOC ships.[75] In addition, over the last three decades of the eighteenth century, the number of British and French vessels came to substantially outnumber those of the Dutch.[76] These ships would typically linger, and this served as an important stimulus to the local economy, especially in Cape Town, the self-styled 'tavern of the seas'. Van Duin and Ross note that the cost of the *pacht* correlated with frequency of the arrival of ships, suggesting that it was sensitive to the demand they stimulated.[77]

The British annexation of the Cape threw up a whole new set of possibilities associated with access to imperial markets. For some, like Robert Percival, who participated in the first British occupation in 1795, there was an opportunity for Britain to reduce its dependency on European wine.[78] The presence of thousands of British troops during the war with France certainly boosted the local demand for wine.[79] Production increased steadily from 9,643 leaguers (1,637 hl.) in 1806 to 14,366 leaguers (2,486 hl.) in 1815, but export levels remained stable at about a third of total production or around 3,500 leaguers (606 hl.) per year.[80] This would suggest that most of the increase continued to be absorbed locally. On an average, between 63 and 78 per cent of the wine produced was despatched to Cape Town in the years between 1811 and 1825, implying that the lesser portion was retained in the rural areas.[81]

The fundamental problem when it came to increasing exports was that Cape wines had cemented a poor reputation, something which Percival and other British observers attributed to the bad habits of the Dutch.[82] A new Governor,

75 Willem H. Boshoff and Johan Fourie, "The significance of the Cape trade route to economic activity in the Cape Colony: a medium-term business cycle analysis", *European Review of Economic History* 14, 2010, p. 475.

76 Van Duin and Ross, *Economy*, p. 40.

77 There were three separate *pachts*: for the right to sell brandy, wine and to sell to foreigners. Van Duin and Ross, *Economy*, p. 55.

78 Robert Percival, *An Account of the Cape of Good Hope* (London: C. & R. Baldwin, 1804), pp. 180–181.

79 There were around 8,000 British troops stationed at the Cape from 1794–1798, and between 1803–1817 the number stood at around 4,000. Van Zyl, *Kaapse Wyn*, p. 103.

80 Van Zyl, *Kaapse Wyn*, p. 106.

81 Rayner, "Wine and slaves", table 1.4, p. 37.

82 Percival, *An Account*, p. 177.

Sir John Cradock, believed that the Cape was capable of boosting its exports provided there was a marked improvement in quality. In 1812, his administration created the position of Taster of Wines, whose seal of approval was needed before any wine, which was now required to be aged for 18 months, could be released for export.[83] Instructions were also issued to assist farmers in improving the quality of their wines and Rayner notes that medals were awarded for those who rose to the challenge.[84] Most importantly of all, British duties were revised in order to give Cape wines privileged access to the British market. Between 1805 and 1812, the British duty on Cape wines was the same as that levied on Portuguese and Spanish wines, at £96 per tun (or 11.46 hl.), but the Cape duty was then dropped by two-thirds to as little as £32 in 1813. Cape wines suddenly enjoyed a substantial price advantage over Portuguese competitors and a very much larger one over French wines which laboured under an eyewatering duty of £114 until 1824.[85] That year, wine duties were reduced across the board, which is sometimes regarded as the first of a series of reversals that sealed the fate of Cape wines.[86] However, over the three decades between 1831 and 1859, the Cape duty of £29 per tun was half of that levied on Portuguese, Spanish and French wines.[87] British imperial preferences ought to have made wine production for export a viable proposition in a manner that had never been the case under the VOC. Moreover, prices paid in Cape Town did fall after 1825, but then they settled at a higher level in the 1830s and 1840s and rose further in the 1850s.[88]

While the Cape should have been well positioned, wine exports faltered in the 1840s and early 1850s, although other overseas markets somewhat compensated, while exports as a proportion of total production widened.[89] If this could not be explained by differential duties, it could be accounted for by the damage done to the reputation of the Cape wines. In 1851, Cyrus Redding laid much of the blame squarely at the door of the merchants in Cape Town:

> Red Cape drunk of a proper age in the country is a sound, good wine. Who would believe this, from the specimens tasted in England? The merchants at the Cape are more careful of their cellars and appurtenances than of the wine they export from them.[90]

But he also blamed the haphazard approach to harvesting the grapes and the process of winemaking, noting in an acerbic aside that the process of

83 Rayner, "Wine and slaves", pp. 13–14. 84 Rayner, "Wine and slaves", p. 15.

85 Ludington, *Politics of Wine*, table A1, p. 264. One tun was equivalent to 252 gallons or 11.46 hl.

86 Van Zyl, *Kaapse Wyn*, pp. 138–146. 87 Ludington, *Politics of Wine*, table A1, pp. 264–65.

88 Van Zyl, *Kaapse Wyn*, p. 111. 89 Van Zyl, *Kaapse Wyn*, p. 170.

90 Cyrus Redding, *A History and Description of Modern Wines* (London: Henry G. Bohn, 3rd ed., 1851) p. 317.

fermentation was 'managed as coarsely as cider-making in Devonshire'.[91] Like Percival before him, Redding identified a missed opportunity for the Cape to carve out a permanent niche at the expense of European wines:

It is, therefore, not wonderful that Cape wines have become depreciated in public opinion. This the more to be lamented, because the mother country possesses no colony where a more congenial soil exists, or where better wines might be grown. The reduced duties, and extent of the home population, would secure a consumption for a superior wine, which would render the Cape in return, pecuniary advantages that could not fail to be felt by the colonists.[92]

Evidence presented to an enquiry set up by the Cape government in 1860 made it abundantly clear that during the years when the Cape had enjoyed a distinct price advantage, wine with added spirit had been shipped in cask and blended into more expensive French wines by merchants in Britain.[93] This had done nothing to cultivate a greater appreciation for Cape wines. In 1865, one informant identified a form of path dependency that proved disastrous in the long run:

My opinion is that if Cape wine, when first produced in this Colony in quantities, had been shipped for consumption in England it would have found a ready market. But it was shipped originally for blending with foreign wines, and since that the farmers have got into the habit of making wine for that purpose alone; the pontac to be blended with port, and the white wine with sherry, madeira etc. Constantia is the only quality that has been sent for consumption and is still exported.[94]

In the late 1850s, Cape wines briefly rallied, as exports to the British market jumped from 860 leaguers (1,249 hl.) in 1853 to 6,576 leaguers (1,169 hl.) in 1859.[95] But in 1860 the British government removed the discriminatory duties on French wines in accordance with the Cobden-Chevalier Treaty. At the same time, William Gladstone, in his capacity as Chancellor of the Exchequer, revised import duties to encourage the drinking of lighter wines. This was construed as a practical and convenient instrument for reducing the consumption of more potent forms of alcohol. Hence in 1861, the levying of import duties was calculated according to alcoholic content. This worked to the detriment of Cape wines by comparison with those imported from France

91 Redding, *History*, p. 317. 92 Redding, *History*, p. 317.

93 Cape Colony, Report of the Select Committee Appointed to Consider the Wine Trade Papers (Cape Town, 1860).

94 Cape of Good Hope, Report of the Select Committee Appointed to Consider and Report on the State of the Wine Trade (Cape Town, 1865), evidence of L. P. Cauvin, p. 18.

95 Van Zyl, *Kaapse Wyn*, p. 154. In the decade after 1960, British imports of French wine increased fivefold. John V. C. Nye, *War, Wine and Taxes: The Political Economy of Anglo-French Trade, 1689–1900* (Princeton, NJ and Oxford: Princeton University Press, 2007), p. 16.

Table I.3. *Average wine price per leaguer at five year intervals, 1870–1900 (in £, shillings and pence)*

Year	Quality Wine	Inferior Wine
1870	£17.9.0	£12.15.0
1875	£25.12.0	£17.9.0
1880	£20.0.0	£11.10.0
1885	£8.3.0	£5.12.0
1890	£11.12.0	£8.6.0
1895	£11.13.0	£9.1.0
1900	£16.1.0	£11.6.0

Source: Reworked from Scully, *Bouquet*, table 4, p. 40.

because they almost always contained a generous dollop of spirit.[96] Henceforth, Cape wine could no longer compete on the basis of either price or quality. Wine exports slumped to 356 leaguers in 1862, and Cape wine thereafter became marginal to the British market.[97] As one informant before the 1865 Select Committee explained:

> One great disadvantage Cape wines labour under is that continental wines can be shipped at a very low strength owing to their proximity to the London market; whereas Cape wines on account of the length of the voyage, have to be fortified before shipped. The foreign wines can be imported into the London market at the 1s. duty.

Most Cape wines incurred the higher duty of 2s.6d per gallon.[98] To compound matters, the opening of the Suez Canal in 1869 meant that the Cape forfeited its role as the 'tavern of the seas'. Meanwhile, the production of wine had increased substantially from 15,829 leaguers (2,739 hl.) in 1840 to 24,736 leaguers (4,280 hl.) in 1860 (see Table I.2). The prices for the better wines remained relatively buoyant until the mid-1870s after which, in the context of the Long Depression, they slid to a third of their former value in 1885 (Table I.3). Consequently, the Cape wine industry was already in a perilous state when phylloxera came ashore.

[96] One informant noted that Cape wines intended for export came with an alcoholic strength of between 12 and 15 degrees. When the wine spirit was added, the strength was raised considerably. Report of the Select Committee Appointed to Consider Wine Trade Papers (1860), evidence of H. C. Jarvis, p. 3. This mattered because under the new duties, wines at over 13 per cent were taxed more heavily while anything over 20 per cent was taxed at the same higher rate as brandy. Ludington, *Politics of Wine*, p. 254.

[97] Van Zyl, *KWV 75 Jaar* (Paarl: KWV, 1993), pp. 6–7.

[98] Cape of Good Hope, Report of the Select Committee Appointed to Consider and Report on the State of the Wine Trade (Cape Town, 1865), evidence of L. P. Cauvin, pp. 17–18.

The Crafting of Wine Science

From ancient times, the makers of wine have been close observers of the relationship between cause and effect without necessarily developing a profound understanding of the reasons why.[99] Hence it was understood that exposure to some air might aid fermentation but could also cause wine to turn to vinegar. The use of sulphur dioxide (SO^2) became more prevalent once wines were committed to bottles. But in the mid-nineteenth century, the production of wine largely remained a process of trial and error. It is only with the foundational research of Louis Pasteur, which saw the light of day in the 1860s, that it was definitively established that yeast was the living organism that converted the sugar to alcohol, whereas other bacteria performed other processes that altered the character of the wine.[100] The authorities charged with improving Cape wines had a ready answer to what needed to be done, which was to address the various points in the winemaking process where harmful bacteria might intrude. Baron Carl von Babo, an Austrian who was recruited as Government Viticulturalist in 1884, believed that the Cape was exceptionally well-endowed for the production of good wine. The real problem, he considered, lay with unhygienic winemaking practices:

> The cutting of the grapes, the separation of the ripe from the unripe grapes, the collection of the grapes before pressing, is all done, with a few exceptions in a careless manner. But the climax of the untidy proceedings is reached in the trampling of the grapes … A number of half-naked coloured men, in a state of active perspiration, are tramping the grapes in the first tub; thus the feet break the grapes, and by the elasticity of the sole, the seeds etc., remain unbroken … From the floor of the wine stores, which are saturated with acetous germs, the trampers carry on their feet a large amount of detrimental substance into the juice, and also the sweat of the man goes into the juice; although the latter does not perceptibly increase the quantity, it certainly imparts a most objectionable bouquet to the wine.[101]

He also found fault with fermentation in open vessels, identifying some of the practices that accounted for the rough taste of the wine:

> Juice, husks and stalks are thrown together into the fermenting tubs, and the astringent harsh tannin is thus extracted from the husks and the stalks, imparting to the wine that unpleasant scratching taste. The fermenting tubs are open, and the juice can absorb from the air any quantity of those germs which are later on a standing danger to the quality of the wine. All the flavour compounds can freely escape during fermentation from the

[99] David L. Thurmond, *From Vines to Wines in Classical Rome: A Handbook of Viticulture and Oenology in Rome and the Roman West* (Leiden and Boston: Brill, 2017).

[100] Harry W. Paul, *Science, Vine and Wine in Modern France* (Cambridge: Cambridge University Press, 1996), ch. 4. Paul notes that, for Pasteur, fermentation and disease were but two sides of the same coin, pp. 169–170.

[101] Von Babo, cited in Leipoldt, *300 Years*, p. 152.

open vessels. These bouquet compounds, which are so characteristic of the Cape grape would also be in the wine, if the making of the wine were better . . .[102]

While the attribution of harsh tannins to the presence of stalks and foreign matter was nothing new (it had been commented on by Percival amongst others), Von Babo was clearly identifying exposure to oxygen as the cardinal error that opened the door to harmful bacteria, which then impacted negatively on the bouquet and flavour of the wine. Von Babo championed the importance of introducing modern presses and much more controlled conditions. By the end of the century, attention turned to the challenge associated with managing fermentations amid excessive heat in the cellars. In 1896, Robert Wallace, Professor of Agriculture at the University of Edinburgh, was commissioned by the Cape government to carry out a survey of agriculture. On the subject of wine, it was his turn to be critical of Von Babo's failure to attend to the temperature of the cellars and the vats. However, he did concede that the Groot Constantia wine farm had adopted some helpful innovations.[103] Underlining the need for both a low and stable temperature, he noted the positive effects of introducing a cooling coil to the vats and taking measures to reduce the temperature of the cellars to around 15.6°C.[104] His description was accompanied by a diagram of the 'attemptator or must cooler' and the copper coil that was passed through the vat. The close attention to temperature control, which was also evident in Algeria at about the same time,[105] reflected a more nuanced understanding of the fermentation process and how it could be nudged in the desired direction. None of this would have been considered orthodoxy only fifty years before.

Although historians and social scientists have enjoyed puncturing myths surrounding the omniscience of Pasteur,[106] the discovery of microbes and the work they perform was revolutionary in its own ways. By contrast, viticulture developed in a much more incremental fashion and largely in response to diseases of the vine. In a kind of revenge against ecological imperialism, the diseases in question originated in American vines that were transported to Europe at a point in the mid-nineteenth century when maritime and rail transport had greatly shrunk geographical distances. The early warning signs

[102] Von Babo, cited in Leipoldt, *300 Years*, p. 152.

[103] Robert Wallace, *Farming Industries of Cape Colony* (London: P. S. King & Son, 1896), pp. 140–141. These innovations may have come after Von Babo left his post. He was succeeded by Clemens Mayer who arrived in 1888 from Geisenheim. Leipoldt, *300 Years*, p. 143.

[104] Wallace, *Farming*, pp. 140–141.

[105] By 1895, Algerian producers were already embracing refrigeration. White, *Blood*, p. 71.

[106] Paul, *Science*, ch. 6. Bruno Latour has observed that more was attributed to Pasteur than could possibly have been the case in *The Pasteurization of France* (Cambridge, MA and London: Harvard University Press, 1988), pp. 41–43.

came with the rapid march of oidium, or powdery mildew, across Europe in the 1850s. This reached the shores of South Africa in 1858 and was apparent in the vineyards of Groot Constantia the following year. Oidium had especially severe consequences for France, which consequently lost ground to some of its neighbours.[107] But this was as nothing compared to the devastation wrought by *phylloxera vastatrix*, the tiny insect that attacks the roots and generally kills the vine. This was described rather memorably by Louis Leipoldt as '[t]his horrible little insect, as hideous as a girl in trousers, [that] has a sex life whose surprising aberrations make, by comparison, the wildest imaginings of modern pornographic novelists appear like anaemic virtuosities'.[108] The insect in question was inadvertently introduced to France on vines imported from the United States and made its way across Europe with remarkable speed in the 1870s and 1880s.[109] Once it had been identified by Jules-Emile Planchon as the cause rather than a symptom of the ailment of the vine, attention turned to various forms of eradication. As is well known, many suggestions were mooted and tested in the field. Given that oidium had been successfully tackled with the application of sulphur, it was perhaps inevitable that many favoured advancing down the chemical route. In France, this entailed the injection of chemicals such as carbon bisulphide into the soil. Having failed to isolate indigenous American vines that were both sufficiently resistant and capable of producing a palatable drink, French scientists and vignerons eventually scored a breakthrough by grafting *vinifera* vines onto American rootstocks that enjoyed an inherited resistance.[110] Needless to say, a great deal of trial and error accompanied the hard science, but once grafting yielded demonstrable results the knowledge was disseminated across the wine world.

The Government of the Cape monitored European developments closely. At various points, it solicited advice from three of the most eminent scientists who served on the Phylloxera Commission that was established in France in 1871, namely Planchon, Maxime Cornu and Pierre Mouillefert.[111] In 1880, specimens were despatched to Cornu who confirmed there was no evidence of

[107] Spain was less affected and to some extent profited at French expense. Simpson, *Creating Wine*, p. 42.

[108] Leipoldt, *300 Years*, p. 142.

[109] Spain was largely spared and benefited accordingly. Simpson, *Creating Wine*, pp. 42, 96. There are also other pockets, for example near Sintra in Portugal and on the small island of Sant'Antioco on the southwest coast of Sardinia, where vines still grow on their own rootstocks.

[110] The development of hybrids was also seen as an option, but the consensus was that the quality was lower. For a definitive account see George Gale, *Dying on the Vine: How Phylloxera Transformed Wine* (Berkeley and Los Angeles: University of California Press, 2011). On the role of science in beating phylloxera, see also Paul, *Science*, ch. 1.

[111] Gale, *Dying*, pp. 18–19.

phylloxera at that time.[112] In October 1881, the Cape government sent a delegate to the International Phylloxera Congress in Bordeaux. At this point, there were hopes that the threat could be kept at bay through the maintenance of a hard maritime border. Having sought Planchon's advice, the decision was taken to ban the importation of vines from countries that were afflicted by phylloxera.[113] However, its local presence was confirmed in 1886, and the best guess was that it had been around for some years. The authorities solicited an assessment from Mouillefert of the French National School of Agriculture. His report concluded that the Cape faced an even greater threat than in Europe because the climate was conducive to faster reproduction of the bug, while the winged females could be active over a space of four months rather than eight to ten weeks.[114] With Mouillefert's wholesome approval, a series of drastic measures was introduced. Teams of inspectors, largely consisting of convicts, were sent to the vineyards and where diseased vines were discovered, sections were cut out. Carbon bisulfide was applied to the soil, although (as in France) the chemicals proved just as likely to kill the vines as the pest itself. Phylloxera-infected areas were also subjected to strict quarantine. Although Cornu had indicated that other plants were not the carriers of phylloxera, with the possible exception of potatoes, the trade in fruit and vegetables across newly established internal boundaries was prohibited. These measures were unpopular amongst the farmers, who complained about unnecessary restrictions on the trade in agricultural goods.[115] A number expressed the belief that it was the inspection teams themselves that were the vector, while one specifically blamed workers from Pniël.[116] Unlike in Russia, where the adherence to chemical solutions rested on a curious Darwinian logic,[117] the farmers at the Cape accepted that the way forward was to embrace American rootstocks. American vines were grown from seed, and some had begun to graft the *vitis*

112 Cape Government Notice No. 783, "Report on the Cape Vines", dated 9 June 1880.

113 Gale, *Dying*, ch. 1.

114 Report by M. O. Mouillefert, dated 30 March 1889, in "Phylloxera in South Africa", *Bulletin of Miscellaneous Information* (Royal Botanic Gardens Kew) 18 (33) 1889, p. 231. Mouillefert apparently visited South Africa much later and allegedly claimed to have seen vines that dated back to the seventeenth and eighteenth centuries, which, if true, would suggest that some older vines survived phylloxera. Paper read by Alan H. Burgoyne MP, "Colonial vine culture", *Journal of the Royal Society of Arts* 60 (3105), 1912, p. 675. I am grateful to Raphaela van Embden for sharing this with me.

115 Amongst those who was critical was a C. L. W. Kohler of Groot Drakenstein. Cape of Good Hope, Preliminary Report of the Phylloxera Commission 1893, Quarantine Regulations, with Proceedings, Minutes of Evidence and Appendix (Cape Town, 1893), pp. 8–9.

116 Evidence of Johannes J. Haupt, 15 November 1892, Preliminary Report, p. 6. A number of other informants mentioned labourers as the vector, although some were more inclined to view wind as the main carrier.

117 Steven V. Bittner, *Whites and Reds: A History of Wine in the Lands of Tsar and Commissar* (Oxford: Oxford University Press, 2021), ch. 2.

vinifera plants to these. At the Phylloxera Commission hearings in 1893 a clear desire was expressed for the authorities to set up nurseries, and to select and disseminate the rootstock most suited to local conditions and to make these available for grafting.[118] In other words, the farmers wanted the Cape government to get a grip.

One important lesson was that the Cape was able to weather the storm because it mostly adhered to the scientific evidence emanating from Europe, rather than seeking to reinvent the wheel. Another was that the Cape was in urgent need of recruiting external expertise, establishing its own research facilities and nurturing educational institutions that could disseminate the new science surrounding viticulture and winemaking. Von Babo's recruitment was a conscious effort to look beyond the talent that was locally available.[119] In 1885, the authorities purchased Groot Constantia as a government farm, and Von Babo was given general oversight. In 1898, the government acquired Elsenburg to establish an agricultural college that would offer training in viticulture, winemaking and a range of other farming activities.[120] In 1901, Elsenburg recruited Frederic Bioletti from the University of California to handle the viticulture and winemaking side of the operation. At that time, Elsenburg had some 40 acres of vines planted on American rootstocks and there were plans for an expansion of production facilities. Bioletti was a noteworthy choice because he was well-versed in the intricacies of phylloxera. Indeed, after three years, he returned to the University of California, where he served as the first Chair of Viticulture and Enology and made a major contribution to the study of phylloxera and resistant rootstocks there.[121] Meanwhile, one Abraham Izak (A. I.) Perold took over the position of head of Elsenburg College in 1912.

That same year, a public debate placed the South African turn to viticultural and oenological research and training into sharp relief. Alan H. Burgoyne, a British Member of Parliament and a director of the wine import company, P. B. Burgoyne & Co., read a paper to the colonial section of the Royal Academy of

[118] For example, evidence of P. C. Le Roux, former member of Phylloxera Commission of 1890, 6 November 1892, p. 13 and Gideon Joubert, farmer from Achter Paarl, p. 14, Preliminary Report.

[119] As Leipoldt indicates, the decision was taken under pressure from the Prime Minister, John X Merriman, who believed that the proposed encouragement of Italian immigrants was not the solution that was needed. Leipoldt, *300 Years*, p. 137.

[120] Anon, "Agricultural education in Cape Colony: The Elsenburg College, a visit and some impressions", *The Agricultural Journal of the Cape of Good Hope* 22 (1) 1903, p. 23.

[121] Biography at https://snaccooperative.org/ark:/99166/w6wq4839 (accessed 26 January 2022). Bioletti published a treatise on phylloxera in 1901, the same year as his move to the Cape. On his subsequent work on phylloxera and resistant rootstocks, see Gale, *Dying*, pp. 161–169.

Arts.[122] The speaker could hold forth with authority on Australian wines given that the company had not only been importing them for some years, but had also purchased its own farms. Burgoyne's brief was to enlighten his audience on empire wines, but this mostly took the form of a comparison between the Cape and Australia.[123] Burgoyne began with a familiar contrast between favourable growing conditions and the 'indolence and ignorance' of the 'Dutch' farmer, which he blamed for a preference for flatlands over hillsides in the pursuit of higher output rather than better quality.[124] He concluded that 'there is no doubt that the Cape market is largely being spoiled by the inefficient and sloppy methods of the winemaker'. In Australia, by contrast, he found meticulously tended vineyards and modern machinery that de-stemmed and crushed the bunches before pumping the must into 'polished cement vats, where fermentation is induced and allowed to take place under the most scientific supervision, and regulated by methods of cooling which it is rare to find in the older established wine-making districts of Europe'.[125] Significantly for our purposes, he linked the advances in modern, scientific methods to the foundation of agricultural colleges in South Australia, Victoria and New South Wales. This presentation elicited a decidedly tetchy response from Charles du Plessis Chiappini, the trade commissioner of the fledgling Union of South Africa. The latter accused Burgoyne of reproducing a caricature of the Dutch farmer that was not based on any first-hand experience. He also countered that while Australian producers deserved credit for having produced 'a commercial type of wine … its quality was not such as to induce South African growers to aim at it as a model'. Indeed, he continued, 'South African wines, as consumed in the clubs and hotels, or in private life, were of a decidedly better quality than Australian wines'.[126] Predictably, he blamed the merchants for any substandard wines that were sold, noting that they took in the wine when it was 10 months old and then 'manipulated it and placed it on the market'. A more surprising observation was that while outside assistance might have served Australia well, 'the foreign experts tried in South Africa has proved to be hopeless failures'. Given that a recent attempt to improve Cape wines was based on the recent contributions of a number of outsiders, from

[122] The original company was founded by Peter Bond (P. B.) Burgoyne in 1871. It became a limited liability company in 1903, with P. B. Burgoyne, Cuthbert Burgoyne, Alan H. Burgoyne and Lennox Stuart Burgoyne as the directors. The company specialized in importing Australian wines; Jennifer Regan-Lefebvre, "John Bull's other vineyard: selling Australian wine in nineteenth-century Britain", *Journal of Imperial and Commonwealth History* 45 (2) 2017, p. 273. The company owned the Mount Ophir farm in Rutherglen, Victoria, which was alluded to in his talk.

[123] On Empire wines see Jennifer Regan-Lefebvre, *Imperial Wine: How the British Empire Made Wine's New World* (Oakland: University of California Press, 2022).

[124] Burgoyne, "Colonial", p. 673.

[125] Burgoyne, "Colonial", p. 678.

[126] Burgoyne, "Colonial", response by C. du P. Chiappini, Trade Commissioner, p. 682.

Von Babo to Bioletti, this was a surprising assertion. However, the point he was presumably trying to make was that it required homegrown talent to propel the industry forward. His intervention brought forth additional comments in favour of either Cape or Australian wines. But it was Burgoyne who made the clinching point:

> The Cape started making wine 200 years before Australia thought of it, and yet as a result of bad methods of cultivation thirty years ago, Cape wines had a bad name today; and it was owing to Australia carrying out the manufacture in a scientific manner from the commencement that they had swept the Cape wines off the markets of the United Kingdom.[127]

Nurturing local talent was now a priority, but this also depended on local experts being well-versed in the world of international wine. The individual who achieved this more than any other was A. I. Perold. The latter is the most revered figure in the history of the twentieth-century South African wine industry by virtue of his practical contributions to viticultural science – not least in the shape of the Pinotage grape which has come down to us as one of the unintended consequence of his experimentation.[128] Perold was very much a product of the Cape winelands milieu, having been born in 1880 in Dal Josaphat, a small wine-farming community located roughly between the towns of Paarl and Wellington. In 1906, when the second Afrikaanse Taalbeweging (Afrikaans Language Movement) was launched, Perold was elected one of the office-holders alongside D. F. Malherbe, the son of the then owner of Kleinbosch, who had been a school friend in Wellington and who went on to author a series of influential works of literature.[129] In his own way, Perold contributed to the elevation of Afrikaans as an appropriate medium for the pursuit of scientific enquiry. In 1906, the young Perold penned his first substantive article comparing the wine industries of South Africa and France.[130] To modern eyes, the orthography is unconventional, signalling that written Afrikaans remained yet a work in progress. Twenty years later, when Perold published his major academic treatise on viticulture, *Handbook oor Wynbou* (1926), he was writing in a language that had assumed a standard

[127] Burgoyne, "Colonial", riposte by Burgoyne, p. 684.

[128] For a biography see R. U. Kenney, *Abraham Izak Perold: Wegwyser van ons Wingerdbou* (Cape Town Pretoria and Johannesburg: Human & Rousseau, 1981). For a selection of his writings, see Peter F. May (ed.), *Perold's Papers*, Vol. 1 (St. Albans: Inform and Enlighten, 2014).

[129] Another member was J. H. H. De Waal, who is credited with writing the first novel in Afrikaans. Giliomee, *The Afrikaners*, p. 389. De Waal became a Member of Parliament in the 1920s and will appear again in Chapter 1.

[130] The article has been re-published as "Di wijnbou in Frankrijk en hier", in May, *Perold's Papers*, Vol. 1.

Figure I.1 A. I. Perold and KWV Colleagues, 1938: De Wet Theron, 5th from left, Perold, 6th, Frank W. Myburgh, 7th, C.J.G. Niehaus, extreme right
Source: Reproduced with kind acknowledgement of KWV, *KWV 1918–1993*.

form and had just achieved official status.[131] In due course, Afrikaans became the language of instruction at the University of Stellenbosch where Perold was installed as the inaugural Professor of Viticulture and Oenology in 1917, at the still tender age of 37 years. The advancement of South African wine science and the progression of the Afrikaans language unfolded in tandem, and both were carried forward in the person of Perold himself (Figure I.1).

Perold took pride in his heritage, but in an obituary penned in 1942, Leipoldt observed that he was also a dedicated cosmopolitan.[132] Perold had completed his doctorate in chemistry at the University of Halle (Germany) in 1904, which he followed up with a year of further study in Paris under the wing of Henri

[131] A. I. Perold, *Handboek oor Wynbou* (Stellenbosch: Pro-Ecclesia Drukkery, 1926). Even at this point, there was considerable resistance to the replacement of Dutch in the absence of a significant literature in Afrikaans. Louis Leipoldt, a renowned writer and friend of Perold, was amongst those who advised caution. Giliomee, *The Afrikaners*, p. 378. The English version of this work has helpfully been reissued as A. I. Perold, *A Treatise on Viticulture* (St. Albans: Inform and Enlighten, 2012).

[132] Kenney, *Abraham Izak Perold*, p. 11.

Moissan, who was to win a Nobel Prize for chemistry shortly thereafter.[133] In 1907, Perold was despatched by the Cape government to conduct a study of viticulture and oenology in Europe, which entailed a welcome step beyond the narrow confines of chemistry. Over a two-year period, he engaged in research stints at the Geisenheim Research Institute in Germany and the Wädenswil Swiss-German Experimental Station, both of which were renowned for their viticultural research. This absence, during a time of upheaval in the South African wine industry, afforded an opportunity to spend several months touring the continent.[134] He targeted leading agricultural, viticultural and oenological institutes, notably at Montpellier University, Belem (Lisbon) and Santarem (Alentejo) in Portugal, and three institutes within Italy, in Alba (Piedmonte) and Portici and Avellino (in Campania).[135] Along the way, he established contact with wine producers in France, Italy, Spain and Portugal. He also took the opportunity to visit Tunisia and Algeria. Whereas the Russian wine experts fixated on all things French, Perold cast his net more widely and translated – in both a literal and figurative sense – the diverse world of European wine for a South African audience.[136]

Perold was fluent in English, Dutch, German and French, learned to speak Portuguese and Spanish and developed at least a reading knowledge of Italian – all of which he put to good use in his academic research and writing. Perold was constantly drawing on Europe both for scientific inspiration and styles of wine that could be replicated under South African conditions. He is credited with having introduced a lengthy list of European grape varieties that were trialled for their suitability before being either adopted or conserved in a kind of living museum of the vine in Stellenbosch.[137] He also championed South Africa's version of fortified wines, which built on his initial engagement with producers in the Douro and in Jerez. And lest it be thought that he had his back turned to the Anglophone world, he personally translated his 1926 treatise into English the following year to bring his labours to the attention of viticultural researchers in California and Australia.[138] At various moments when the

[133] May, *Perold Papers*, p. 17.

[134] His itinerary, based on his personal diary, is discussed at length in Kenney, *Abraham Izak Perold*, pp. 5–6.

[135] Kenney, *Abraham Izak Perold*, pp. 56, 63–67.

[136] Much of this was in the shape of articles he wrote for the industry magazine *Wine and Spirit*. See the bibliography in Kenney, *Abraham Izak Perold*, pp. 143–145.

[137] In his obituary, Leipoldt mentioned that Perold was responsible for importing no fewer than 60 cultivars (comprising both wine and table grapes) from Europe and North Africa. A figure that is three times higher is widely cited. Perold also introduced the Barlinka table from Algeria which became a significant export from South Africa. Leipoldt specifically mentioned Grenache Noir and Barbera. Kenney, *Abraham Izak Perold*, p. 11. Barbera was probably introduced by Perold after he joined Elsenburg College in 1912. The cultivar secured a small niche in Durbanville where it was planted at Altygedacht around 1920.

[138] Kenney, *Abraham Izak Perold*, pp. 8, 10.

country seemed to turn in on itself, Perold stood for a distinctive version of Afrikaner cosmopolitanism that was firmly grounded in international wine science.

In conclusion, what emerges from this introductory analysis is that the trajectory of Cape wine was shaped in fundamental ways by the structures and practices of the VOC in which slavery was always at the centre of the frame. As the Cape entered the British imperial orbit, wine farmers were required to adapt successively to the ending of the slave trade, emancipation and the exigencies of free trade. But slavery continued to cast the longest of shadows in the shape of an almost caste-like system of labour relations. The history of other wine regions beyond Europe reveals a very different story. The Argentinian wine industry, centred on Mendoza, was shaped by targeted immigration from Italy, while conscious efforts were made to attract Italians, Germans and others with knowledge of the vine to California and Australia.[139] At the same time, the Cape was caught up in successive global crises precipitated by phylloxera, war and economic depression. There was a conscious effort to draw on European experience, not least with respect to the new science emerging around viticulture and oenology. But it is no less significant that government officials charged with responsibility for the wine industry also looked to California and Australia for examples of how to train up the next generation of wine producers.

Skipping through Fields and Meeting Dead-Ends

In every humanities project there are active choices as well as pragmatic adjustments that are required to deal with the inherent unpredictability of conducting research. Elements of both are embedded in the current study. One of the active choices was to pay less attention to labour issues, certainly not because these were unimportant, but simply because so much excellent work already existed. At a later stage in the writing process, it was tempting to engage closely with the recent collaborative work of Xabier Itçaina, Antoine Roger and Andy Smith.[140] The latter seeks to account for recent transformations within the European wine industry, combining elements of historical institutionalism with Pierre Bourdieu's conception of fields. The attraction of their model is that it enables one to unravel the languages and practices that are specific to each field – economic, bureaucratic and scientific – while

139 Uttam Bajwa, "Frontier enterprise: immigrant winemaking in Mendoza, Argentina (1884–1914)", unpublished PhD thesis, Johns Hopkins University, Baltimore, 2012; Julie McIntyre and John Germov, *Hunter Wine: A History* (Sydney: New South Books, 2018), ch. 5.

140 Xabier Itçaina, Antoine Roger and Andy Smith, *Varietals of Capitalism: A Political Economy of the Changing Wine Industry* (Ithaca, NY and London: Cornell University Press, 2016).

demonstrating how historical change might arise from the alignment (or lack thereof) between them. The model helps one to appreciate why experts who might be able to drive transformations in their own domain, such as viticultural research, might have limited influence upon regulatory bodies. The serious dearth of good planting material in the 1980s is a good example of what happened when scientific, bureaucratic and economic actors were pulling in different directions. Table I.4 represents what a rendering of the fields might look like when modified for the South African case. As can readily be seen, there were structural tensions, for example, between the imperative for farmers to expand the market for wine and the pressure on government to tackle alcohol abuse, or between the desire of merchant–manufacturers to achieve vertical integration and the wish of government to prevent monopolies from taking root in the alcohol sector. All these tensions are teased out in the pages of this book and the reader may find it useful to return to this table as a kind of user's manual. However, I have ultimately decided against writing a book that turns on the articulation between fields. One reason is that race and consumption are difficult to attribute to any one field. Another is that while such a highly structured approach is an aid to understanding moments of change, and periods of stasis, it does not lend itself to the kinds of individual stories I wish to tell. I, however, have cause to return briefly to this model in the Conclusion.

The choices that were forced upon me took the form of an unexpected paucity of archival materials. When I embarked on the project, I looked forward to grappling with a plethora of documentary sources. There turned out to be little in the National Archives in Cape Town covering the decades after Union in 1910, and most of what there was in Pretoria related to the country's external relations. The reason seemed to be that with the devolution of regulatory powers to the KWV, it became the keeper of the relevant documents. After 1940, the KWV collected data on every farm where wine grapes were produced, and it enforced its rules by means of a team of inspectors who certainly kept detailed records. When I sought access to the KWV archives, I was variously told that there were no records, or that files existed but were not in the public domain. Given that the KWV had performed statutory functions, it arguably should have deposited its files with the National Archives when it converted to an entirely private company devoid of public functions. However, these records were quite likely the collateral damage that was inflicted at a time when the KWV feared a government takeover (as outlined in Chapter 7). In all probability, the single most important set of records documenting the recent history of the Cape winelands has therefore been lost forever. My persistent enquiries did yield access to a few files that contained more recent material relating to cooperatives. Moreover, I was grateful for the opportunity to access the photographic collection of the KWV. But that was as far as I was able to progress.

Table I.4. *The Cape Wine industry and its fields*

Elements	Scientific	Economic	Political/Bureaucratic
Interventions	Viticultural research	Grape growing	Regulation of production
	Oenological research	Winemaking	Regulation of consumption
	Outreach to farmers, including farm trials, disease treatment	Wholesale distribution	Taxation – excise duties
		Wine retail	Quarantine
		Wine exports	Rural policing
Institutions and Actors	University of Stellenbosch, Department of Viticulture and Oenology (1917)	Individual grape growers and farmers	Ministry of Agriculture – general oversight and quarantine
	Elsenburg College (1898)	Cooperatives	Ministry of Justice – regulation of liquor consumption and licensing
	Nietvoorbij Viticultural and Oenological Research Institute (1955)	Merchant-manufacturers (e.g. SFW and Distillers)	Department of Customs and Excise
	KWV	Liquor outlets, bottle-stores, hotels	KWV – devolved regulation of distilling wine (1924) and drinking wine (1940)
	International collaborations, e.g., Geisenheim, Weinsberg, University of California–Davis	KWV (brandy), wine merchants (wine)	
Competing Discourses	Promoting better varietals and planting material	Protecting viability of small farmers	Curbing output whilst improving quality
	Virus eradication	Improving quality of wine	Helping wine farmers to regulate themselves
	International scientific collaboration	Expanding domestic market for wine	Preventing alcohol abuse, including dop
		Achieving greater efficiencies in distribution through vertical integration	Oversight of labour relations, enforcing racial laws in winelands
		Developing exports	Taxing at a level that would not threaten viability of small producers
		Making wine profitable	Preventing monopolies in distribution

At a point when the prospects for the project looked bleak, my attention was alerted to the existence of the Distell Archive in Stellenbosch by two influential figures who had worked for the SFW in the past, namely Duimpie Bayly and Dave Hughes. The archive turned out to house a diverse collection of files relating to the various companies that ended up being folded into the SFW and Distillers over many decades. Its main strength was that it provided an insight not only into the relationship between the wine companies and their trusted farmers, but also into their market research, marketing and advertising strategies. It was this that led me to take an even greater interest in the consumption side of the wine story. I also delved deeply into the magazine that was directed to the farmers. In its initial incarnation as *Wine and Spirit*, and subsequently as *Wynboer*, it became easier to trace emerging trends, follow debates and identify links between the Cape and the rest of the wine world. Because *Wynboer* was acquired by the KWV, it also afforded an insight into the mindset of those who regulated the industry. Through its pages, the KWV sought to persuade farmers and consumers of the need to embrace the latest trends and contemporary innovations.

My other adaptation involved engaging more closely with the history of specific farms. In the end, I was able to do this for only two, namely Joostenburg and Rustenberg, but this proved invaluable for understanding moments of transformation in the vineyards and cellars. In addition, I was able to read these against the SFW's *Boereboeke* (Farmers' Books) that detailed the interactions with the farmers who made wine for the largest company. It also meant that I could piece together an account of production to sit alongside the substantial material I had gathered on the distribution of wine. Over the years, I also had the good fortune to interview a good number of the leading figures within the industry, often more than once over. Finally, I have paid particular attention to moments when issues relating to the wine were in the public eye. This has entailed poring over Parliamentary debates and Commissions of Enquiry which often crystallized the points of contention in the pithiest ways. In the end, this partially compensated for the lack of a wine archive in the conventional sense.

It remains to clarify that this book adopts a broadly chronological approach, but with chapters structured around thematic strands. I begin with an issue that was acutely contentious at the end of the nineteenth century, namely whether the Government of the Cape should intervene to relieve the distress of the wine farmers or should rather further restrict access to all forms of alcohol as temperance activists vociferously demanded.

1 Contesting the Moral High Ground

Overproduction and the Temperance Onslaught, 1880–1928

> It cannot for a moment be denied that the world's overproduction of grapes has considerably increased during the last quarter of a century. This has been caused by a more intensive cultivation in the wine countries like Algeria, Tunis, California, The Argentine, Chili [sic] and other South American States, and to a certain extent, Australia and South Africa ... Unfortunately, for the wine-grower, the consumption of wine has on the whole fallen considerably. This is due to a number of causes, of which I mention the propaganda in favour of total prohibition, which culminated in its adoption by the United States of North America ... To this rule our country is no exception. It is no use arguing that we suffer from under consumption and not over-production. So long as production exceeds consumption – inclusive of exports – there is over production.[1]
>
> (Perold, 1931)

In their analysis of the eighteenth-century Cape economy, Pieter Van Duin and Robert Ross maintain that there was no systemic problem of overproduction, in large part because of the robust demand for wine in Cape Town.[2] As we have seen, the second half of the nineteenth century witnessed the loss of export markets and the reduced significance of the city as a maritime hub. Given the expansion of production that could find no ready outlet, it must have felt very much like there was a crisis of overproduction by the 1860s. The onset of phylloxera dealt with that problem in a summary fashion, wiping out investments in vineyards and compounding the financial plight of many producers. However, farmers quickly took to replanting vineyards in the 1890s, such that the production levels at the moment when phylloxera struck had already been exceeded by 1907. This is perhaps surprising when the prospects looked so uncertain. However, this reflected a global trend, as A. I. Perold – alert to the bigger picture, as always – indicated in 1931. But Perold also put his finger on something else, which was the reality that consumption in many countries had been buffeted by the impact of global temperance.

[1] A. I. Perold, "The South African wine industry and overproduction", *Wine and Spirit: A South African Review*, no. 2, November 1931, p. 35.

[2] Van Duin and Ross, *Economy*, pp. 50–51.

In this chapter, I consider both sides of the equation – that is, the efforts of the temperance movement to restrict wine consumption and the efforts of the KWV to increase the market for wine whilst balancing the interests of different rural constituencies. I begin this account by situating the South African story within the contentious politics that followed the ending of the phylloxera crisis in Europe. Here, I deploy France as a foil for understanding the range of possibilities that were present at the Cape.

Wine, Regulation and Temperance in Comparative Perspective

France was the first to be struck by phylloxera and here, arguably more than anywhere else, the future configuration of the wine industry was shaped by the contestation that surrounded restructuring. Under the onslaught of phylloxera, wine production dwindled, exports of wine plummeted and import of wine surged by a factor of 25 between 1870 and 1889 – all of which redounded to the benefit of Spanish and Italian producers before they too succumbed.[3] As the solution of grafting to American rootstock found favour, significant changes ensued across Europe. James Simpson observes that the costs associated with grafting, and the need for greater chemical use, led to increased barriers to (re-)entry.[4] Whereas those with sufficient capital could opt for the development of superior wines in favoured locations, the mass of ordinary producers had to pay close consideration to financial viability. Hence many opted to plant cultivars that guaranteed a high yield and were considered more resistant to disease. There was also an orientation towards regions where land was relatively cheap. Hence French producers faced renewed competition from Spain and Italy, where plantings and the output of wine increased significantly at the close of the nineteenth century.[5] At the same time, there were significant shifts in the centre of gravity within all these countries, assisted by improvements to transport infrastructure. In France, the output was heavily dominated by the Midi (south of France), where the Aramon grape – which reputedly yielded up to seven times more volume per hectare – was planted more widely than ever before.[6] It is telling that the total area under vines in France was significantly lower in 1905 (at 1,669,000 hectares) than it had been in 1878

[3] Lachiver, *Vins*, p. 48; Simpson, *Creating Wine*, p. 42.

[4] Simpson, *Creating Wine*, pp. 38–39. [5] Simpson, *Creating Wine*, pp. 41–48.

[6] Charles Warner cites Chares Gide's estimates in the greater yields for the Aramon grape. Charles K. Warner, *The Winegrowers of France and the Government since 1875* (New York: Columbia University Press, 1960), p. 10. Plantings of Aramon preceded phylloxera but was more widely planted thereafter. As a whole, yields in the Midi in the first decade of the twentieth century averaged 49 hl. as opposed to 27 hl. in the rest of France. Simpson, *Creating Wine*, table 3.2, p. 66.

(2,296,000 hectares), whereas the output of wine had climbed back to pre-phylloxera levels by 1913.[7]

An oversupply of ordinary wines exerted downward pressure on prices. In the end, it required a measure of state intervention to square the circle. In France, there were two diagnoses of the underlying problems and two related sets of solutions. The first was that there was a veritable epidemic of fraud that greatly augmented the volume of what was being sold. This assumed the shape, firstly, of wine shipped in from further afield that was passed off as French, and secondly, it entailed various forms of adulteration. Warner cites one estimate that fraudulent wines accounted for as much as 40 per cent of French national production in 1902.[8] Adulteration also damaged consumer confidence which was reflected in reduced exports to the British market.[9] Part of the difficulty was that the issue divided constituencies within France. Producers in the Midi presented themselves as the hapless victims of unscrupulous *négociants* who adulterated wines with imports from neighbouring countries, as well as Algeria.[10] This came to a head in the much memorialized revolt of the Midi in 1907. Meanwhile, *vignerons* in Champagne complained that their own reputation was being sullied by inferior wine from the Midi being passed off as their own.[11] A priority was to define practices that were blatantly fraudulent and to introduce legal sanctions. As important was the sanctioning of discrete territorial appellations, following the passage of a framework law in 1905. Demarcating the boundaries could be a fraught exercise, as the protests in Champagne in 1911 amply demonstrated, but it was fundamental to the campaign against fraud.[12]

The second diagnosis was that *vignerons* were simply producing too much ordinary wine for a saturated market.[13] Here, the solution was to push for an improvement in the quality of wines from designated appellations, while imposing limits on fresh plantings and promoting shy-yielding varieties. Under the rules sanctioned by the Appellation d'Origine Contrôlée (AOC) system, farmers could only plant designated cultivars, were required to restrict yields and had to respect certain winemaking rules. In regions where more bulk wine was produced, smaller producers were encouraged to join cooperatives that could draw on concessionary loans to invest in the cellars and

[7] Lachiver, *Vins*, pp. 582–583; Simpson, *Creating Wine*, pp. 36–38, figure 2.3, table 2.3; Warner, *Winegrowers*, table 4, p. 15.

[8] Warner, *Winegrowers*, p. 14.

[9] Simpson, *Creating Wine*, pp. 92–98.

[10] Harvey Smith, "Agricultural workers and the French wine growers revolt of 1907", *Past and Present* 79, 1978; Smith, *Terror*, ch. 1.

[11] Guy, *When Champagne*, p. 121.

[12] Guy, *When Champagne*, chs. 5–6.

[13] In France, the struggle to prevent overproduction had a long history. In the eighteenth century, France had witnessed a rapid expansion of production at the expense of quality, mostly driven by peasant households, despite the best efforts of local authorities and central government to outlaw fresh plantings. Lachiver, *Vins*, pp. 335–336.

equipment that would enable better wine to be made. Progress was slow, but by 1914, there were 79 wine cooperatives in France.[14] In 1944, a separate category of Vin Delimité de Qualité Supérieur (VDQ) was created to meet the needs of the cooperative sector. At the same time, the Statut de la Viticulture which was 'promulgated by the government, between 1931 and 1935 and modified by various decrees since' addressed the root causes of overproduction.[15] The Statut imposed restrictions on fresh plantings and established subsidies for uprooting vines, with financial penalties for farmers who allowed yields to rise above a specified level. It also provided for the enforced distillation of surplus wine and the blockage of wine sales when prices fell below a specified point.[16] The surplus had to be surrendered to a government agency that distilled it and found other inventive uses for the wine.[17]

France threw up its own version of the temperance movement, but as Joseph Bohling demonstrates, the defenders of quality wine and temperance advocates ultimately found common cause in the assault on spirits – with wine being marketed to the public as a healthy alternative.[18] The French model was therefore one that recognized the necessity of embracing a spectrum from *premier cru* Burgundies and top-growth Bordeaux at one end, to table wines at the other. Whereas much of the premium wine would continue to be exported, the expectation was that *vin ordinaires* would be consumed by ordinary French men and women as part of their daily diet. The premise was that a high level of export and domestic production would together address overproduction and guarantee everyone's livelihoods.

At the Cape, the issues were posed rather differently around the turn of the century. Imports of wine were negligible, and the question of fraud did not really arise – except in the shape of Cape wines that were blended into French wines. At the Cape, three main issues were at stake. The first was the indifferent quality, which had been a stock complaint since the nineteenth century. By all accounts, Cape wines tasted different by the time they were reached Europe, but even at home the vast majority were deemed to be lacking in character. The diagnosis remained largely the same: namely that farmers who lacked modern pressing facilities allowed stalks and foreign matter to enter the must, while the resulting wines were often described as being overly alcoholic.

[14] Simpson, *Creating Wine*, pp. 72–73. [15] Loubère, *Wine Revolution*, pp. 126–136.

[16] Loubère, *Wine Revolution*, p. 132. A separate category of *vins de pays* was recognized in 1968 and was not covered by these rules.

[17] This included the production of petrol and fuel for cars. Joseph Bohling, *The Sober Revolution: Appellation Wine and the Transformation of France* (Ithaca, NY and London: Cornell University Press, 2018), p. 31. On this and subsidies for uprooting see Loubère, *Wine Revolution*, pp. 131–133.

[18] This was immortalized in the slogan "Drink Well, Drink a Little, in Order to Drink for a Long Time". Bohling, *Sober Revolution*, p. 100.

In parallel with France, the solution was sought in the promotion of cooperative wineries that could bear the cost of installing modern production facilities. In 1905, following the establishment of a Commission of Enquiry, the Cape government made concessionary loans available to cooperative wineries. These initially struggled to become viable and, by 1913, after the government was forced to write off the original advances, the number had fallen from nine to five in total. But some of these became well-established and steadily cemented a reputation for producing wines of dependable quality.[19]

There was also a question about whether the varietals that were planted were conducive to achieving superior quality. Von Babo was of the view that Semillon, Chenin Blanc, Pontac and Muscadel were all eminently capable of making delicate and aromatic wines, provided the highest standards of vinification were observed.[20] Groendruif/Semillon had been the dominant grape in the nineteenth century. In 1823, William Bird reckoned that there were 11 types of grape that were grown at the Cape. He estimated that out of a total of 25.2 million vines, Semillon – 'the common green grape' which in practice was often reddish in colour because of genetic mutation[21] – accounted for no fewer than 21 million vines.[22] This was the grape from which Cape Madeira was produced. The second most planted cultivar was Muscadel, which was the source of sweet wines and accounted for 525,000 vines, presumably including both the white and the red, mutated version. Pontac, a dark red varietal that Bird (half wrongly) associated with Cote Rôtie and the Douro, ranked third with 270,000 vines.[23] Bird noted that Chenin Blanc, 'which gives the full-bodied steen wine, so-called from the same grape of the Rhine and which is well-adapted for wine, but not productive',[24] accounted for 180,000 vines. The remainder was made up of Hanepoot, or Muscat d'Alexandrie, grapes that were considered unsuitable for wine production, and some lesser varietals.

[19] The five that remained were the Drakenstein (near Paarl), Bovlei (near Wellington), Wellington, Drostdy (Tulbagh) and Helderberg cooperative wineries. Union of South Africa, Report of the Wine Commission (Pretoria: Government Printer, 1937) [U/G. No. 25, 1937], pp. 8, 18 [hereinafter *Wine Commission*].

[20] Leipoldt, *300 Years*, p. 138.

[21] Perold observed that 'red Greengrape' pre-dominated in the 1870s. A. I. Perold, "Historical notes on the Cape wine industry", in *Wine Book of South Africa* (Stellenbosch: Wine & Spirit, 1936), p. 93, reflecting on the evidence given by Charles G. Marais of Jonkershoek to a questionnaire and published in *Het Zuid-Afrikaansche Tijdschrift*, November 1878.

[22] William Wilberforce Bird, *State of the Cape of Good Hope in 1822* (London: John Murray, 1823), p. 112. The provenance of these figures is left unclear other than they supposedly emanated from a reliable source.

[23] Pontac is actually Teinturier. It is indeed used in Douro wines under the name of Tinta Francisca, but Côte-Rôtie wines are made mainly from Syrah grapes, with some including Viognier. Robinson, Harding and Vouillamoz, *Wine Grapes*, pp. 1040–1041.

[24] Bird, *State*, pp. 112–113. Clearly, Chenin Blanc is associated with the Loire rather than the Rhine.

Unfortunately, there seem to be no reliable profiles for the decades that followed. But anticipating the possible arrival of phylloxera, the Vine Diseases Commission of 1881 conducted a census and provided highly incomplete figures for the areas planted with each of the main varietals. From the indicative figures in Table 1.1, it can be seen that Semillon remained dominant but faced greater competition than before. Hanepoot placed a distant second and Steen/Chenin Blanc came in third. Of the red varietals, only Pontac featured in the list.

Following the replanting of the vineyards after phylloxera, the vineyard profile shifted. The data in Table 1.2 is expressed in terms of production levels rather than numbers of vines, but it reveals the relative importance of particular cultivars by 1909. It can be seen that Semillon remained the most significant of the cultivars, accounting for 39.5 per cent of production. But what is striking is that the second most important cultivar was now Chenin Blanc, which accounted for 5,473 leaguers (31,633 hl.), or 20.1 per cent of wine produced. An even more striking transformation is that a red cultivar came in a close third, namely Hermitage/Cinsault, which contributed as much as 17.5 per cent of production. Palomino and red Muscadel were the only other varieties of real significance. Unlike in parts of France, it would be difficult to argue that there had been a downgrading in the quality of the cultivars. Indeed, the opposite is probably the case.[25] It is true that of the so-called noble varieties, only Cabernet Sauvignon and Sauvignon Blanc made the list. Nevertheless, Chenin Blanc was capable of producing exceptional wine – with Cyrus Redding noting that some of it 'is really excellent when about seven years old' and Baron von Babo crediting it as 'a most delicate wine'.[26] The replacement of Pontac by Cinsault as the red grape of choice was probably an improvement if the intention was to create table wines.[27] Some of the most distinctive wines in South Africa today are made from Cinsault as well as from Chenin Blanc. Hence it was much less a question of the intrinsic attributes of the cultivars than the attention paid to viticulture and winemaking. However, by 1909, much of the grape production was channelled into the production of brandy. Some of the brandy was made from wine spirit and some from the whole grapes, while a coarser version was distilled from the husks. Brandy could be distilled from any of these grapes but was most likely to be made from Semillon and Palomino. Where farms were geared to brandy production, high yields were privileged and much less attention was paid to the quality of

[25] Both White Muscadel/Muscat de Frontignac and Pontac were phased out under Von Babo and his successor, Clemens Mayer. Estreicher, "Brief history", p. 526.

[26] Redding, *History*, p. 316; Leipoldt, *300 Years*, pp. 110, 138.

[27] The plantings of Muscat de Frontignan/Muscat Blanc à Petits Grains, which had been associated with the most delicate Constantia wines, appear to have declined in significance. Aramon seems never to have been planted.

Table 1.1. *Reported number of vines in 1881*

Division	Groendruif (Semillon)	Steen (Chenin Blanc)	Muscadel	Hanepoot >(Muscatd' Alexandrie)	Pontac	Fransdruif (Palomino)	Total
Bedford	–	–	–	–	–	–	1,500
Cape	392,200	521,000	492,250	453,250	71,000	137,300	2,656,300
Caledon	86,500	500	500	15,000	–	–	1,318,900
Clanwilliam	–	–	–	–	–	–	160,500
Calvinia	600	–	–	44,800	–	–	150,200
George	–	–	81,600	74,600	–	34,000	211,200
Jansenville	–	–	–	–	–	–	134,400
Malmesbury	611,000	157,000	52,000	64,000	–	18,000	2,478,000
Paarl	12,042,500	454,000	112,250	1,172,000	272,000	168,000	18,203,300
Piquetberg	–	–	–	–	–	–	560,000
Prince Albert	–	–	62,000	132,000	–	24,000	591,000
Robertson	246,000	9,000	560,900	597,700	–	133,000	4,143,900
Riversdale	–	40,300	119,400	49,900	–	70,800	280,400
Stellenbosch	6,911,500	1,221,000	74,000	135,000	529,000	160,000	14,651,800
Swellendam	161,000	–	9,000	–	–	20,000	294,000
Tulbagh	46,000	39,000	–	–	–	–	630,000
Uniondale	–	–	105,500	164,800	–	94,500	413,500
Uitenhage	–	–	–	–	–	–	1,000
Willowmore	71,000	–	4,900	9,800	–	5,500	174,500
Worcester	1,247,000	–	120,000	2,086,500	22,000	–	5,548,800
Total	21,815,100	2,442,300	1,795,050	5,600,450	894,000	867,000	52,603,400

Source: Extract from Report of Vine Diseases Commission, 1881, in Perold, "Historical notes", p. 110.

Table 1.2. *South African wine and brandy production leaguers and morgen, and areas under vine, 1909*

Area	Pontac	Hermitage	Cab Sauv	Steen	Sauv Blanc	Green Grape	White French	White Muscadel	Red Muscadel	TOTAL WINE	Brandy – Dop	Brandy Grape	Brandy Wine	TOTAL Brandy	Areas under vine morgen
Caledon	8	53	...	115	3	328	20	23	...	550	68	14	...	83	225
Cape	15	843	117	553	4	70	9	7	6	1,626	60	70	23	154	714
Ceres	...	13	...	...	...	133	...	...	...	147	1	58	...	60	95
Ladysmith	...	...	...	2	...	...	70	22	...	95	3	51	...	55	47
Malmesbury	...	215	8	39	...	1,507	68	1	30	1,869	131	...	1	133	900
Montagu	13	...	...	...	...	35	84	88	1,195	1,416	92	645	2	739	331
Oudstshoorn	...	...	...	...	...	...	...	...	...	...	...	118	4	122	102
Paarl	201	1,627	45	927	16	1,888	222	89	37	5,053	469	...	29	499	2,223
Piquetberg	...	11	...	267	...	231	17	...	6	533	32	...	...	33	329
Port Albert	...	...	...	...	...	6	...	...	17	24	8	...	...	36	26
Riverdale	...	...	...	...	...	1	8	...	9	18	83	27	...	101	25
Robertson	6	112	...	1,087	...	146	618	65	1,024	3,059	477	17	46	1,532	684
Stellenbosch	113	892	69	2,322	251	1,101	9	1	2	4,762	200	1,008	...	209	1,621
Swellendam	...	...	...	...	...	12	27	...	8	48	...	8	...	189	145
Tulbagh	1	128	...	67	...	774	73	3	52	1,100	65	188	1	67	364
Wellington	12	306	6	...	...	2,348	...	...	...	2,673	201	...	...	201	805
Worcester	55	567	12	91	...	2,150	1,013	111	206	4,206	244	...	8	1,017	1,478
Grand Total	425	4,769	257	5,473	275	10,735	2,239	411	2,594	27,179	2,141	2,974	115	5,230	10,120

Source: Cape Archives (CA), AMPT PUBS C/1/2/1/149, "Annexures to the Votes and Proceedings of the House of Assembly: Report of Commission of Enquiry into the Economic Condition of the Wine Districts of the Cape Colony" [G-47-1909].

the grapes. Conversely, it was in the areas where grapes were destined for wine production that more rigorous tending of the vines was likely to result in better wine from the cultivars that were available at the start of the twentieth century.

The second set of issues turned on the volume of wine that was produced. During the VOC years, one of the barriers to the extension of the vine had been entirely physical. It was relatively easy to transport wines from Stellenbosch, Wellington, Paarl and Franschhoek to Cape Town by waggon, but the high chain of mountains that lay beyond placed practical limits on further expansion. But in the nineteenth century, the construction of mountain passes altered the spectrum of possibilities. The Bain's Kloof Pass, which afforded a direct connection between Wellington and the Breede River Valley around 1849, initially catered to horse-drawn waggons and subsequently to motorized traffic. Moreover, a railway from Cape Town was routed through Worcester and Matjiesfontein in the direction of Beaufort West – the first leg of which was opened in 1877. This imparted greater economic potential to the valley and the expanse of the Karoo to the east. However, it was by no means certain that this was an area best suited to the vine. The Breede River Valley is naturally arid because the rains mostly fall on the other side of the mountains, and it experiences a very high rate of water loss through evaporation.[28] Most of the seasonal rain and snow falls in the mountains and the water then runs off through a multiplicity of streams that feed into the Breede River. In the nineteenth century, the river would overflow its banks during the winter months, creating a substantial floodplain, while in the summer it effectively dried up. The attraction of the valley initially resided in the access to pasturage for cattle and horses. With the ostrich boom of the later nineteenth century, driven by the fashion for feathers in Europe, many turned to rearing or produced lucerne as fodder. Lucerne makes heavy demands on water, and this placed a greater premium on management of the river. Farmers planted vines on the mountain slopes where numerous springs ensured a supply of water during the dry months.[29] By the 1860s, some had begun to cut irrigation furrows that diverted the waters of the Breede River. The figures presented by the Commission of Enquiry into the Economic Conditions of the Wine Districts (Table 1.2) revealed that Worcester could already lay claim to having the third largest area of land under vines by 1909, behind Paarl and

[28] Eric H. Bolsman, *Bertrams Guide to South African Wines of Origin* (Cape Town: Bertrams, 1976) estimated annual rainfall at 85 cm for Constantia and 35 cm for Robertson but falling to 21 cm on the eastern side of the Worcester district, bordering the Karoo (pp. 53, 65, 72). Contemporary estimates tend towards 40 cm for Robertson and Worcester and 52 cm for Stellenbosch. Groot Constantia claims to receive 110 cm, a high estimate that is widely repeated.

[29] Interview with Abrie Bruwer, 16 October 2009.

Stellenbosch.[30] The Commission believed the total number of vines was probably more in the region of 100 million rather than the 52 million that was reported. This would have represented a tripling of plantings since the 1820s, which seems highly unlikely. What these rather notional statistics do reveal is that vineyards were planted across a very wide area including the Karoo, but also stretching to Willowmore, Prince Albert and Graaf-Reinet in the eastern Cape and as far north as Calvinia.

Inevitably, concerns were expressed about the likely impact on overall production if vineyard planting accelerated. The same Commission concluded that in the Stellenbosch, Paarl and Wellington districts, 'there are no crops or subsidiary industries which would give the farmer in these districts the same return from a limited area as the vine does under normal conditions, nor are there any other agricultural pursuits capable of maintaining on a similar area of land so dense a population as the viticultural industry . . .'.[31] But it maintained that there were encouraging signs of diversification on the other side of the mountain, where the vine was being abandoned in favour of lucerne and ostrich farming.

> As regards the Worcester, Robertson and Montagu Districts, however, the position, as stated before, is being entirely altered by the increased area of land that is being brought under irrigation, and the constant influx of farmers with capital from the Oudtshoorn District. The farmers too are here, as a rule, more extensive and more adaptable to stock and mixed farming generally, with the result that wherever it has been found possible to bring the rich Karroo soil under irrigation this is being done and viticulture is being abandoned for the, at present, more profitable lucerne growing and ostrich farming – some instances coming to the Commission's notice where farmers who formerly derived practically their whole income from the vine have now uprooted whole vineyards, in many instances healthy vines, and put down lucerne instead.

This assessment proved to be less than prescient because in 1914 the second ostrich boom collapsed, and with it the viability of lucerne production. The crash culminated in a retreat of farmers from the Karoo into the Breede River Valley, many of whom turned to planting vines, benefiting initially from the enhanced soil fertility bestowed by lucerne.[32] More significantly, thoughts turned to the possibilities for irrigation. After the Boer War, an individual initiative to settle former soldiers and immigrants on an irrigation scheme at what is now Bonnievale had been a qualified success because of the low water levels in the summer months, and associated salinity.[33] The solution was to

[30] Perold, "Historical notes", p. 110. In his recapitulation, Perold indicated that only the returns for Stellenbosch, Malmesbury, Tulbagh, Worcester and Robertson were complete.

[31] CA AMPT PUBS C/1/2/1/149 "Annexures to the Votes and Proceedings".

[32] Wessel Visser, "White settlement and irrigation schemes: CF Rigg and the founding of Bonnievale in the Breede River Valley, 1900–c.1953", *New Contree* 68 (2013), p. 22. Lucerne added nitrogen to the soil. Interview with Abrie Bruwer,16 October 2009.

[33] Visser, "White settlement", p. 25.

construct a freshwater dam that could supply water during the dry months. The Zanddrift Irrigation Board raised the bank loan that eventually enabled the Brandvlei Dam (or Lake Marais) to be completed near Worcester in 1922. This investment, along with subsequent improvements, transformed the valley. As might have been predicted, the option to irrigate led to a marked increase in vineyard plantings, along with substantially higher yields, in Worcester and Robertson.

The third set of issues turned on the thorny issue of consumption. As has already been indicated, rural Afrikaners were not great imbibers of the wine they produced. In Cape Town and its surrounds, it was often claimed that the merchants had killed their own market. Through tied houses, they were able to keep prices artificially high and so, it was said, deterred people from drinking more wine. But an even greater threat resided in the temperance movement whose societal influence was second to none at the end of the nineteenth century.[34] The Temperance International, as we might reasonably call it, was a worthy successor to anti-slavery in the mid-nineteenth century. Temperance spawned a dense network of associations that spanned continents, linking the United States and Britain;[35] colonies of White settlements such as Canada, New Zealand, Australia, Natal and the Cape, but also encompassing India, British West Africa, South America and East Asia. The leading organization was the Women's Christian Temperance Union (WCTU), which had its origins in the 'women's crusade' in Ohio in 1874, but went global shortly after its formation.[36] The International Order of Good Templars (IOGT), founded in the United States in the 1850s, was less prolific, but also managed to spread well beyond its original heartlands.[37] Finally, in the years after the

[34] The following draws substantially on Paul Nugent, "The temperance movement and wine farmers at the Cape: collective action, racial discourse, and legislative reform, c.1890–1965", *Journal of African History* 52 (3) 2011.

[35] Brian Harrison, *Drink and the Victorians: The Temperance Question in England* (London: Faber & Faber, 1971), pp. 101–104, 196–199; Jeffrey M. Pilcher, "The globalization of alcohol and temperance from the gin craze to prohibition", in Carol Helstosky (ed.), *The Routledge History of Food* (London: Routledge, 2014).

[36] Catherine Gilbert Murdock, *Domesticating Drink: Women, Men, and Alcohol in America, 1870–1940* (Baltimore: Johns Hopkins University Press, 1998). By the 1920s, the WCTU had affiliates in more than 40 countries and operated across the British Empire. Ian R. Tyrrell, *Woman's World/Womans Empire: The Woman Christian Temperance Union in International Perspective, 1880–1930* (Chapel Hill: The University of North Carolina Press, 2006), p. 2. See also Ian Tyrrell, "Women and temperance in international perspective: the World's WCTU, 1880s–1920s", in Susanna Barrows and Robin Room (eds.), *Drinking Behavior and Belief in Modern History* (Berkeley, Los Angeles and Oxford: University of California Press, 1991).

[37] David M. Fahey, *Temperance and Racism: John Bull, Johnny Reb and the Good Templars* (Lexington: University Press of Kentucky, 1996).

First World War, a renewed international campaign was launched by the World League Against Alcoholism (WLAA), which agreed a platform for cooperation with the WCTU.[38]

The IOGT commenced operations at the Cape in 1873, and by the end of the 1890s it was reputed to have 10,000 members, with more than 12,000 additional members subscribing to the International Order of True Templars (IOTT), which had been created for a specifically 'non-white' membership.[39] The IOTT became a powerful force in the Eastern Cape, campaigning strongly against *utywala* (so called 'kaffir beer'), whilst advancing the claim that European drinks threatened a weakening of the bonds of African society. At the same time, the IOTT provided an important vehicle for African nationalists who were keen to shed the paternalism of the White leadership.[40] The IOGT/IOTT remained formally distinct from the WCTU whose arrival at the Cape dates from a visit by Mary Leavitt during her world tour on behalf of the World Union in 1889.[41] The first affiliates were established here, as well as in Natal and the Orange River Colony that same year, followed by the Transvaal two years later. After the creation of the Union of South Africa in 1910, these separate chapters merged into one national body.[42] The latter remained in close touch with the World WCTU through the receipt of literature and visiting speakers and participation in the regular cycle of conventions in the USA.[43] The final body that is worthy of specific mention is the South African Temperance Alliance (SATA) that was established in 1893. SATA positioned itself as an umbrella body seeking to coordinate the efforts of the IOGT/IOTT, the WCTU and a multiplicity of church-based groupings – Methodist, Anglican, Baptist and Presbyterian.[44] The relationship between the White leadership of these bodies was close. The leading light in the IOGT,

[38] Ian Tyrrell, *Reforming the World: The Creation of America's Moral Empire* (Princeton, NJ and Oxford: Princeton University Press, 2010), p. 211.

[39] Jennifer Pearce, "The origins of the temperance movement in Cape Town in the 1880s" (BA Hons. long essay, History Department, University of Cape Town, Cape Town, 1985), p. 11. On the race issue, see Fahey, *Temperance*.

[40] Wallace G. Mills, "The roots of African nationalism in the Cape Colony: temperance 1866–1898", *International Journal of African Historical Studies* 13 (2) 1980.

[41] On the significance of Leavitt's tour, see Tyrrell, *Woman's World*, p. 1.

[42] I will simply refer to the WCTU from this point on, except where this would cause any ambiguity.

[43] Emilie Solomon, who served as president of the Cape WCTU and was national president from 1919 to 1925, was elected vice-president of the World WCTU from 1925 to 1931. Tyrrell, *Woman's World*, p. 72.

[44] Rev. Cook was released by the Methodist Church in 1919 to become the chairman of SATA, a position he occupied until 1930 (Ruby Adendorff, "A Knight without Fear and without Reproach" (undated), typescript). I am grateful to A. T. McCutcheon for sharing this document and allowing me to view the other family documents in her possession.

Theophilus Schreiner, became a vice-president of SATA, while as a Member of Parliament (MP)[45] he counted on the vocal support of the WCTU. All three bodies attempted to keep their members abreast of global developments. The list of invited luminaries included no less a figure than William 'Pussyfoot' Johnson of the Anti-Saloon League who took time out from his campaign on behalf of the WLAA, in Europe and India, to tour Southern Africa with Rev. A. J. Cook in 1924.[46] Another was Bishop Cannon of the WLAA, who accepted an invitation from Cook and SATA to lend his weight to the campaign for Local Option.[47] At the same time, South African campaigners made their own temperance pilgrimages. Cook, for example, covered a swathe of the United States in 1920 to study the progress of Prohibition, and in 1928 he visited Britain on behalf of SATA.[48]

The internationalism of the temperance movement contrasted with the more limited horizons of the farming community. Very few farmers had any direct experience of the wider world, although they kept abreast of developments in the European wine regions through the local press.[49] The topography of the winelands and generations of intermarriage meant that the perspective of many farmers focused on a particular valley or district.[50] Following the creation of the Afrikaner Bond in 1883, the interests of the wine farmers found a political outlet. But party structures were poorly institutionalized and MPs, who tended to be drawn from an urban elite, conducted themselves with patrician independence.[51] Whereas the temperance movement (with the notable exception of IOTT in the Eastern Cape) tended to be urban, largely female and English-speaking, the wine farming communities were dominated by Afrikaner men who were mostly staunch adherents of one or other iteration of the Dutch Reformed Church (DRC). SATA purported to embrace an ecumenical vision, seeking to enlist not just Afrikaners, but also Muslims and Jews. But while SATA boasted Dr. Abdullah Abdurahman

45 The name for the legislature shifted over the twentieth century. For reasons of simplicity, I will refer to the Parliament throughout.

46 Cook and Johnson are said to have travelled 7,000 miles and to have addressed 55,000 people. CA A1696 "Women's Christian Temperance Union", File 98: Correspondence A-C (1913–1941), "A Brief History of the Women's Christian Temperance Union in South Africa" (Cape Town, 1925), p. 35; Tyrrell, *Reforming*, p. 217.

47 Tyrrell, *Reforming*, p. 215. Local Option had enabled temperance campaigners to turn large areas of America dry well in advance of Prohibition.

48 A. T. McCutcheon, "Rev. A.J. Cook and temperance" (undated), typescript in Cooke papers, shared by author.

49 They maintained an acquaintance with international events through the Afrikaner press. On the press and Afrikaner nationalism, see Hermann Giliomee, "Western Cape wine farmers and the beginnings of Afrikaner nationalism, 1870–1915", *Journal of Southern African Studies* 14 (1) 1987, pp. 60–61.

50 In 1878, a Wine Farmers Association was established to oppose an excise tax on brandy, but it did not endure.

51 J. L. McCracken, *The Cape Parliament, 1854–1910* (Oxford: Oxford University Press, 1967), pp. 50–51, 110–112; Giliomee, "Western Cape".

as one of its vice-presidents, it was patently a vehicle for English-speaking Protestants.[52] Although a solid body of the DRC was opposed to alcohol, there was lingering sensitivity about Anglophone domination that was reflected more broadly in campaigns to redress the marginalization of the Afrikaans language. Moreover, the fact that WCTU campaigned for a qualified but non-racial and gender-equal franchise, was not likely to endear it to many farmers.[53] But, by far, the greatest source of concern was its relentless targeting of the *dop* system. The temperance movement in South Africa could never have gone down the French route of strategic accommodation because the worst cases of chronic alcoholism emanated from the wine districts, where farmworkers were dependent on wine rather than brandy. The defence of the farmers was typically to fall back on the logic of paternalism – insisting that they had always exercised a moral responsibility for the welfare of their Coloured wards,[54] which included regulating daily access to liquor. In what follows, I now work through the three-way struggle for supremacy between the temperance movement, farmers and merchants.

A Glass Half-Empty or Half-Full?

The Battle over Consumption

At the turn of the century, the relationship between the temperance movement and the wine farmers became decidedly fractious. The farmers were sensitive to anything that might squeeze further life out of the internal market. In the context of mounting complaints about public drunkenness in Cape Town, however, temperance activists sought to persuade the authorities of the need to introduce stricter controls.[55] Their campaigns bore fruit in the Liquor Act of 1891, which included prison sentences for repeat convictions, and the introduction of Local Option provisions. The law required that applications for new licences be supported by a majority of voters for the relevant district council, and imposed a stipulation that licensing courts reject applications for renewal where two-thirds of voters in a district, municipality or ward signed a memorial objecting.[56] In an amendment of 1898, licensing courts were empowered to

[52] On Abdurahman, see Vivian Bickford-Smith, *Ethnic Pride and Racial Prejudice in Victorian Cape Town: Group Identity and Social Practice, 1875–1902* (Cambridge: Cambridge University Press, 1995), pp. 205, 213.

[53] This is dealt with in detail in June McKinnon, "Women's Christian Temperance Union: aspects of early feminism in the Cape, 1889–1930", unpublished MA thesis, UNISA, 1995, ch. 4.

[54] In this text I refer to 'White', 'Coloured' and 'Black' - categories that are rooted in segregationist and apartheid discourse, but which are impossible to avoid using because they have meaning for the actors themselves. See the 'Note on the Text' on page vi for more detail about the history and use of this term in South Africa.

[55] Pearce, "Origins", p. 14.

[56] Act to Amend the Law Relating to the Sale of Intoxicating Liquors (Act 25 of 1891), published in Percy T. Jones (ed.), *The Liquor Laws of the Colony of the Cape of Good Hope with Notes of Cases Decided Thereon* (Cape Town: Juta, 1907), pp. 89–91.

impose additional conditions on the sale of liquor to 'natives', while fresh restrictions were placed on the brewing of 'kaffir beer' in the rural areas.[57] At each stage, temperance activists instigated mass petitions and lobbied MPs. Indeed, the movement can be credited with transforming politics into the legitimate concern of a wider populace, most of which was formally excluded from the franchise at the time.[58]

In 1905, SATA drew up a joint programme of action. The latter contained 11 action points, which can be collapsed into four for the sake of simplicity. The first was to apply pressure upon the Cape government to introduce a consolidated liquor law that would bring about 'the prohibition of the sale of intoxicating liquor to the native races' and a further reduction of access to alcohol by White people.[59] The second was to actively exploit the provisions of existing legislation, by attending licensing courts *en masse* and challenging the rubber-stamping of applications. The third was the furtherance of public education, combined with pressing the demand for temperance teaching in schools. The final aspect consisted of promoting 'counter-attractions' to the canteen.[60] The WCTU sponsored tea-rooms, coffee houses and outlets for the sale of wholesome fruit juices. The only concession to the embattled wine farmers was the contention that grapes could be used to produce healthy alternatives such as cordials, juices and *moskonfyt* (grape syrup).[61] In 1909, SATA reported the willingness of certain farmers in Stellenbosch to cooperate in producing a bottled grape juice. Indeed, SATA even hired a tent at the Rosebank Show and encouraged visitors to sample a product called Golden Vintage that could be consumed mixed with water or soda water.[62]

This renewed activism coincided with lobbying by distressed wine farmers and merchants for government intervention in their favour. In 1907, the year of the revolt in the Midi, a Colonial Wine-Farmers and Wine Merchant' Association was formed. This came in the context of extremely volatile prices: whereas prices for quality wines in 1903 were higher than they had been since

[57] The Bill was sponsored by James Rose-Innes. The final Act defined a 'native' as 'any Kafir, Fingo, Basuto, Damara, Hottentot, Bushman or Koranna'. See Act to Amend the Law Relating to the Sale of Liquor (Act No. 28 of 1898), article 5, in Jones, *Liquor Laws*, p. 111. The courts regarded physical appearance as crucial to determining whether someone was Coloured or 'native'.

[58] The WCTU submitted 28 petitions in support of the 1898 Act (McKinnon, "Women's Christian", p. 114). White women did not acquire the full franchise until the Women's Enfranchisement Act of 1930. A relatively small number of Coloured and African men who met the qualifications could vote.

[59] SATA singled out theatres, music halls and circuses for exclusion.

[60] The expression is borrowed from Harrison in relation to the pub. See Harrison, *Drink*, pp. 297–298.

[61] The WCTU subsequently introduced an annual 'Grape Day'.

[62] CA AGR 498 C.65 "Grape Juice and Most Konfyt (1909–1911)", "Golden Vintage" (pamphlet, 1909). W. C. Winshaw was one of those who agreed to explore the possibilities.

Table 1.3. *Average wine prices per leaguer, 1880–1907 (in £.shillings.pence)*

Year	Quality Wine	Inferior Wine
1880	£21.3.0	£11.10.0
1885	£8.3.0	£5.12.0
1890	£11.12.0	£8.6.0
1897	£12.0.0	£8.10.1
1898	£13.0.0	£8.18.1
1899	£10.8.0	£7.19.0
1900	£16.1.7	£11.6.0
1901	£14.15.0	£10.14.0
1902	£14.12.0	£10.13.0
1903	£23.3.0	£15.16.0
1904	£16.8.0	£10.7.0
1905	£27.15.0	£15.17.0
1906	£9.8.0	£6.3.0
1907	£8.6.0	£4.19.0

Source: Reworked from Scully, *Bouquet*, table 4, p. 40.

1875, they plummeted in 1907 to a third of what they had been the previous year, heralding a reprise of the hardships of the early 1890s (see Table 1.3). The chairman of the Association was C. W. H. Kohler, a farmer from the Drakenstein Valley, who had only recently left active parliamentary politics and was destined to play a dominant role in the decades to come.[63] C. F. Sedgwick, one of the principal wine merchants, was elected vice-chairman, underlining the extent to which the depression was hurting all sides. Whereas the temperance movement had managed to gradually reduce the supply of liquor over the previous decade, the wine lobby now attempted to reverse the flow. The association demanded a revision of the laws that inhibited wine sales and the appointment of a Select Committee to enquire into the state of the industry.[64] The following year, a private Light Wines Bill was brought to Parliament. This was designed to assist the farmers by lengthening the hours of sale and permitting them to sell wine from the farm-gate.[65] The temperance movement mobilized all its resources to assist Schreiner in fighting the Bill. The WCTU had previously enjoyed some success with written petitions, but now decided to embark on more direct action. Having collected signatures

[63] Annette Joelson (ed.), *The Memoirs of Kohler of the K.W.V.: Politician, Traveller, Founder of the South African Wine Industry* (London: Hurst & Blackett, 1946).

[64] Joelson, *Memoirs*, p. 75.

[65] The Liquor Laws Licensing Act of 1883 had permitted the sale of light wines from grocery stores. McKinnon, "Women's Christian", p. 120.

under its Women's 1907 Temperance Campaign, the WCTU marched on Parliament where its leaders presented a petition, sparking an impromptu debate about whether their actions underlined or undermined the case for women's enfranchisement.[66] The unprecedented demonstration stung the wine farmers into mounting their own 'anti-temperance crusade' in Wellington.[67] This was a rare occasion on which the farmers prevailed. The final iteration of the Act permitted farmers and cooperatives to sell wine in volumes of not less than 4 gallons (18.2 litres) without a licence. Moreover, such sales could be made to Black consumers who were registered voters, as well as to Coloured ones – although not to the rest of the Black population for whom wine and brandy was prohibited.[68]

In 1908 John X. Merriman became Prime Minister in association with the Afrikaner Bond, which had historically identified with the interests of the farmers.[69] Although a wine farmer himself, Merriman was critical of the tendency of most producers to place volume ahead of quality.[70] Moreover, he was unyielding over the demand that the government rescind the excise tax on wine. His reasoning was partly that measures designed to help the struggling farmers might merely provide an incentive to further boost production rather than engaging with more viable alternatives. Taking a leaf out of WCTU's book, the farmers decided to resort to more direct methods of persuasion. On 14 April 1909, Kohler led a demonstration of some 3,000 farmers and supporters onto the streets of Cape Town. This culminated in a mass meeting in City Hall, followed by what the *Cape Times* described as a 'howling demonstration on the steps of Parliament'.[71] The farmers demanded an audience with Merriman, which he granted only grudgingly.[72] In the heated exchanges that ensued, Kohler was scathing about the refusal of Merriman to make a firm commitment to assisting the farmers, and insisted that the underlying problem was not overproduction, but excessive regulation:

[66] Schreiner argued that this action provided the fitness of women to receive the vote. There was a second petition that presumably related to the franchise itself given that the enfranchisement of women was one of the main objectives of the WCTU. McKinnon, "Women's Christian", pp. 121–122.

[67] A large gathering at the town hall in Worcester passed a resolution condemning those who 'worked against their interests by attacking the only industry which would support the population of the Western Province'. "The wine farmers: anti-temperance crusade", *Cape Argus*, 9 September 1907.

[68] Act to Provide for the Sale without a Licence of Certain Liquors Made by Persons Engaged in Viticulture on Their Own Property (Act No. 8 of 1907) article 2, in Jones, *Liquor Laws*, p. 127.

[69] Giliomee, "Western Cape", pp. 44–48.

[70] Merriman owned Schoongezicht, which was originally part of the Rustenberg farm in Stellenbosch and is so today. Although McKinnon rightly observes that Merriman rejected the right of women to petition in chauvinistic terms, her claim that he treated the farmers preferentially is questionable. McKinnon, "Women's Christian", pp. 121–122.

[71] The figure is cited in Van Zyl, *KWV*, p. 20.

[72] "Wine farmer's demonstration: a great gathering", *Cape Times*, 15 April 1909.

If the same quantity of wine cannot be consumed to-day, it is clearly due to legislative enactments which have so restricted the dealings in your product that the consumption is less to-day than it was twenty-five years ago.[73]

The specific demand was for the repeal of the excise duty, but Kohler was also making a thinly veiled reference to the pernicious influence of the temperance movement. In chiding Kohler, the *Cape Times* observed that J. H. Hofmeyr of the Afrikaner Bond, whom the farmers had been counting on for moral support, had himself cast doubt on the likelihood that ending the excise would make a material difference. He was also quoted as reflecting that consumption of alcohol had come 'not only through the efforts of the temperance societies, your Abbeys and Theo. Schreiners ... [but because] many who used to take their cordial at eleven o'clock and even with their lunch, are now satisfied with a cup of tea or coffee or beef tea'.[74] This implied that temperance campaigning had won genuine converts. The newspaper further cited Hofmeyr as pointing out that demand had once hinged on the sale of cheap alcohol to Black consumers in the eastern Cape. Given that nobody wanted a return to this 'abominable traffic', it was necessary for the farmers to be realistic. The report ended by pointing out that Merriman had already set up a Commission of Enquiry and had solicited expert advice from Lord Blyth, a British expert on the wine trade.[75]

Part of Blyth's remit was to investigate the temperance claim that Cape 'light wines' were high in alcohol, whilst simultaneously addressing the myriad problems that were holding the industry back.[76] Julie McKinnon quotes a *Cape Times* article that appeared to confirm Blyth's opinion that Cape wines were indeed highly alcoholic, but in fact the thrust of his report was far from favourable to the temperance campaign. Referring specifically to concerns about drinking amongst the 'coloured races', he tackled standard objections head-on, citing evidence for the health benefits of wine consumption. Ironically, he invoked none other than William Gladstone, whose desire to promote good drinking wine as an alternative to stronger alcohol had killed the export market for Cape wines:

It would, I believe, be impossible for anybody, be he black or white, to become intoxicated by drinking Natural Wine, and all our great legislators, such as John Bright, Cobden, Disraeli and Gladstone, have recognised their health-giving properties

73 This quote from the *South African News* is reproduced in Joelson, *Memoirs*, p.76. In an open letter the previous month, Kohler had claimed that drunkenness by Africans in the Cape was almost certainly lower than in New Zealand, which was held up as citadel of temperance virtue.

74 "Wine farmer's demonstration".

75 Blyth had married a daughter of the family of W. & A. Gilbey, which specialized in Cape wines until the end of colonial preference, when it diversified its portfolio and became a leading retailer of wines in Britain. Asa Briggs, *Wine for Sale: Victoria Wines and the Liquor Trade, 1860–1984* (Chicago: University of Chicago Press, 1985), pp. 62, 68.

76 McKinnon, "Women's Christian", p. 123.

and availed themselves of every opportunity of advocating their consumption on the score of temperance. There is no more sober nation than France, and yet with a total population of 40 millions the average consumption per head is considerably over one hundred bottles of Natural Wine per annum, and the feeling prevails to-day more strongly than ever, both in France and in England, that Natural Wines, rather than Beer or any other stimulant, are indispensable to the health of those of sedentary habits.[77]

When it came to the market for Cape wines, Blyth's advice was to concentrate less on trying to break back into the British market and to look to alternatives across southern Africa. However, his report also maintained that the government could do more to assist the industry by boosting sales at home:

It seems to me that the future Government of the Union could render a great service to the Wine Industry of South Africa in setting an example by instituting a system whereby both Red and White Natural Wine of good marketable quality and in perfect maturity for consumption could be obtained at all railway stations and restaurant cars, or wherever the Government has jurisdiction, at a low fixed price per bottle, the same to bear the Government official stamp as a guarantee of genuineness.

Blyth's report was a rebuke to the temperance movement and provided some support for those demanding freer distribution.

For its part, the Commission of Enquiry into the Economic Condition of the Wine Districts confirmed that financial distress was rife. It observed that in the heartlands of Stellenbosch and Paarl, relatively few farms had been placed on the market, but only because these had been heavily mortgaged. In its view, there would likely have been a serious depreciation in property value if these farms had been sold on the basis of their current financial return.[78] On the other hand, it observed that 55 farmers in Robertson and Montagu had uprooted 500,000 vines. The implication was that if winemaking was confined only to the coastal areas, a solution might yet be found to the scourge of oversupply. Nevertheless, the Commission did not recommend active intervention by the government to steer the farmers down a more desirable path, and far less did it recommend financial subsidies to the producers.

In October 1909, the WCTU responded to the farmers' demands with a counter-march through Cape Town to express opposition to any dilution of the liquor laws.[79] However, with the consummation of the Union of South Africa

[77] CA AGR 498 C.67 "Cape Wine Commission and Lord Blyth's Report on Cape Wine Industry" (1909).

[78] It referred specifically to the case of a 300-morgen farm in the Paarl district, for which the owner had been offered £10,000 a few years earlier, but which had since changed hands for £3,500, and only then because the buyer had been willing to go beyond the effective market value of £2,500 to secure land for his sons. CA AMPT PUBS C/1/2/1/149 "Annexures to the Votes and Proceedings" (1909).

[79] McKinnon, "Women's Christian", p. 125.

in 1910, a temporary suspension of hostilities ensued. Thereafter, both sides were forced to adjust to the enlargement of the political arena that injected new sets of interests and perspectives into the political equation. The temperance movement had the most to gain from Union – certainly Schreiner believed so – because it became that bit easier to coordinate campaign strategies across the region. However, whereas English speakers had dominated the Cape legislature, the Union Parliament was certain to be controlled by Afrikaners.[80] Hence the WCTU and SATA needed to find a way of making common cause rather than presuming to speak for Afrikaners. This did not come naturally, as is reflected in the tardiness with which the WCTU adjusted to publication in the Afrikaans language.[81] As for the wine farmers, their MPs now represented a relatively small group within Parliament who could not necessarily count on government backing when other vested interests were competing for attention. It became apparent, therefore, that they needed a strong collective voice outside of Parliament if they were to effectively neutralize the active propaganda of SATA and the WCTU.

After 1910, much of the effort of the WCTU was directed towards offering alternatives to alcohol for servicemen and policing the extension of liquor licences.[82] Moreover, campaigners continued to draw attention to alcohol abuse amongst the Cape Coloured population. This culminated in the creation of the (Baxter) Select Committee in 1918, before which Schreiner made a plea for bringing Coloured people under the restrictive provisions of the 1898 Act, subject to a right of exemption for 'respectable' elements.[83] In addition, Schreiner attempted to pass a Direct Vote Bill that would have extended Local Option by transferring powers from licensing courts to communities. Predictably enough, Schreiner pointed an accusatory finger at the wine farmers when his Bill failed to pass. As for the latter, the lack of any functioning association impeded efforts to effect a change to the law in their favour. In 1912, Tielman Roos did endeavour to pass a Bill that would have permitted Black drinkers freer access to 'kaffir beer' and light wines and would have allowed coffee shops and boarding houses to apply for licences and extended the hours of sale.[84] The failure of this Bill led to farmers' leaders shifting the emphasis away from an expansion of the market for wine towards seeking higher prices. This reduced some of the points

80 In 1908, English speakers still made up 54 per cent of MPs. McCracken, *Cape Parliament*, table 3, p. 53.

81 Very little temperance material was translated into Afrikaans before the Second World War. Ruby Adendorff, one of the leaders of the WCTU, eventually published *Alkohol – Wat Dit is en Wat Dit Doen* (Paarl: WCTU, 1946).

82 McKinnon, "Women's Christian", pp. 92–94.

83 This was the Select Committee on Drunkenness in the Western Districts of the Cape Province. The Baxter report recommended regulation rather than abolition of the dop system.

84 McKinnon, "Women's Christian", p. 129.

of friction with the temperance lobby, but it increasingly pitted the farmers against their other great adversary, namely the merchants.

The Battle over Pricing: Wine Farmers against the Merchants

Temperance campaigners and wine farmers had recourse to a very similar rhetoric when criticizing what they regarded as noxious monopolies pervading the liquor trade. The former complained of an excess of canteens dispensing cheap wine, coupled with the monopolistic inclinations of the liquor firms. The WCTU and SATA both alleged that licensing courts deferred to vested interests and were rife with corruption. As for the farmers, a common complaint was that the merchants acquired wine at the lowest possible prices and sold it on to consumers at a lucrative mark-up. In his memoir, Kohler also claimed that the merchants were able to exploit a buyer's market by stockpiling supplies and then driving the hardest possible bargain at the end of the season when the farmers were desperate for money.[85] To some extent, these critiques of the merchants were contradictory: for temperance activists, wine was too cheaply available, while for farmers the price to the consumer was unjustifiably high. But both agreed that it was merchants who elevated crude profit above some conception of the greater good.

Some of the issues surrounding distribution had been specifically addressed by the 1909 Commission. The latter estimated that 'fully 70 per cent of licensed houses (exclusive of bottle stores) are tied or controlled by breweries or wholesale wine and spirit merchants'.[86] One consequence was that there was often a preference for the sale of imported spirits over Cape brandy. Another was that tied houses tended to increase the cost of wine and brandy to the consumer:

> Owing largely to the tied house system . . . the Commission finds that the product of the viticulturalist has generally to pass through two, and in some cases three middlemen ere it reaches the consumer's hands, with a corresponding increase in the price which the consumer has to pay.

However, as with the dop system, identifying a set of abuses was one thing, while bringing them to an end was quite another. Hence the question of cartels in the liquor trade remained unresolved during the first decade after Union.

The First World War brought renewed difficulties for farmers, as prices plummeted to an average of £2.10 to £3 per leaguer between 1915 and 1917.[87] This served to reinvigorate efforts to found an association to represent the

[85] Joelson, *Memoirs*, p. 83.
[86] CA AMPT PUBS C/1/2/1/149 "Annexures to the Votes and Proceedings".
[87] *Wine Commission*, p. 8.

interests of wine farmers. What Kohler envisaged was the formation of a cooperative society that could bargain with the merchants over the price to be paid for wine. In 1916, a planning meeting was held, and in November 1917 the Constitution of the KWV was signed. In 1918, the KWV was formally registered as a company in the absence of any legislation providing for the formal registration of cooperatives at that time. With a membership of 1,807 farmers by April of that year, the KWV seemed to have gained widespread initial acceptance. In his memoirs, Kohler claimed that '(W)e had great difficulty in getting the merchants to join us and accept our Constitution. They kicked hard against the co-operative movement and would have nothing to do with it.'[88] He also maintained that the KWV forced the merchants to the bargaining table by threatening to enter distillation in competition with them. In fact, the firms were not averse to dealing with a single farmers' association. In November 1917, the Board of Sedgwick passed a resolution approving the principle of fixing a 'reasonable minimum price' for wine, for disposing of the surplus and for taking measures to prevent the sale of wine below the agreed price. Its policy was to adopt 'a reasonably sympathetic but non-committal attitude'.[89] In addition, the firm decided to not enter into any fresh contracts with farmers pending the inauguration of the KWV. Furthermore, a number of the leading merchants, including Sedgwick, agreed to seek an arrangement with the KWV, provided the latter could secure control over at least 80 per cent of total production and provided the firms of E. K. Green & Co. and H. C. Collison's came on board.[90] But attacking the liquor firms, much like targeting the mining companies,[91] was guaranteed to secure a sympathetic audience.

In the first year, the KWV and the merchants managed to come to terms. The merchants agreed to pay a minimum price of £4.15s for distilling wine and £5.5s for 'good' (or drinking) wine.[92] The KWV passed this price on to the farmers, less 10s on each leaguer of wine and a pro rata deduction for wine that was estimated to be surplus to the requirements of the trade. Both parties were conscious of the need to maintain internal discipline: if the farmers agreed to supply firms at beneath the minimum price, there was a likelihood that both the KWV and the newly formed merchants' association would unravel. In 1918, the actual price for wine fluctuated between £4.15s and £6.10s per leaguer for

[88] He made an exception of Mr Jooste of Jooste and Bryant who even made a loan to the KWV. Joelson, *Memoirs*, p. 88. The KWV was distinct from the cooperative wineries.

[89] Distell Archive, "The House of Sedgwick" (unpublished typescript, 1951), p. 29.

[90] "House of Sedgwick", p. 31.

[91] Boonzaier's cartoon image of Hoggenheimer, representing a fictitious Jewish mining magnate, became a regular feature in *Die Burger*. Giliomee, *The Afrikaners*, p. 331. There was no liquor equivalent, but the over-representation of Jews in the trade did not go unnoticed.

[92] The firms which signed up were the major players, notably E. K. Green, Castle Wine and Brandy Co, H. C. Collison's, J. Sedgwick & Co. and the Van Ryn Wine and Brandy Co. Van Zyl, *KWV*, p. 26.

distilling wine, while the price for good wine inched up to around £8.[93] With a return to relative optimism, farmers began to replant their vineyards. Whereas there were estimated to be 86.9 million vines in the Cape Province in 1918, this had risen to 101.2 million in 1921. The volume of wine produced also rose steeply from 96,750 leaguers (559,215 hl.) to a high of 128,473 leaguers (742,574 hl.), which rather gave the lie to Kohler's earlier claims that overproduction was not an issue.[94]

In 1920, responding to rumours of a short vintage, the firm of W. C. Winshaw secretly signed contracts with as many farmers as it could, in effect undercutting the compact between the KWV and the larger firms. Winshaw then announced that he controlled 60 per cent of the harvest and invited the other merchants to join him in a combine. The latter spurned the offer, and some like Castle Wine and Brandy Co. decided to actively compete, thereby pushing prices to a level where farmers began turning every kind of grape into cheap wine.[95] The anticipated shortfall was thereby transformed into a veritable glut overnight. As the firms attempted to divest themselves of excess stocks, prices suddenly plummeted. A number of companies were bankrupted in 1920, including W. C. Winshaw and Myburgh, Krone & Co. The companies that had been more cautious or were better capitalized, notably Sedgwick, Castle Wine and Brandy Co., Paarl Wine and Brandy Co. and Van Rhyn's survived and bought up the assets of those that had failed.[96] This shakeout further exemplified a long-term tendency towards concentration in the liquor industry.

The reaction on the part of chastened farmers and merchants alike was to renegotiate a price agreement. The leading merchants formed the South African Wine and Spirit Corporation with a view to eliminating the competitive bidding that had landed them in trouble. At the same time, the KWV, which had decided to try to take control over the 1921 and 1922 vintages, saw an advantage in price stability. The terms of the new agreement were that the merchants would pay £9 per leaguer (£1.56 per hl.) for distilling wine and £11 (£.1.90 per hl.) for good wine to the KWV, which would pay the farmers at £3 a leaguer (£0.52 per hl.) for distilling wine, supplemented with an additional £2 (£0.35 per hl.) premium for good wine. The difference between the sale price and what the farmer received reflected the quantity of wine that was surplus to the trade, which the KWV was mandated to dispose of. Between 1921 and 1923, no less than 27.9 per cent of total wine production, for which

93 *Wine Commission*, p. 9. 'Good wine' referred to wine that was intended for drinking rather than distillation.

94 *Wine Commission*, p. 9.

95 The Wine Commission cites a figure of £30 per leaguer (£5.19 per hl.). *Wine Commission*, p. 9.

96 Castle Wine and Brandy Co. acquired Collison's, while Jooste and Bryant from Johannesburg acquired Sedgwick & Co. Distell Archive, "House of Sedgwick", p. 18.

no use could be found, was physically destroyed.[97] The logic underpinning the agreement was that prices would not be pushed upwards by rampant speculation but would reflect the level of effective demand. This was reassuring for the nervous merchants. Equally by disposing of the surpluses, the KWV ensured that the market was not ruined by chronic over-supply. This was a crucial guarantee for the struggling wine farmers. But the balancing act was only likely to work if merchants were not tempted to seek supplies at a lower price and if the KWV could find some way of reducing the overall surplus – whether by actively discouraging the farmers from producing more or by finding new markets that did not step on the toes of the merchants.

In reality, both parties experienced acute problems in disciplining their members. In 1922, Sedgwick broke away from the Corporation, thereby signalling a return to competition between the merchants. Although the other firms remained formally committed to their agreement with the KWV, it was alleged that certain of them began to cut secret deals. On the other hand, many farmers believed that the KWV was creaming off too much for itself. The higher-quality producers in Constantia, in particular, insisted that the surplus disposal should not apply to 'good' wine and they should receive the full price handed down by the merchants. Indeed, one of them successfully took the KWV to court over the issue.[98] With increasing numbers signalling their intention to resign from the KWV, the leadership struggled to prevent the association from unravelling. As Kohler indicated in his autobiography, some time was bought by means of a mixture of cunning, subterfuge and sheer bluff. When the KWV was registered under the Co-operative Societies Act of 1922, it was able to insert a clause that bound all members to the surplus arrangements. However, when the merchants declared their own intention to withdraw from the pricing agreement, the KWV realized that its strategy was in deep trouble. The only solution appeared to be to solicit government support for underwriting a system of statutory control. From such chaotic origins was the Leviathan of regulation born.

In his official history of the KWV, Diko Van Zyl observes that while Kohler claimed credit for what subsequently transpired, it was Charlie Heatlie, KWV director and South African Party (SAP) MP for Worcester, who approached Jan Smuts, as he was about to travel to the United Kingdom, with a proposal for devolving regulatory powers to the KWV.[99] Smuts signalled that he was prepared to oblige, provided such an initiative enjoyed the support of the

[97] Joelson, *Memoirs*, p. 92. No fewer than 91,656 leaguers (15,857 hl.) were destroyed between 1921 and 1923, 39,830 (6,891 hl.) of them in 1923 itself. Figures from *Wine Commission*, p. 9.

[98] The association lost two court cases against its own members who disputed the applicability of the surplus contributions to good wine and the right of the directors to enforce compliance. Van Zyl, *KWV*, pp. 36–37.

[99] Van Zyl, *KWV*, pp. 45–49.

majority of KWV members and as long as the NP did not turn the enabling legislation into a partisan affair in Parliament. Leading figures within the KWV brokered discussions between SAP and NP politicians, and only when a deal was in the offing did they inform Kohler. When Smuts arrived back at Cape Town docks, the KWV directors were able to present Smuts with detailed proposals. The prime minister agreed to personally bring a Bill to Parliament at the earliest opportunity rather than postponing a decision until the following season.

When he stood up to introduce the second reading of the Wine and Spirits Control Bill, Smuts acknowledged the storm that the proposed legislation had provoked: 'Judging from the daily press and the letters and communications which have appeared in it, I am afraid that I have put my head into a hornet's nest.' He also mused that:

> Discussion of wine produces almost as much heat as the consumption of wine. I therefore appeal to hon. members to approach this dangerous subject in a good temper. It is a difficult one; it is one involving not only large principles but large interests . . .[100]

During the subsequent debate, the leader of the opposition, J. B. M. Hertzog, did not register any objections other than to urge the appointment of a Select Committee to thrash out the details. But the proposal was vigorously attacked by MPs from both sides of the house. Smuts conceded that many of the criticisms of the KWV were valid but insisted that it was better for government to support the industry in putting its own house in order rather than exercising direct control. In this, he was repeating a line that had once belonged to Merriman. This made little impression on opponents of the Bill who pointed out that if the industry was truly to be self-regulating, then logically both the farmers and the merchants should be involved. Morris Alexander even went as far as to label it a 'Bolshevist Bill' intended 'to take away everybody's rights and interests in the wine and spirits industry'.[101]

Predictably, Smuts' most vocal supporter in Parliament was Heatlie, who had only just ceased being a KWV director, and whose fingerprints were all over the legislation. One MP explicitly took up the case against the merchants on the basis that a couple of companies, which also owned the hotels and 'canteens', were able to maximize the difference between the price paid to the farmers and the sale price.[102] The MPs who were sympathetic to the merchants

[100] Jan Smuts, Prime Minister, moving second reading of the Wine and Spirits Control Bill, 6 February 1924, Union of South Africa, Debates of the House of Assembly (Cape Town: Cape Times, Parliamentary Printers, various years), p. 105 [hereinafter *Assembly Debates*].

[101] M. Alexander, MP for Cape Town-Castle, *Assembly Debates*, 6 February 1924, p. 112.

[102] He claimed that farmers received 4d. a bottle for wine that was sold by E. K. Green at 2 shillings. J. W. Roux, MP for Ceres, *Assembly Debates*, 8 February 1924, p. 146.

regarded the legislation as pandering to the narrow interests of the KWV leadership. No less fierce was the criticism that emanated from the ranks of the wealthier producers. Prominent farmers in Constantia had long opposed regulation, arguing that this was tantamount to rewarding the producers of low-quality wine. M. Bisset, the SAP MP for South Peninsula, which included Constantia, maintained that the system of surplus control in effect meant that the makers of good wine ended up subsidizing the producers of 'absolute muck':

> In that particular year that I am dealing with, the price for good wine was £11 a leaguer, and if they were liable for surplus contribution they would have to pay two-thirds of that which would have left the maker of 'good wine' £9 per leaguer. People I represent in Constantia say it is almost impossible to make good wine at that rate. They say their cost is very much higher than elsewhere, and in some parts you get three times as many leaguers from a given number of 'sticks' as you do at Constantia.[103]

Bisset reminded the House that the Constantia farmers had won a court case over the issue, but that the KWV had changed its constitution when the Co-operative Act of 1922 came into force to nullify the judgement and render it difficult for farmers to leave.

The context was a shift in the balance of forces within the KWV towards the producers of distilling wine *anderkant die berg*.[104] Major Van Zyl made the point that regulation was a slippery slope because it might merely increase the tendency towards overproduction:

> We make 135,000 or 150,000 leaguers of wine per annum, while the consumption in the Union is 80,000–90,000 leaguers, which means we are at the present paying for the 140,000 leaguers to consume 80,000, and with regular increasing production this means that at the end of three years we shall be led into a most serious position, for the surplus will be enormous; and what are we going to do then? . . . The whole of the community will have to suffer for the farmers who make bad wine, and what are we going to gain by it?[105]

Although these figures were not terribly accurate, the most compelling indictment of the KWV was that it had done nothing to check the hike in production. In 1918, when the association was founded, the total vintage was equivalent to 96,750 leaguers (559,215 hl.) while in 1923 it stood at 110,544 leaguers (638,944 hl.).[106] Although Smuts had made it clear that the government was prepared to make exceptions for drinking wine, Bisset insisted that this did not resolve the issue of whether the quality producers would be subjected to the

[103] M. Bisset, *Assembly Debates*, 8 February 1924, p. 145.
[104] Literally 'on the other side of the mountain', but a shorthand for the Breede River Valley.
[105] These estimates were not particularly accurate. Maj. G. B. Van Zyl, Cape Town-Harbour, *Assembly Debates*, 6 February 1924, p. 120.
[106] *Wine Commission*, p. 9.

KWV regime and forced to participate in the surplus contribution. Another MP underlined the conflicting interests between producers in the different districts which was fast becoming a significant political issue:

There are many farmers in Caledon, Stellenbosch, Paarl and nearby that make good classes of wine and they receive £6 for their wine, which is the nominal worth, but they have to give £3 to the co-operative; but the man who is sitting on the other side of the mountain can simply let the wine flow; I say that what happens is an encouragement for the production of the lowest classes and quality of wine.[107]

This MP was the only one to raise specifically the impact of restrictive liquor laws, noting the difficulties even for White people of acquiring wine in a restaurant. During the debate, the KWV was roundly criticized for managing its affairs so poorly. J. H. H. De Waal even alleged that Kohler and other directors had cut their own private deals with the merchants so that they would be excluded from the terms of any pricing arrangement by virtue of the fact that they had been made before the Bill.[108] Smuts was forced to concede that the wine industry had been its own worst enemy, and in some respects his assessment was just as damning as that of Bisset:

A good deal of the stuff we produce to-day is not fit for distillation, and to use a vulgar expression, is only fit for the gutter, and the result is that a natural industry is in a very parlous condition. Another danger, owing to our having gone in more for brandy and neglecting the wine production, a tendency in this country is to drink less wine – the market, even in South Africa does not expand, and we have the danger, and it is difficult to pull an industry like this out of the mire. To my mind, if ever there was a case for regulating an industry, which is to some extent absurd, and which is also over-produced in large quantities, it seems to me the very article should be subject to regulations.[109]

However, Smuts was also desirous of keeping the state at one remove from the regulatory process.

Only one pro-temperance MP spoke in the debate, and that was Will Stuart, a self-professed 'prohibitionist' and relative of Schreiner, who actually supported the prime minister on the basis that the Bill was likely to lead to the production of less harmful forms of brandy.[110] The silence of Dr. D. F. Malan was deafening, given his leadership of the temperance campaign in Parliament (see below). This striking failure to line up on the side of those who claimed to be advancing the cause of quality wine, whilst stemming the flood of distilling

[107] Le Roux van Niekerk, *Assembly Debates*, 8 February 1924, p. 121.

[108] De Waal claimed that Kohler had signed an agreement for 10 years with the firm of E. K. Green to sell wine at £14 per leaguer. J. H. H. De Waal, MP for Piquetberg, *Assembly Debates*, 6 February 1924, p. 118.

[109] Jan Smuts, *Assembly Debates*, 6 February 1924, p. 106.

[110] W. H. Stuart, MP for Tembuland, *Assembly Debates*, 8 February 1924, p. 148. The Bill required brandy to be matured for three years.

wine, is at first surprising because temperance advocates were concerned about the health and social effects of spirits. It is possible that the pro-temperance MPs simply wished to visit a plague on both houses. But there are three more likely reasons why they remained silent and ultimately voted with Smuts across party lines. One is that they may have hoped for reciprocal support for Local Option legislation that stopped short of prohibition. Another is that in the eyes of the anti-liquor lobby, the real enemies were the wine merchants whose growing economic might threatened to make alcohol more cheaply available through a greater number of outlets. If the net effect of empowering the KWV was to push up the purchase price of alcohol, that might have a depressing effect on consumption. Finally, the fact that Smuts and Hertzog had come to a backroom deal meant that senior Nationalist MPs who broadly favoured temperance were not prepared to rock the boat.

Following criticism of the Bill, the sting was taken out of the opposition through a resort to two expedients. Despite his initial reluctance, Smuts gave way to demands for the appointment of a Select Committee to thrash out some of the serious points in contention. This enabled the producers of 'good' wine to advance their case, which culminated in drinking wine being specifically excluded from the legislation. In addition, Gerald Jooste from Sedgwick & Co. was able to present the case for the merchant community. Secondly, and in parallel, Smuts succeeded in bringing the KWV and the merchants to the bargaining table. The merchants agreed to accept the role of the KWV in controlling the price of distilling wine and to deal with the surplus, in return for a guarantee that the KWV would not enter the retail trade directly. The amended Bill required the KWV to sell to bona fide distillers or merchants.[111] The merchants also agreed to terminate the contracts they had already made for the coming year, with personal pressure being applied to Castle Wine and Brandy Co. by Smuts.[112] The KWV clearly received the better end of the bargain, and while there remained significant criticism of the legislation, the Wine and Spirits Control Act duly passed through Parliament. The future of the KWV was apparently secure. However, this merely brought the issue of consumption back into focus.

Liquor Control Redux: Temperance Campaigning and the 1928 Liquor Act

In the early 1920s, the triumph of Prohibition in the United States following the passage of the Volstead Act, brought liquor to the forefront of public debate. Although few imagined that South Africa would suddenly 'turn dry',

[111] Statement by Smuts at committee stage, *Assembly Debates*, 27 February 1924, p. 488.
[112] Van Zyl, *KWV*, p. 56.

the temperance movement turned its attention to Local Option as a halfway house towards outright prohibition. The pre-eminent Parliamentary champion was Dr. D. F. Malan, the future prime minister of South Africa. Malan's father had been the owner of the Allesverloren wine farm in the Swartland, but hardly any wine or brandy was consumed there.[113] Ownership ultimately passed to his brother, S. F. Malan, in part because his father did not consider that he possessed the necessary business acumen. D. F. Malan instead studied theology and became a dominee, or DRC minister, before turning his hand to journalism and politics. He later recalled that his conversion to the temperance cause came during his duties tendering to the flock in rural Montagu when he witnessed the devastation wrought by drink on the Coloured population.[114] Malan introduced a Local Option Bill in 1923 that was opposed by many MPs as a slippery slope to prohibition. Morris Alexander, for example, pointed out that the law already provided for a version of Local Option, given that licensing courts were required to withhold licences if two-thirds of the ratepayers objected. The Bill was narrowly defeated, as it was in the following year when Malan re-introduced it.[115] These near-misses brought home the importance of mobilizing public support so that wavering MPs would be more inclined to back the Bill when it resurfaced.

It was partly in response to the Parliamentary debates that SATA sponsored a conference on 'The Drink Problem in South Africa' in Cradock – historically a prominent temperance town – the aim of which was to advance the case for Local Option. Papers were read that dealt with the experience of local option in far-flung realms of the Empire like Scotland, Canada and New Zealand, as well as with the record of Prohibition in the United States. This underlines the extent to which the South African activists imagined themselves as marching in step with a global movement. Hence Rev. A. J. Cook rather optimistically claimed that South Africa 'had caught the spirit of the age' and was destined to become a global leader in the fight for temperance.[116] Rev. A. W. Eckard acknowledged that 'the wine farmers are, without exception, opposed to Local Option', which he attributed to fears concerning the loss of their livelihood. But since the American experience demonstrated that there were paying alternatives to wine, he argued, there was a realistic basis for cooperation.[117]

[113] The farm was dedicated to production of a version of port wine. Wine proper was only drunk on special occasions. Interview with Danie Malan, 2 November 2009.

[114] "Echo from the Past – Extract from an Address by the Hon. D.F. Malan, Stellenbosch 1912", Stellenbosch University Document Centre.

[115] Malan lost the vote by nine votes in 1923. *Cape Times*, 16 March 1923.

[116] Rev. A. J. Cook, "The American experiment and its meaning for South Africa", in *The Drink Problem in South Africa: Addresses and Papers Delivered at the Local Option Congress Held at Cradock on December 5th and 6th, 1923* (Cape Town: SATA, 1924), p. 99.

[117] Rev. A. W. Eckard, "Local option and the wine farmer", in *Drink Problem*, pp. 124–125.

The president of the WCTU, Emilie Solomon, spoke on the effects of alcohol on the home and on infant mortality, and finished with a remarkable flourish concerning the effects upon racial vitality.[118] Rev. W. J. Naude of the DRC contrived to find the hand of God working through medical research, which demonstrated the devastating effects of alcohol on the human body:

> By natural science, and especially by medical science, the Lord is teaching us more and more that alcohol is injurious and unnecessary for the human body . . . [and] that so far from being a direct gift of God, it is nothing less than a distinct poison, and must be regarded as such and avoided.[119]

He also claimed that the Bible had been mistranslated and that references to the drinking of wine referred to a non-alcoholic grape syrup, in effect turning the wedding at Cana into a kind of temperance gathering. Finally, Dr. J. Van Schalkwyk offered a lengthy medical treatise, and repeated the assertion that 'alcohol must not be regarded as an enjoyment or as a food, but as a poison or a medicine which may be prescribed to patients under proper supervision.'[120] The congress finished by passing a number of resolutions. One advocated forging better links with the DRC. Another proposed sending a letter to farmers' leaders expressing 'friendly greetings' and urging cooperation around the production of non-alcoholic beverages.[121]

Much like the rival demonstrations in Cape Town in 1909, the Cradock congress galvanized the defenders of wine into staging a rival meeting in Paarl in May 1924. The formal agenda was that of promoting moderation, but the gathering was clearly intended as a broadside against the Local Option campaign. It was addressed by an impressive list of luminaries that included A. I. Perold; Louis Leipoldt, the doctor and poet; W. C. Winshaw, the merchant who went on to found the SFW; and a couple of churchmen. But while the speakers were all wine advocates, no farmers' representatives actually spoke, possibly because the KWV was otherwise preoccupied. The closest approximation was Perold, who was by then South Africa's pre-eminent expert.[122] In his contribution, Perold argued for the benefits of moderate consumption and attacked Local Option as the thin end of the wedge:

118 "One of the greatest problems in our country is how to keep the white races efficient and fit to take their part in the uplift of the less advanced races of this vast sub-continent. Drink is the greatest cause of race deterioration . . .", Miss E. Solomon, "Alcohol and the home", in *Drink Problem*, p. 60.

119 Rev. W. J. Naude, "The Bible and alcohol", in *Drink Problem*, p. 19.

120 His lumping of tea and coffee with other 'substances' like cocaine, tobacco, morphine and alcohol raised doubts about the WCTU's promotion of alternatives to alcohol. J. Van Schalkwyk, "The medical aspect of the drink problem", in *Drink Problem*, p. 53.

121 Resolutions in *Drink Problem*, p. 176.

122 Perold was instrumental in the meeting and the subsequent publication. He moved to the KWV in 1928.

Some opponents of drunkenness believe that the principle of moderation is not sufficiently effective to fight the abuse of liquor successfully; and therefore they plead for total prohibition, as it is now generally called. Their favourite means to this end is the fine-sounding term 'local option' which aims at the local total prohibition of the sale of liquor in order to make the whole country gradually dryer and dryer, until as a whole, it will be ripe for total prohibition. Everyone who is against total prohibition should therefore also oppose this local option, the more so as its supporters, as recently happened at the Cradock conference, no longer hide the fact that their final goal is prohibition.[123]

Perold recalled that when he had challenged 'Pussyfoot' Johnson on the record of Prohibition, pointing out that increased prices were due to the fact that Californians were making wine in their own homes, the campaigner had been unwilling to admit the truth. Perold concluded that '*this looks uncommonly like intentionally misleading an unsuspecting public*' (emphasis in original).[124]

Professor E. E. Van Rooyen from the Theological Seminary in Stellenbosch gleefully shot holes in the assertion that Biblical wine was unfermented and maintained that the Bible was clear about the lawfulness of alcohol consumption. In his words, 'The principle of moderation is Scriptural and therefore Christian.'[125] Legislating against wine, he reasoned, took away the moral obligation on the individual to actively practise moderation. The same point was made even more forcefully by Rev. Harrington Johnson who, in a speech entitled 'Why I am not a Prohibitionist', insisted that 'prohibition is based on a non-Christian view of the world'. This insistence on the thinking Christian subject was at least as compelling as the notion that there was a scriptural embargo, especially when the Biblical texts appeared to indicate the exact opposite. As probably the only American present at the meeting, Winshaw drew attention to the failure of Prohibition in the United States and presented South Africans with the following dire spectre:

Could sunny South Africa become a nursery of fanatics, paring down the joys of life with perhaps two and a half hypocrites to a family – one awful vast Kansas? Let us rather climb the golden stairs before our time than to live under such gloom – and probably have to pay heavily for it into the bargain, in increased taxes, first to make good the loss to revenue due to prohibition, and afterwards to raise every year more and more money to pay for the increasing cost of enforcement which fails to enforce.

But perhaps the most subversive refutation of the Cradock declaration came from Leipoldt, who made a case for consumption based on medical evidence:

123 Perold assumed joint responsibility for seeing the papers through to publication. A. I. Perold, "The social aspect of the liquor problem", in *Wine and Drunkenness: The Social Problem of the Day* (Cape Town, 1924), p. 162.

124 Perold, "Social aspect", p. 166.

125 W. C. Winshaw, "The effect of Prohibition in America", in *Wine and Drunkenness*, p. 10.

Alcohol is a normal constituent of blood. Every bit of sugar, every bit of starch we eat as food, must be changed into alcohol before the body can make use of it. This is also precisely what the body does . . . The time occupied by the change of alcohol to acetic acid is very brief and this accounts for the relatively small amounts of free alcohol that we find in the human blood. But that such free alcohol actually does exist in the blood is now no longer doubted in the least.[126]

Far from being a poison, he insisted, alcohol was wired into the very physiology of human beings. He then clinched the argument by pointing out that moderate consumption of alcohol was an aid to digestion and contained vital nutrients. He concluded by declaring that: 'I therefore consider it our duty to encourage the use of light wines.'[127]

With these opening salvoes duly exchanged, the debate returned to the Parliament floor. In February 1924, Leslie Blackwell introduced the latest version of the Local Option Bill, having paid tribute to D. F. Malan's previous unsuccessful efforts.[128] He rehearsed the argument about endemic drunkenness amongst the Cape Coloured population, and added the threat to the welfare of 'poor whites'. He also restated the supposed failings of the licensing courts. Confirming Perold's assessment, Blackwell observed that while the time was not ripe for the introduction of prohibition, the creation of 'a few dry patches' would 'set in motion a process of becoming dry', leading eventually to the dry areas outnumbering the wet and the creation of a public mood favouring outright prohibition. He was unapologetic, stating that, 'I am a prohibitionist and I see in this Bill the half-way house to prohibition, and I believe it will pave the way ultimately for going dry.' Such forthrightness provoked a ferocious response from MPs representing wine-farming constituencies, who warned that they could not be expected to vote for such legislation. Tielman Roos was especially emphatic, adding that the Bill was anachronistic given that Smuts had only just introduced legislation intended to assist the wine farmers.[129] After a passionate debate, the Bill narrowly failed to carry the necessary support, losing on this occasion by 53 to 51 votes.

Shortly thereafter, Parliament was dissolved, and Smuts took the country to a general election which he proceeded to lose. When Parliament reconvened in 1924, an alliance between the National and Labour parties commanded a

[126] C. Louis Leipoldt, "The medical aspect of the moderate consumption of alcohol", in *Wine and Drunkenness*, p. 120. Leipoldt was a genuine polymath. He wrote on the subject of diet and critiqued both temperance thinking and vegetarianism. Controversially for South Africa, he also maintained that it was perfectly acceptable to give light wine to healthy children at dinner. C. Louis Leipoldt, *Common-Sense Dietetics* (London: Williams & Norgate, 1911), p. 148.

[127] Leipoldt, *300 Years*, p. 135.

[128] Strangely, Blackwell's autobiography makes no mention of his leadership in the anti-liquor debates. Leslie Blackwell, *Blackwell Remembers: The Memoirs of the Hon. Leslie Blackwell Q.C., M.C.* (London: Howard Timmins, 1971), pp. 47–48.

[129] Tielman Roos, *Assembly Debates*, 7 February 1924, column 129.

majority and Smuts was consigned to the opposition benches. Within the Pact Government Roos assumed the Justice portfolio, while Malan became the Minister of Interior, Public Health and Education. It was now Roos who made the running, but in a rather different direction from Malan. In 1925, a private Local Option Bill was introduced for the fourth year in succession but it failed by a wider margin, which confounds any simple notion that Nationalists were naturally more disposed towards temperance. It now fell to Roos to table legislation that would consolidate the liquor laws, a demand that had been repeatedly made since Union in 1910. Introducing his draft Liquor Bill in September 1926, Roos went on the offensive by openly criticizing the temperance campaigners as 'self-appointed reformers'. In particular, he singled out a public protest that had been called by the temperance lobby to oppose his Bill.[130]

The Bill conceded something to both wine-farming interests and the temperance lobby, but at the risk of alienating both. On the one hand, Roos proposed an extension of the dop system to the Transvaal, on the basis that outright prohibition for Black people had proved a singular failure and that it would help to stem the drift of labour to the cities. In addition, his Bill envisaged government canteens through which liquor could be made available to 'non-whites' under controlled conditions. Part of the intention was evidently to expand the market for 'light wines', a longstanding demand that Roos had previously championed. The Bill conspicuously omitted a Local Option clause and went further by excluding teetotallers from serving on licensing boards. This was a very direct affront to temperance campaigners. Finally, White people were to be permitted to purchase wine and beer from cafés and restaurants without complicated licensing restrictions. But to balance the ticket, the Bill was supposed to phase out licences for stand-up canteens over a five-year period. The Bill would have permitted Coloured people in the Cape to drink in licensed canteens in the interim, while banning them from purchasing off-sales alcohol, thereby addressing some of the concerns about liquor abuse over weekends in rural areas. Crucially, all Black people in the Cape were to forfeit the right to freely purchase 'European alcohol', regardless of whether they qualified to be on the voters' register. Roos had already pre-empted the debate by announcing that the Bill would be referred to a Select Committee. Over the next two years, the WCTU and SATA kept up sustained pressure through petitions and public meetings, targeting aspects of the 'Roos Bill' that they deemed unacceptable. The draft that returned to Parliament in 1927 was shorn of its more liberal aspects and reflected much more of the temperance agenda. While Blackwell continued to oppose

[130] He further lamented the waste of Parliamentary time resulting from repeated attempts at legislating for Local Option. Tielman Roos, Minister of Justice, introducing second reading of Liquor Bill. *Assembly Debates*, 10 February 1926, column 460.

particular sections, the temperance lobby kept up the pressure outside Parliament. At a 'mass meeting' at City Hall, which was led by the Archbishop of Cape Town, speakers celebrated the withdrawal of 'two-thirds' of the offending articles from the Bill, notably on the composition of the licensing boards and the sale of liquor through cafés and restaurants.

By contrast, it is somewhat puzzling that the KWV failed to articulate a public case in favour of wine and spirits. In Parliament, Heatlie and J. H. H. De Waal made lengthy contributions to the debate, but given the latter's hostility to the KWV, it is perhaps understandable that they struggled to find a unified voice. The one specific item on which these MPs mounted a defence was in relation to the dop system.[131] However, this was more about justifying established practice in the Cape than supporting an extension to the north. While Blackwell wished to exclude all Black people from the dop, Heatlie insisted that it was impractical to separate Coloured and Black farmworkers in this way. He also asserted that the dop was conducive to law and order because it kept farmworkers away from the canteens.[132] For defenders of the dop, the cardinal principle remained that the farmer was the best judge of the welfare of his workers. As Jeremy Martens has indicated, the debate also elicited fundamental differences of opinion as to whether the Coloured population should be treated on a par with the White one.[133] While some defended the rights of Coloured people to consume on the basis of non-racialism,[134] those who represented wine interests were conscious of the fact that they were the principal consumers of unfortified wine. At the same time, the abandonment of the right of Black voters in the Cape to drink was a further nail in the coffin of a shared citizenship.[135] Temperance campaigners, who had formally supported the political rights of Black people in line with the traditions of Cape liberalism, had contributed to this outcome by abandoning equality before the law in the pursuit of eventual prohibition.

In 1928, the temperance movement had chalked up a significant victory over the wine farmers and the merchants alike, and in ways that were to have profound consequences for the next three decades.[136] Under the 1928 Liquor Act, all Black people were henceforth excluded from the purchase of wine, bottled beer and

[131] One MP shrewdly observed that many MPs who were vocally opposed to the dop system had previously voted against Local Option. Gilson, *Assembly Debates*, 2 May 1928, column 3595.

[132] Charlie Heatlie, MP for Worcester, *Assembly Debates*, 2 May 1928, column 3590.

[133] Jeremy Creighton Martens, "Conflicting views of 'Coloured' people in the South African Liquor Bill debate of 1928", *Canadian Journal of African Studies* 35 (2) 2001, pp. 313–338.

[134] Maj. G. B. Van Zyl referred to a petition signed by 10,344 Coloured people, many of whom were temperance supporters, objecting to any distinction on the basis of colour. Van Zyl, *Assembly Debates*, 20 February 1928, columns 1181–1182.

[135] Black voters in the Cape, whose rights had rested on a qualified franchise, were removed from the common roll in 1936.

[136] Muriel Jones, "Roos Liquor Bill", *White Ribbon* XXXVIII, no. 9, June 1928; CA A1696 "Women's Christian Temperance Union".

spirits, which represented a significant reversal of the position in the Cape where those who qualified to vote had previously been exempted, even if permits of exemption could still be applied for in exceptional circumstances.[137] And yet, for temperance campaigners, there were three lingering sources of discontent. The first is that they had failed to prevent the legalization of municipal beer halls selling a version of 'kaffir beer' on the Witwatersrand. Secondly, the dop system remained in place in the Cape and the Orange Free State, albeit subject to formal regulation. Thirdly, Coloured people in the Cape and Natal (and Asians) were still permitted to purchase alcohol from canteens and off-licences. However, the Act provided that all canteens would close within three years, except for those that were converted into hotel licences, which was likely to reduce Coloured people's access to alcohol before very long. Also, they had failed to entrench their preferred version of Local Option. But the hours of sale were reduced, and while the wine farmer's licence survived, it was restricted to larger volumes consumed off-premises. On balance, it was evident that Blackwell and the temperance lobby had forced Roos into a humiliating retreat through a skilful mixture of public campaigning and the application of pressure to individual MPs. As one Parliamentarian later described the outcome: 'The Bill which Mr Roos introduced . . . at that time was introduced as a Liquor Bill, but it left the House as a Prohibition Act. It was introduced as a Roos Bill and went out as a Blackwell Act.'[138] The wine farmers had avoided an even worse fate, perhaps, but the provisions that were intended to expand the market for light wines had been stripped out. What this meant was that the internal market for wine was even more precariously balanced on the consumption of White and Cape Coloured people, whose capacity to drink would also be inhibited by stricter licensing laws. The 1928 legislation was equally a defeat for the merchants who avoided a curb on 'tied houses' but faced greater constraints on their ability to sell wine and spirits.

Conclusion

Across the wine-producing world, as Perold rightly observed, there was a steep increase in production around the turn of the century that was not matched by a comparable rise in demand.[139] Unlike in France, a generic problem was compounded by South African legislation that was designed to prevent a majority of the population from acquiring access to alcohol, including wine

[137] The exemptions covered a period of 12 months. Act to Consolidate and Amend the Laws for the Control of the Supply of Intoxicating Liquor (Liquor Act) (No. 30 of 1928), section 101 (3).

[138] A. J. Stals, *Assembly Debates*, 9 February 1933, column 511.

[139] See Kym Anderson and Vicente Pinilla, "Global overview" in Anderson and Pinilla (eds.), *Wine Globalization*, table 2.1, p. 27.

and brandy. The 1928 Liquor Act marked both the demise of a lengthy campaign to establish an exception for 'light wine' and victory for the temperance lobby over the wine farmers and merchants alike. It was not a total victory because White and Cape Coloured drinkers could still purchase wine. But it narrowed consumption at a time when production was surging as a consequence of the opening up of the Breede River valley to irrigated farming. The government was reluctant to intervene directly, and so it fell to the KWV to address an oversupply of basic wine destined for distillation. In the next chapter, I assess how far the KWV proved capable of fulfilling its devolved mandate after 1924, and the door to the advancement of a quality agenda remained open.

2 'South Africa Calling the World'*

KWV Regulation and the Struggle over Quality, 1924–1940

In Chapter 1, I addressed the three-way tussle between wine farmers, merchants and the temperance movement in the first two decades of the twentieth century. Even more than in France, the Cape and post-Union governments were reluctant to intervene directly in the industry, preferring to broker agreements between the principal players and devolve regulatory functions rather than taking the initiative directly. This had profound consequences for the long-term configuration of the industry, as we shall see in detail. The 1924 Wine and Spirits Control Act and the 1928 Liquor Act were the two legislative cornerstones that imparted structure to the industry over the coming decades. In this chapter, I focus on the impact of the 1924 Act, with a specific focus on the success with which the KWV endeavoured to reconcile three imperatives: namely, securing sustainable prices for farmers, tackling the endemic threat of overproduction and improving the quality of Cape wines. The latter assumed a particular importance in the context of efforts by wine merchants and quality producers to re-enter the export market. In the second section of the chapter, I consider a recurrence of problems in the wine sector that ultimately (and unexpectedly) led to a further extension of KWV powers in 1940.

A Mixed Scorecard: KWV Custodianship of the Wine Industry

Having secured statutory rights of control over distilling wine in 1924, the KWV leadership faced the task of rebuilding its credibility. It had not merely to win back the trust of the farmers, many of whom were deeply disillusioned, but also to demonstrate that it possessed both the inclination and the capacity to carry out regulation in a manner that would be acceptable to farmers and merchants alike. The KWV was also keen to justify the confidence that Jan Smuts had placed in it, even if he was no longer in office following the

* 'South Africa Calling the World' was the name of an ambitious special issue of *Wine and Spirit* designed to place South African wine squarely in the centre of international frame.

1924 election defeat.[1] In its various efforts to answer its detractors, the KWV went beyond the narrowest interpretation of its remit and sought to develop a coherent long-term strategy for the development of the industry.

Given that the rationale for the creation of the KWV in the first place had been to protect the interest of the ordinary farmers, it is hardly surprising that its priority was to tilt the pricing regime in their favour. The Wines and Spirits Act empowered the KWV to fix minimum prices for distilling wine and required all purchases to be made with its consent. The merchants were therefore required to comply with a pricing mechanism that they were excluded from shaping. However, they *were* given the right to take the final decision to a Board of Appeal if they felt that the declared price was unjustified. In his memoir, Kohler recalled that the merchants appealed as soon as the KWV fixed its first minimum price of £7.18s.9d per leaguer, but they lost the case and became reconciled to their fate.[2] For some years thereafter, the price was pegged at the same level, imparting a degree of much needed stability to a volatile market. The farmers did not, of course, receive the full minimum price, but one that took account of the need to dispose of the underlying surplus. Each year, the KWV made a calculation, based on orders by the merchants and an estimate of the harvest, of what the wine surplus was likely to be. The surplus declaration became the determinant of what the farmers received for the wine that they sold – although most were only selling grapes. The formula divided the total amount paid by the merchants for all the distilling wine they purchased by the total quantity of wine produced, yielding a price per leaguer that the farmers received. As the 1937 Wine Commission explained:

> ... the underlying principle of the control exercised by the K.W.V. under Act No. 5 of 1924 as far as distilling wine is concerned, is that the portion of the vintage which is sold for local consumption, in any particular year, pays for the whole distilling wine vintage of that year.[3]

The farmers were only allowed to sell wine to distillers with the consent of the KWV, and they were required to surrender their share of the estimated surplus to the KWV at no cost. After 1924, the price paid to the farmers varied from a high of £5.0s.6d in the years between 1926 and 1928 to a low of £3.3s.3d over 1932 and 1933. On an average, prices were fractionally higher than they had been during the earlier crisis years, which represented a modest benefit to most farmers. Whether the system was sustainable in the long run, however, depended on the dimensions of the annual surplus. If this were to increase over time, the net effect would inevitably be downward pressure on the producer price – even if the KWV could choose to cushion short-term swings with its accumulated financial reserves.

[1] Joelson, *Memoirs*, p. 101. [2] *Wine Commission*, p. 98. [3] *Wine Commission*, p. 19.

Secondly, the KWV came up with creative ways to dispose of the surplus. In 1924 and 1925, the association resorted to destroying stocks of excess wine but many, including Kohler himself, regarded this as inherently wasteful, and greater attention was directed to finding alternative outlets.[4] One option, which the temperance movement had long been advocating, was to develop the market for grape syrup (*moskonfyt*) and grape juice. There was some local demand and the KWV enjoyed success in opening sales to Britain. However, Diko van Zyl observes that the KWV decided not to focus unduly on grape juice production, preferring instead to develop its capacity to handle wine.[5] Another option was to pay greater attention to the development of the market for Cape brandies. The association purchased distilleries in Worcester, Montagu and Robertson, and improved existing facilities for the distillation and maturation of brandy in Paarl and Stellenbosch. In this manner, it was able to channel a large part of the surplus into a very substantial brandy operation. Under the Act, the KWV was not permitted to compete with merchants in the South African market, or indeed in Africa south of the equator, which meant that it had to carve out an export niche further afield. Here again, the KWV enjoyed a measure of success. In total, brandy exports rose steeply from a meagre 1,350 gallons (61.4 hl.) in 1924 to 20,970 gallons in 1934 (954.1 hl.). The private merchants controlled the largest market, which was Southern Rhodesia (19,386 gallons or 882.1 hl.), whereas the KWV predominated in sales to Canada (17,232 gallons or 784.1 hl.) and to Britain (6,995 gallons or 318.3 hl.).[6] In addition to brandy, the KWV also produced some gin, but this was of marginal significance.

In 1927, the British government re-instituted preferential duties on wine from the Empire, which made it realistic for the KWV to contemplate re-entering a lamented lost market. Because the KWV did not have any control over 'good wine', it bought its supplies from farmers in the normal manner, cellared the wine and sold the product under its own labels. It held no particular advantage over private merchants who competed in exporting some of their own wines. Counter-intuitively, the onset of the Great Depression enlarged the British export market because lower duties on Empire wines was the quid pro quo for reduced tariffs on British manufactures. Hence there was a significant increase in South African wine exports to Britain after 1928, as indeed there was from Australia.[7] A significant initiative was the development of what was essentially a new line in Cape Sherry. This was assisted by the introduction of four different strains of *flor* from Spain that enabled South

[4] However, wine did need to be destroyed again in later years. [5] Van Zyl, *KWV*, p. 74.

[6] *Wine Commission*, table xvi, p. 79.

[7] This is correctly identified by Regan-Lefebvre, *Imperial Wine*, p. 173.

Table 2.1. *South African exports of wine and spirits, 1923–1935 (bulk gallons)*

Year	Brandy	Liqueurs	Light and Sparkling Wines	Port, Sherry and Other 'Heavy' Wines
1923	3,396	2,637	139,971	532,236
1924	1,350	1,666	120,845	325,331
1925	3,264	2,146	38,034	129,355
1926	1,210	1,907	57,320	111,855
1927	1,785	1,704	167,246	212,439
1928	1,332	1,737	91,546	266,218
1929	2,531	1,326	181,137	393,606
1930	2,621	904	116,546	529,791
1931	6,754	1,067	197,789	701,572
1932	6,536	470	161,445	669,705
1933	12,742	948	209,753	1,072,418
1934	20,970	1,532	135,357	1,173,586
1935	48,759	1,248	132,658	1,231,929

Source: *Wine Commission*, table XVI, p. 79.

African versions of sherry to be developed.[8] The KWV significantly augmented its production in the mid-1930s. It also paid greater attention to the development of port and madeira styles of fortified wine.[9] In the mid-1930s, there was a significant increase in exports of fortified wines by both private merchants and the KWV (see Table 2.1). Although Britain was the main market, these fortified wines made some headway in Denmark, Sweden, Canada and New Zealand, the last two of which had not yet become significant wine-producing countries.[10] In 1927, the KWV came to an agreement with a British importer, Vine Products Ltd, for the supply of fortified wine. This effectively made the company the sole distributor of KWV products in the British market.[11] Four years later, the company and the KWV established a jointly owned company, the South African Wine Farmers' Association (SAWFA) to handle the business. Finally, the KWV was imaginative in developing new outlets for the products of the vine, including the production

[8] The strains were imported by Dr C. J. G. Niehaus, then at the University of Stellenbosch (he moved to the KWV in 1937). He himself explained that what had previously been called sherry was really nothing of the kind. True sherries involve a secondary process after the initial fermentation, when the wine is left to develop a film through which certain yeasts produce chemical reactions in the wine that impart a distinctive flavour to the sherry. Niehaus considered White French/Palomino as the most suitable grape. C. J. G. Niehaus, "South African sherries", *Wine and Spirit*, February 1937, p. 2988.

[9] Leipoldt, *300 Years*, pp. 199–200.

[10] *Wine Commission*, p. 80. The wine merchants handled the exports to New Zealand and Southern Rhodesia.

[11] Van Zyl, *KWV*, p. 68.

Table 2.2. *Spirits used for fortification by KWV and merchants (in leaguers of wine at 20 per cent proof)*

Year	Total Spirit Used for Fortification	Total Spirit Used for Fortification of Export Wines	Total Spirit Used for Fortification of Wines for Local Consumption
1924	21,090	–	21,090
1925	20,127	–	20,127
1926	23,507	–	23,507
1927	27,610	4,235	23,375
1928	31,459	6,347	25,112
1929	33,451	1,076	22,475
1930	38,080	14,376	23,704
1931	43,758	21,048	22,710
1932	42,382	120,182	22,200
1933	46,420	22,901	23,519
1934	65,408	38,368	27,040
1935	58,132	25,314	32,818

Source: *Wine Commission*, table XIII, p. 42.

of motor fuel and *eau de cologne*, although these experiments were later abandoned as uneconomic.[12]

One indicator of how successful the KWV was lies in the total volume of distilling wine that was taken out of the system. Between 1924 and 1935, the volume of spirits consumed within South Africa hardly budged. However, the total volume of spirits that was used nearly doubled, from 71,300 leaguers (412,114 hl.) to 130,823 leaguers (756,157 hl.), between those years. Around 44 per cent of the latter figure was accounted for by using wine spirit in fortification, which underlines how important the new export trade in sherry and port was to the KWV's overall strategy (see Table 2.2). However, the figures were to some extent an optical illusion, in the sense that the KWV was gambling against the future by building up substantial stocks of spirits and fortified wines that it hoped to find a market for at some point in the future. In the mid-1930s, this seemed like a not unreasonable risk to take (Table 2.3).

The third area in which the KWV sought to contribute was in the general improvement of the quality of wine produced. Strictly speaking, this lay beyond its official remit, but given that government intervention was half-hearted, the KWV endeavoured to fill the vacuum. Moreover, as the representative of the great majority of the wine farmers, the KWV considered it incumbent upon itself to assist members to improve their viticultural and

[12] The South African Motor Fuel Supply Co. ran at a loss and had to be liquidated. Joelson, *Memoirs*, p. 95.

Table 2.3. *Exports of fortified wine by KWV, 1926–1935 (bulk gallons)*

Year	Export Wines Made	Wines Exported
1926	245,433	23,104
1927	349,983	145,142
1928	643,160	205,144
1929	1,208,551	338,926
1930	1,197,085	511,779
1931	1,543,975	633,498
1932	1,254,213	658,294
1933	1,495,171	987,852
1934	3,620,130	1,015,879
1935	2,135,950	1,109,171

Source: *Wine Commission*, table IX, p. 38.

oenological practices and to churn out less distilling wine. During the interwar years, there were improvements in vineyard management. Although most of the vineyards were still under bush vines, there was a movement towards modern trellising that enabled yields to be more effectively controlled and facilitated harvesting with less damage to the grapes. However, a recurrent complaint from the merchants was that farmers continued to harvest before the grapes were fully ripe. In the cellars, the wider use of *egrappoirs* meant that fewer stalks – reputedly the source of much of the harshness of Cape wines – found their way into the juice.[13] However, the most intractable problem remained the heat of the cellars during the harvesting season, which was detrimental to the quality of the wine and conducive to the proliferation of all manner of harmful bacteria. The KWV could not claim the credit for all the improvements that ensued, but it played an important role in raising the awareness of the farmers. The industry magazine that it sponsored with effect from 1931, *Wine and Spirit*, contained many pages of advertisements showcasing state-of-the-art equipment, as well as publishing articles and advice on the latest trends in viticulture and oenology. It also contained regular updates on trends in other parts of the wine-producing world, including France, Germany, Italy and Australia, but also much further afield, including Russia. This reinforced the message about the need to keep abreast of the latest innovations. Although it is difficult to measure its influence, the fact that *Wine and Spirit*'s opinion leaders were often picked up in the national press would suggest that it was widely read, and most especially by the farmers who

[13] An *egrappoir* separates the stems from the grapes.

were the intended audience. Its role in disseminating knowledge about improved practices should not, therefore, be underestimated.

In his own illuminating account, Louis Leipoldt observed the catalytic effect of wine shows which put on display the best of what the Cape had to offer. These emerged as a strand in the Western Province Agricultural Show, but the first special show for wine was held in 1912.[14] After a slow start, the idea caught on and by the 1930s the wine show, which was often held in Rosebank, had become the most important event in the social calendar. Its value, as *Wine and Spirit* saw it, was as a source of knowledge dissemination:

> Sound competition, so essential to the progress of the Wine industry, is promoted by shows. Even [for] the farmer who does not exhibit his wine but who is interested in the industry, the show is both useful and instructive. When shows no longer receive support there will be retrogression in many directions.[15]

The trophies that were competed for reveals something about how wine was conceptualized at that time. The basic distinctions were between white and red wines, with a preponderance of the former, and these were then broken down according to their sweetness, 'lightness' and whether they were fortified, and only then according to the varietal. Hence, at the 1932 show, there were eight classes of white wines evaluated – 'dry white wine, light-bodied Hock type', 'dry white wine, full bodied unfortified sherry type', 'sweetest white wine full bodied, fortified', 'white Jerepico, Muscadel grapes', 'white Jerepico, Hanepoot grapes', 'white Jerepico, non-Muscat type', 'dry white wine, Muscat flavour, unfortified', 'dry white made from one variety of grape'. Amongst the red wine categories, one is struck by categories such as 'dry red wine, light bodied, Claret type' and 'dry red wine, full bodied, Burgundy type', which make very little sense in contemporary wine parlance.[16] But it is in the residual categories for red wine – 'made from one variety not mentioned in the previous classes' – that one can detect the first serious attempts to produce wine from Shiraz and even Petit Verdot, as opposed to Cinsault or Chenin Blanc which had become the default grapes. Moreover, there was a category specifically devoted to Cabernet Sauvignon, which is evidence of changes afoot in some of the vineyards. One can also observe direct evidence for the renewed engagement with export markets in the creation of a series of special trophies. The most prestigious were two silver trophies donated by the London-based wine importers P. B. Burgoyne & Co., for white and red wines of 'export quality'. As we have seen in the Introduction, this company had

[14] Leipoldt, *300 Years*, p. 164.

[15] [Anon.], "The value of shows" (information), *Wine and Spirit*, October 1932, p. 515.

[16] [Anon.], "Catalogue for 1932 Wine Show", *Wine and Spirit*, November 1932, p. 525. It is difficult to imagine a Burgundy-type in the absence of Pinot Noir and Chardonnay grapes.

pioneered the export of Australian wines to Britain in the later nineteenth century. Despite earlier reservations about the quality of South African wine, the company elected to open a second line in Cape wines and took steps to incentivize quality. The patriarch of the company by this point was Cuthbert Burgoyne, who paid a highly publicized visit to South Africa in 1920 with a view to sourcing wines and meeting with interested farmers. He also held discussions with the KWV, which culminated in the first efforts by Frank W. Myburgh to produce export wines.[17] That year, none other than C. W. H. Kohler was the proud winner of the Burgoyne cup for 50 leaguers of 'dry white wine suitable for export'. Most of the other prizes were donated by local merchants, farmers and others involved in the sale of equipment to the industry.[18] The KWV was not the main organizer of the Cape wine show, which remained the pride of the Western Province Agricultural Association. However, the KWV donated its own special trophies. Moreover, its wine experts were a permanent fixture amongst the judges, most notably A. I. Perold and Frank Myburgh. It made a difference that *Wine and Spirit* accorded generous coverage to the show and placed its winners in the spotlight.

The contributions of Perold and Myburgh go much deeper, and their lives became closely entwined through their employment in the service of the KWV.[19] Myburgh had inherited the historic Elsenburg farm in Stellenbosch from his father Phillipus Albertus Myburgh, a farmer and politician who Pamela Scully describes as 'a good example of the traditional elite of the Stellenbosch district'.[20] Like many, Frank Myburgh had been forced to sell up in 1898 after running into financial difficulty. The Cape government stepped in to purchase the property which, as we have seen, was converted into Elsenburg Agricultural College.[21] Myburgh subsequently took up the position of manager of the Drostdy Co-operative Winery in Tulbagh, and in 1909 he produced the first bottles of what ultimately became South Africa's first genuine wine brand, *Witzenberg*, in the 1920s.[22] The latter was a white wine modelled on sweeter German styles and quickly became the market leader, in large part by

17 Phillip Myburgh, "Frank Myburgh: a tribute from his son", *Wine and Spirit*, November 1945, p. 6401.

18 The coopers, O. Bakke and Castle Wine and Brandy Co. were amongst those who donated trophies.

19 Kenney, *Abraham Izak Perold*; Peter F. May, *Pinotage: Behind the Legends of South Africa's Own Wine* (St. Albans: Inform and Enlighten, 2009).

20 P. A. Myburgh had also owned Meerlust and Mariendahl farms. Scully, *Bouquet*, p. 18.

21 According to his son, Myburgh had previously been exporting Pontac to France where it had been used by Bordeaux *négociants* for blending purposes. Myburgh, "Frank Myburgh – a tribute", p. 6399. The financial problems that led to the sale of Elsenburg were associated with the failure of the Stellenbosch banks. Frank's father had been a director of the Stellenbosch District Bank. Scully, *Bouquet*, p. 18.

22 André Rossouw, "Drostdy, Suid-Afrika se eerste kooperatiewe wynkelder: van 'palmietsop' tot puikwyn", *Wynboer*, December 1975, pp. 34–36. Rossouw noted that it was Jannie Viljoen,

deploying the distribution channels of the merchants, E. K. Green.[23] After some years of promoting *Witzenberg*, Myburgh took up an offer of a job as a wine expert in the employ of the KWV in 1920. Myburgh assumed responsibility for assisting the farmers to improve their winemaking practices, allegedly covering 3,000 miles a month in the process.[24] His services were sold at 5s per leaguer of wine made under his supervision, a fee which was waived if the product was not sold as good wine.[25] Myburgh became particularly closely associated with Rhodes Fruit Farms (RFF), which had bought up twenty-nine farms around Paarl and Stellenbosch, including much of the Drakenstein valley and the prestigious Boschendal estate that bordered onto Pniël.[26] The RFF scooped up no fewer than six of the trophies in 1932, which no doubt owed something to the close assistance offered by Myburgh. With an orientation that was more practical than scientific, Myburgh was widely revered for his knowledge of the global wine industry and of what yielded the best results locally.

As we have already seen, Perold's background was that of a researcher with an intimate knowledge of viticulture and the many afflictions of the vine. However, his wider knowledge can be gauged from his regular and highly varied contributions to *Wine and Spirit*. Even more than Myburgh, Perold was alert to what South Africa could learn from other parts of the wine world. But at the same time he also believed that the Cape manifested its own specificities, which meant that careful attention needed to be paid to adapting viticultural and oenological knowledge to local conditions. After his first European sojourn, Perold had been appointed to the position of Government Viticulturalist. He tried in vain to persuade the government of the importance of establishing a properly equipped oenological institute in Paarl. Although the government did acquire a farm, there were lengthy delays in repairing the

who was trained by Myburgh who launched Witzenberg in the 1920s. However, the trademark was registered in 1913.

23 E. K. Green had shown an early interest in the cooperative, but after a first disastrous exercise in winemaking had withdrawn. Rossouw, "Drostdy", p. 35. In the 1920s, however, Green became a major distributor of *Witzenberg*. The dominant grape was Palomino.

24 Myburgh, "Frank Myburgh: a tribute", p. 6401.

25 J. F. Knott-Craig, "Quo vadis? The K.W.V. after a quarter of a century", *Wine and Spirit*, July 1943, p. 5710.

26 Scully, *Bouquet*, p. 29. An unexpected discovery during my fieldwork in 2009 was that Myburgh struck up a relationship with a woman from neighbouring Pniël, which had a troubled relationship with RFF. The children took the Myburgh name but had no formal contact with the rest of the family. Informal meeting with descendants of Myburgh, Pniel. I am grateful to Matthew Cyster for helping me solve this puzzle. The relationship between RFF and the people of Pniël was often a tense one. In 1915, the custodians of the Pniel Institute unsuccessfully initiated legal proceedings against RFF after the latter erected a fence on lands bordering onto the Dwars River. CSC 2/1/1/760 ref 120 "Illiquid Case. Henry John Cyster versus Rhodes Fruit Farms Ltd. Action for a Declaration of Rights", "*Henry John Cyster (Plaintiff) vs Rhodes Fruit Farms (Defendant)*", in Supreme Court, Cape of Good Hope Provincial Division, 1 June 1915.

dilapidated buildings and making budgetary provision for all the equipment that Perold considered essential. Evidently frustrated at the lack of urgency, Perold resigned and took up the position of head of Elsenburg in 1912. He subsequently became the founding dean (and professor) of the Faculty of Agriculture in 1917 at the University of Stellenbosch.[27] An experimental farm was established at the same time at Welgevallen, in close proximity to the University, for the purposes of teaching and research on viticulture. Perold was responsible for the introduction of a wide array of European varietals, some of which found favour and others of which had to wait nearly a century before being taken up commercially.[28] In 1928, Perold was lured away from the University to become the chief wine and scientific expert with the KWV in Paarl, where he continued to carry out independent research and writing. It is partly to Perold that the South African fascination with German styles can be traced. Perold believed that excessive heat during harvesting made it difficult to emulate the best dry white wines, but that the Cape was well-suited to sweet wine production in the German manner.[29] But while Germany always loomed large for Perold, he was equally interested in the sweet whites and red wines of France, and he made repeated visits there. He embarked on a tour of Bordeaux, Burgundy and the Rhône in 1935 and paid close attention to what he observed and tasted.[30] Although his diary indicates that he found the white Burgundies less fragrant than German whites of the Mosel and the Rhine, he was impressed by the reds, to which he was treated to a tasting by M. Latour.[31] He commented in particular on the colour of the Burgundies which he attributed to the fact that they were handled in very cool cellars, adding, 'We must do the same!'[32]

Perold displayed a particular fascination with Pinot Noir, the varietal associated, above all ,with Burgundy. He had it growing in the experimental vineyard at Welgevallen, and he later remarked on a successful wine made with grapes from another experimental farm in Malmesbury.[33] But the trials with Pinot Noir do not seem to have gone well overall. It is a notoriously

[27] Elsenburg, which retained its autonomy, ran degree courses concurrently with the University of Stellenbosch, whose Faculty of Agriculture staff were similarly civil servants, between 1926 and 1973. To this day, the Elsenburg Agricultural Training Institute remains a college under the control of the Western Cape Department of Agriculture.

[28] Many derived from Italy, like Aglianico, Barbera, Nebbiolo and Trebbiano. For a list of varietals during the time of C. J. Theron, which were mostly introduced by Perold, see Dine Van Zyl, *Prof. C.J. Theron, Pionier van ons Wybou* (Kaapstad: SFW, 1982), pp. 19–20.

[29] A. I. Perold, "Cape wines and their origin", *Wine and Spirit*, August 1932, p. 380.

[30] Extracts from the diary may be found at Kenney, *Abraham Izak Perold*, pp. 108–115.

[31] He considered that a 1923 Côte de Nuits tasted a bit like old wine and unlike anything produced in South Africa, except by Manie Malan. Kenney, *Abraham Izak Perold*, p. 111. He was also particularly fond of the wines and especially the port of Portugal, which he also visited in 1935.

[32] Extract from diary. Kenney, *Abraham Izak Perold*, p. 111.

[33] Perold, *Handboek*, p. 239.

temperamental grape that does not fare well in hotter locations, which is why the best examples in South Africa today are produced in the cool climate zones along the east coast. However, these areas were off the cognitive map at the time Perold was engaged in his quest to find a suitable home for Pinot Noir. Although Perold apparently encouraged G. P. Canitz to persist with planting Pinot Noir at Muratie in Stellenbosch, where the first wine from the grape was made in 1927, this lead was not followed by other farmers.

In fact, it was the modification of Pinot Noir for which Perold is perhaps most famous. The Pinotage story has been much embellished over the years, but the version that seems to have won acceptance is one that comes down to accident as much as to design. Perold's university residence was located in Welgevallen. He considered that the Cinsault grape was capable of producing acceptable quality, especially on the hills around Constantia and Stellenbosch, but only under conditions of low yield and on the right soils.[34] It had the great advantage of being relatively disease-resistant. On 17 November 1924, amongst several experimental crossings, he successfully fertilized a Hermitage (Cinsault) flower with pollen from the Pinot Fin variant of Pinot Noir.[35] Perold managed to produce four seeds, which he proceeded to plant in his own garden, and then promptly forgot about them. After he left for Paarl, it may have been Dr. Charles Niehaus of the University who spotted them in the overgrown garden, which was about to be cleared. They were then looked after at the Elsenburg nursery by Professor C. J. Theron, who had succeeded Perold. Theron grafted them onto Richter 99 rootstocks and planted them in Welgevallen. It was Theron who later revealed the existence of the vines to Perold. The latter rekindled his interest in developing what came to be known to the world as Pinotage.[36] Only one of the four vines was considered viable. Further planting material was propagated from this vine, and in 1941 the first experimental wine was made at Elsenburg by a lecturer there, C. T. de Waal. However, the first commercial plantings did not follow until some years later.[37] The larger lesson from the Pinotage story is that Perold was engaged in constant experimentation and developed close working relationships with particular farmers whom he persuaded to plant varietals that he considered

[34] In his handbook, he observed that in the south of France, where it produced good wine, the yield was between 4.5 and 9 leaguers per morgen, but in the Cape, it was more like 10–15 leaguers in the absence of trellising. He referred to a farm in Durbanville where it yielded 43 leaguers, commenting that, 'The wine here is thin, light red and without much character. This is the highest yield from Hermitage per morgen in our country and possibly in the world.' Perold, *Handboek*, p. 248.

[35] This is clear from Perold's detailed diary entries. May, *Pinotage*, pp. 58–59. See also the brief account given by C. J. Theron in Van Zyl, *Prof. C.J. Theron*, pp. 10–11.

[36] The name was evidently an amalgam of 'Pinot' and the last three letters from 'Hermitage'.

[37] May, *Pinotage*, pp. 78–79. The first vines were shared with Muratie and with Paul Sauer (Kanonkop) and Piet Morkel (Bellevue) in Stellenbosch. Van Zyl, *Prof. C.J. Theron*, p. 11.

suited to particular locations, based on soil type and rainfall patterns. Like Myburgh, Perold did not believe that the Cape was only capable of producing the sweet white wines that many saw as the future of the industry at the Cape. Indeed, they were both aware that the finest sweet wine, along the lines of Sauternes, could not actually be emulated because of an anomaly in the regulations that required wines containing 20 grams of sugar to be fortified.[38] The mounting interest in red wines also owed something to Myburgh and Perold during their most productive collaboration at the KWV in the 1930s.

The threads that I have identified thus far conveniently converge in a story of three friends whose shared pursuits exemplify some of the important transformations that were underway in the vineyard and the cellar. It is also a tale of global connectivity. Our story begins at the Alto farm, which nestles at the foot of the Helderberg mountain in Stellenbosch. In the early 1920s, the farm was planted entirely with Cinsault vines. H. J. ('Manie') Malan, the son of the owner, had been in the first graduating class from the Faculty of Agriculture at the University where he studied directly under Perold. In 1923, he was given responsibility for his first harvest. Malan boldly invited Perold and Myburgh to sample the wine that resulted.[39] They were so impressed that a sample was sent to P. B. Burgoyne & Co., who offered Malan a five-year contract to supply them. Unusually for the time, Malan now proceeded to plant experimental blocks of Cabernet Sauvignon, Shiraz and Pinot Noir with Perold's advice and assistance. Malan won the Burgoyne trophy in 1924 for 'the best dry red wine approximating to the Burgundies of France'.[40] He later recalled that he won the trophy six years in succession, and to recognize the singular achievement of back-to-back triumphs in 1929, 1930 and 1931, he was presented with a replica of the trophy in June 1932. By this point, Malan was producing a red blend that consisted of 50 per cent Cinsault and 20 per cent each of Cabernet Sauvignon and Shiraz. The photograph of the celebration in Alto in 1932 (Figure 2.1) shows a relaxed Manie Malan standing alongside Senator F. S. Malan (seemingly no relation), representing Messrs Burgoyne, and a benign-looking Frank Myburgh.[41] In his

[38] This no doubt helped to dispose of some of the surplus wine spirit but did not allow the emulation of European styles.

[39] Manie Malan is profiled in Barrie Biermann, *Red Wine in South Africa* (Cape Town: Buren, 1971), pp. 99–102.

[40] It would appear that it was a blend that did not include Pinot Noir.

[41] The significance of the latter observation lay in the fact that farmers at the Cape had routinely added quantities of spirit to their wine in order to prevent it turning sour. During the debates of 1924, one MP claimed that most of what was sold as wine was a 'camouflaged brandy' which was 'incapable of being sold save when drugged with brandy with a full percentage of oil or vitriol or fusel oil, and which is foisted on the unfortunate consumer as light wine'. Senator F. S. (or Frans) Malan is not to be confused with Senator S. F. (Fanie) Malan, the owner of the farm Allesverloren and brother of D. F. Malan, the Prime Minister from 1948. F. S. Malan held a

Figure 2.1 Frank W. Myburgh, Senator F. S. Malan and Manie Malan at Alto, Stellenbosch, June 1932
Source: Copy in Distell Archive.

speech honouring the young pioneer, the Senator pointed to the latter as an example of what could be achieved by greater effort, stating pointedly that, 'Mr Malan has proved that South Africa can produce a natural, good white wine and place it on the London market without fortification.'[42] Malan was

number of ministerial portfolios and, according to his biographer, he twice passed up the opportunity to become Prime Minister of the Cape. He had a particular interest in wine and in 1909, when wine farmers protested about their plight in the streets of Cape Town, the task of pacifying them fell to him. See Bettie Cloete, *Die Lewe van Senator F.S. Malan (President van die Senaat)* (Johannesburg: Afrikaanse Pers-Boekhandel, 1946), pp. 206, 212, 215. Fanie Malan was elected a director of the KWV as early as 1917. Apart from his role in various farming associations, he was also a director of SANLAM and SANTAM, the two great Afrikaner insurance corporations. In 1952, he was elected deputy chairman of the KWV, thus underlining the linkage between political interests and the wine industry. In 1956, he became a Senator. [Anon.], "Oom Fanie Malan: 'n leeftyd in diens van die wynboere", *Wynboer*, February 1960, p. 5; Van Zyl, *KWV*, p. 150.

42 [Anon.], "Trophy for the best wine: Stellenbosch farmer's achievement", *Die Burger*, 3 June 1932, copy in collection of clippings and photographs donated by Phillip Myburgh, Distell archive.

ahead of his time in using a water cooler to permit fermentation at lower temperatures, and he was reputedly an absolute stickler for cleanliness in the cellar.[43] His wines therefore travelled better and did not require inoculation, which was very much to the liking of Messrs Burgoyne. In his acceptance speech, Malan took up the theme, commenting that good wine 'was more susceptible to disease than a baby'. He also risked reopening an old wound by asserting that, unlike Burgoyne, local merchants were not really interested in the promotion of quality. Manie Malan publicly thanked Myburgh for all his help, while the latter in turn praised his protégé for being willing to take advice. In a separate speech, Alfred Appleyard of RFF, who had similarly benefited from the assistance of Myburgh, commented rather tartly that, 'One successful good wine maker will contribute more to the success of the wine industry of South Africa than any amount of restrictive legislation'.

On the back of this triumph, a visit to Britain was arranged for September of that same year. Myburgh represented the KWV, while Manie Malan travelled as the representative of a new organization called the Quality Wine Growers' Society. They were accompanied on a remarkable tour of the European winelands by André Simon, who was destined to become the world's most influential wine expert before the ascent of Robert Parker. In his autobiography, Simon recalled that he had travelled to the Cape no fewer than half a dozen times between 1919 and 1931 – on each occasion by means of the Union Castle shipping line – and had made many contacts in the country.[44] This presumably included Myburgh who, together with Perold, was the most respected local authority. On this occasion, Simon led his South African guests through Germany, Champagne, Burgundy and Bordeaux, a tour which included access to the world's most famous cellars, tastings of some of the most exalted vintages and dinner at the most prestigious chateaux.[45] The tour came at a crossroads in Simon's own life and career. Simon had been the London agent of the Pommery champagne house since 1902 but had been caught short when Britain came off the gold standard in 1931 and the pound plummeted against the franc. In November 1932, only 10 months before this tour, Pommery had summarily terminated the relationship, which must have been the source of some regret and embarrassment to Simon. As he later wrote,

[43] The use of cool fermentation is mentioned in Manie's Malan's recollections in Biermann, *Red Wine*, p. 101.

[44] André L. Simon, *In the Twilight* (London: Michael Joseph, 1969), p. 19. Simon also recalled that these were good days for champagne sales in South Africa, suggesting that he was engaged in business as well as pleasure.

[45] This tour is recounted in Frank W. Myburgh, "Through the wine country of France and Germany", reprinted from *Cape Times*, 30 December 1933 and 4 January 1934 [copy in Distell Archive].

he had lost both his firm and his job.[46] One can only wonder what might have passed between the three friends as they wandered together through the famed chalk cellars of Pommery.

Back in London, Myburgh and Malan set out to make an impression, extolling the virtues of Cape wines to the British press at every available opportunity. Malan sought to disabuse the British public of the uncherished notion that 'native labour was used for foot-pressing of the grapes', and asserted that 'to-day we have the most efficient machinery in the world'. He also declaimed that South Africa was on the verge of a breakthrough in quality and that her wines were now comparable with any, except for the very finest from Europe. A number of British newspapers ran reports on the visit. The *Birmingham Post*, for example, observed that a revival in Cape wine was being led now not so much by the sweet wines for which Constantia was so famous, but by newly introduced varietals. The confidence that Malan and Myburgh exuded underlined an important point, namely that they did not see themselves as entering from the margins of the wine world to pay homage to their French and German masters. Rather, they positioned themselves as serious players who might have a thing or two to teach the Europeans. Myburgh, who wrote an account of the visit for the *Cape Times*, was evidently not in awe of what he tasted or witnessed. He was critical of an 1870 Chateau Lafite, of which he wrote that the 'body was firm, the bouquet clean, but the finish was perhaps a little dry'. The vintage of the previous year he considered excellent, but disappointing on the nose. As for Chateau Y'quem, he found the wines of 1930 and 1932 'very poor and of 1931 none too good'. It is doubtful whether many other South African wine producers have dared to pronounce on the quality of Europe's best wines in quite the same way since. In one respect, however, the visitors deferred to their European counterparts and that was in the healthy respect for wine that they considered to be deeply ingrained in European culture. In his reflection on dining in the Moselle valley, Myburgh observed that:

> [W]ine is consumed in amazingly large quantities. Yet nowhere was the slightest sign of intoxication. Would that South Africans showed the same preference for the wines of their own country ... The impression formed, apart from the preference for the local product, was at the back of the appreciation of a pleasant and healthful beverage was a lively patriotic sentiment which we do well to cultivate in South Africa ... Sitting there, my thoughts reverted to sunny South Africa, land of pleasant vineyards and well-stocked cellars, filled with as fine a product as ever came from the juice of the grape, yet scarcely appreciated by a people who, as yet, do not appear to have cultivated a wine sense, and would scarcely know the difference between what was really good and what was simply mediocre.[47]

[46] Simon, *In the Twilight*, p. 50.

[47] Myburgh, "Through the wine country", p. 7.

To add insult to injury, he complained, South Africans were being encouraged to drink tea, a commodity that 'has caused more dyspepsia in the world than any other beverage'.

After their return to London on 20 September, Myburgh and Malan parted company with Simon. Possibly, this was the last time Simon met Myburgh because he apparently ceased to be as regular a visitor to the Cape, and it is unlikely that Myburgh, who died in 1945, ever made it back to Europe. After the European wine tour, Simon returned to England and embarked on a new chapter of his life at the age of 55. The following month, he co-founded the Wine and Food Society and cemented his reputation as a restless advocate for fine food and wine. Myburgh and Malan returned to the Cape with a greater appetite than ever for developing quality wines, with Malan winning the Burgoyne trophy on three successive occasions once again and becoming the company's agent in South Africa. By the time Simon returned to the Cape in 1965, Manie Malan was no longer actively farming, having retired in 1957, but he had recruited and trained up a new winemaker for Alto, namely Piet Du Toit.[48] Myburgh was already 64 years old when he returned, but he remained committed to the cause of good wine. In 1944, he finally retired from the KWV after 24 years of service. At a lavish ceremony held in his honour, Myburgh urged a younger generation to carry the concept of the wine show forward, and in a re-iteration of his earlier views about the importance of fostering a genuine wine culture he finished with a rhetorical flourish that possibly reflected aspiration more than reality: 'Wine farming is national in South Africa; wine is our national drink.'[49]

Lest it be thought that the upbeat statements attributed to Myburgh and Malan reflected their purely personal aspirations, it is helpful to turn to *The Wine Book of South Africa*, which was a glossy publication produced by *Wine and Spirit* to coincide with the Empire Exhibition in Johannesburg in 1936.[50] This volume, which contained a good number of photographs, predates the better-known guides to Cape wines by around half a century. The publication represents a very conscious effort to sell the Cape wine industry on the basis of its venerable historical lineage. Hence claims to being 'The Empire's Oldest Vineyard'[51] are interspersed with references to Cape Dutch homesteads and to the 'inherited virility of French Huguenot wine makers'. But the book was also at pains to accentuate the thrusting modernity of the South African wine

[48] Piet du Toit was the father of Hempies Du Toit, the Springbok rugby player, who succeeded his father at Alto.

[49] "K.W.V. neem afskeid van Mnr. Frank Myburgh, vader van Witzenberg", 21 March 1944, newspaper clipping in Phillip Myburgh papers, Distell Archive.

[50] A forerunner was a special issue of *Wine and Spirit* entitled "South Africa Calling the World", August 1933.

[51] Terence P. O'Donoghue, "Wine from the Empire's oldest vineyards", in *Wine Book*, p. 131.

industry. The most bullish contribution by Terence O'Donoghue acknowledged the difficulties of the past but asserted that South Africa was unusual in having reconstructed itself on the basis of placing quality ahead of quantity. The author quoted the Empire Wine Commission as stating that:

> The increase in South African wine exports in recent years, as compared with other countries, is due to the different policy pursued. South Africa is building up quality; others are selling at low prices by means of artificial aid.[52]

The author went on to repeat Manie Malan's earlier claim that South African producers were harnessing science in the pursuit of quality and credited the KWV – described as a 'veritable fairy Godmother' – for having prepared the foundations for a world-leading industry:

> In fact, there are many wine-producing countries which lag far behind South Africa when a comparison of the methods of manufacture is made. The highly-technical and delicate art demands skilled effort and workmanship and an army of experts and specialists is employed for this purpose by the industry. Science plays a fulsome part in the production of quality wines at the Cape although the greatest care is taken to preserve unsullied their natural inheritance.

The conscious balancing of the science and nature is striking. There are also direct references to the special advantages attached to the climate of the Cape. In interesting ways, this echoed the pitch for Australian wines that Alan H. Burgoyne had made in 1912 (see Introduction).

One contribution quoted none other than André Simon as declaring that the Cape enjoyed the most favourable conditions for achieving vintages of consistency, while another recalled his assessment of Cape wines that, '[I]n some of them I have found the flavour and bouquet of the best wines.'[53] This was maybe not the most ringing endorsement, but coming from Simon, it was useful ammunition. Referring presumably to the white wines, another article observed that

> They are not French nor German wines altogether: their character, bouquet and palatability differs essentially from Continental vintages. They are the pure wines of the Cape, made lovingly from the juice of the ripe grape by men who take pride in their labour. They are improving year by year, so that now it is possible to identify all the French and Rhone characteristics from time to time in vintages from the hills and valley land of the Cape, yet possessing that robust character that is distinctive of all wines from South Africa.

In a nutshell, the message was that South Africa was at the forefront of a veritable oenological revolution that was set to place the Cape on level terms

[52] O'Donoghue, "Wine", p. 134.

[53] Major Leslie Cox, "The Western Province of the Cape and its wine industry", in *Wine and Drunkenness*, p. 16.

with some of the world's leading producers. Given the ownership of *Wine and Spirit*, it can safely be concluded that this positive message was one that the KWV itself wished to propagate. Clearly, there was a great deal of self-promotion afoot, but an emerging generation of quality producers genuinely felt that there were abundant opportunities for South Africa to sell wine to the world.

The KWV Once More Embattled

Although there was no hint of lurking difficulties in the pages of *The Wine Book of South Africa*, the vexed question of overproduction had already reared its head some years before. In 1931, *Wine and Spirit* announced an essay competition, with a prize of £25, in which contributors were invited to come up with creative suggestions for what could be done to 'overcome and prevent the wine surplus'. Two issues came to be hotly debated in this forum and elsewhere. The first was how to deter an acceleration of new plantings, while the second was what might be done to promote quality ahead of quantity. In his memoirs, Kohler indicated that he was constantly mindful of the first issue and referred to a speech of 1925 in which he warned the membership of the associated dangers:

> I would like once more to point out to members as I have done at most annual meetings although my voice is as one crying in the wilderness, that it is impossible to continue for long to create an artificial price for an article unless you can control the production of that article. If the members imagine that you can go on planting vines galore and continue to receive the price they are getting for their wines today, they are living in a fool's paradise and we must wake up one day to find ruin staring us in the face. Members must face up this issue to-day. Do not keep putting it off each annual meeting.[54]

The threat posed by the mass production of distilling wine was something that Kohler was equally conscious of. In an editorial of January 1933, *Wine and Spirit* observed that in most countries the producers of inferior distilling wine had gone out of production because of the lack of buyers. But it went on to assert that in South Africa, too, many farmers were intent on pursuing their own self-interest:

> Similarly, matters in South Africa will not fully improve until such time as everyone has learnt to do his duty. Producers must supply that for which there is a demand. They must study the interest as of their Co-operative as well as those of the wholesaler and the retailer. Only by doing so will the individual benefit in the long run.[55]

[54] Joelson, *Memoirs*, p. 99.
[55] [Anon.], "Editorial: ourselves in the world picture", *Wine and Spirit*, January 1933, p. 611.

However, this evidently begged the question of why it was in the interests of Cape farmers to continue delivering 'inferior wine'. One straightforward reason is that the vast majority were operating on a limited scale and found it more remunerative to maximize their output at a modest rate of return than to restrict yields in pursuit of a higher unit price. Here it is of some interest to take cognizance of deeper historical continuities. According to Mary Rayner's estimates for Stellenbosch in 1823, 96.5 per cent of farmers were producing less than an average of 72 leaguers of wine (416.2 hl.).[56] A little more than a century later, in 1936, 73.4 per cent of farmers across the country were still producing less than 100 leaguers (578 hl.), and only 3.2 per cent accounted for more than 300 leaguers (1,734 hl.). The average for all producers sat at a modest 83 leaguers (479.7 hl.).[57] This comparison suggests that while overall production was increasing, the vast majority of farms were still operating on a marginal scale.

In their submission to the essay competition, a group of farmers from Robertson identified the fundamental problem as a pricing policy that encouraged farmers to produce more distilling wine rather than either good wine or raisins for which there might be a market. Their preferred solution was for the KWV to pay subsidies for the uprooting of 'distilling wine vineyards' and the promotion of export wines.[58] Such proposals were hotly debated within the farming community and came to divide the membership of the KWV. In 1931, the Minister of Agriculture, General Kemp, appointed a Wine Committee under the chairmanship of W. J. Lamont from the Department of Agriculture, with a broad mandate to consider the marketing of wines at home and overseas; producer and consumer prices; and other matters affecting the industry. Kohler was invited to represent the KWV, alongside a delegate from the merchants, another from Customs and Excise and a judicial advisor.[59] Kohler submitted a lengthy memorandum that merits closer consideration. It confirmed that production of wine had risen from 110,000 leaguers (635,800 hl.) in 1923 to 162,369 leaguers (938,493 hl.) in 1930. Over the same time, the consumption of spirits had contracted from 928,363 gallons (42,204 hl.) to 841,846 gallons (38,271 hl.). Even factoring in the consumption of good wine, this pointed to significant overproduction, which Kohler finally acknowledged.[60] However, he made two further observations. The first was

[56] Rayner, "Wine and slaves", table 1.8, p. 33a.

[57] These figures included a large number of producers of table grapes, but only includes the distilling wine component. *Wine Commission*, table III, p. 15.

[58] [Anon.], "Essay no. 4 on how to overcome and prevent the wine surplus" by B. Burger, De Hoop, Robertson "on behalf of a number of wine farmers", *Wine and Spirit*, November 1932, pp. 543–544.

[59] [Anon.], "Trade notes: Wine Committee", *Wine and Spirit*, 1 November 1931, p. 45.

[60] Report by C. H. Kohler to Chairman of the Government Liquor Commission, 1931, reprinted in *Wine and Spirit*, May 1932, p. 254.

that spikes in production in 1929 and 1930 had taken place despite a falling producer price. In his view, this proved that the KWV's pricing policy was not to blame. The second was that there were distinct regional variations. That is, while production in Stellenbosch and Paarl had fallen since 1921, output in Robertson had leapt from 12,000 leaguers (69,360 hl.) to 29,000 leaguers (267,620 hl.) in 1930, while over the same period the production of Worcester had jumped from 29,000 (167,620 hl.) to 40,000 leaguers (231,200 hl.). More worryingly, Kohler observed that farmers in outlying eastern districts such as Riverdale, Graaf-Reinet and Oudtshoorn, were actively planting vineyards once more because of the lack of paying alternatives rather than because of high prices.[61] The memorandum went on to observe that the effect of the surplus on prices was bound to impact most on the farmers of Paarl and Stellenbosch whose yields were lower. Whereas they could normally expect a yield of 2 leaguers (11.56 hl.) per 1,000 vines, their counterparts in Robertson and Worcester received yields of twice that amount. Hence in the former cases, a producer price of £5 represented a virtual break-even point, while in Robertson and Worcester it still paid to plant vines at £3.11s.6d.

Kohler also addressed the marketing side of the equation, claiming that part of the reason why the producers of 'good wine' were struggling was that the merchants were reluctant to pay them a decent price. In support of this contention, he mentioned the case of a farmer who had taken a series of prizes at the annual Wine Show, but had been so disgusted at the offer of £4.10s for his quality wine that he had uprooted his vines.[62] Kohler also denied that the local merchants were being shut out of the export market, pointing out that Burgoyne & Co. paid substantially more than them, but had nevertheless developed a successful trade to Britain.[63] The elephant in the room was, of course, the 1928 Liquor Act which had restricted access to 'light wines', a provision that was currently under review by a Select Committee. The Wine Committee made a number of significant recommendations, most notably that good wine should be brought under the pricing mechanism of the KWV; that farmers should be paid their distilling wine according to a sliding scale;[64] that there should be a three-year moratorium on plantings; and, finally, that 'light wines' should be made more freely available to Black consumers in controlled 'wine shops'. On the latter point, the Committee had been impressed by the lack of any signs of public drunkenness during a field visit to Lourenço

[61] Report by C. H. Kohler to Liquor Commission, p. 256.
[62] Continuation of Kohler's report, *Wine and Spirit*, June 1932, p. 292.
[63] Report by C. H. Kohler to Liquor Commission, *Wine and Spirit*, May 1932, p. 254.
[64] The proposal was that the proportion of his output that the farmer supplied as distilling wine would determine the price he was paid per leaguer. A farmer who supplied mostly good wine would therefore receive greater remuneration and thereby a financial incentive.

Marques, the capital of Mozambique, where the population was allowed to purchase wine freely. No doubt anticipating a temperance backlash the Lamont report was suppressed by Kemp, with the result that the recommendations concerning production control were kicked into the long grass as well.[65]

Meanwhile, the KWV was attempting to forge some consensus within its own ranks over the need to limit production. A special committee was established which recommended that new vines should only be planted under permit and subject to the proviso that the total acreage of an existing farm could not be extended. This proposal provoked a fierce debate at the annual general meeting of the KWV in December 1931. Rial (Gabriel) Kloppers from Robertson led the charge, alleging that the farmers of Robertson and Worcester were in effect being victimized.[66] Given the ferocity of the response, in which Kohler was personally criticized, it was decided to constitute a more inclusive body, the Brëe (or Expanded) Committee, to go into the matter again. The Committee consisted of no fewer than 12 KWV directors and 24 farmers, chosen on the basis of two members per district. This Committee considered the proposal for restrictions on the planting of vines and recommended that each farm be allocated a production quota based on output over the previous three years. Moreover, farmers would be paid the official price only for the first 50 leaguers, and a reduced amount for the remainder of their crop. The package was then placed before a general meeting in Paarl in March 1932, where it was adopted after some negotiations. The fundamental problem remained, however, that in the face of resistance from some quarters, it would require legislation to augment the powers of the KWV. However, Kemp was not inclined to favour the KWV, and declined to bring enabling legislation to Parliament. Even the threat of direct action by the KWV, along the lines of the demonstration of 1909, failed to sway the Hertzog government.[67] It is worth noting that readers of *Wine and Spirit* would have been well aware that sustained pressure from farmers had culminated in government legislation to limit new plantings and to tax excessive yields in France.[68] In South Africa, not only was the government reluctant to take matters in hand, it was equally unwilling to concede greater powers to the KWV.

In an attempt to keep the Brëe Committee recommendations alive, Dr. A. J. Stals proceeded to bring a private members' Bill to Parliament. One clause placed a moratorium on the planting of vines for a period of three years with associated penalties for infringement, while a second sought to bring 'good

[65] Kohler recalled that they were not even permitted to print private copies of the report. Joelson, *Memoirs*, pp. 111–112.

[66] [Anon.], "Wine farmers' conference", *Wine and Spirit*, January 1932, p. 115.

[67] Van Zyl, *KWV*, p. 106.

[68] [Anon.], "Trade notes: the new French Law of Viticulture and the wine trade of the 4th July, 1931", *Wine and Spirit*, February 1932, p. 145.

wine' under KWV control. Stals sought to sell his Bill on the basis that the farmers were not seeking government subsidies but were merely asking for the means to help themselves. He also maintained that it was the low price for good wine that was driving the farmers to sell their output as distilling wine.[69] Hence, granting the KWV control over both good and distilling wine was the only realistic means of saving the industry. Despite this pitch, there was lukewarm support from either side of the House. Jan Smuts, now serving as the Leader of the Opposition, had personally steered the 1924 Act through the Assembly, but was distinctly unenthusiastic about the Bill. He noted that the decision to exclude good wine from statutory control had been agreed upon after detailed investigation and ought not to be summarily abandoned. Unlike Stals, he saw the pricing policies of the KWV as the fundamental cause of overproduction, and expressed his doubts as to whether the proposals would actually have any offsetting effect.[70] Other MPs opposed the Bill on grounds that it constituted an interference with the rights of private property, or that it would create an unfortunate precedent for other industries in distress.[71] Predictably, the MP for Oudtshoorn was adamant that the proposals did not enjoy the support of small farmers in places like Oudtshoorn, Calitzdorp and Ladysmith. He maintained that the latter had not attended the farmer's meeting at Paarl and claimed that the representatives of Worcester and Robertson had only given their consent on condition that concessions were made, but these were not contained in the Bill.[72] The upshot was that the Stals Bill was talked out in Parliament without a positive result.

Meanwhile, internal discord became yet more visible. In 1934, a report on Commission of Enquiry into Co-operation and Agricultural Credit served up a damning indictment of the KWV's handling of the relationship between pricing and overproduction. It had concluded that:

> From these statistics it is very evident that the very problem which the control measure was instituted to overcome, viz., overproduction, has been accentuated and aggravated through control. Complete control over the Industry at once created in the minds of producers the psychological atmosphere for expansion an aspect which was further strengthened by the price policy followed by the controlling Vereniging. As pointed out previously the price ruling for distilling wine prior to legislative control was about £3 per leaguer. When the Ko-operatiewe Wijnbouwers Vereniging took control in 1924 it

[69] Dr A. J. Stals moving second reading of Wine and Spirits Further Control Bill, Union of South Africa, *Assembly Debates*, 27 April 1932, columns 3795, 3800.

[70] Smuts agreed to vote for the Bill on the basis that if the farmers wanted to help themselves, they should be given the chance. *Assembly Debates*, 27 April 1932, columns 3806–3807. Prime Minister Hertzog was no more enthusiastic.

[71] One MP commented that the powers would be handed over to 'Stals-Stalin Co.' Mr S. P. Le Roux, *Assembly Debates*, 27 April 1932, column 3813. Another referred to 'Bolshevism run riot'. Mr M. M. Kentridge, *Assembly Debates*, column 3818.

[72] Mr S. P. Le Roux, *Assembly Debates*, 27 April 1932, column 3815.

immediately raised the price for distilling wine to the producer to £4.4.8 and considerably higher in subsequent years.

And again:

There does not exist the least doubt in the mind of the Commission that the policy followed by the Vereniging definitely encouraged the production of an inferior article. This applies particularly to the newer areas of wine production, viz., Montagu, Robertson and Worcester, where lower land values and higher yields made distilling wine prices very lucrative as compared with the older wine districts.

A special meeting was convened by the KWV at Paarl that rejected the findings by a large majority.[73] *Wine and Spirit* indicated that a meeting in Robertson, where there had been the fiercest opposition to the KWV strategy, had itself condemned the report.[74] The sense that all was not well with the KWV was confirmed when Rial Kloppers was removed from his directorship in April 1934. In the special meeting that was convened, Kohler indicated that the leadership had been reluctant to take action despite the fact that Kloppers had conflicting interests in a Sweet Wine Association, for fear of offending the farmers of Robertson. At the hearing, Kloppers received support from other farmers in the area who warned against administering a slap in the face to the farmers of Robertson.[75] However, in an unprecedented move, the overall majority decided that he should be removed from his position. At this point, the KWV seemed more divided than ever.

In 1935, following the installation of the Fusion Government, a more receptive Minister, in the shape of Deneys Reitz, fielded representations from the KWV leadership. Reitz proceeded to announce the formation of a Wine Commission in 1935 with a broad remit to enquire into the state of viticulture as well as the operations of the Wine and Spirit Control Act of 1924. This included a possible extension of statutory control to cover good wines as well as raisins and sultanas. Whereas the Acts of 1924 and 1928 had effectively treated statutory control and liquor distribution separately, the Commission was tasked with tackling both sides of the equation. The five-member Commission included Alfred Appleyard of RFF (which was now owned by Abe Bailey) and Sidney Frank Waterson, an MP who sat on the board of Sedgwick.[76] In 1937, the Wine Commission delivered by far the most detailed

[73] [Anon.], "Wine growers' great victory: great confidence in Co-operative Wine Growers' Association", *Wine and Spirit*, April 1934, p. 1365. The meeting was allegedly attended by 1,400 members with only 19 voting against the resolution.

[74] [Anon.], "Troubles of the wine co-operative: a leader of the Cape Times", *Wine and Spirit*, April 1934, p. 1367.

[75] [Anon.], "Groot vergadering in Paarl besluit om Mnr. Rial Kloppers as KWV direkteur te ontstel", *Wine and Spirit*, May 1934, pp. 1414–1415.

[76] Waterson had spoken in Parliament against the Stals Bill.

report on the state of the wine industry in the twentieth century. It was based on evidence tendered by the KWV, individual farmers and the wine merchants.

The report confirmed the worst fears of all parties concerned. According to the KWV's own figures, the number of vines had increased from 71 million in 1927 to 102.2 million in 1935, representing an expansion of 44 per cent.[77] The biggest increases were indeed *anderkant die berg*, where the wine was mostly consigned to distillation. In the Montagu/Robertson district, there was an increase from 12,395 vines to 22,807 vines (an 84 per cent increase), while in Worcester the number rose from 15,955 to 25,814 (a 61.8 per cent increase). In total, the latter two districts accounted for 48 per cent of the total number of vines under bearing by 1935. Moreover, these were areas where irrigation was changing the face of viticulture. The completion of the Brandvlei dam in 1922 had transformed the possibilities for irrigated agriculture in the Worcester District, leading to many more plantings on what had hitherto been marginal arid land.[78] The advance of irrigated farming in the 1930s threatened to unleash vast quantities of distilling wine onto the market. According to KWV statistics, in the Stellenbosch District, 16,434,600 vines produced 27,404 leaguers (158,395 hl.) of wine in 1935, yielding an average of 960 litres or 1.67 leaguers per thousand vines. In Worcester, 25,813,600 vines produced 48,940 leaguers (282,873 hl.) or an average of 1,100 litres or 1.90 leaguers per thousand vines. However, Kohler's own estimates had suggested that yields might be considerably higher than that. Moreover, these figures did not fully reflect the reality that the vineyards in the irrigated districts had not yet reached their full bearing potential. The Worcester, Robertson and Montagu districts accounted for 102,190 leaguers (590,658 hl.) of wine out of a total of 226,982 leaguers (1,311,956 hl.) produced in 1934, or 45 per cent of total production. But this was likely to increase substantially in the coming years. In Robertson, production had spiralled upwards, from 8,533 leaguers (49,320 hl.) to 34,806 leaguers (221,987 hl.) in the 10 years between 1924 and 1934 (see Table 2.4). Finally, the introduction of irrigated settlement schemes along the Orange River – which had been motivated by the need to offer practical solutions to the urban drift of 'poor whites'[79] – posed an additional threat given that raisins,

[77] *Wine Commission*, p. 11. [78] *Wine Commission*, p. 49.

[79] The 'poor white problem' had been a serious political issue since the Union was formed. It grew more serious in the wake of the First World War, and more so again during the Great Depression. The scale of the problem was exposed by the Carnegie Commission which reported in 1932. The Pact Government embraced irrigation in the 1920s, and during the 1930s dam construction provided employment for those who had been rendered destitute. Wessel Visser, "Water as agent for social change, 1900–1939: two case studies of developmental state approaches in establishing irrigation schemes", *Historia* 63 (2) 2018. Permitting settlers to grow grapes was initially on the understanding that no wine would result.

Table 2.4. *Production in leaguers of wine by district, 1924–1935*

District	1924	1934	Increase	Per cent Increase
Caledon	1,445	2,497	1,052	72.8
Ceres and Tulbagh	3,853	6,284	2,431	63.1
Cape (incl. Constantia)	3,052	10,537	7,485	245.3
Malmesbury	6,548	10,653	4,105	62.7
Stellenbosch	17,059	27,355	10,926	64.1
Paarl	27,507	42,388	14,881	54.1
Worcester	20,088	48,312	28,224	140.5
Montagu	7,126	19,072	11,946	167.6
Robertson	8,533	34,806	26,273	307.9
Total wine	95,211	202,444	107,233	112.6
	(550,320 hl.)	(1,170,126 hl.)	(619,807 hl.)	
Total including raisins and dried grapes	115,558	226,982	111,424	96.4

Source: *Wine Commission* (1937), table II, p. 12.

sultanas and, to some extent, table grapes might enter the distilling pool. The summary of the overall problem by the Commission is worth recording in full:

> . . . [I]t is apparent that the period 1924 to 1935 witnessed the expansion of viticulture of an unprecedented scale throughout the Western Province, but more especially in the Districts of Worcester, Robertson and Montagu. During this period too, viticulture has become re-established on an extended scale in the Districts of Ladismith, Calitzdorp and Oudtshoorn, while the vine, more particularly for raisin and sultana production was also introduced to the Irrigation Settlements along the Orange River at Upington, and is making rapid progress in these areas . . . The continued rapid increase of production during the past ten years, as well as the heavy further plantings of vines during 1935 and 1936 in the case of some districts – notably where the vine is grown under irrigation – clearly seem to indicate that the saturation point in increased production has not necessarily already been reached.[80]

On the other side of the equation, the Commission confirmed that consumption of the products of the vine was more or less static. Although there had been a significant increase in purchase of good wine, much of this reflected stockpiling by the KWV in the expectation of breaking into the American market after the end of Prohibition. The Commission found that the demand for spirits used for making brandy, gin and liqueurs for local consumption and export was also more or less constant. While the KWV was stockpiling wine that might not actually find a market, the Commission also observed that its various means of

[80] *Wine Commission*, pp. 13–14.

disposing of distilling wine surpluses were probably loss-making in purely economic terms. Even then, the surplus remained had increased from around 7 per cent of total production in 1924 to around 30 per cent in 1935.[81] In a nutshell, the industry was teetering on the brink of a further crisis, placing the livelihood of some 3,000 grape/wine farmers at risk.

Whereas Kohler and Stals had sought to refute the charge that the KWV was at fault by artificially boosting the price for distilling wine, the Wine Commission identified injudicious pricing policies as the principal cause of overproduction. The decline of alternatives in the Karoo was certainly one factor in the equation. According to Rial Kloppers, a revision of rail rates following Union in 1910 had undermined the advantages for particular crops, while motorized transport had impacted negatively on the breeding of horses and mules.[82] However, the Commission concluded that the real impetus towards replanting came from 'the relative profitability of the profits of the vine'.[83] This then raised the question of why the KWV had persisted with a policy that was essentially self-defeating. The underlying reality was that all wine farmers had a right to join the association and to vote for its directors. As production increased, the district maps needed to be re-drawn to take account of the shifting demography. The net result was that the directors representing the expanding districts *anderkant die berg* were in a position to block proposals aimed at restricting production. As the venerable Mrs. A. W. Albrecht, representing the Constantia producers, informed the Commission:

> While we believe that the directors of the Ko-operatiewe Wijnbouwers Vereniging appreciate the seriousness of the present position they are powerless to alter it, due to being elected directly by popular vote. Did they antagonise that vote by paying muck prices for muck, or by other drastic restriction, they would lose their directorships. It is absurd to suppose that the makers of distilling wine who constitute the great bulk of the membership, will vote themselves out of existence or reduce the income from their product.[84]

The representatives of the Quality Wine Growers Society, including Manie Malan, concurred. Their own written submission quoted extensively from the Commission of Enquiry into Co-operation and Agricultural Credit that had criticized KWV's custody of the industry.

The Commission also heard complaints to the effect that the development of the export market was being unduly hampered by the business tactics of the

81 *Wine Commission*, table XV, p. 45.

82 CA A517 "Wine Commission: Evidence Given before the Commission", Volume I, Farmers and Farmers' Organisation, A-K, evidence of Gabriel Jacobus Kloppers, 27 September 1935.

83 *Wine Commission*, p. 50.

84 CA A517 "Wine Commission", Memorandum from Mrs A. W. Albrecht, Honorary Secretary Constantia Fruit Growers Association, 6 September 1935.

KWV. There had already been some litigation between the Central Co-operative Wine Exporters of Robertson and the KWV over access to cheap wine spirit needed for fortification.[85] Seizing the moment to exact some revenge, Rial Kloppers informed the Commission that the KWV was deliberately over-declaring the surplus in order to receive substantial quantities of wine at no cost, which it could then use to pursue its own trade monopoly in concert with Vine Products.[86] The Quality Wine Growers Society similarly claimed that the KWV had effectively driven the independent exporters out of the market for sweet wines. It also expressed concern at the efforts by the KWV to enter the export market for dry wines in competition with its members. Once again, it cited the Commission of Enquiry into Co-operation, which essentially accused the KWV of having abused its position. Finally, the memorandum from the Society maintained that the KWV had failed more generally to understand what was required to build the wine industry on the basis of quality, which was fundamental to the international reputation of Cape wines.

> In the course of the K.W.V.'s representations it has been suggested that quality be defined on spirit strength which we submit is contrary to the art of wine-making as this is a matter of technical and individual skill which cannot be expressed along mass production lines.[87]

Their position was broadly supported by the merchants who had no desire to see any widening of the regulatory powers of the KWV.

Having analysed the evidence before it, the Wine Commission came to some rather surprising conclusions. On the one hand, it vindicated many of the criticisms of the KWV. It accepted that in the absence of any controls, production and consumption would probably have come into alignment of their own accord. The fact that this had not happened was directly attributable to the effects of regulation that 'indicates an interference with the economic laws of supply and demand'. Moreover, it accepted that the fixed price for distilling wine had created a 'psychological effect' that led farmers in the irrigable districts to revert to the vine. Furthermore, the report hinted at a contradiction between the desire to improve the lot of the ordinary producer and the imperative to regulate the industry:

> While the control exercised by the K.W.V. under the Wine and Spirits Control Act of 1924 has up to the present therefore succeeded in returning a better price to the producer, it has failed to achieve the object of stabilising the industry – there exists in the country to-day an ever-widening margin between production and economic

[85] Joelson, *Memoirs*, p. 112. [86] Evidence of Gabriel Jacobus Kloppers, 27 September 1935.
[87] CA A517 "Wine Commission", 'Memorandum to Chairman and Members of the Wine Commission, 1935, by Quality Wine Growers' Society'.

consumption. Indeed . . . the very fact that it has succeeded in improving the price to the producer created an incentive for further production.

The report equally endorsed the logic of Mrs Albrecht's argument about the inability of the KWV to override the vested interests of its majority. It recognized that the elected directors were beholden to their members, a large number of whom would stand to lose out if the system was altered.

On the other hand, the Wine Commission proceeded to back away from the logic of its own analysis. Part of the context here was a global shift towards intervention in agricultural pricing in the wake of the Great Depression, which came to be reflected in South Africa's own Marketing Act of 1937.[88] Hence the Commission maintained that a policy of leaving everything to market forces was a hypothetical option, but that it would rebound on farmers in the older districts like Stellenbosch, whose financial margins were tighter. In addition, the Commission argued that the prices for good wine had been disappointing primarily because of the oversupply of distilling wine. This was the opposite of what Stals had previously posited, but the conclusion was essentially the same. The report reasoned that:

[s]ince it would be impossible to withdraw the existing control without causing the entire collapse of the industry, the Commission considers that the only way in which the position of the good wine producer can be stabilised in relation to that of the distilling wine producer is by the control of good wine.[89]

This vindicated the claim that Kohler had been making since 1924. On the question of overproduction, the Commission expressed its opposition to a ban of fresh plantings and quotas, on the basis that this would be discriminatory towards the emergent districts. It argued instead in favour of creating incentives for the production of better quality wine from shy-bearing varieties, the responsibility for which should rest with whatever statutory body was established.

That left the thorny question of what kind of body would be most appropriate to preside over regulation. The Commission maintained that if it had been asked to design a system from scratch it would have preferred a properly representative Board to manage the industry, but recognized that it was presented with a fait accompli. Since the KWV was already exercising partial control, enjoyed the support of the farmers and had accumulated useful experience, it was preferable to stick with it:

Subject to certain reservations . . . the Commission therefore recommends that the K.W.V. should retain the control of distilling wine, and that the control of good wine

[88] I am grateful to an anonymous reviewer for pointing out the influence of the Roosevelt administration's programmes. Nick Vink, "The long-term consequences of agricultural marketing legislation in South Africa", *South African Journal of Economics* 80 (4) 2012.

[89] *Wine Commission*, p.60.

should also be assigned to it, and the commission suggests that the Wine and Spirits Control Act, 1924 (Act No. 5 of 1924) be amended in order to place the control of good wine under the K.W.V.[90]

The reservations were marginal. Rather than giving the merchants direct representation, it recommended that the Appeal Board on pricing be chaired by a government representative. Secondly, it suggested that the performance of the KWV be reviewed after a seven-year period. Finally, to be on the safe side, it recommended that raisins and sultanas be controlled by a regulatory body separate from the KWV, and that their conversion into alcohol be explicitly prohibited. The only genuine concession to critics of the KWV was the suggestion that in trying to develop the export market for fortified sweet wines, with distinct brand identities, exporters should be given access to wine spirit at a reasonable price.[91] In a nutshell, the KWV had managed to persuade the commissioners that there was no alternative to its preferred solutions. And, as in 1924, it had been rewarded for failings that had been exposed in the starkest of terms. Although the Commission upheld the opinion that the real affliction was overproduction rather than under-consumption, it lent its support to the voices calling for a revision of the 1928 Liquor Act to retain the canteen and create a special category of 'light wine' licences for cafés and restaurants. It also supported the case for reduced freight rates to give some financial relief to the industry. Finally, the Commission gingerly expressed the view that if the ban on Black consumption was ineffective, there ought to be a review of the Liquor Act rather than allowing such an unsatisfactory situation to continue.

All in all, the KWV could feel encouraged, if not exactly vindicated. The next step was to ensure that government passed the necessary legislation with a minimum of delay. For this to happen, Kohler and his colleagues were aware of the importance of avoiding the impression that the farmers were divided. Hence the KWV made a concerted effort to reassure the 'quality producers' that they would benefit from fixed prices and that it was serious about the promotion of quality in the industry. In contrast, it was now the merchants who became the principal obstacle to reform. Having crossed swords with Kohler on the Lamont Committee, they renewed their opposition to any extension of KWV powers. In 1938, there were renewed complaints about the prices being offered for good wine by the merchants, and in November at a farmers' conference in Worcester disappointment was expressed at the failure of the government to proceed with legislation.[92] Eventually, the government mandated a committee to draft a Bill in 1939. In the process, it attempted to broker

[90] *Wine Commission*, p. 74.

[91] Contrary to the impression created by the KWV, the Commission noted that the expansion in exports had mostly been in bulk for use in blending.

[92] Van Zyl, *KWV*, p. 121.

an understanding between the KWV and the merchants that would smooth the way. However, the merchants refused to sign up to a deal – in part because of their concern about proposals for a £2 gap between the price for distilling wine and good wine, and a further £2 gap for something called 'quality' wine.

Towards the end of 1939, following a rift in the government over entering the war, Smuts returned to office as Prime Minister. In April 1940, a Wine and Spirits Control Amendment Bill was finally brought before Parliament and justified in terms of protecting the interests of good wine producers.[93] The real battle, however, played out in the Select Committee. The proposal that the KWV be empowered to set quotas for production was again opposed by farmers from Oudtshoorn who reminded the Committee that this was historically a wine-making area and insisted that quotas based on recent production patterns would work to their detriment.[94] Their preference was for curbing production by means of a sliding scale of prices paid according to output. But the most trenchant criticism came from the ranks of the merchants. In April 1940, A. T. Hudson, Dr. M. L. Ashton and H. S. Ashton stated the merchant's position on behalf of Sedgwick, Castle Wine and Brandy Co., E. K. Green, H. C. Collison and Van Ryn. Hudson maintained that whereas the earlier discussion had considered practical issues for improving standards in wine-making, none of this had been written into the Bill.[95] The merchants also argued that the KWV's stance was antagonistic and it could not therefore be trusted to manage the industry in an even-handed manner. For its part, the KWV repeated the mantra that, '[T]he goal of the merchant is to buy as cheaply as he can and to sell for the highest possible price' [my translation].[96]

The draft legislation envisaged that the KWV would set separate prices not just for distilling and good wine, but also for 'quality wine'. Whereas good wine was simply that which was consumed as such – including so-called canteen wine that was directed at the low end of the Coloured market – Kohler and his colleagues insisted that it was important to provide a price incentive to genuinely superior wine.[97] The spokesman for the merchants opposed this provision on the basis that

[93] Statement by the Minister of Agriculture and Forestry, Colonel Collins, in second reading of Wine and Spirits Control Amendment Bill, *Debatte van die Volksraad*, Deel 38, 4 Maart–12 April 1940 (Cape Town: Cape Times, Parliamentary Printers), p. 4495.

[94] Evidence of Jurgens and John Schoeman, Unie van Suid-Afrika, *Verslag van die Gekose Komitee oor die Kontrole oor Wyn en Spirtiualieë Wysigingsontwerp* [SC 7-'40] (Cape Town: Cape Times, 1940), pp. 1–10.

[95] Evidence of A. T. Hudson, 15 April 1940, *Verslag*, 11 April 1940, p. 13.

[96] Evidence of S. E. Warren of the KWV, *Verslag*, 14 April 1940, p. 32. As evidence, Kohler noted that when the KWV purchased large stocks of good wine, it paid substantially more than the merchants who bought at close to the distilling wine price. Evidence, 18 April 1940, *Verslag*, p. 46.

[97] In this text I refer to 'White', 'Coloured' and 'Black' - categories that are rooted in segregationist and apartheid discourse, but which are impossible to avoid using because they have meaning

the draft legislation provided no definition of 'quality wine'. Moreover, the Bill permitted the KWV to specify a minimum of quality wine that the merchants would be forced to buy at a declared minimum price, with the likely effect that farmers would be able to offload more basic wine at a premium. Kohler, for his part, alleged that the firms were increasingly buying grapes from the farmers rather than finished wine – becoming merchant–manufacturers in the process – and that this threatened a dangerous drift towards the Australian model. By requiring the companies to buy wine from the farmers, and by stipulating that some of this had to be quality wine, the KWV would be serving the general interest. In Kohler's words: 'In the event that no percentage of quality wine is specified the merchants will say that they do not need that sort of wine. If it is left up to them the wine farmers will not sell a drop of quality wine.'[98] The merchants, on the other hand, continued to insist that they worked closely with selected farmers to improve quality, and it was the KWV that had consistently rewarded volume over quality. Again, whereas the merchants regarded themselves as expanding the market for the products of the vine, Kohler accused them of monopolistic practices that had precisely the opposite effect. By targeting the business practices of the firms, the KWV turned the tables, arguing that the real barriers to the freedom of commerce were the liquor firms themselves.

In the final event, the merchants lost the argument, and the Bill passed its third reading without any significant amendments. Hence the law of 1940 brought good (and quality) wine within the purview of the KWV. This meant that the merchants were forced to comply with the prices laid down by the KWV, albeit subject to a right of appeal. They were also required to purchase a minimum percentage of 'quality' wine at a price determined by the KWV. At the same time, the Act empowered the KWV to set quotas on production, giving it the necessary leverage over sections of the farming community who were determined to continue planting vines willy-nilly. After nearly a decade of campaigning, the KWV had finally got what it had been angling for: namely, complete regulatory powers over the wine industry, albeit bound by a period of seven years in the first instance. What it had not succeeded in doing was rolling back the restrictive liquor laws. This was, however, to be focus of a renewed effort over the decade that followed, as we will see in the next chapter.

Conclusion

In this chapter, I have exposed the uneven record of the KWV in exercising its functions under the 1924 Wine and Spirits Control Act. On the one hand, the

for the actors themselves. See the 'Note on the Text' on page vi for more detail about the history and use of this term in South Africa.

[98] Evidence of Kohler, 17 April 1940, *Verslag van die Gekose Komitee*, p. 32.

KWV could claim some credit for improving standards in viticulture and oenology at a time when A. I. Perold and Frank Myburgh worked closely with individual farmers. This emboldened a minority in areas like Constantia and Stellenbosch to reorient their vineyards and techniques of production with a view to capturing a foothold in the export market. Manie Malan was one of those who embraced red cultivars and established a close working relationship with P. B. Burgoyne & Co. But ultimately this burst of innovation stalled in the face of the renewed spectre of overproduction. The looming crisis led to deepening rifts within the farming community as well as renewed disagreements between the KWV and the merchants. As the Wine Commission acknowledged, the KWV was effectively paralysed because the elected representatives of districts *anderkant die berg* were opposed to reforms that might serve to restrict production. When the breakthrough finally came in 1940, it was because the KWV was able to persuade the Smuts government (for a second time) that an extension of devolved regulatory powers was preferable to the uncertainty that would follow complete deregulation. This was a fateful decision that made it much less likely that the Cape wine industry would be built on the principle of quality first.

3 Orchestrating a White Wine Revolution

Merchants, Farmers, Co-operatives and Consumers, c. 1940–1962

In Chapter 2, I considered the efforts of the KWV to re-establish its credibility after assuming statutory control functions in 1924, as well as the manner in which the British wine importer, P. B. Burgoyne & Co., sparked renewed interest in the export market after a lengthy hiatus. This chapter pursues a parallel story. In the first section, I briefly consider the ways in which the KWV reinterpreted its mandate following the enlargement of its regulatory powers in 1940. I then shift the focus to the relationship between the merchant-manufacturing firms, the cooperatives, and the independent farmers. In particular, I investigate a wave of innovation that was more far-reaching than that of the 1920s and early 1930s. On this occasion, it was a conjuncture between innovations in the cellars and a shift in the drinking patterns of White consumers that produced the first real breakthrough on the domestic market.

The KWV and the Reimagination of Wine

Following the passage of the 1940 legislative amendment, the government continued to play a hands-off role. A rare publication designed to engage with the wine farmers, entitled *Wine-Making*, was published by the Ministry of Agriculture in 1947.[1] However, most of the useful information was disseminated through the pages of *Wine and Spirit* and specialist publications.[2] The KWV itself pursued a number of intersecting strategies designed to place the industry on a more secure footing, two of which are worthy of further elaboration. Firstly, and somewhat belatedly, the KWV endeavoured to persuade ordinary farmers of the need to reorient their production away from distillation and towards wines that might find favour amongst both domestic and foreign consumers. The sharpest instrument at its disposal was the pricing

[1] C. J. Theron and C. J. G. Niehaus, *Wine-Making*, Farmers' Bulletin, Series No. 130. Union of South Africa, Department of Agriculture [GPS 11337, 1947].

[2] See, for example, C. B. Henning, "A guide to the various wines and spirits produced in South Africa", *South African Wines, Spirits and Liqueurs: A Handbook on Their Composition, Preparation and Serving* (Stellenbosch: Wine, Spirit and Malt, 1958).

mechanism, which enabled it to create financial incentives for farmers wanting to focus more on quality. The greatest deficiency of the 1940 legislation was that it did not provide a means for the KWV to phase out the high-yielding cultivars or to prescribe production methods, whether limits on irrigation or rules about trellising, pruning, or harvesting. In that sense, the industry was deprived of some of the benefits of a system of appellations that was adopted in France and elsewhere. In 1943, J. F. Knott-Craig, Assistant General Manager of the KWV, vented his frustration at the mindset of many farmers:

> Act 23 of 1940 has had little effect in halting the mad and indiscriminate planting of vines, and the 1943 auction sales of vine cuttings and young vines have been distinguished by the record prices – as much as five times their normal value – paid by the growers anxious to secure vines. Apparently, the Scheme for the Limitation of the Production of Wine and its implications are not understood by growers, or else some of them live blissfully in the hope that the Scheme is not intended to apply to them, but only to their neighbours.[3]

While bemoaning this tendency, the KWV was also complicit. An unforeseen problem was that the growers in the riverain settlement schemes, having lost their external market during the war, demanded alternative outlets. The Deciduous Fruit Board was empowered to turn table grapes into wine for supply to the KWV, which threatened to greatly increase the volume of distilling wine. The KWV was subjected to intense political pressure to accommodate a de facto expansion of the winelands. Faced with the spectre of a further addition to the wine supply, the KWV began working on the details of the 'Scheme for the Limitation of the Production of Wine', more popularly known as the quota system. The idea was that maximum production figures were to be established for each farm 'based on the proved past maximum performance of the vines in respect of those in full bearing'. The system was made applicable to the table-grape producers. Although the KWV expected to roll out the quota from 1944, the association felt that it needed to carry out a systematic survey of national production before introducing a scheme that was bound to be highly controversial. I return to the quota system in Chapter 5.

Secondly, the KWV endeavoured to raise the consciousness amongst the White public about the desirability of drinking wine alongside the intake of food rather than regarding consumption as an exceptional event or as necessarily deleterious to health. The imperative of transforming consumption habits had already become a recurring theme in *Wine and Spirit* in the 1930s. However, this was pursued in a more sustained manner after 1940, when numerous public information booklets were disseminated. When KWV officials travelled to southern Europe, they never ceased to remark on the fact that

[3] Knott-Craig, "Quo vadis?", p. 5707.

while wine was drunk in significant quantities, there was little evidence of public drunkenness. The explanation was that wine was considered as an integral component of the daily intake of food. The KWV repeated the claim that European civilization itself had been built around the vine and maintained that this heritage was something that ought to be consciously re-appropriated by White South Africans. KWV publicity campaigns targeted women because they shopped and prepared the daily meal but were also thought to bear the responsibility for entertaining guests. The informational literature sought to demystify wine and suggest appropriate pairings between wine and food. One such pamphlet addressed the female host on how to prepare a cheese-and-wine party:

> Dear Hostess, have you considered giving a wine and cheese party? They are becoming increasingly popular nowadays, but they will always have the charm of novelty about them. Ours is the ideal country for this sort of party: a wonderful variety of Cape wines and South African cheeses to offer for the enjoyment of your guests. How much wine should you order? Estimate about 12 bottles of wine for 18 persons. This allows almost 4 good-sized wine glasses for each person. For a party which includes women, provide two bottles of white or rosé for each bottle of red. Women generally prefer the lighter, sweeter whites and the rosés to the more robust reds.[4]

That men and women had very different taste preferences was an unquestioned assumption. Whereas the KWV had tended to shy away from an open confrontation with temperance interests, *Wine and Spirit* also launched a counterattack in the 1940s. The KWV therefore faced both ways at once – at one moment coaxing and cajoling the farmers over their errant ways, and at another demanding a better deal for the farmers and chastising the temperance movement for its unwarranted attacks on a European cultural patrimony.

Whites on Whites: Shifting Consumption Patterns

Although the passage of the 1940 Amendment to the Wine and Spirits Control Act was dictated by a sense of wartime urgency, it is ironic that a period of relative prosperity ensued that was scarcely connected to the legislation. This reflected favourable developments both within the export and domestic markets. An immediate consequence of the war was that the British demand for wine and table grapes was threatened. However, European wine production and supply lines were also adversely affected by the conflict. This helped open up alternative markets for Cape brandy, and to a lesser extent for wines. In the post-war years British demand recovered quickly, while the Scandinavian countries, Canada, British West Africa and even Germany assumed a greater

[4] KWV, *Planning a Wine and Cheese Party* (Paarl: KWV, 1967), pp. 1–2.

Table 3.1. *Consumption of spirits in South Africa, 1938–1965 (proof gallons)*

Year	Brandy	Total Spirit
1938	1,101,819	1,240,690
1948	2,515,280	2,568,635
1949	2,640,321	2,700,989
1950	3,017,570	3,090,976
1951	3,214,325	3,377,659
1952	3,399,592	3,595,325
1953	3,621,994	3,734,412
1954	3,842,349	3,936,233
1955	3,946,619	4,084,576
1956	4,082,331	4,406,077
1957	4,082,277	5,013,411
1958	3,243,866	4,839,969
1959	2,914,531	4,121,484
1960	3,065,536	4,298,255
1961	3,259,585	4,331,273
1962	3,291,024	4,143,339
1963	3,760,599	4,874,351
1964	4,224,834	4,901,723
1965	–	4,780,623

Source: KWV, *A Survey of Wine Growing in South Africa 1965–66* (Paarl: Public Relations Department), p. 54.

significance. On the domestic market, brandy consumption more than doubled in the 10 years before 1948 and continued on an upwards trajectory for the next 10 (Table 3.1). An unexpectedly large hike in the excise duty on wine spirit to the tune of over 90 per cent in 1958 had a long-term depressive effect on the domestic market for brandy.[5] Moreover, whereas the consumption of fortified wine flattened out after 1946 and the demand for sparkling wine remained relatively constant, the demand for unfortified wine increased year on year, with the result that consumption had nearly trebled 10 years later. In 1953, its sales passed those of fortified wine by volume for the first time and the gap continued to widen in the years thereafter (Table 3.2). This represented the first tangible evidence of a shift in drinking habits amongst White consumers. In the 1950s, the country was undergoing an economic boom, while the newly installed National Party (NP) government more or less guaranteed full employment for Afrikaners. As the 'poor white' spectre receded, a more confident Afrikaner middle class, ensconced in new housing

[5] Van Zyl, *KWV*, p. 143.

Table 3.2. *Wine consumption in South Africa, 1945–1959 (bulk gallons)*

Year	Fortified	Unfortified/Drinking	Sparkling	Total
1945	8,724,644	3,583,047	120,608	12,428,299
1946	10,374,313	3,826,106	136,607	14,337,026
1947	7,839,472	4,810,796	94,590	12,744,858
1948	7,505,408	4,959,060	105,323	12,569,791
1951	7,157,358	6,308,797	160,614	13,626,769
1952	7,193,613	7,160,142	190,389	14,544,144
1953	7,014,853	7,948,167	176,980	15,139,730
1954	7,079,072	8,707,494	194,845	15,981,411
1955	6,925,928	9,316,644	195,505	16,438,077
1956	7,107,306	9,676,870	195,053	16,979,229
1957	7,214,086	10,015,440	216,612	17,446,138
1958	8,035,466	11,131,530	230,774	19,397,770
1959	9,138,763	12,513,243	234,070	21,886,076
1960	9,586,805	13,930,788	251,312	23,768,905
1961	9,855,288	14,768,781	240,922	24,963,991
1962	9,313,157	14,815,579	243,701	24,372,437
1963	10,804,272	17,904,599	261,704	28,970,575
1964	11,363,204	22,525,156	282,446	34,170,806
1965	10,441,139	22,293,178	293,761	33,028,078

Source: KWV, *A Survey of Wine Growing in South Africa 1965–66*, p. 54.

estates and passing time in gleaming new shopping centres, announced its arrival. Whereas middle-class White people embraced wine and the good life that it stood for, the temperance movement seemed out of kilter with the times. The KWV and the merchant-manufacturers were quick to identify this shift and capitalize upon it.

These developments were associated with more favourable prices for wine producers. In the case of distilling wine, there was a steep increase in the price from £4.2s.5¾d per leaguer in 1941 to £11.10s.2¼d in 1951. The prices then stabilized at around £10 per leaguer in the mid-1950s before rising again to £12.9s.9d in 1959. The significance of these prices, of course, lies in the comparison with corresponding prices for good and quality wine. Prices for good wine climbed steadily from £6 in 1941 to £12 in 1952, inched upwards through the 1950s and reached £16.3s.6d in 1959. In the mid-1950s, the difference between the price for good wine and for distilling was typically less than £2 per leaguer, although the gap widened at the end of the decade. The producers of 'quality' wine generally received an additional £2 per leaguer through the decade. However, it is a moot point whether the pricing structure shifted the weight sufficiently against distilling wine to produce the intended shift in production habits. In it its annual *Survey* for 1959–1960, the KWV distinguished between the Coastal Belt (Constantia, Stellenbosch, Paarl,

Tulbagh, Ceres and Malmesbury) and the Little Karoo (Worcester, Robertson, Montagu, Oudtshoorn). In the first case, the average yields were 3–6 tons of grapes per acre, while in the second they averaged 6–10 tons per acre. If we assume that a distilling wine farmer received 10 tons, a good wine farmer 6 and a quality producer 3 tons per acre, it is clear that the financial incentives remained skewed in favour of mass production. Be that as it may, the KWV felt that it did not have any immediate need to depart from a policy of gradualism. Overall production remained stable between 1945 and 1953, but in the second half of the decade there was a significant spike that continued through to the early 1960s. Nevertheless, the surplus declarations between 1947 and 1954 dropped to 25 per cent, and the market situation remained healthy in the early 1960s. Indeed, there was even a brandy shortage that necessitated a rationing of supplies to the merchants. The relative optimism that prevailed in the early 1950s provided the backdrop against which the first significant breakthroughs in quality occurred in relation to white wine. I turn now to changes in the sphere of distribution and their relationship to innovations in the cellar.

The Logic of Vertical Integration

As has already been indicated, the 1928 Liquor Act had very significant consequences for the way the products of the vine were distributed. It is true that a pronounced tendency towards oligopoly, arising out of a combination of acute competition and price volatility, had already set the tone well before the 1920s. This was linked to strategies of vertical integration in which the same companies that dominated the supply of wine to the market sought to control the points of sale. The struggle became intense once the Act pegged the number of liquor outlets to population size. This meant that it was imperative for the liquor firms to control as many outlets as possible, either by outright acquisition or through the operation of 'ties' that effectively required a hotel or bar owners to exclude the stock of rival companies. The 1937 Wine Commission distinguished between 'manufacturing' wholesale merchants and 'purely distributing' wholesale merchants. At that time, there were formally 16 manufacturing wholesalers involved in the liquor trade, of whom 6 produced wine alone.[6] However, the market was effectively controlled by two dominant players. The so-called Combine, which was established in 1934 and brought together the Castle Wine and Brandy Co and E. K. Green, commanded a market share of 57.5 per cent. Jooste and Bryant, and Sedgwick, which had amalgamated but maintained their distinct brand identities, controlled another 22.5 per cent. Finally,

[6] Board of Trade figures cited in *Wine Commission* (1937), p. 25.

Santhagens and the remainder of the smaller firms accounted for 20 per cent of the market. On the side of the 'distributing' wholesale merchants, the Wine Commission observed that only 31 of the 68 firms were entirely independent firms, with another 30 being essentially linked in to the bigger merchant-manufacturers. In terms of the retail outlets, many of the bottle stores were owned by the firms directly or were tied. For those that were not, there was furious competition to curry favour with the retailers.

The firms would typically purchase the wine from the farmers, mature and blend it, and then transport it in bulk to depots in the interior. Whereas wine and brandy had historically been transported in large vats, either by road or by train, the firms began to acquire tankers in the late 1940s that could convey the product in larger volumes and considerably quicker. The wines would then be bottled and labelled at the depots or by the retailers themselves. Alfred Baumgartner of Distillers recalled that the wine was 'tapped by a rubber pipe from the delivery cask into the bottle which was closed with a tapered cork which in turn was banged into the bottle neck with a piece of wood'.[7] The bottles were of various shapes and sizes, having previously served another purpose. One of the long-standing employees of Sedgwick recounted something very similar:

> They had very few things such as tankers in those days and they would come in huge vats ... Hogsheads were the largest, about 70-odd gallons and there was a variety of casks used in those days, ranging from kegs (4 gallon), anker (7 gallons), half aum (about 15 gallons). And then you had the quarter cask (30 gallons) [and] hogshead (70 gallons). [They were transported by] rail and lorries and they would pump them from there into the big maturing vats. And also we used to sell in casks because stacks and stacks of bottle stores and hotels used to bottle their own products and actually at that stage we had an agreement with the various hotels and bottle stores and their name actually appeared on the label. We had 'Sedgwick's Muscadel Wine' bottled by '....' and people used to buy this stuff in bulk, and do their own bottling. But people became more concerned about the hygiene because it was very conducive to fiddling ... I think that only stopped in 1959 – it was quite late. It was a big trade, bulk supply.[8]

Round about 1947, E. K. Green acquired road tankers, the stainless steel containers of which held as many as 2,100 gallons (9,555 litres/95.6 hl.) or the equivalent of 32 hogsheads. Apart from the greater speed associated with the tanker, the spoilage was also considerably reduced.[9]

A strategic role was attached to the 'travellers', whose job was to cement a friendly working relationship with the independent retailers. The staff magazine of the Combine firms, called the *Wine Press*, underlined the importance of

[7] A. Baumgartner, *The First 35 Years of Distillers Corporation (SA) Limited within the Oude Meester Group* (Stellenbosch: Distillers Corporation, undated), p. 16.
[8] Distell Archive, "Interview with Wally Sterry, Glencairn, 14 July 1982".
[9] L. Gorfinkel and G. Skelton, "Wheels of wine", *The Wine Press*, IV (7) 1948, p. 26.

establishing a rapport with those who really mattered, notably the bottle-store owners and hoteliers. One cartoon depicted a customer asking for 'Commando Brandy', being asked to try 'El Blotto' instead and walking away with a case of the latter with a satisfied smile on his face. The accompanying text read: 'However well you know your Licencees [sic] and Proprietors, never underestimate the selling power of the retail assistant or barman.'[10] The magazine also underlined the importance of vigorous advertising 'to keep the names of our products before the public, to maintain our century old prestige, and to convince existing and potential customers that our brands are quality brands worth consuming.'[11] The investment in advertising was considered essential to conjure demand, and was valued highly by the retail outlets whose premises were brightened up at no cost to themselves. Indeed, one leader in the *Wine Press* claimed that the goodwill created in the mind of the general public led the owner of one formerly tied house to request a fresh tie for his new premises, without financial support, such was the impact of company advertising on his overall business.[12] Finally, the Combine convened a regular series of meetings for the bottle-store managers of the outlets they owned, in which considerable discussion went into the importance of attractive window displays in which the prices were readily apparent for specific products.

The standard criticism of the wine merchants before 1940 was that their pricing strategies deterred consumers from embracing the pleasures of unfortified wine. Consequently, it was claimed, South Africans paid far more than their counterparts in somewhere like Britain, despite the fact that they were living in a wine-producing country. However, it was clear that the firms were adapting to the distortions created by the 1928 Liquor Act. Because White people consumed relatively little wine and Black consumers were off-limits, the profits of the firms depended heavily on plumbing the lower depths of the market. Here, there was no incentive to be innovative or to pursue quality for its own sake. Hence much 'good wine' – so called only because it was not distilled – was actually distinctly ordinary. Much of it was simply labelled as 'Boerewyn' (literally farmers' wine), with no indication as to what a given bottle contained. This wine was targeted primarily at Coloured consumers and was sometimes administered as part of the dop.[13] As Baumgartner proudly recalled:

> The 'big business' in respect of volume sales on the lower market was the trade with 'Boer-wine' as well as lower priced semi-sweet fortified wines. Boer-wine was a dry white vin ordinaire, of no specific character but of good quality. The Coloured

[10] Depicted in *The Wine Press*, IV (7) 1948, p. 16.

[11] [Anon], "What is advertising", *The Wine Press*, IV (7) 1948, p. 15.

[12] [Anon.], "Goodwill and the group", *The Wine Press*, date unknown, p. 6.

[13] In this text I refer to 'White', 'Coloured' and 'Black' - categories that are rooted in segregationist and apartheid discourse, but which are impossible to avoid using because they have meaning for the actors themselves. See the 'Note on the Text' on page vi for more detail about the history and use of this term in South Africa.

community were the main consumers with 175 litres per capita per annum, an undisputed world record, displacing the French with 124 litres to second place.[14]

On the higher end of the market, the merchants resorted to names that they felt would have some resonance amongst those consumers who had a passing acquaintance with French and German wines, and who might thereby be persuaded to pay more. Hence recourse was had to terms such as 'Burgundy', 'claret' and 'champagne'. This misleading nomenclature was also reflected in prizes awarded at the Cape Wine Show, which created categories that made little intrinsic sense. The fact that a Burgundy and a claret could both be made from Cabernet Sauvignon grapes – and the compounding distinction between the former as 'heavy' and the latter as 'light' – meant that even if there had been an inclination by White consumers to embrace wine for its own sake, it must surely have been a rather confusing experience.

The development of specific brands was a process that took some time to work itself out, and it had everything to do with the standardization of quality and packaging, and the cultivation of distinct images associated with the products. The pioneer was the Drostdy Co-operative whose *Witzenberg* brand, with which Frank W. Myburgh was originally associated, had won local recognition and carved out a limited export market around the time of the First World War.[15] This was closely followed by a wine from the Sedgwick stable called *White Leipzig*, which was made from Palomino grapes grown by the Rabie family on the Leipzig farm at Nuy.[16] Sedgwick enjoyed some success with this brand and its labels proudly paraded the prizes it had chalked up at the Cape Agricultural Show and the Brewers' Exhibition competition in London – against Australian rivals. In the early 1920s, Sedgwick added *Karavan White* and *Karavan Red*, which prospered for some time before being taken off the market to make way for alternative brands.

But the real impetus to take branding seriously came with French pressure in the early 1930s in defence of its own appellations. The demand that Empire wines respect protected names came at precisely the moment when Cape products were beginning to make some headway. British wine merchants sought to stiffen the resolve of the British government to rebuff French demands, with Cuthbert Burgoyne insisting that the names in question had been used in the empire trade for a very long time. For whatever reason, the South African government decided to cut a deal with the French government in 1935, whereas other wine-producing countries continued to hold out. Under

[14] Baumgartner, *First*, p. 19.

[15] In July 1964, Distillers took over the Drostdy Co-operative Winery Ltd.

[16] Romi van der Merwe, *A Magic Blend: SFW 1925–2000, Its People, Products and Places* (Stellenbosch: SFW, 2000), p. 102. The *White Leipzig* and *Karavan* labels were registered in 1925. These labels may be found in a Black Guardbook at the Distell Archive.

the so-called Crayfish Agreement, South Africa received favourable tariffs for the export of fruit and crayfish in return for respecting designated French names of origin.[17] The KWV fought unsuccessfully against this agreement, maintaining that names such as Burgundy were well-established in the trade. At the end of 1942, following a speech to the KWV, Kohler entered a somewhat fractious newspaper debate with George Simon, Managing Director, Courvoisier in London, over the use of French names. Kohler noted that South Africa had been producing champagne for the past 40 years and went on to state that:

> The winegrowers of Champagne were pretty cute in naming wine made in that district 'Champagne', the name of the district, although it is merely a class of wine which can be made in any country which grows suitable grapes, and then getting the Government to exclude and prevent all the rest of France from making and selling champagne. Now that is all very well for France. She can do what she likes in her own country and for her own people. She is now not satisfied with that proud position. She now wants to impose those same restrictions upon winegrowers of other countries by means of treaties with their Governments. I don't suppose she got off as cheaply in other countries as she did in South Africa, which bartered a birthright of its winegrowers for a few tons of crayfish ...[18]

Kohler suggested that the qualifying words 'South African' be added to ensure that there could be no confusion in the mind of the consumer about the provenance of the product. He went on to warn, rather implausibly, that if the government would not abrogate the agreement, there was nothing to stop South Africans renaming one of their districts 'Champagne'. Simon countered by insisting that champagne referred to a product with a very specific regional origin and that South Africa had all along merely been producing a form of sparkling wine.[19] Another contributor to the debate ('Disinterested'), who was, in all likelihood, Phillip Myburgh, the son of Frank Myburgh, was more forthright:

> The very name 'South African Champagne' is a joke. Being interested in the matter I once asked the maker of one of our local 'Champagnes' how long the process took, from the time the wine arrived in his cellars until the finished article was ready for the market, and his reply was 'About ten months at present, but we hope as time goes by to reduce it still further'.[20]

[17] Anne Stern, "The protection of geographical indications in South Africa", in *Symposium on the International Protection of Geographical Indications: Cape Province 1999* (Geneva: World Intellectual Property Organization, 1999), pp. 31–32.

[18] The initial salvoes were reproduced in *Wine and Spirit*, alongside an editorial supporting Kohler's position. *Wine and Spirit* February 1943, pp. 5587–5591.

[19] Distell Archive, "South African Champagne, from M, George Simon", undated from "Files of Phillip Myburgh".

[20] Distell Archive, "Champagne" from 'Disinterested', undated from "Files of Phillip Myburgh".

What he failed to underscore was that whereas champagne was produced through a secondary fermentation that occurred in the bottle, most South African sparkling wines derived from the addition of carbon dioxide.[21]

In 1935, anticipating a change to the law, Sedgwick announced a competition for the renaming of its wines and brandies.[22] However, the change to government legislation was considerably delayed and it was only in February 1950, when new rules were imminent, that Sedgwick finally approached the advertising company, J. Walter Thompson, for advice on renaming their *Sparkling Burgundy* and *Le Roi Champagne*.[23] Sedgwick seems to have paid greater attention to the use of varietal names at this time, although what went into the bottle was probably more of a blend. A common strategy was for the firms to conjure up names that hinted at an association with France or Germany, but without falling foul of the regulations. *Witlingsheim* and *Tafelheim*, which were launched by Sedgwick in 1958 and 1961, respectively, hinted at a German style,[24] but were none too specific. J. Walter Thompson's advice was to find a creative way around the law, for example by retaining coded allusions to Burgundy:

> I think it is almost essential to retain the word 'Sparkling' and you may be permitted to coin a word which is similar to 'Burgandy' [sic]. I am thinking of 'Sparkling Burgoine' or 'Sparkling 'Burgundia'. Another idea is to try and imply the fact that this wine is red by selecting a name such as 'Sparkling Rougeot' or 'Sparkling Rougeais'. I also quite like 'Sparkling Romanie' or 'Sparkling Red Romanie'.

The advertising firm also suggested possibly replacing 'champagne' with a name such as 'Beaujolie' or 'Grand Fleur' or, more simply, 'Sedgwick's Extrasec'. It was doubtful, however, whether any of this really helped build a strong identity for the wines in question. The controversy over the right to use the term 'champagne' was one that did not go away quickly, but by the early 1950s the search was on for new brand identities that were more locally grounded.

Over the 1950s and 1960s, there was a further push towards concentration within the industry as the merchant-manufacturers sought to forge fully integrated liquor interests. Whereas the Rembrandt Group had made its money in tobacco, it went on to create a substantial liquor concern when Oude Meester

21 In 1947, Distillers had imported a champagne fermentation plant from France and came up with four different champagne-type wines under the label of *La Residence*. These were produced without the introduction of carbon dioxide. Baumgartner, *First*, pp. 36–37.

22 Distell Archive, "Names and Label Designs", advertisement entitled "Wanted a Name", advertisement, August 1935.

23 Roland T. Wentzel, J. Walter Thompson and Co to D. King, J. Sedgwick and Co., 23 February 1950, Distell Archive, "Names and Label Designs". *Le Roi* was registered as a brand name in 1935.

24 The labels may be found in a Black Guardbook at the Distell Archive.

was formally launched by Anton Rupert in 1965. The biggest part of its liquor operation was accounted for by Distillers Corporation, which was established in 1945 and proceeded to absorb the struggling Combine firms of the SA Distilleries and Wine Group in 1969.[25] In 1964, Distillers also acquired the Drostdy Co-operative Winery in Tulbagh at a time when wine was in short supply and subject to purchasing quotas.[26] Subsequently, the holding company acquired Consolidated Western Wines Ltd, P. J. Joubert Ltd, Roadside Hotels Ltd as well as wholesale interests and interests in dozens of small-scale liquor outlets across the country. The main rival to Oude Meester/Distillers was SFW which was re-registered as a company in 1935 and began to build a distinctive portfolio of its own.[27] In 1966, SFW acquired Monis Wineries, followed by Sedgwick Tayler in 1970, with the Stellenbosch Wine Trust established as the holding company.[28] At this point, the latter claimed to account for 70 per cent of all unfortified wine that was sold in South Africa. The rethinking of brands was apparent in the clear strategies adopted by the SFW, which began to pay closer attention to distinct segments of the consumer market. In 1936, W. C. Winshaw, the founder of the company, had launched a Chablis-style wine called *La Gratitude*, made from Chenin Blanc grapes, in an attempt to capitalize on an expanding market for unfortified wines. This was followed by *Angelica*, which had to be labelled *vin ordinaire* in order to satisfy export-labelling requirements.[29] Also, in 1936, the SFW had introduced *Tassenberg*, which was intended to create an identifiable brand for the much smaller red wine market. The latter was produced from Cinsault grapes and quickly cemented its position in the market for red wine. It acquired a longstanding reputation for being a cheap but dependable product and is still going strong to this day.[30] In the 1940s and 1950s, the SFW attempted not merely to develop brands at the middle and top ends of the market, but to solidify its base amongst Coloured consumers whose loyalty was crucial to the overall profitability of the firm. This was reflected in the launch of a dry white, but brown-coloured, wine called *Oom Tas* in 1952 which, in its flagon format, went on to become a firm favourite amongst the Coloured population in the Western Cape.[31] These innovations in marketing and advertising signalled a

[25] [Anon.], "Rembrandt expands into liquor", *Wine, Spirit and Malt*, November 1969, p. 5.

[26] The takeover entitled Distillers to a larger quota of wine. Distell Archives, "Distillers Corporation Expands" (Circular letter, 8 July 1964).

[27] The previous company had involved a partnership with the Krige family. They were bought out in 1935 and the company was re-launched.

[28] [Anon.], "S.F.W. – Sedgwick Tayler state policy", *Wine Spirit and Malt*, September 1970, p. 7.

[29] Van der Merwe, *Magic*, pp. 16, 48.

[30] Circular letter by Sales Manager, SFW (2 May 1955), Distell Archives, "Sales Letters, 1951–1962".

[31] Van der Merwe, *Magic*, p. 70.

step shift in the sphere of distribution and were the precursor to a greater transformation that occurred at the level of production, to which I now turn.

Cool Fermentation and Cellar Innovations

Whereas the main advances in the interwar years had taken place in the vineyards, driven by the likes of Manie Malan of Alto, the focus of innovation after 1940 shifted to the cellars. Some advances were made in the handling of the grapes in a manner that helped to extract the juice more efficiently, facilitate skin contact and reduce the influence of extraneous matter. One significant local innovation was the development of continuous presses that could handle a much greater volume of grapes. The McKenzie pneumatic press was developed in South Africa and was being rolled out by 1960, although the family business subsequently moved to Australia and continued to market its products from there.[32] But it was, above all, the 'cool fermentation' revolution that is credited with facilitating a breakthrough in quality for white wines. In many renditions of this history, N. C. Krone from Twee Jonge Gezellen in Tulbagh is cited as the first to really grasp the underpinning science. Having graduated from the University of Stellenbosch, Krone worked for a number of farmers and became acutely aware of the problem caused by excessive heat during the fermentation process. In 1955, his own research demonstrated that wines made from grape juice fermented at 10°C retained up to 75 per cent more of the esters, and in this way the delicate aromas and flavours were preserved.[33] For farmers seeking to replicate Rhine winemaking styles, this was a crucial insight. When the attempt to pipe river water as a cooling agent failed to produce the desired effects, Krone installed a cooler in the cellar which kept the entire space at the desired temperature. At the 1959 Cape Wine Show, Krone swept the board, winning no fewer than eight trophies including the Burgoyne trophy for the highest number of points awarded for a dry white wine, and the Frank Myburgh trophy for the best sample of a hock-type dry white wine.

The 'discovery' of cool fermentation is, of course, a misnomer. The dangers caused by excessive heat had long been understood and mechanisms to cool the fermenting must by means of the circulation of cold water had been in existence since the late nineteenth century. In the 1950s, much of the emphasis was placed on the encouragement of natural yeasts. What was not taken full

[32] Interview with Dave Hughes, 31 March 2009. Simon Jonathan Nordestgaard, "Phenolic extraction and juice expression during white wine production", unpublished PhD thesis, University of Adelaide, 2011, pp. 88–89.

[33] Bennie Howard, *Vader en Seun, Wingerd en Wyn: 'n Studie oor Vyf Families in die Wynbedryf*, Cape Masters of Wine project, June 1983, p. 2.

account of is that fermentation at 70–80°F (21–27°C) might help the yeast to go about its work, but it also tended to destroy the esters that imparted the aroma to the wine. This was not a problem in Germany, where the cellars were naturally cool, but in South Africa the farmers struggled to keep the temperature down. While farmers endeavoured to keep cellars cool by the free circulation of cool air and fermenting in open tanks, very few had installed cooling pipes. Although *Wynboer* magazine credited Krone with the breakthrough, there were other contenders for the mantle.[34] For example, Johann Georg Graue, the German owner of Nederburg, had experimented with cool fermentation in the early 1950s and was, arguably, a forerunner to Krone. Certainly, the wines of Nederburg began to win more accolades at around this time. The official KWV history gives Graue the credit for having recognized the general principles, but notes that it was Krone who installed dedicated cooling tanks and other equipment.[35] Baumgartner claims that Distillers scored a 'first' following the introduction of temperature-controlled fermentation according to the 'Geiss' method, combined with the cultivation of pure yeast culture, that permitted a transformation in quality around 1951.[36]

The debate about who was first misses a more fundamental point, which is that it was the merchants who were driving innovation. They detected an expanding market for drinking wine and were eager to secure a product of sufficiently reliable quality to sustain brands. Hence, when Santhagens took out an advertisement in *Die Wynboer* congratulating Krone on his singular achievement at the Cape Wine Show, they quietly slipped in the message that they had played their part by placing their expertise at his disposal.[37] From the moment of its entry into the wine industry, Distillers established a close working relationship with a handful of farmers that could be trusted to supply wine of an even quality, in which temperature control was fundamental. This included Alto in Stellenbosch, which was eventually acquired by the company. It also included working with A. W. Jordaan of Theuniskraal and De Wet Theron of Montpellier, both of whom were in Tulbagh and hence were neighbours of N. C. Krone. All of these remained loyal to Distillers over the decades, which led to the company marketing wines under labels that also bore their names. This was the first systematic attempt to build brands around specific production sites – or what would eventually become known as 'estates'. In addition, Distillers introduced the innovation of subsidized study tours to Europe for people within the liquor industry. The first of these took

[34] [Anon.], "Droë wyn en verkoeling", *Wynboer*, January 1960, p. 3. Another claimant to the mantle was the owner of what is now called Oak Valley in Elgin.

[35] Van Zyl, *KWV*, p. 60. Interview with Duimpie Bayly, 17 February 2011.

[36] Baumgartner, *First*, p. 51.

[37] [Anon.], "Gelukwense aan N.C. Krone", *Wynboer*, September 1959, p. 4.

place in 1962 and involved 85 tourists, most of whom were company employees, hoteliers and bottle-store owners.[38] These tours provided a further stimulus to emulation and experimentation while helping build goodwill with the trade.

The proactivity of the merchants can be traced in considerable detail through the *Boereboeke* (or Farmers' Books) of the SFW. The latter bought from a larger segment of the farming community than Distillers did and, probably as a consequence, it felt the need to be stricter in the demands that it made. These ledgers describe every tank and whether the wine was fit only for distillation or was of sufficient quality for the SFW to have an interest in purchasing it. At the end of every year, W. J. (Bill) Winshaw made an assessment of the standard of winemaking as well as recommendations for future improvement. These records indicate that the SFW took a firm line with the farmers, often chastising them and demanding that they adhere to the advice that was proffered. Close attention was paid to whether the grapes were ripe enough when harvested and whether rotten berries were present. The greatest threat was posed by harmful bacteria, which was reflected in high levels of volatile acidity in the cellar. The farmers were browbeaten into using enough SO^2 to reduce the threat and warned to be careful about the re-use of the large wooden vats – *stukvats* or *foudres* – that could incubate bacteria. But the SFW went much further. It advised the farmers on which varieties to plant according to soil type. This close attention to detail can be seen in the case of the Zonnebloem farm in Simondium (Drakenstein), which the SFW always believed had great potential. Its owner, Willem Furter, had been a member of the Quality Wine Growers' Society and had supplied P. B. Burgoyne & Co. with wine for export until 1930, at which point he switched to supplying the KWV.[39] Zonnebloem had become a regular prize-winner at the Cape Wine Show in the years that followed. On Furter's death in 1940, his 21-year-old daughter, Marie, assumed the mantle of winemaker, initially with the assistance of Frank Myburgh, and continued selling to the SFW and winning prizes at the Wine Show. After her marriage to Maurice Crouse in 1942, the farm was sold to John De Villiers who further cemented Zonnebloem's reputation. In 1945, the farm produced what was discovered much later to have been a stand-out Cabernet Sauvignon from low-yielding bush vines.[40] After the accidental death of De Villiers in

[38] "Big study tour starts today: 84 to go on Distillers Corpn trip", *Rand Daily Mail*, 9 March 1962; and circular entitled "1964 Toer Na die Buiteland", 15 January 1964, Distell Archive.

[39] Chris Venter, *The Story of Zonnebloem Wines*, unpublished manuscript, 2010, Distell Archive, pp. 4–5.

[40] This was discovered much later because SFW had cellared some of the wine which was opened decades later. Michael Fridjhon, *The Penguin Book of South African Wine* (London: Penguin, 1992), p. 38.

1948, Marie and Maurice Crouse returned to rent the farm and began making wine once again – before buying the farm outright in 1956.

However, by this point the SFW began to have its doubts about the willingness of Maurice Crouse to adhere to the highest standards. In 1954, Bill Winshaw indicated that although the white wines had potential, the farmer was not making the most of his grapes and was therefore producing rather disappointing wine:

> Most of CB [Clairette Blanche] is good but grapes were picked too early & FA [Fixed Acidity] too low. The French, Steen and Green grapes are not qual[ity] wines and should be removed from [SFW] contracts as such. With ref[erence] to Cab[ernet] their wines are not made to specification & is becoming a vin ordinaire wine. Should Mr Crouse not be able to follow instructions he should contact the winery & not remain negative to a procedure which will make or break his wine. The present method will prod[uce] a reasonably good wine which will not cont[inue] to improve in vats or bottle.

The following year, Winshaw repeated that there was a need for greater care in harvesting, especially 'separating of musty or earth-tainted bunches of grapes in the vineyard'. He also recommended the planting of more Cabernet Sauvignon on the farm. In 1956, Winshaw suggested that the white grapes should be taken in by SFW which would makes these wines itself, while leaving the farm to produce better quality Cabernet. In 1960, Winshaw recommended a full enquiry into the reasons why the white wines were so lacking in quality:

> The quality of the Riesling wines is extremely poor & we must assume that the fault lies in the condition and state of the grapes. We suggest a thorough analysis of soil, fertilizing, & method irrigation and a method of pruning the vine. The same applies to the Cl[airette Bl[anche] the quality which normally carries this farm.

Winshaw came around to the view that the key to putting things right lay with temperature control. Hence, he recommended simply buying the best Riesling and Clairette Blanche grapes and taking in much of the rest once the must had settled in order 'to submit the Zonnebloem wines to the correct temperature control and culture innoculation'. He went on to state that 'other wine making cellars are now introducing refrigeration & this may be the answer'. By 1962, Winshaw had come to a more resolute opinion: 'It is now absolutely certain that this method of producing wine (A) without refrigeration (B) in stuk vats is producing a wine not comparable with the delicate fruity wines being marketed e.g. Tasheimer.' As in the case of Distillers, the preference of SFW was increasingly for taking some of the grapes directly from the farmers and making the wine directly. Consider, for example, the following response to problems at Schoongezicht/Rustenburg:

> Possibly fair nose – unsound palate – faint cloud. Because of low SO2, white wine affected by air. In our opinion will not keep unless by extra SO2. This cellar has a

tendency towards unsoundness which makes it difficult for us to decide on a definite price. Would Mr Barlow consider selling some of his grapes to us next year?[41]

Although Rustenburg subsequently sold some of its grapes to SFW,[42] it endeavoured to maintain its independence.

In 1960, an excessively hot summer led to a crisis in the cellars across the winelands and confirmed Winshaw in his conclusion that the introduction of refrigeration was the only way forward. The SFW was also an early convert to the use of stainless-steel tanks which had a range of advantages: they could be easily cleaned, the temperature could be controlled and fermentation could be carried out under pressure. Hence the farmers were encouraged to abandon open fermentation and to embrace the new technologies. The problem was that the Crouse family did not have the resources to modernize their cellar. Chris Venter notes that Maurice Crouse solicited advice from none other than André Simon about whether it made sense to embrace the new fashion for 'semi-sweet' white wines, which implied abandoning the old *stukvats* and investing in new cellar technologies. Simon was apparently sceptical about the current fashion. When the SFW declined to loan the money that was needed, the decision was taken to cease making wine altogether at Zonnebloem.[43] The link with SFW was severed and the farm sold its grapes to a cooperative winery from 1965. Ironically, however, the *Zonnebloem* brand name became more closely associated with the SFW which copyrighted it in 1964. Single varietal wines were henceforth marketed under the *Zonnebloem* label, but using grapes sourced from many other farms whose owners were carefully tutored, thereby mirroring the strategy being pursued by Distillers.

At the end of the 1950s, the South African wine industry was very much in the vanguard of innovation, and this continued through the 1960s. Vernon Singleton, one of the pioneers in wine science at the University of California-Davis, recalled:

I was in S.A. I think the first time was 1962 and I had 3–4 extended stays there ... As far as I know there is no 'record' of Californian interactions with South Africa, but it was frequent ... I do think SA was in the forefront of cool fermentations. I did some work on it when I returned to Davis ... As an Enologist I am not well versed in the management of vineyards, but I suspect SA was slower in this area.[44]

There was, in fact, an intricate web of connections linking California, Germany and South Africa. N. C. Krone had studied under Professor Hugo Schanderl, an esteemed wine microbiologist, in Geisenheim and regarded him as a

[41] SFW, *Boereboeke* 1955/56.

[42] This is apparent from the Rustenburg farm records. In 1968, for example, the Chenin Blanc and Clairette Blanche were delivered to the SFW.

[43] Venter, *Story*, p. 26. [44] E-mail from Vernon Singleton, dated 26 October 2010.

lifelong mentor. The files of Maynard Amerine, the other leading figure in Californian wine research, indicate that there were close links between Schanderl and researchers at Davis. Like Singleton, Amerine spent time in South Africa in the 1960s, to match his three visits to the Soviet Union that have recently been detailed by Steven Bittner.[45] Amerine also published specifically on the subject of cool fermentation and was in correspondence with Robert Mondavi who went on to become one of the leaders of the wine revolution in California.[46] Nicky Krone, who inherited Twee Zonge Gezellen, recalls that at one point Mondavi beat a path to Tulbagh to acquaint himself with the innovations that were underway at the farm.[47] It is perhaps not too far-fetched to posit that Amerine was the source of the information that Mondavi may have acted upon.

After 1959, cool fermentation became the watchword of the farmers and co-operatives alike. For example, Bernard Podlashuk installed air-conditioning into his cellars at Bellingham in 1960.[48] In the case of Schoongezicht/Rustenberg, which had been attempting to produce export quality wine from the interwar period, the surviving farm records make it possible to date the introduction of cool fermentation very precisely. In February 1960, a new cooling system arrived and was installed, to some excitement. The entry for 5 March simply reads: 'COOLED! WK2 from 73°F ⇒ 68°F between 7.15 and 9.15 a.m.' On 28 February, the outside temperature was 90°F (32°C) while in the cellar it was still a considerable 70°F (21°C). The introduction of the cooler subsequently made it possible to bring the must down to around 48–50°F (8.9–10°C). Although the cooler was only circulating cold water and the introduction of refrigeration would follow later, it presumably made a significant difference to a farm which, at that time, was largely a white wine producer.[49] Although the farm diaries do not indicate that the farm was under any particular pressure to change its methods, Santhagen's purchased much of the wine and presumably was in favour of making such an investment. Whereas N. C. Krone continued to make use of wooden vats within a temperature-controlled cellar, Frans Malan, the owner of De Hoop (the precursor to Simonsig), laid claim to being the first individual farmer to adopt stainless steel fermentation tanks. Indeed, he installed no fewer than 10 tanks

45 Bittner, *Whites*, ch. 6.

46 Maynard A. Amerine Papers, University of California–Davis, D-060, Box 2, Folder 2 (1959–1960). Maynard Amerine worked at Davis, becoming Professor of Viticulture and Oenology, between 1936 and 1974.

47 Interview with Nicky Krone, 28 September 2009.

48 This was done at Bellingham in 1960. R. L. Scott-Hayward, "Slow fermentation makes finer wine", Wine News, supplement to *Wine and Spirit*, June 1965.

49 In 1958, the only red grapes were Cabernets and Red Frontignac, whereas the rest was made up of white varieties: Stein (for good wine) and, Hanepoot, Clairette Blanche, South African Riesling for sale to the KWV as distilling wine. Rustenberg Farm Records for 1958.

over 1963/64 at a time when there remained some scepticism about the benefits relative to cost.[50] These refrigerated tanks were supplied by the engineering firm, Consani, which became a world leader and a significant exporter of tanks to other countries.[51] Those farms which could afford stainless steel concentrated on producing white wine for which there was rising consumer demand.[52] Hence, Van Zyl recalls that De Hoop was dedicated to the production of Cape Riesling (Crouchen Blanc), Chenin Blanc and Clairette Blanche and had only small plantings of Cinsault.[53]

A select number of farmers were able to take advantage of the conjuncture between rising quality and increasing consumer demand by bottling and selling wine under their own labels. In 1960, Peter Barlow of Rustenberg sold wine directly to bottle stores such as Solly Kramer, particularly in the Johannesburg area, but also despatched wine as far as Swaziland and Southern Rhodesia.[54] A pioneer was Sydney Back whose family had purchased the Klein Babylonstoren farm near Paarl. The Backs began producing 'sherry' from Palomino, Semillon and Clairette Blanche grapes, under the guidance of Dr. Niehaus of the KWV, as well as sweet red wine from Cinsault grapes. Sydney Back recalled that around 1943/44 he won the Burgoyne trophy for the best sweet red wine. As he took greater control of the farming operations, Sydney Back aspired towards bottling his own wine. His father relented, but insisted that it would be necessary to inform Niehaus personally of the decision. What follows in the narrative is instructive:

> I made an appointment with Dr Niehaus and went to see him. I explained to him the way I was thinking and in his normal gentlemanly fashion he listened to all I had to say. When I was finished, he got up, put his hand out to me and said to be 'Sydney, my boy, if you leave the KWV once, you leave the KWV for good.' Far be it from me to believe that Dr Niehaus intended to harm me in any way but what he did for me was probably the best thing the KWV has ever done for me. He threw me in at the deep end. I either had to sink or I had to swim and I didn't have the slightest intention of sinking.[55]

[50] Diko van Zyl, *Frans Malan Van Simonsig: Visionêre Baanbreker en Leier in die Moderne Suid-Afrikaanse Wynbedryf en Landbougemeenskap*, unpublished manuscript (Stellenbosch, 2002), p. 41.

[51] Interview with Bennie Howard, 17 March 2009.

[52] In Australia, the shift towards cool fermentation similarly led to a shift in the direction of white wines and the targeting of female consumers. Kym Anderson, "Australia and New Zealand", in Anderson and Pinilla (eds.), *Wine Globalization*, p.341.

[53] Van Zyl, *Frans Malan*, p. 29.

[54] Rustenburg Farm Records, May 1960. The farm also sent some wine to individuals, including the Archbishop of Cape Town and the Bishop of Johannesburg.

[55] Phyllis Back (ed.), *Sydney Back, 70 Years of My Life, 1926–1996*, unpublished document (Klapmuts, 1996), p. 14.

In the 1950s, the Backs applied for a farmers' licence, bottled their own wine and delivered much of it to consumers by road. In the 1960s, an Italian winemaker at the Franschhoek Co-operative winery by the name of Alberto Agostinis encouraged Back to begin copying the style of a bottled semi-sweet white wine. Back created *Mardi Gras*, which he proudly noted preceded the SFW's *Lieberstein*, as well as being the country's first Perlé wine. However, at this time it was an uphill battle for a small outfit to sell its own wines in competition with the big players and the business was eventually sold in 1969.

The vast majority continued to sell to the large companies, but those who had invested in new cellar technologies increasingly felt that the returns from the leap in quality were being unevenly shared. Hence, Frans Malan who had been on the receiving end of Winshaw's withering critique in the mid-1950s,[56] began to bottle his own wine under the Simonsig label in 1968. The following year he joined forces with Spatz Sperling from Delheim and Sydney Back from Backsberg to form what became the Cape Estate Wine Producers Association (CEWPA),[57] in effect reviving the agenda of the Quality Winegrowers' Society of the 1930s. This put the aspiring wine farmers on a collision course with the firms whose labels often implied that they were selling wine from a single estate whereas they were drawing on diverse sources. At the other end of the spectrum, the adoption of cool fermentation was associated with the revival of the wine co-operatives. The five cooperatives that existed at the time of the Wine Commission were joined by another two towards the close of the 1930s, and a further 25 in the 1940s. The addition of a further 25 cooperative wineries in the 1950s and 1960s was related to structural changes within the industry. Because smaller farmers could not afford the investments required, they sold their grapes to the local cooperative that was able to invest in modern cellaring equipment by virtue of concessionary loans. The SFW often preferred to purchase its wine from the cooperatives rather than from individual farmers because they were regarded as being more consistent in the quality of the wine they delivered.

The technical breakthroughs that took place in the late 1950s and early 1960s enabled the merchant-manufacturers to pursue their branding strategies more effectively, and none more so than SFW. In the 1950s, a great deal of effort went into promoting new quality wines, including a Cabernet Sauvignon and a Riesling from the Zonnebloem farm (and labelled as such) and *Chateau Libertas*. In 1959, the SFW took its most significant step forward with the introduction of *Lieberstein*, a sweet white wine made from Chenin Blanc grapes. This capitalized on the improvements associated with cool fermentation, enabling the SFW to market a thoroughly consistent product in

[56] This is clear from the pages of the *Boereboeke*. [57] Van Zyl, *Frans Malan*, pp. 43–44.

prodigious quantities. The bottling plant, which 'hot bottled' under sterilized conditions, took a leaf out of the book of the dairy industry which was accustomed to handling large volumes. Indeed, the machinery consisted of modified milk fillers imported from the Netherlands.[58] The sales pitch for *Lieberstein* emphasized value for money. Initially it was sold at the same price point as the others and *Golden Alibama* (*sic*),[59] and was made available in quarts, gallon and half-gallon jars. Within a few years it was being targeted at a middle range of consumers at a lower price point, and to maximize sales it was sold in cooler units in bars. *Lieberstein* was explicitly intended to appeal to both the White and Coloured consumers. After enjoying considerable success in the Western Cape, *Lieberstein* was rolled out in other parts of the country. A confidential sales directive for the representatives in Port Elizabeth stated quite explicitly that:

> The objective which we have adopted for Lieberstein in the Port Elizabeth market is a significant market share of both the European and non European lower priced wine potential. It must be emphasized that the objective is to establish Lieberstein firmly in both racial sectors of this market and that the basis of our expected sales should not be confined to one racial group.

The letter went on to state that the intention was to install cooler units in every canteen catering to Coloured people, and that in the public relations campaign 'our Coloured representative should be used to the maximum'.[60] The role of the sales representatives was, as we have seen, crucial and they are credited with much of the success. As one former employee of SFW observed:

> The liquor reps in those days were perhaps some of the finest men you could ever find on the road . . . [They were] real friendly sociable types. You could go all over the place and find that everyone knew the liquor rep wherever he went. I think it was Ronnie Nienaber who told me that when they were trying to promote Lieberstein, how they used to go into the pubs after work . . . and chat to people and say 'How about tasting this new wine?'[61]

At this time, the SFW also began to inject substantial resources into marketing, which included the offer of attractive window displays at liquor outlets, newspaper placements and advertisements on the radio. The intention was to make *Lieberstein* a truly household name. In September 1961, the SFW bought

58 Apparently, the large bottling line was unusual. Gallo, for example, had a number of smaller bottling lines. Interview with Dave Hughes, 31 March 2009.

59 Circular sales letter by R. D. Burmeister, Assistant Sales Manager (10 October 1960). Golden Alibama was marketed as a sweet 'golden-coloured' wine, Distell Archives "Sales Letters, 1951–1962".

60 Circular sales letter by J. M. Watkins, General Sales Manager (2 March 1962), "Sales Letters, 1951–1962".

61 Distell Archive, "Interview with Wally Sterry, Glencairn", 14 July 1982.

a series of quarter and half-minute advertising slots on Springbok Radio that began and ended with the German folksong *Ach du liebe Augustine*. The advertising jingle that became seared into the consciousness of all South Africans went: 'Get together with Lieberstein, any day any time'.[62] This drove home the message that wine was something intended for everyday conviviality, and crucially by both men and women. This campaign was spectacularly successful. The SFW gleefully reported that sales had rocketed from 6,637 gallons (302 hl.) in 1959 to 6,936,139 (315,594 hl.) in 1964, by which time it commanded 36.3 per cent of the domestic wine market.[63] In the early 1960s, *Lieberstein* had reputedly become the world's largest single wine brand.[64] Given that most South Africans were forbidden from drinking wine, that was no mean achievement. Inevitably, however, *Lieberstein* eventually lost its appeal to more affluent White consumers as new products came onto the market – and this increasingly meant wines that were less sweet and increasingly red. This is a theme that I will return to in greater detail.

This inevitably brings us back to the question of the extent to which there had been a shift in the centre of gravity from distillation to the production of wine for consumption. The KWV's own statistics reveal that the size of the distilling pool was relatively constant between 1945 and 1955, but then began to edge upwards once more (Table 3.3). Conversely, the production of good wine remained stable until around 1958, when there was a significant spike. Within the industry this period is remembered as a time when consumers could not get enough, and this is reflected in the fact that the consumption of drinking wine more than doubled between 1955 and 1965, whereas the consumption of spirit in its various forms remained static (Tables 3.1 and 3.2). The uptake in wine drinking played a crucial role in shrinking the wine surplus in the 1960s. With the de-racialization of the liquor laws, which is addressed in the next chapter, there seemed every chance that the industry could carry off the kind of transition that C. W. H. Kohler had promised.

Conclusion

In this chapter, I have been concerned with identifying the drivers of change in the wine industry from the 1940s to the early 1960s. In the scientific arena, international collaborations served to create a more nuanced understanding of the ways in which temperature affected the fermentation process and the aroma compounds that were embodied in the resulting wine. This, together with the

[62] Circular sales letter by R. D. Burmeister, 26 September 1961, "Sales Letters, 1951–1962".

[63] Stellenbosch Farmers Winery, *Die Natuurwyn-revolusie* (Stellenbosch: SFW, 1965), p. 2.

[64] Although Gallo presumably sold much more, its products were marketed under many different labels.

Table 3.3. *Production of good and distilling wine, 1945–1965 (leaguers)*

Year	Good Wine	Distilling Wine	Percentage Surplus Declared
1945	146,002	254,427	39[a]
1946	179,930	244,435	39[a]
1947	182,565	187,680	25
1948	190,118	232,937	25
1949	180,526	221,752	25
1950	153,443	258,143	25
1951	158,814	294,292	25
1952	180,478	171,612	25
1953	190,438	277,176	25
1954	186,418	284,747	25
1955	184,393	345,742	24
1956	172,414	419,116	24
1957	161,082	357,835	35
1958	194,956	339,839	24
1959	214,697	302,541	35
1960	254,490	341,827	28
1961	232,599	295,272	19
1962	243,564	360,899	18
1963	243,181	363,777	26
1964	316,179	330,087	15
1965	369,743	403,859	15

[a]Figures rounded upwards.
Source: KWV, *A Survey of Wine Growing in South Africa 1965–66*, p. 49.

technical breakthrough that came with the introduction of temperature-controlled stainless-steel tanks, facilitated a quality leap for white wines. But innovation also came at a financial cost, and this lent greater stimulus to the cooperative wineries that could draw on the financial resources that most individual producers could not. It also created its own form of path dependency because it converted the majority of producers into grape growers rather than wine producers in the strict sense. These developments were accelerated by systemic changes in the sphere of distribution. A handful of large firms dominated the domestic market for wine through their control over bottle stores and hotels. The KWV bemoaned this trend and claimed the credit for improvements, but the evidence strongly suggests that it was the companies that were driving innovation in close cooperation with specific farms. By the time André Simon returned to the Cape in 1965, there was a self-confidence in the industry that had not been witnessed since he had toured Europe in the company of Manie Malan and Frank W. Myburgh three decades earlier.

4 De-racializing the Liquor Laws

Temperance, Wine and the Consumption of Race, 1928–1964

> A glance at the Liquor Act reveals how fuddled were the minds of the legislators that passed it . . . Its repeal, which is imperatively necessary in the interests of all concerned, can only be brought about by educating the public to realize that the proper way to eliminate drunkenness is to promote the consumption of light, natural wine, and to check thereby – and not by prohibition – the consumption of spirituous liquor.[1]
>
> (Leipoldt, *300 Years*, 1952)

At the time these words were penned by Louis Leipoldt, the liquor question was beginning to animate public debate once again. After the victory of the National Party (NP) in 1948, the KWV was presented with a Prime Minister, Dr. D. F. Malan, who was a staunch advocate of Local Option. But at the same time, the KWV could count on influential friends within the ruling party. The merchant-manufacturers continued to enjoy a fractious relationship with both the temperance movement and the KWV. Although they had their own defenders in Parliament, they lacked the political clout of their opponents. But because of their economic might, they were relatively confident that government would leave them with a free hand to handle the distribution of wine. The balance of forces was, therefore, broadly stable in the two decades following the 1928 Act. However, this changed in the 1950s as criticism of the liquor laws became increasingly vocal, and occasionally from unexpected quarters. In this chapter, I am interested in the reasons why it became possible for the KWV and the merchants to persuade government to de-racialize the liquor laws at precisely the moment when apartheid legislation was reinscribing race in all walks of life. I also seek to account for the reasons why restrictions on the distribution of alcohol were relaxed after the repeal of the 1928 Act despite the misgivings of the Dutch Reformed Churches and the temperance lobby.

[1] Leipoldt, *300 Years*, pp. 212–213.

One Volk, Many Drinkers: The Enigma of Apartheid

During the interwar years, the tightening up of segregationist legislation and practice further compartmentalized populations that were already subject to stratified political rights, carried out different kinds of work for unequal rates of pay, and were required to live in physically separate areas. The fear that Black urbanization would eventually bring about the dissolution of the boundaries between the population groups contributed in large part to the election of the NP in 1948. Apartheid was, in effect, an attempt to go beyond ad hoc responses, and to create a coherent system that would keep the designated racial groups separate from one another and, by controlling the flow of the rural Black population to the cities, maintain the spatial foundations of White supremacy.[2] At an ideological level, apartheid made a virtue out of supposedly innate cultural differences. According to Hendrik Verwoerd, the architect of apartheid, the constituent races had distinct aptitudes, cultural values and legitimate expectations, which meant that Black and White people necessarily had to revolve within a series of parallel, but spatially distinct, orbits.[3] During his premiership (1958–1966), a whole battery of laws was introduced to regulate and control every aspect of the lives of Black South Africans, while resistance was met with increasingly severe repression after the Sharpeville killings of 1960. But while South Africa was becoming a distinctly illiberal country, the liquor laws moved in the direction of greater liberalization. Surprisingly little has been written about this aspect of the nexus between alcohol and apartheid.[4] Most of what there is frames the linkage in terms of the imperatives of financing urban apartheid. Given that the profits from municipal beer halls and bottle stores were what helped to defray the cost of implementing the provisions of the Group Areas Act, they came to stand as symbols of oppression, as reflected during the SOWETO uprising of 1976 when they were torched.[5] But much of the urban population gained access to alcohol through illicit shebeens. While the NP government was ostensibly worried about their

[2] Dubow, *Apartheid*; Deborah Posel, *The Making of Apartheid, 1948–1961: Conflict and Compromise* (Oxford: Oxford University Press, 1991); Dan O'Meara, *Forty Lost Years: The Apartheid State and the Politics of the National Party, 1948–1994* (Johannesburg: Ravan Press, 1996).

[3] Henry Kenney, *Architect of Apartheid: H.F. Verwoerd, an Appraisal* (Johannesburg: Jonathan Ball, 1980).

[4] Monographs that have focused on apartheid as a system of regulation have had so little to say about liquor control. See, for example, Adam Ashforth, *The Politics of Official Discourse in Twentieth-Century South Africa* (Oxford: Clarendon Press, 1990), and Ivan Evans, *Bureaucracy and Race: Native Administration in South Africa* (Berkeley: University of California Press, 1997).

[5] Baruch Hirson, *Year of Fire, Year of Ash – The Soweto Revolt: Roots of a Revolution?* (London: Zed Press, 1979), pp. 264–266.

proliferation, shebeens also came to be tolerated and actively courted by the liquor industry. The apartheid regime, which went to inordinate lengths to regiment other aspects of African lives under the Act, was often quite candid about the difficulty of eradicating the shebeens. The government also resisted pressure to prevent bottle stores in White areas from selling alcohol to 'non-whites' on the basis that the liquor industry had made significant investments, and that imposing additional limitations would merely stoke the illicit trade.[6] Much of this is counter-intuitive and needs to be properly explained.

Consumption, Race and Nationalism

Following the passage of the 1928 Liquor Act, the temperance movement and the wine farmers reconciled themselves to an uneasy stalemate. The remaining point of friction was over the high levels of alcohol consumption amongst the Coloured population of the Western Cape.[7] The temperance movement continued to push for stricter controls on Coloured people's drinking but also for an end to the dop system that was seen as the driver of all manner of social problems. In 1937, two separate Commissions of Enquiry were constituted. The first was the Wine Commission, which has already been discussed in Chapter 2.[8] The Commission made a number of observations and recommendations that were intended to be helpful to the wine industry. It found fault with aspects of the existing legislation that it considered 'unnecessarily irksome'.[9] It specifically proposed that the prohibition on the sale of wine through cafés and restaurants be repealed and that special licences be provided that would be exempt from quotas imposed under the Liquor Act.[10] Anticipating a temperance backlash, the Commission clarified that 'the supply of natural dry wines, of low alcoholic strength in limited quantities with meals only' would educate 'young people in the proper use of alcoholic liquor'; indeed, so the reasoning went, it would teach the youth how to practise temperance.[11] In addition, the Commission dared to broach the question of whether it was time to revisit the ban on Black people being allowed to purchase alcohol, given that there was abundant evidence to suggest that they were already doing so:

> Ineffectual prohibition is a demoralising and costly state of affairs – it creates criminals, involves considerable State expense and breeds a contempt of authority. The

[6] In 1967, the Minister of Justice, Mr. Pelser, resisted pressure from the Cape congress of the party. [Anon.], "Apartheid in retailing not realistic", *Wine, Spirit and Malt*, November 1967, p. 19.

[7] In this text I refer to 'White', 'Coloured' and 'Black' - categories that are rooted in segregationist and apartheid discourse, but which are impossible to avoid using because they have meaning for the actors themselves. See the 'Note on the Text' on page vi for more detail about the history and use of this term in South Africa.

[8] *Wine Commission* (1937), p. 98. [9] *Wine Commission*, p. 90.

[10] Anticipating opposition from the hotel industry, the Commission suggested that this experiment in expanding the availability of light wine be maintained for an initial period of five years.

[11] *Wine Commission*, p. 100.

> Commission is accordingly of the opinion that either prohibition should be completely enforced or that if that is impossible, then the fact should be squarely faced, and the necessary steps taken to see that facilities are provided for the supply of liquor, of moderate alcoholic strength, to natives in reasonable quantities under adequate supervision and decent surroundings.[12]

The Commission also expressed the opinion that the scheduled termination of bar and canteen licences in 1937 would impose an unnecessary burden upon the Coloured population. The Commission was clearly tackling a number of delicate issues head-on. Surprisingly, temperance organizations did not give evidence, and seemingly they did not react to its findings.

The second enquiry was infused with a rather different tone. The Cape Coloured Commission was set up to investigate 'the social factors affecting the well-being of the Cape Coloured population', the economic position of skilled and unskilled workers, and the economic position of farmworkers and rural dwellers.[13] Although the alcohol question comprised only a small part of the overall enquiry, its work was informed by the debate about whether a lack of social cohesion was due to some biological deficit, poverty or the destructive consequences of drink. The six-member Commission included Dr. Abdurahman, who had long been associated with the temperance cause.[14] The commissioners took evidence from a variety of quarters, and came to the conclusion that while Cape Malays, being Muslim, did not drink and the artisanal classes were generally moderate in their consumption, many of the "unskilled labouring type" were experiencing a reduction of their wage-earning capacity as a consequence of their 'physical and moral deterioration'. The Commission was sceptical that abolishing the dop would, in and of itself, address the problem, but nevertheless recommended it as part of a coordinated drive to improve rural living conditions. Its pragmatism was also reflected in the balance struck between opposition to total prohibition for Coloured people, which it considered un-enforceable, and advocacy of an end to bulk sales for off-site consumption and a reconciliation of the hours of sale. In effect, the Commission deployed some longstanding temperance arguments whilst borrowing from critics who maintained that ill-chosen legislative intervention was doomed to failure. Probably reflecting the personal influence of Dr. Abdurahman, the Commission rejected a racialized reading of alcohol addiction and placed its faith in the leadership of 'the upper Coloured classes' in fostering a social stigma towards intemperance amongst the 'lower classes'. In effect, the Commission returned to the mantra that temperance was best achieved by positive example rather than through the dead hand of legislation. This was

[12] *Wine Commission*, p. 91.

[13] Union of South Africa, *Commission of Enquiry Regarding* [*the*] *Cape Coloured Population on the Union* (1937).

[14] South African Temperance Alliance, *Red die Kleurling Volk!* (Cape Town: SATA, 1937), p. 6.

not so different from the Wine Commission's own conception of what temperance meant: namely something that was actively practised rather than being imposed from above. The difference is that while the Wine Commission envisaged legislative reform, the Cape Coloured Commission was committed to upholding the status quo. Nobody was seriously suggesting that the laws ought to be made any more draconian.

In the same year that these two commissions reported, the South African Temperance Alliance (SATA) published a document that signalled the beginnings of a discursive shift. *Red die Kleurling Volk* (or *Save the Coloured People*) repeated a familiar position that the Coloured population was under a particular threat from the ravages of alcohol, but it also echoed the Wine Commission in pointing to shifting demographics arising from Black immigration to the Western Cape.[15] By 1945, when the Cape Coloured Liquor Commission (CCLC) published its report, Coloured people's drinking and African shebeening had become thoroughly intertwined in official thinking.[16] In many ways, this report merely rehashed the work of the Cape Coloured Commission, but in a much less nuanced fashion. Strikingly, it fell back on crude notions of innate biological dispositions derived from 'Hottentot blood'. But by broaching the matter of the illicit trade, it laid down a marker of its own. The Commission made two specific claims, one tendentious and the other more firmly grounded. The first was that Coloured people had become "so enfeebled" through drink that they were no longer capable of performing heavy farm work, thereby opening the door to Black labour.[17] The second was that because Black people could not legally acquire access to 'kaffir beer' in the Cape, they were tempted to purchase wine and brandy illegally and with the assistance of Coloured middlemen.[18] Having opened this particular can of worms, the CCLC came down on the side of advocating no immediate change to the law. But it did recommend that the government consider the 'native' liquor question in the Cape at the same time as it addressed Coloured people's consumption.[19]

The liquor industry was well aware of the growing importance of the shebeens and actively pushed the case for legalization. Whereas in the 1920s the WCTU and SATA would have faced down these demands, they struggled to convince the White population that the solution was to impose more rigid

[15] *Red die Kleurling*, p. 11.

[16] Union of South Africa, *Report of the Cape Coloured Liquor Commission of Inquiry* (Pretoria: Government Printer, 1945) [hereinafter *Cape Coloured Liquor Commission]*.

[17] The Report claimed that farmers would have found themselves in a predicament had it not been for the availability of Italian prisoners of war. *Cape Coloured Liquor Commission*, p. 2.

[18] *Cape Coloured Liquor Commission*, p. 18.

[19] It also urged the phasing out of the dop system over a period of two years. Its more concrete recommendations were for the creation of a Central Liquor Board, to provide better co-ordination between Licensing Boards; even more restrictive licensing hours; the closure of canteens catering to Coloured women; and the teaching of temperance in schools.

restrictions on Coloured people's access to alcohol. Over the next decade, the temperance movement increasingly found itself on the back foot. To understand why it was losing ground, a number of factors need to be taken into account. The first is that the WCTU had become a victim of its own success. It had creatively linked the demand for the women's franchise to the campaign against alcohol. When White women were enfranchised in 1930, this removed one of the planks that had sustained popular support for the WCTU. Because the WCTU did not take up the right of 'non-whites' to vote, it was effectively restricted to single-issue campaigning. Moreover, while the national and provincial leadership of the WCTU continued to reproduce itself, it struggled to hold onto a younger generation of activists at lower levels. An internal history indicates that the low conversion rate from the youth unions (the 'Ys') to full membership after the war proved decisive.[20] In 1957, the chairman of the Cape WCTU, M. E. Duguid, alluded to efforts to resuscitate moribund unions and to revive relations with SATA. She also hinted at some internal carping:

> Some of us rather enjoy living in the past – getting 'a kick' out of recalling its past glories or moaning over its failures. Have we not all heard about the 'W.C.T.U. being on its last legs'? Do we listen? Do we believe it? Do we contradict it? That we have been in existence for a long time is true, as we began in 1889, and there is still lots of work for us to do.[21]

In particular, she referred to the difficulties associated with preaching the doctrine of abstinence to youth who were seduced by the glamour of liquor advertising – singling out the current Miss South Africa as someone who frequented all too many drinks receptions. Some of the events in question would no doubt have been hosted by the KWV, which sought to associate wine with the intake of food, but also with glamour, beauty and the good life.[22] The reality was that the stock of ideas that had previously attracted youth to the temperance banner seemed out of kilter with the times. But whereas the White chapter of the WCTU failed to attract younger members, its relevance seemed much more obvious in the Coloured areas. For example, 'WCTU (Coloured),

[20] WCTU, *The Women's Christian Temperance Union in South Africa 1889–1989* (Cape Town: WCTU, undated), p. 49.

[21] M. E. Duguid, "Chairman's address at Cape Province convention by Mrs M.E. Duguid", *White Ribbon* 64 (1), Nov./Dec. 1957.

[22] The pages of *Wynboer* in the 1960s and 1970s regularly featured successive Miss South Africa's featuring alongside fashion models on the front cover and inside pages. The WCTU attempted to counteract these images with its own advertising campaign, with variable success. The WCTU placed posters at 39 railway stations between Cape Town and Kimberly in 1962, and in subsequent years it continued to target these public spaces. This included an iconic poster that read "You May Think Alcohol Puts Springs Under You But It Always Lets You Down". *Women's Christian Temperance Union*, p. 60.

Cape Province' campaigned against the opening of a restaurant, lounge and bar for Coloured travellers at Cape Town Station in 1960.[23] It also opposed the expansion of liquor outlets in Coloured townships and took a particular interest in the ending of the dop system in the rural areas. The activism of the Coloured chapter in the Cape, under the leadership of Mrs. E. Achilles, also led to friction over the perceived paternalism of her White counterparts. In 1963, WCTU (Coloured) applied for direct affiliation to the WCTU of South Africa rather than having to work through the Cape Province WCTU.[24] This was an indication that the balance of power within the WCTU had shifted away from the White leadership, but with the inevitable consequence that its political leverage was also more limited.

Secondly, the shifting balance of power within the White population worked to the detriment of the temperance movement. As we have already seen, the WCTU was overwhelmingly led by White English speakers and, although SATA made more of an effort to publish its materials in Afrikaans, a stigma remained attached to the movement as a whole. This counted much more after 1948 because the government was made up almost entirely of Afrikaners. The combination of public campaigning and lobbying of MPs had served the WCTU and SATA well in the past. But once the NP had built up a hefty majority in Parliament, individual MPs tended to be less susceptible to pressure. Moreover, the NP preferred to deal with competing political demands behind closed doors rather than in public. This meant that being on the outside of the charmed circle greatly restricted the level of influence that could be exercised. For its part, the KWV leadership was careful to cultivate a special relationship with the NP and its ancillary structures. This included membership of the Broederbond in the case of successive KWV chairmen, and the ongoing practice of directors holding parliamentary seats for the ruling party.[25] Although the Dutch Reformed Churches were in favour of temperance, they had never lobbied strongly for legislative solutions. However, their stance did infuse the attitudes of individual MPs who opposed proposed changes to the Liquor Act. And indeed, it is within Parliament, rather than outside it, that temperance ideas held the greatest sway by the end of the 1950s.

In contrast with the waning influence of temperance bodies, the KWV spearheaded a campaign to make wine one of the integral ingredients of a nation-in-distillation. Public displays of Afrikaner nationalism were a notable

[23] [Anon.], "Coloured bar on station opposed", *Cape Argus*, 19 August 1960. The Coloured chapter was established in 1949.

[24] CA A1696 "Women's Christian Temperance Union", S. Pritchard, WCTU.CP (Coloured) to Secretary of WCTU of S.A. (25 June 1963).

[25] In the 1960s, André J. Du Toit, was a member of the Broederbond. When he stood down in 1984, he was replaced by Pietman Hugo who was not just the representative for Worcester, but also the MP for Ceres.

feature of the post-war years, and nowhere more so than in the Cape winelands that were construed as the cradle of the *volk*.[26] The KWV took full advantage of the tercentenary of the arrival of Jan Van Riebeeck in 1952 to promote a National Vine Festival that commemorated the first plantings of *vitis vinifera*.[27] As part of the festivities, a *Nooientjie vir die Wingerd* (Maiden of the Vine) was crowned from amongst hopefuls drawn from each of the wine districts.[28] At around this time, the KWV instigated annual wine festivals in the main towns in the winelands. These additions to the calendar celebrated Dutch heritage, but also highlighted the unique Huguenot contribution to the making of wine and the Afrikaner volk. Although the references were South African, the motifs suggest that these festivals were quite likely modelled on those that were initiated in Burgundy in the 1930s.[29] The forging of an Afrikaner nation under specifically African conditions drew freely on European symbols and strategies. The festivities typically included processions of floats – depicting giant bunches of grapes, vats and period dress – led by drum majorettes (see Figure 4.1). The townspeople would gather at the exhibition grounds where wine was consumed alongside meat from the *braai*, which was the distinctively South African touch. The dignitaries typically included local NP politicians, government ministers and, of course, KWV directors. The temperance movement had nothing to match this reappropriation of Afrikaner cultural politics in the service of wine, which merely compounded a failure to engage with an emergent youth culture. To complete this picture, it is also important to underline the importance of an emergent Afrikaner middle class in the post-war years.[30] As the spectre of the 'poor white' mired in alcoholism faded from view, it became possible to trumpet the virtues of pleasurable consumption. The wine festivals triangulated history, culture and consumption in a way that made ordinary people feel proud to be Afrikaners. But this packaging of consumption also raised significant questions about how other South Africans might relate to wine: was the possibility of living a civilized lifestyle through appreciation of the products of the vine to be confined to Afrikaners – or to White drinkers in general – or could it work its magic on South Africans of all racial hues? This is where the wine lobby began to enter some potentially choppy waters because even raising the

[26] Leslie Witz, *Apartheid's Festival: Contesting South Africa's National Pasts* (Bloomington: Indiana University Press, 2003).

[27] Van Zyl, *KWV*, pp. 54–55. [28] Distell Archives, copy of *Paarl Post*, 25 February 1955.

[29] Whalen, "'Insofar as the ruby wine seduces them'", pp. 67–98. As Laferté has demonstrated, La Confrérie des Chevaliers du Tastevin was founded in 1934 by some of the leading figures in the wine business who sought to revive the fortunes of Burgundy by hitching the performance of history and culture to a project that was quintessentially modern. Laferté, *La Bourgogne*.

[30] See Albert Grundlingh, "'Are we Afrikaners getting too rich?': Cornucopia and change in Afrikanerdom in the 1960s", *Journal of Historical Sociology* 21 (2/3), September 2008.

(a)

(b)

Figures 4.1 (a) Paarl (1955) and (b) Robertson (undated) Wine Shows
Source: Reproduced with kind acknowledgement of KWV.

question of whether there might be a large nation of consumers touched on the domain of politics.

Back to Parliament

In South Africa, liquor legislation had a habit of turning out very differently from what was inserted into the draft Bill. In the 1950s, an attempt to confront the reality of oligopolies in the liquor industry ended in the abolition of racially configured liquor legislation and the widening of access to products of the vine.

In 1955, the government set up a commission to revisit the issue of liquor boards and tied houses. This led to the passage of the Liquor Further Amendment Act (Act 61 of 1956), the most important provision of which was the termination of ties in the liquor trade, which was to be fully implemented over a six-year period. I will have occasion to return to this in the next section. While some of the original remit of the Commission was hived off to a separate enquiry led by the Board of Trade and Industry, the life of the Commission was then extended with a brief 'to inquire into and report on the general distribution of liquor and the selling prices thereof'.[31] Although distribution was an important dimension of the report, even greater historical significance resides in its reconsideration of whether drink should be made freely available to all South Africans regardless of race and province. The cross-party Commission was chaired by Dr. Avril Malan, a former academic, serving MP, member of the Broederbond and someone who was eminently sympathetic to the wine farmers. Because the membership of the Commission changed over time, Malan's personal influence was probably greater than it would otherwise have been. The Commission received direct evidence from no fewer than 314 witnesses. The wider context was the liberalization of comparable liquor laws in Southern Rhodesia and the reality of a flourishing illicit trade to Black townships. To learn more about the relationship between regulation, consumption and illegality, the Commission beat a path to Salisbury, Lourenço Marques, Blantyre (Nyasaland), Elizabethville (Belgian Congo), Lusaka and Ndola (Zambia). In the case of Southern Rhodesia, the Commission was struck by the fact that allowing Africans to purchase liquor had led to a brief upsurge in wine and beer sales followed by a subsequent return to 'kaffir beer'. In the case of Mozambique, the Commission found minimal restrictions on Africans purchasing alcohol, and evidence of moderate consumption of wine. It concluded that there was no reason to believe that

[31] Union of South Africa, *Report of the Commission of Enquiry on the General Distribution and Selling Prices of Liquor*, May 1960 [henceforth Malan Commission], unofficial translation prepared and issued by the Western Province Bottle Store Keepers Association, p. 1.

making alcohol more freely available would necessarily lead to an increase in consumption in the longer term. The secret was to ensure that alcohol was consumed in places that were conducive to healthy drinking patterns. Another conclusion was that the existing legislation was both counter-productive and ineffective. It was counter-productive because denying beer and wine to Africans made them want it all the more:

> The economic condition of the natives has improved to such an extent that they can, inter alia, afford the white man's drink. The status and living conditions of many of them in their own community have improved accordingly, so that the refusal to let the natives have the white man's drink have caused so much resistance that infringement of the law – viz. by obtaining drink illegally – gives them a certain amount of pleasure.[32]

It was ineffective because the authorities did not have the means to prevent 'an illicit liquor trade which transcends the wildest flights of the imagination'.[33] The net result was that the same amount of alcohol was consumed (albeit at a higher price for the Black community), more people were criminalized for infringements of the 1928 Liquor Act, and a minority of people – Coloured in the Cape and White elsewhere – became rich on the basis of trafficking. The Commission estimated that, in some areas, up to 60 per cent of the liquor trade passed through illicit channels (although Malan later hinted that this was a high estimate), while the merchants volunteered an estimate of 40 per cent.[34] Predictably, the Commission drew on its reading of the experience of Prohibition to make the point that the South African liquor question had to be seen in an international context:

> One's first reaction may be that such an illicit trade is a sad reflection on the ability of the police and at the same time forget to pay attention to the flaws and shortcoming of the existing legislation, which have simply made its application impossible. Today the law demands that which is practically the non-supply to by far the most numerous group in the country – indeed, a group almost three times the size of the remaining groups collectively. Is it reasonable or just as impossible of application as the laws which the United States of America introduced a number of years ago when they made abolition the law of the land with the intention of making it work? Along the road the Americans had to learn that the outrageous evils which came into being in the U.S. were the result of bad liquor laws which, with the exception of two states, they eventually had to revoke.

The Commission reasoned that, given the realities of the situation, the existing system could only be made to work if prohibition was extended to all racial groups, but this was not a realistic option because most White people insisted on their right to drink. The alternative was to excise the racial provisions of the

[32] Malan Commission, p. 17. [33] Malan Commission, p. 10.
[34] Malan Commission, p. 14.

Liquor Act and to direct consumption into legal channels where it could better be regulated: 'Be lenient with the number of points of distribution but relentless with the standards maintained, also in respect of infringements of the Liquor Law – with stress on drunkenness.'[35] Drinkers, Black as well as White, should be encouraged to embrace light wines and malt beer, but not spirits.[36] The Commission did not come down in favour of absolute uniformity, reasoning that 'the conditions do not as yet justify the free supply of liquor to non-Europeans in certain provinces'. However, a unification of practice was deemed to be the ultimate objective.[37] In the interim, the Commission recommended that light wine and beer in the Transvaal and the Free State be made available to Black people only for on-site consumption in formal beer halls, with special permits (as before) being required for off-site consumption. In the Cape and Natal, it recommended that existing 'privileges' be maintained, although it proposed that the hours of sale for White and non-White people be aligned.[38] When it came to White people, the Commission found that the consumption of spirits was considerably higher than for 'comparable' countries in Europe and Australasia. It reasoned that the strategic objective should be one of shifting consumption away from 'strong drink'. The means to do this was to improve the ease of access and reduce the price for beer and wine which had a lower alcohol content and were 'relatively harmless to the human system'.[39]

The proposal that special licences be introduced for the sale of natural wines and beers in restaurants, cafés and hotels was bound to be controversial, not least because it would reverse the victories chalked up by the temperance movement in 1928. Not surprisingly, the WCTU and its allies sought to rebut the claim that there was any alcohol that could be considered benign. As Mrs. Duguid stated in her chair's address in 1957: 'Alcohol is a narcotic drug, a dehydrant and a solvent, no matter how it is disguised.' Whereas the KWV was actively seeking to associate wine with food, the WCTU considered that normalization of alcohol posed an even greater threat:

> *Wine in our cafes:* Has every parent here present begun to think what this will mean to our young folk? Even now, you must know how much glamour is being connected with liquor. Its sociability, the seeming necessity of it at any social function, dance, braaivleis or party. And if all gathering, even in cafes, will also include wine, and you realise what will happen?

However, the Commission adopted a radically different tack, and argued that because healthy drinking was linked to the consumption of food, 'natural alcoholic types' should logically be available for purchase at grocery stores

[35] Malan Commission, p. 19.
[36] Malan Commission, p. 26.
[37] Malan Commission, p. 33.
[38] Malan Commission, p. 39.
[39] Malan Commission, p. 48.

as well.[40] Through the very act of shopping, a new attitude towards drink would be instilled: 'Its abuse at home is unthinkable and for that very reason it would be convenient and right if the housewife could order both simultaneously from the same shop.'[41] For those with a sense of history, the logic was gloriously Gladstonian. For the temperance movement, it constituted nothing less than an assault on the integrity of the family.

Remarkably, the Verwoerd government did not merely accept the diagnosis and the somewhat cautious recommendations but went considerably further in amending the 1928 Liquor Act. This took place in two stages, during which the various interests in the liquor question struggled as best they could to shape the agenda. In 1961, the Minister of Justice, F. C. Erasmus, brought forward an amendment to the 1928 Act that was intended to extend the right to purchase alcohol to all racial groups. Rather coyly, he presented it as 'an experiment' which would need to be assessed in the light of future evidence. The amendment permitted Black people to purchase not merely beer and wine, but spirits as well. This erased the clear distinction that the Malan Commission had drawn between 'natural' drinks and strong drinks. Moreover, Black consumers over the age of 18 years would be permitted to drink not only in designated beer halls, but also to purchase liquor for off-site consumption from licensed premises that municipal authorities were required to construct.[42] At the same time, Coloured and Asian consumers across the country were to be treated on an equal footing as White communities across all four provinces. The rules for on-site consumption by Black people, and the creation of separate regulatory authorities, was all that would remain of the racial provisions of the 1928 Act.

The Minister drew heavily on the Malan Commission in arguing that the most realistic means of curbing trafficking was to allow Black South Africans to freely purchase alcohol. But to balance the ticket, he proposed the simultaneous introduction of tougher penalties on illegal brewing and shebeens, thereby increasing the potential costs to illegality. The ostensible objective was to facilitate a liquor trade that was more efficiently managed. On the face of things, it seems curious that the government should impose something as complex and costly as the Group Areas Act with scarcely a qualm, only to fall back on the argument that the police were unable to make the liquor laws stick. However, part of the intention was to free up police time to carry out other duties that arose directly as a consequence of that Act. In addition, the liquor amendment was consistent with the desire of the government to erect a system of controls along the optimal line of defence, which was thought to be the point

[40] Malan Commission, p. 73. [41] Malan Commission, p. 73.

[42] Introduction to second reading by Minister of Justice, *Debatte Van Die Volksraad*, 16 June 1961, p. 8466.

of sale. Everything, therefore, hinged on an effective system of licensing that would operate within the spatial parameters set by the Group Areas Act.

Although the Bill was introduced as a non-party affair, in practice the United Party (UP) MPs opposed the amendment – including one who had sat on the Malan Commission – whereas those of the NP tended to support it. The disagreements clustered around two main sets of issues. The first was the question of who stood to benefit from an end to racial prohibition. Some MPs supported the claim that the Bill had been brought forward to 'fill the pockets' of the wine farmers and merchants. Having wrecked the bodies and souls of the Coloured population, Dr. D. L. Smit asserted, the drinks industry was intent on doing the same to the Black one. Interestingly, a very similar point was made by Black opponents of the Bill outside of Parliament, both those who belonged to temperance organizations as well as the African National Congress (ANC).[43] The charge that the government was doing the bidding of wine interests was vehemently rejected by W. C. Malan, who represented the wine-farming constituency of Paarl. He insisted that the pressure to change the law came from the police, who had indicated that they were unable to cope with the workload.[44] On their part, the defenders of the Bill took up the position that when the law was so blatantly and routinely transgressed, it also threatened the moral fabric of the entire community. This reinforced the contention that heightened criminality was the logical outcome of a law that was not considered legitimate by the mass of the population.

Secondly, there was a fundamental disagreement as to how different racial groups related to alcohol. The Malan Commission asserted that the living standards of Black people had improved to the point where they now expected to be able to buy 'the white man's drink'. Dr. Smit asserted that, on the contrary, most Africans were living on the breadline, which meant that there would inevitably be a trade-off between alcohol and the essentials of life.[45] Invoking a much older paternalistic discourse, he argued that alcohol posed a particular threat to people 'emerging from barbarism'. Colin Eglin was less emphatic on this score, but while agreeing that the 1928 Liquor Act had been drafted at a time when South Africa was a rather different country, he argued that the economic conditions of Africans would have to be uplifted significantly before it was

[43] Anne Kelk Mager, *Beer, Sociability and Masculinity in South Africa* (Bloomington: Indiana University Press, 2010), p. 17. Albert Luthuli was one of those opposed to the change to the law.

[44] W. C. Malan, *Debatte*, 16 June 1961, columns 8479–8492.

[45] Dr. D. L. Smit, *Debatte*, 16 June 1961, column 8471. Mager notes that Smit, the son of a missionary was the voice of prohibition in the early 1960s. Mager, *Beer*, p. 16.

realistic to treat everyone on an equal footing.[46] He supported the position of Dr. Frans Cronje, who had served on the Malan Commission in its later stages, that an elaboration of the existing system of permits was preferable, especially as the Malan Commission had itself indicated that the system had been subject to relatively few abuses.[47] This was related to the larger question of whether there was actually a racial convergence, whether measured in terms of lifestyle or desires. Counter-intuitively, it was Nationalist MPs who were inclined to argue that the gap had narrowed significantly, while their UP counterparts were inclined to fall back upon the paternalist position that most Black people were still on the road to 'becoming civilized'. The lessons to be drawn from consumption patterns of the Coloured population in the Cape were deployed opportunistically on either side of the debate. Those opposed to the Bill held up endemic alcoholism among Coloured people as the imminent spectre that loomed over the Black population if they were permitted freer access to liquor. In contrast, the Malan Commission had asserted that there were fewer per-capita convictions under the liquor laws amongst the Cape Coloured population than amongst those in the Transvaal, where they were subjected to prohibition. While those opposed to the Bill wished to keep Black people away from liquor in general, they were implacably opposed to spirits. While not disputing the argument about their adverse effects, W. C. Malan reasoned that Black people had been attracted to brandy precisely because when purchasing drinks was illegal, there was an incentive to maximize the alcoholic content. Conversely, once brandy became freely available, there was likely to be a turn to healthier alternatives, most notably wine.[48] Although this Bill demonstrated that there remained a strong residual concern amongst many MPs and the churches about the likely effects of ending racial prohibition, the Bill passed surprisingly easily, and came into effect in August 1962. Within a year, the new Minister of Justice, John Vorster, was pointing to falling convictions for liquor offences as evidence that the experiment had been a success.[49]

The second amendment was introduced by Vorster himself the following year. The ostensible purpose was to instil a healthier drinking habit into South Africans by moving them away from hard liquor and towards natural wine. This sounded innocuous enough, but the debate became a heated affair in which the divisions crossed party lines. One reason is that it touched directly on the consumption habits of White people. But it also brought what Vorster

46 Colin Eglin, UP Member for Peninsula, *Debatte*, 16 Junie 1961, column 8524. Eglin was later a leading light in the Progressive Federal Party that constituted the main parliamentary opposition.

47 Cronje was later appointed by SAB to its African sales division and eventually chaired its Board. Mager, *Beer*, pp. 19, 32.

48 M. C. Malan, *Debatte*, 16 June 1961, column 8491.

49 Vorster, *Debatte*, 10 June 1963, column 7911.

called clashing interests (*botsende belange*) into direct competition with one another. The merchant-manufacturers felt that they had been on the receiving end of recent amendments. As I have already indicated, the 1956 amendment had required them to relinquish their ties in the retail trade by 1962. The companies that nested under South African Breweries (SAB) had sought to persuade the Malan Commission that their greater interests lay in the hotel industry and that this should not be covered by this amendment. However, the Commission regarded these as being covered by the anti-tie rules, given that many hotels operated off-licences. Because the new law was focused largely on the hotel industry, the merchant-manufacturers were concerned that their business interests would be directly threatened. The Bottlestore Owners Association was most obviously affected by the Bill and mounted a public campaign to defend its members' interests. For its part, the KWV continued to oppose any form of vertical integration, which had the effect of creating monopolies that drove up the price of wine and brandy to the consumer. At the same time, the KWV had an interest in the expansion of the number and range of liquor outlets where the products of the vine could be freely purchased. And, finally, this was the last chance for the churches and temperance movement to shore up the foundations of the 1928 Liquor Act. It was clear that many MPs had been lobbied by the various interests involved, presumably in the knowledge that the matter would be debated along no-party lines.

The objective of the Bill was to expand the distribution points for wine through hotel off-licences, restaurants and grocers. Vorster began his speech with an open attack on vested interests. He singled out the Bottlestore Owners Association for having launched a press campaign against the proposed Bill. On the other hand, he made little secret of the fact that he was sympathetic towards the wine farmers. He stressed that he was not bringing the amendment on their behalf, but he expected them to benefit from its provisions. Tellingly, he alluded to the fact that in the previous years some 30,000 leaguers of wine needed to be distilled for want of a market.[50] Permitting wine to be sold in restaurants and hotel bottle stores, but also at grocery stores, was intended to facilitate ease of access to the products of the vine. Vorster also explicitly praised the KWV for advancing the cause of good wine, despite the fact that this was not within its formal remit.[51] The most telling omission from the Bill was the freer distribution of beer, which had been considered on equal terms by the Malan Commission. Apart from supporting the case of the wine farmers, Vorster expressed a desire to do something for the struggling hotel industry, which would also serve to promote tourism. His solution was not to

[50] Vorster, *Debatte*, 10 June 1963, column 7920.
[51] Vorster, *Debatte*, 10 June 1963, columns 7918–7919.

allow the merchant-manufacturers back in, but rather to make the hotels more profitable in their own right. Under the proposed amendment, hotels would not only be permitted to sell wine to their customers but could also operate off-sales facilities, which might be physically located away from the hotel buildings for the reason that the latter were often deliberately situated in quiet locations. This posed a threat both to the wholesalers and the bottle-store owners, who came together in what one MP described as an 'unholy alliance' with the supporters of temperance.[52] Indeed, it was even alleged that bottle-store owners paid certain churchmen to write letters of petition against the amendment, ostensibly on the grounds of temperance.[53]

On this occasion, Mr. Bowker led the charge against what he described as a 'revolutionary' Bill. He claimed that he had never received so many letters as he had received from temperance and welfare organizations expressing their vehement opposition.[54] Bowker invoked some predictable temperance arguments. The first of these was that the Minister was pandering to sectional interests by encouraging people to imbibe the wine surplus, while at the same time collecting more tax revenue for government.[55] The second is that families, the building blocks of the nation, were threatened by the prospect that grocers' shops would render alcohol more freely available.

> We must protect our children: that is our first duty. If we don't build up a strong and powerful people here in the country we are doomed, and now we want to permit that wine may enter people's houses as part of their grocery order. It will be found that people who can just about afford to feed their children reasonably well, who order groceries will also include wine in the order at the expense of certain essential foodstuffs.[56]

The claim that wine was benign was disputed by Dr. Van Nierop who maintained that alcoholics did not start by drinking spirits, but typically began with wine before progressing to the hard stuff.[57] He also questioned the repeated references to positive European models, arguing that France had a higher rate of alcoholism precisely because of its preference for light wine. Conversely, he maintained that in countries where restrictions had been placed on alcohol, there had, in fact, been a decline in drunkenness.[58]

[52] One MP who supported the Bill dubbed it an "Unholy alliance" between the bottlestore owners and the church. Muller, *Debatte*, 10 Junie 1963, column 7934.

[53] W. C. Malan, *Debatte*, 10 Junie 1963, p. 7968.

[54] Bowker, *Debatte*, 10 Junie 1963, p. 7929. [55] Bowker, *Debatte*, 10 Junie 1963, p. 7932.

[56] Bowker, *Debatte*, 10 Junie 1963, column 7928.

[57] Van Nierop, *Debatte*, 10 Junie 1963, p. 7940. In response, Avril Malan insisted that no alcoholic began with light wine, which repeated an assertion by Wine Commission. *Debatte*, 11 Junie, column 8022.

[58] Some MPs, who backed the Bill on pragmatic grounds, agreed that more could be done to promote the cause of sobriety with the help of the churches.

While generally supportive of the Bill, B. Coetzee pointed to the anomaly of excluding beer from grocers' shops, given that the alcoholic content of beer was lower than wine. Since beer was subjected to a higher excise duty, the wine producers already enjoyed an advantage over the brewers which he, and some other MPs, considered unfair.[59] Avril Malan defended the special case for wine on the basis that while beer was a thirst-quencher, wine had to be viewed in terms of its special relationship with the intake of food. Moreover, whereas beer was always going to remain popular, wine had become the Cinderella of the liquor industry despite being so integral to the culture of the volk.[60] At least one MP maintained that it was unfair to favour the grocers over the bottle-store owners who had done their bit for the industry over the years. At the same time, while the merchant-manufacturers were being kept out, some MPs could foresee a point when chain stores (in effect supermarkets) would create monopolies of their own.[61] The hoteliers were not spared their share of criticism either. One compelling argument was that because their markups tended to be substantial, they had proven to be a deterrent to the wider dissemination of wine.

In the end, Vorster had his way and the Bill passed into law with some minor modifications. What the debate underlined is that while the temperance movement was not an entirely spent force, it had lost ground to players in the liquor industry.[62] The controversy surrounding the 1964 amendment had also underlined that these interests were ranged against each other. One reading of the outcome is that wine farmers, represented by the KWV, had wheedled their way into a much more favourable position in the pecking order. Although the hotel industry was an ostensible beneficiary of the legislation, this was arguably secondary to the need to find fresh outlets for wine. The bottle-store owners were amongst the principal losers, and their position was perhaps not helped by the fact that they could not so easily call on the backing of the merchant-manufacturers. The debate had also pointed to the ways in which the future of wine was linked to that of beer. This was the prelude to a much more radical restructuring of the liquor industry, as we will see.

The final observation is that the elephant in the legislative chamber, namely the future of the dop system, was not tackled head-on, despite the fact that the White and Coloured chapters of the WCTU continued to campaign vociferously on the issue. Vorster was evidently unwilling to intrude on the

[59] B. Coetzee, *Debatte*, 10 Junie 1963, p. 7951. He was supported by Mr. Moore, and Mr. Gay, the MP for Simonstown (including Fish Hoek), *Debatte*, 10 Junie 1963, column 7955, 7971.

[60] Dr. A. I. Malan, *Debatte*, 11 Junie, column 8014.

[61] Smit, *Debatte*, 11 Junie, column 8040.

[62] Fish Hoek had its own restrictive liquor by-laws that provided a model for Local Option, and remained a bastion of the WCTU. During the debate of 1963, Vorster was visited by a deputation from the town demanding that if the law should pass, liquor licences should still not be issued there. Vorster, in *Debatte*, 11 Junie 1963, column 8059.

established relationship between the farmer and 'his workers'. This was perfectly illustrated by the fate of a Dutch immigrant, B. E. Kok, who endeavoured to organize a Western Cape Farm Workers' Association in the mid-1960s. He began in the Drakenstein Valley and hoped to branch out from there to the rest of the winelands. In 1965, Kok sparked a debate in the letter pages of the *Cape Argus* about the operations and consequences of the dop system. Amongst other things, he maintained that because a worker was typically paid 65 cents, and only 5 cents less if he accepted the dop, there was an incentive to take the drink that was on offer. The response of a number of farmers was highly defensive. His future plans for public campaigns were bound to cause particular offence. For example, he proposed an anti-wine festival to the WCTU which would, in effect, have turned the standard fare of the normal run of wine festivals upside down:

> To combat the reign of alcohol I have worked out an idea of an 'anti-wine week' with a terrible witch as 'Aunty Wine' who pulls the people into the grave. For this we need big posters, films, lectures, and the choosing of Miss Berg River Valley, as well as organising sports, strong men competitions and boxing, in short offering such things that will interest the people more than drink, which are very few, but surely there must be something ... Leaflets are not the answer, many cannot read, and certainly do not read small type matter. To combat our enemy we have to propagate OUR product as the liquor people do i.e. with attractive or shocking pictures and with very fitting slogans.[63]

Kok received moral and financial support from the WCTU and SATA. Where he crossed the line was in seeking to gain direct access to farmworkers. In 1966, Kok was apprehended on a wine farm, beaten unconscious and then eventually deported on the basis that it was not in the public interest for him to remain in the country. Evidently, he had stepped on some influential toes, and the summary manner of his expulsion indicated that the government was inclined to side with the farmers, despite the fact there were many in the DRC who had their own moral misgivings about the dop system.

Conclusion

With the amendment to the 1928 Liquor Act in 1962, all South Africans were legally entitled to drink wine, spirits and bottled beer, regardless of their racial classification, even if drinking spaces remained strictly segregated. Curiously, racialized prohibition was ended at precisely the moment when the NP government was doubling down on apartheid. In this chapter, I have attempted to explain this apparent disjuncture. It is significant that the most far-reaching

[63] CA A1696 "Women's Christian Temperance Union", B. E. Kok. Western Cape Farm Workers Association, Paarl, to President, WCTU of SA and Rhodesia (17 April 1965).

change to the liquor laws started out as a more narrowly focused attempt to block vertical integration within the liquor industry – a longstanding preoccupation of the KWV. Although some of that agenda stuck, the decision to enquire more broadly into the state of the alcohol industry led to the opening of an altogether juicier can of worms.

The Wine Commission played a catalytic role in that it publicly acknowledged that the existing liquor laws were being routinely flouted, traffickers were garnering substantial economic rents, and the police were being stretched to breaking point. Evidently, there was a pragmatic calculus lurking behind the amendment, given that freeing up access to alcohol would enable the authorities to concentrate resources on implementing other aspects of urban apartheid. But it also marked a significant departure from the principle that Black people were inherently different and could never be treated as akin to citizens bearing equal rights. Not surprisingly, legislative debates skirted around the question of the right to drink, but what was striking was an acceptance that all putative racial groups were ultimately driven by similar desires and calculations as to the benefits of remaining within the law. Finally, the wine lobby, realizing that the temperance cause had lost ground, sensed that the moment was ripe for a revision of the laws in its favour. Although the farmers were the intended beneficiaries, the merchant-manufacturing interests were presented with the enticing prospect of selling wine to a greatly enlarged consumer market.

5 Bureaucracy without the State

The KWV System and Its Discontents, 1962–1986

In Chapter 6, I reveal how the structures of marketing and patterns of consumption altered, following the revisions to the liquor laws in the early 1960s. But before doing so, I will dissect what we may reasonably call the 'KWV system'.[1] It was systemic in the sense that it comprised a series of interlocking components that were devised to address the structural problems confronting the wine industry. The regulatory framework drew on models that had a wider currency, especially in Europe. Nevertheless, the manner in which the pieces were assembled, together with the sequencing thereof, reflected significant differences. This merits meticulous analysis because the KWV system set the parameters within which innovation was variously facilitated and impeded, rewarded and punished.

Whether the net consequences were positive or regressive has tended to elicit rather different responses. No less of a luminary than Maynard Amerine could assert that the KWV was the singlemost important factor driving the improvement in quality in South African wines.[2] In his own finely documented history of the KWV, published on the eve of its demise, Diko Van Zyl could still argue for the overall beneficial effects of stabilization.[3] Even Spatz Sperling, who will feature prominently as this chapter unfolds, could look back on the system as a historical necessity that avoided cycles of boom and bust.[4] However, as the industry faced up to the realities of overproduction in the mid-1980s, many were inclined to blame an excess of misplaced intervention. This shift of opinion was especially evident amongst the ranks of

[1] The KWV was not responsible for every element, but it had a stake and a say across the board. The fact that it considered its role holistically is apparent from its own public documents. See for example, KWV, *Some Aspects of the Functions of and Control Exercised by the K.W.V.* (Paarl: KWV, 1969).

[2] Amerine bemoaned the fact that in California it was the Universities rather than the industry that were left to channel innovation. Maynard Amerine, University of California–Davis lecture 10 (undated, but possibly in 1972), www.youtube.com/watch?v=S-e7zNQ0p3Yfrom minute 37. In the same lecture, he highlighted the difficulty of dissuading Californian producers from planting grapes in the wrong places – such as Pinot Noir in Fresno.

[3] Van Zyl, *KWV*, pp. 292–293.

[4] Interview with Spatz Sperling, 20 April 2007.

independent producers who strove to chisel out a niche in the interstices between the cooperatives and the merchant-manufacturers.

Much as international influences shaped regulation, the impetus for change was driven by an awareness of emerging trends elsewhere. At a purely technical level, South Africa benefited from the exchange of information that was afforded by its membership of l'Office International du Vin at le Vigne (OIV) with effect from 1962.[5] The latest trends were amply documented in the pages of *Wynboer*, but a feeling that things could be managed differently was also fed by the annual cycle of European study tours and research exchanges with overseas institutions, notably Geisenheim and the University of California-Davis. It is surely no coincidence that many of those who helped to articulate the need for change came from outside the charmed circle either because they were immigrants, like Sperling or Giorgio Dalla Cia, or because they were English-speaking and/or Jewish, as was the case with Cyril and Sydney Back. Recent immigrants also exercised an influence out of all proportion to their numbers. Leading the way were two Hungarians, Dr. Julius Laszlo of the Bergkelder, and Desiderius Pongracz, initially of the Viticultural and Oenological Research Unit (VORI) in Nietvoorbij. They vied for influence with another German immigrant and Weinsberg graduate, Günter Brözel, who had been appointed winemaker in Nederburg in 1956, and cemented his authority within the SFW over the course of the 1970s.[6] At a time of increasing international isolation, their European contacts were of fundamental importance in the reception and dissemination of the latest thinking. More specifically, their activism emboldened an emerging generation of farmers to embrace new cultivars, especially those that were both red and 'noble', and to embrace the use of oak barrels in maturation. The frustration they gave vent to threw into sharp relief the heavy-handed manner in which regulation was applied in practice.

The KWV and the State

In the case of France, Leo Loubère describes the Institut National des Appellations d'Origine (INAO) as a 'private organization with a public mission'[7] – private in the sense that it was composed of representatives of the producer associations, or *syndicats*, but public in that it was sustained by subsidies. In South Africa, the KWV enjoyed a greater degree of operational autonomy from government, while there was nothing comparable to syndicats at the district level. This strengthened the hand of the KWV in sometimes

[5] Piet Venter brokered this before moving to Distillers the following year. Chris Venter, *History of Die Bergkelder* (unpublished and undated manuscript), Distell Archive, Stellenbosch, p. 18.
[6] Interview with Günter Brözel, 18 August 2009. [7] Loubère, *Wine Revolution*, p. 123.

surprising ways.[8] Successive National Party (NP) governments were content to leave the KWV to get on with things, which is one reason why there are precious few documents relating to wine in the archives. The Minister of Agriculture typically adjudicated only when disputes arose. According to Phillip Myburgh, the owner of Joostenberg and an opposition MP through the 1970/80s, wine was only ever discussed in Parliament when duties were debated as part of the budget.[9] The state had a direct financial stake in the shape of the excise duty, which often contributed handsomely to government coffers. Despite furious lobbying on the part of the KWV, the duties on spirits, sparkling and fortified wines almost doubled in 1958, and in 1962 these were applied to drinking wine as well. The excise duties continued to climb until the late 1970s, when there was a decline again.[10] Raising duties exposed the limits of KWV influence, but the flip side was that it could be used to justify a countervailing case for favourable consideration in other areas. Because many Cabinet ministers were drawn from the farming community and KWV leaders were members of the Broederbond,[11] those in power were naturally sympathetic to the wine-farming interest and protective of the KWV.

The KWV mimicked the language and practices of the state despite the fact that it was formally a cooperative performing devolved functions. By maintaining an operational distance from the bureaucracy, it forced the government to accept its right to author the script and to assign roles to the various actors in the industry. At the same time, the KWV also operated as a commercial entity which contributed to the tense relationship with the merchant-manufacturers, who complained that it combined the role of gamekeeper and poacher. The KWV's obsession with manipulating the 'world of paper' resided in the micro-management of the fundamental unit of production, namely the individual wine farm. By extension, it also came to know a great deal about every producer who was necessarily a member of the association and, in all likelihood, also a member of a cooperative. If, to use James C. Scott's felicitous phrase, the state had an interest in rendering the population legible,[12] the KWV had an equal interest in minutely documenting the activities of its members. The latter could apply pressure to the elected directors, but the professional managers sought to maintain their operational autonomy,

[8] Danie de Wet recalled that André du Toit issued ultimatums that resulted in the summary sackings of two Cabinet Ministers. Interview, 16 October 2009.

[9] Interview with Philip Myburgh Snr, 27 February 2009.

[10] KWV, *Some Aspects*, p. 15.

[11] Interview with Philip Myburgh Snr, 27 February 2009. Curiously, studies of Afrikaner nationalism have said little about the KWV. There is a passing reference in Dan O'Meara, *Volkskapitalisme: Class, Capital and Ideology in the Development of Afrikaner Nationalism, 1934–1948* (Cambridge: Cambridge University Press, 1983), p. 99. More surprisingly, the KWV receives no mention in Giliomee, *The Afrikaners*.

[12] James C. Scott, *Seeing Like a State: How Certain Schemes to Improve the Human Condition Have Failed* (New Haven, CT: Yale University Press, 1999), p. 2.

which inevitably created some internal friction with the membership.[13] The way in which the KWV snooped on individual farmers and went after those who were regarded as being in breach of the regulations became a source of constant irritation even to those who considered themselves loyalists. But the KWV leadership had also learned something from its near break-up in the interwar years and was generally sensitive to serious rumblings of discontent. A preference for not airing dirty linen in public meant that even when there were disagreements, they scarcely went beyond the four walls of the headquarters in Paarl. It helped that the Afrikaans-language press, most notably *Die Burger*, was disinclined to cause embarrassment to the NP or the KWV. In what follows, I will provide a detailed anatomy of some of the constituent elements in the KWV system and show how the pieces worked together to forge a highly elaborate system of regulation.

Curbing Production: The Quota System

As I have already indicated, it was the looming spectre of overproduction that justified the passage of the Wine and Spirits Control Amendment Act (No. 23) of 1940.[14] The main purpose of the legislation was to extend the principle of minimum pricing to 'good' wine, but it also empowered the KWV to fix the maximum quantity of wine that the holder of a permit was allowed to produce.[15] The KWV understood perfectly well that overproduction was the greatest threat to the long-term viability of the industry. The quota allocation was initially supposed to be based on the maximum quantity produced by a farmer in the previous couple of years along with an assessment of the number of vines planted at the time of the coming into force of the legislation in November 1940.[16] A Quota Committee was vested with responsibility for carrying out inspections on each farm. However, the system was not implemented immediately, in part because there was actually a shortage of wine spirit which required the introduction of a form of rationing (or 'pooling'). But when production levels began to climb steeply in the early 1950s, the imperative to restrict production returned. The KWV felt that the existing legislation was cumbersome because it tied the quota to the person of the farmer whose circumstances might change from year to year. For this reason, the Minister of Agriculture was persuaded to introduce a further legislative amendment that bound the production quota to the farm itself. The Wine and Spirits Control Act (No. 38) of 1956 redefined the quota as 'the maximum quantity of wine calculated at a strength of ten per cent which may be produced on such farm or

[13] I am grateful to an anonymous reviewer for pointing this out.
[14] This was replaced by the Wine and Spirit Control Act, No. 47, of 1970. [15] Article 9.
[16] Van Zyl, *KWV*, p. 133.

Figure 5.1 Malmesbury Quota Committee 1957
Source: Reproduced with kind acknowledgement of KWV. Copy in author's possession.

subdivision during any year'.[17] An additional amendment of 1957 (No. 49) tidied up the supporting legislation. The KWV then set about estimating the production potential of each wine farm, considering the number of vines that had already been purchased for planting and those that were still coming into bearing (Figure 5.1).[18] The sheer complexity of the exercise meant that the system only became fully operational in 1960.

The rolling out of the quota system was intended to produce a comprehensive mechanism for collecting data and policing compliance. This was achieved by requiring the farmers to keep thorough records and to submit regular updated returns to the KWV. Although the quota was initially designed to take into account historical production figures, it was not intended to freeze

[17] The initial formulation was 20 per cent, which was a reference to the sugar reading on the saccharometer. This was subsequently amended to refer to 10 per cent strength by volume. The relevant clause states that "one hectolitre of wine of a strength of 20 per cent shall from 1 January 1981 be reckoned to be the equivalent of one comma one five (1,15) hectolitres of wine of a strength of ten per cent alcohol by volume."

[18] Van Zyl, *KWV*, p. 142.

the map of production for all time. Provided the demand for wine was sufficiently robust, there was an expectation that fresh applications for quotas would be entertained from time to time, as indeed they were.[19] Equally, where vineyards went out of production, the farms would forfeit their quotas, thereby helping to restore the overall equilibrium. On applying, a farmer was required to submit to the KWV a sketch plan that clearly laid out the boundaries of the farm in question. Thereafter it was allocated a number and a quota which considered what had previously been produced and the extra output that might be expected to accrue from immature vines. Kallie Hickman, a retired senior quota inspector, recalls that some account was also taken of the quality of the soil, whether the grape varietals in question were heavy- or shy-bearing and the marked differences in the productivity of the vines in particular districts. All this information was used to work backwards to a notional tonnage of grapes that a farm might be expected to produce.[20] In the event that the quota committee did not have all the information it required, it was empowered to issue a provisional quota. Only once a quota was formally approved was the farmer issued with a permit to produce wine. Over time, the system was rendered somewhat more flexible, to take account of a scenario where a farmer over-produced in one year but under-produced in another, or where the introduction of new machinery and methods of production led to greater efficiency. Moreover, where there seemed to be enough slack in the system, the Minister of Agriculture could invite applications for conditional additional quotas.[21] These were to be valid for a period of 66 months and, on their expiry, farmers were entitled to apply for a permanent additional quota. Appeals against quota allocation could be made to a board of appeal, whose ruling was considered 'final and binding'.

In addition to gathering basic data on individual farms, the KWV went to great lengths to update the records and to monitor any changes in the profile of a farm. Firstly, the farmers were given 15 days from 30 October of each year to supply detailed information about the vineyards on a form known as KC1. The farmer was required to specify the grape varieties, the number of vines that were or were not irrigated, the hectarage that was or was not trellised as well as details on rootstocks. The farmer was also obliged to provide details on the vines that were a year old or more, those which had been planted more recently and others that had been uprooted in the preceding 12 months. Where a

19 Statement of Minister of Agriculture during second reading of *Debatte van die Volksraad*, 7 June 1957, column 7772.

20 Interview with Kallie Hickman, 16 January 2009.

21 The KWV was concerned that any new plantings resulting from the additional quotas should be from varieties deemed suitable to the soil and climate, although it had little control over that aspect. "New Year's Message from André J. du Toit (Chairman of the K.W.V.)", *Wynboer*, January 1972, p. 13.

previous return had been submitted, the farmer filled out a version of the form that updated the return from the previous year in a manner that was only slightly less onerous. With this information, it was possible for the KWV to anticipate what the grape production of an individual farm was likely to be and, therefore, whether or not it would comply with the quota that had been allocated. Secondly, farmers were expected to apply before 31 July for a permit to produce wine in the coming year, and then they were given up to 14 days after 30 November to submit form K3 that provided details on the upcoming vintage. The farmers needed to estimate the tonnage of grapes intended for winemaking, consumption as grapes and the making of raisins, sultanas or currants. Once the wine was produced, the farmers were required to submit form KC 11, detailing all the good and distilling wine that had been produced. In addition, the farmer had to submit form KC12 which detailed the 'gross mass of grapes of each variety … and the average degrees sugar (Balling) of each such variety'. Cooperatives took in the grapes from their members and carried out the vinification in their own cellars. In this case, they were obliged to submit form KC19 which documented the grape varieties, the weight of the grapes and the sugar reading with respect to each delivery they received. They also needed to submit a return detailing the types of wine and quantities produced (KC14), ideally after pressing had been completed, but certainly before 30 June of each year.

On-site inspection was routinely carried out by officials from Customs and Excise, which removed some of the burden of cross-checking from the KWV. For this reason, Hickman recalled that a team of KWV inspectors initially only consisted of four people, although this later increased along with the work-load.[22] The linkage between the Excise and the KWV was an important one because the information that was supplied to the former was routinely shared with the latter. Moreover, the KWV was legally mandated to act with the same authority as Excise officers. Hence the legislation stated that:

> Any excise officer authorised thereto in writing by the Commissioner of Customs and Excise, and any official of the vereniging so authorized by the vereniging may at any time enter upon any premises occupied or used by any such person, distiller or holder of a permit, and may examine and take stock of any article whatsoever on such premises.[23]

KWV officials were entitled to inspect vineyards and cellars without notice and to demand samples and access to stock books, while non-compliance was a criminal offence. The latter is illustrative of the state-like properties assumed by the KWV. Some farmers who received a criminal record for failing to

[22] Interview with Hickman, 16 January 2009. I am grateful to him for talking me through all of these forms.

[23] Article 11 of Wine and Spirits Amendment Act of 1946.

supply the KWV with the relevant documentation, took a certain vicarious pleasure in subverting the micro-regulation that the KWV revelled in.[24]

The quota system was fundamental to keeping overall production within the bounds of what could be absorbed on the domestic market or otherwise exported. But it inevitably created rigidities. Firstly, there was a de facto bias towards farms that were already in production as against possible newcomers. It equally tended to privilege older districts over newer ones, with one major exception. There is general agreement that the fateful decision to allocate quotas to the Orange River was driven by acute political pressure applied to André du Toit by the Minister of Agriculture, Dirkie Uys.[25] Hickman recalled that the farmers of Vredendal subsequently considered that they had been poorly treated in the initial allocation of quotas because they were not producing much wine in 1960. They also considered it especially unjust that fresh quotas were allocated to producers in Upington who they considered had less of a claim because they did not have a previous history of wine production.[26] Secondly, it was often the case that a farm with considerable potential received an inadequate quota whereas a farm that was less endowed received a more favourable allocation. There were suspicions that people who were politically connected influenced the way in which the quotas were allocated. Brözel noted that there were striking anomalies, such as when a farmer with a hundred hectares received a quota of 2,000 tonnes whereas another farmer with a thousand hectares was allocated 150 tonnes.[27] In Paarl, Fairview received a relatively generous quota, which Charles Back attributed to the probable influence exercised by a member of the Broederbond who happened to own a farm nearby.[28] An inadequate quota meant that wine farmers often had to engage in other kinds of farming activity to make a profit. Two cases in point are Joostenburg (Stellenbosch) and Backsberg (Paarl), which resorted to pig and chicken farming, respectively.[29] Many farmers also resorted to fruit production to make ends meet, as was the case at Simonsig.[30]

Inevitably, farmers sought to find creative ways around the quota regulations. One tactic was to acquire a farm that had reached the ceiling of its permitted production and another that was under-producing. While a case

24 Interview with François Malan, Stellenbosch, 25 July 2009. Van Zyl, *Frans Malan*, p. 76.

25 Interviews with Braam Van Velden, 5 August 2009, and with Danie de Wet, 16 October 2009.

26 Interview with Kallie Hickman, 16 January 2009.

27 Interview with Günter Brözel, 18 August 2009.

28 Presumably because it would have looked like corruption if only his farm benefited, all the farmers in the vicinity received more favourable quota allocation. Interview with Charles Back, 17 April 2007.

29 The Joostenburg farm records are suggestive, but this was also confirmed in interview with Phillip Myburgh Snr, 26 February 2009. For Backsberg, see Back, *70 Years*, pp. 23–29.

30 Simonsig had 60 hectares under fruit on account of the lack of quota. Interview with François Malan, 25 July 2009.

could be made for increasing the quota on the first farm, it might also be possible to pass off some of the over-production to the second farm. It was precisely for this reason that strict rules were imposed that made it compulsory to press the grapes on the specified farm unless they were delivering them to a cooperative cellar. Farmers were expressly prohibited from sharing cellar facilities, and in one instance Spatz Sperling of Delheim and Frans Malan of Simonsig were caught red-handed as they were moving grapes from one farm to the other.[31] In an obvious manner, the control system was self-defeating. It was in the interests of farmers to push their production to the limits of the quota, lest it be cut back, but also because that made it possible to apply for an additional quota. Crucially, the farmers had no incentive to curb yields to optimize quality. Over time, the KWV introduced more flexible rules that, for example, enabled quotas to be consolidated between farms that belonged to a single owner. Right at the end, it even became possible to buy and sell quotas independently of the farms. But, as Hickman recalled, the system was extremely complex, and each reform created fresh anomalies and further incentives for evasion.

The broad lesson is that while the quota system successfully restricted the extension of vineyards to new districts, it did not serve to scale back plantings or overall production. Hence, during the 1970s, when the regulatory system was in full flight, the number of new vines planted consistently exceeded the number of vines that were cut out (see Table 5.1). The cumulative impact of a year-on-year augmentation of the stock of young vines inevitably translated into rising levels of production. Whereas the total wine crop increased rather modestly from 5,308,041 hl. in 1965 to 6,639,015 hl. in 1975, it climbed to as much as 8,766,753 hl. in 1987 (Table 5.2).

Price Control and Surplus Disposal

The quota system was always intended to operate alongside two of the original pillars of KWV regulation, namely, a system of minimum pricing and a mechanism for the disposal of the annual surplus. The first was supposed to balance the need to secure a viable income for the farmer, with the imperative of discouraging mass plantings. The second was designed to ensure that any excess wine would not be released onto the domestic market. After 1940, there was never any question of the KWV destroying the surplus as it had done in

[31] KWV, *Quota Control Survey* (Paarl: KWV, 1988), p. 11. They were caught by KWV inspectors as they sought to move grapes from Delheim to Simonsig because of a problem of capacity on the former farm. Discussion with Spatz Sperling, 21 April 2007. Frans Malan was a long-standing critic of the quota system, but agreed to stand as one of the two KWV directors for Stellenbosch in 1983 when Niel Joubert of Spier stepped down. He served until 1991.

Table 5.1. *Vines planted and cut out, and production, 1970–1981*

Year	Hectares Planted	Hectares Cut Out	Increase in Hectarage of Vines
1970	3,726.70	2,564.00	1,162.7
1971	5,103.34	2,407.38	2,696.06
1972	8,275.60	2,133.62	6,141.99
1973	9,073.43	2,452.37	6,621.06
1974	8,280.24	3,714.80	4,565.44
1975	10,103.54	2,562.04	7,451.50
1976	5,604.50	2,432.40	3,172.10
1977	4,459.04	3,405.07	1,143.97
1978	5,370.50	3,585.86	1,784.64
1979	5,174.04	3,902.67	1,271.37
1980	4,471.52	3,393.88	1,077.64
1981	5,163.07	5,572.69	−409.62

Source: KWV, 'Statistieke van Wingerdstokke', published in *Wynboer*, various years.

Table 5.2. *Total wine harvest, 1965–1987*

Year	Wine Harvest, Hectolitres @10% Alcohol by Volume
1965	5,308,041
1970	5,071,363
1975	6,939,015
1976	6,930,204
1977	5,538,321
1978	7,162,316
1979	7,237,339
1980	8,243,554
1981	7,594,573
1982	8,929,988
1983	9,117,804
1984	8,976,171
1985	8,262,259
1986	7,619,418
1987	8,766,753

Source: KWV, *Statistics Survey Nr 12: 1988*, table, 2.5.1., p. 9.

the early years. Each year, the KWV would estimate what percentage of national production could be absorbed and how much of it was surplus.[32] The latter had to be delivered free of charge to the KWV, which distilled the alcohol into brandies and used wine spirit for the fortification of liqueurs.

32 The assumption was that all 'good wine' would be absorbed by the market while the remainder was channelled into distillation.

To ensure that the merchants did not subvert minimum pricing, another layer of bureaucracy was introduced by the KWV. A farmer was obliged to keep a stock book that could be inspected at any time, which provided details on the good wine and fortified wine in their possession. This had to be updated at the beginning and close of very month. Where a merchant wished to purchase wine, a contract of purchase was drawn up (KC8A for good and KC8C for distilling wine), which had to be approved by the KWV. Samples were also taken because the price was determined according to the alcoholic strength of the wine in question. The merchants were free to pay producers at above the minimum prices but were not allowed to drop below them. The purchase price was calculated as a cellar-door figure and the date for delivery of the wine was fixed. Where there was a delay in collection, the price to the merchant was increased to take account of storage costs and interest.[33] The entire transaction was mediated by the KWV, which issued the invoice to the merchant on behalf of the farmer or co-operative and monitored the completion of the transaction. All wine that was removed from a farm under a purchase agreement had to be documented on the relevant forms. The wholesale merchants were also required to submit a monthly return both to the KWV and the Excise office, detailing where they had acquired their stock from, listing the farmer/cooperative, contract number and price.

The surplus disposal mechanism was intended to be flexible enough to allow for an adjustment after the wine had eventually been disposed of. Although the farmers or cooperatives were paid according to the declared annual surplus, they would receive an *agterskot*, or bonus, on distilling wine that was successfully disposed of by the KWV. By agreement with the merchant-manufacturers, the KWV was not permitted to sell its products in the South African market, which placed a premium on developing an export market for brandy and liqueurs. It was these sales that enabled the KWV to top up the earnings of the farmers. However, the growing force of the international boycott of South African goods from the late 1970s onwards squeezed these alternative outlets. The danger was that if the KWV was too generous in its pricing policies and too accommodating in its management of the quotas, it would be left drowning in a veritable brandy lake.

Certification of Origin

The third piece in the regulatory jigsaw was the certification of Wines of Origin (WO), which came into effect in September 1973. This needs to be

[33] In practice, the SFW and the farmers who supplied them were content to store the wines on the farms until the next harvest. This meant that company did not need to maintain greater storage capacity, while ensuring that the vats were full reduced the risk of contamination for the farmers. Interview with Braam Van Velden, 5 August 2009.

viewed against the backdrop of European pressure for designation of origin and accurate information about specific varietals contained in imported wines. South Africa had already agreed to renounce the use of French names such as Champagne and Burgundy, under the Crayfish agreement of 1935, and this was reconfirmed by government notices in 1962.[34] But it became increasingly clear that South Africa needed to formulate its own nomenclature if it wanted to secure non-discriminatory access to the European market.[35] The pressure intensified with the expected accession of Britain, a leading export market, to the European Economic Community (EEC). However, the Chairman of the KWV, André du Toit, indicated that the scheme had been introduced partly also in response to demands from farmers in the historic wine-producing areas. He observed that the expansion of wine production in new districts, notably along the Orange and Olifants rivers, carried serious implications for the established districts:

> Production has in recent years also expanded to new districts in the hinterland regions with much higher production, under irrigation, per unit area of land. I would not claim that they cannot make good wine, I would not even claim that they cannot make such good wines as the Western Cape can make. What I would claim is that their wine will necessarily differ from that of the Boland; it will be of a different character; and that they will still have to show what they can deliver. They will still have to deliver the proof that they will obtain the same reputation here and overseas in terms of their quality that the wines of the Western Cape have gained.[36]

Du Toit was evidently treading carefully, acknowledging the aspirations towards quality production in the older districts whilst taking account of the demands for equal treatment in the newer, irrigated ones. That this remained a contentious issue is clear from the following statement made by Sperling as he reflected on the significance of the WO legislation after its first year in operation:

> It should now also be possible for one district to prove that its Pinotage, for instance, is better than Pinotage from another district. As a Stellenbosch farmer I was concerned for the survival of the older wine districts. With this legislation we can now prove that wines from Stellenbosch are, indeed, different from or 'better' than wines from newer or lesser-known regions. Again speaking subjectively, it would have been terrible had wines from areas with lower production costs such as the Orange River and Northern

[34] In the 1950s, South Africa also came under pressure to agree to renounce the use of the terms 'sherry' and 'port', while in the early 1960s Italy and West Germany were similarly pushing for protection on their own names. Secretary for Commerce to Secretary for Agriculture (15 March 1963), National Archives (Pretoria), TS 18/11 Vol. 1: "Wine Industry".

[35] The threat was the EEC would impose penalties on wine from outside the Community that did not conform to its specifications. Van Zyl, *KWV*, p. 205.

[36] Quoted in Reg Weiss, "The truth on wine labels", *Wynboer*, June 1974, p. 51.

Cape been able to swamp the expensively-produced wines form the traditional areas. If the new wine-producing areas can prove themselves superior so much the better.[37]

Strictly speaking, the production costs were higher in the irrigated areas, but the yields were also considerably more bountiful. In the 1972–1973 season, the highest production and labour costs were estimated to fall in Regions III *anderkant die berg* (Rawsonville, Robertson and Bonnievale) and IV (Orange River and Olifants River). The lowest costs were incurred in Region I (Stellenbosch, Paarl, Wellington and Malmesbury). But whereas a farmer might harvest 7.6 tonnes of grapes per hectare in Region I, a farmer in Region IV could expect 21.8 tonnes, while the national average stood at 11.65 tonnes.[38] It was therefore important for farmers in Region I to be able to protect their claim to be quality producers based on their more parsimonious yields. The WO system can therefore be seen as the outcome of a much older struggle to balance the interests of different wine-producing districts by acknowledging their distinct endowments.

The third reason for the introduction of the legislation resided in active lobbying by an emergent coterie of independent producers. In the late 1960s, farmers became increasingly dissatisfied with being forced to deliver their wines to the merchant-manufacturers and/or the cooperatives. They aspired to produce wine in their own cellars, and to bottle and market it under their own labels. This was, in turn, related to anticipated shifts within the consumer market. At the more affluent end of the drinking spectrum, there was mounting interest in red wines and with cultivars such as Cabernet Sauvignon and Shiraz that were most closely associated with France. Despite the Huguenot heritage to which many Afrikaners liked to lay claim, the cultural links with France were limited. This began to change, partly because of rugby touring in the 1960s. Given that there was such a close connection between rugby and winemaking in the South African context,[39] the importance of sport as a vector of fashion should not be underestimated. Initially, consumers were less familiar with French wines, but this changed as greater numbers of White South Africans took holidays abroad or merely read about European wine in glossy magazines. At the same time, some winemakers like Jan 'Boland' Coetzee opted to go to France for their overseas training, which was important in terms

37 Spatz Sperling quoted in Weiss, "The truth", p. 63.

38 [Anon.] "Produksiekoste van wyndruiwe in die produksiejaar 1972/73", *Wynboer*, May 1974, p. 27.

39 Many players who represented Western Province or Boland and played for the Springboks were winemakers and farmers. This included Jan 'Boland' Coetzee, Jannie Engelbrecht of Rust en Vreede and Hempies du Toit of Alto. Rugby was equally strong in French wine-growing regions, which solidified the bond.

of bringing about a shift in the basic approach to winemaking. As Giorgio Dalla Cia explained:

> In '74 I came here in South Africa and in '78 I went to Meerlust. And in '78 I started to apply French technology, contrary to the technology that was still taught at the University here. As an example of the red wine, they were fermenting the red wine down to 8 Ballings, from 24 let's say, down to 8, and then drawing off and finishing the fermentation in the tank. In the very beginning they were very much against the malolactic fermentation. That was a typical German approach, where I went completely the opposite and went to the French approach. And I started to win all the prizes in the wine show. Then a lot of people realized it's much better to ferment completely it dry on the skin and then they learned to keep it a little longer on the skin.[40]

Meerlust was one of the earliest to adopt the maturation of wines in French oak barrels. This shift was closely connected with a surge in interest in the classic French red varietals.

Those who considered themselves aficionados were increasingly attracted to associations that were exclusive in character. Again, it was France rather than Germany that provided the point of reference. A handful of South Africans, who were involved in the wine trade or in wine writing, had become honorary members of the Confrérie des Chevaliers du Tastevin in Burgundy.[41] One of these, Tinus Van Niekerk, initiated the Les Chevaliers du Tastevin de Pretoria in the early 1960s, with restrictive membership rules and elaborate rites of passage along the lines of the Burgundian parent.[42] The Stellenbosch Wine Circle was formed at almost the same time and the two groups vied for the claim to being the first such association. In 1964, Les Tastevins du Cap was launched as a separate chapter and was later enabled to publish its newsletter in the pages of *Wynboer*. In the 1970s, wine appreciation societies proliferated on university campuses and in the principal towns across the country, as can also be gauged from the information pages of *Wynboer*. For the participants, it was all about (re)connecting to a wine world, at a time when White South Africa was smarting from isolation. For those who really invested in the cult of Bacchus, the tastings would typically involve the best wines that Europe had to offer pitted against their up-and-coming South African equivalents. Bragging rights resided in being the first to discover a new wine before anyone else had come to know of its existence. François Naudé, who at various points chaired the Pretoria Tastevins and the Stellenbosch Wine Circle, claims that it was the feedback that the wine guilds imparted that encouraged the farmers to

[40] Interview with Giorgio Dalla Cia, 17 March 2009.

[41] Interview with François Naudé, 31 August 2009.

[42] Van Niekerk was later awarded Officer of the Ordre du Mérite Agricole by the French government for his services to the industry. After an academic career, he joined the Rebel Liquor Group and was responsible for the importation of champagne and other premium French wines.

embrace noble red cultivars.[43] The wine companies were quick to spot emerging fashions and encouraged their favoured farmers to plant red cultivars that would do particularly well under South African conditions. Brözel was forthright about where he felt the future lay:

> I do not like to make an Olympic Games out of comparing wines but even the French would be impressed if they were to discover what the standard of our red wines in South Africa really are [sic]. I am referring specifically to our Cabernet Sauvignon, which does better in South Africa than France, but the same applies to our other noble red wines. Cabernet Sauvignon is singularly outstanding in South Africa and with a little selection and care in our vineyards it would be difficult for anyone to beat us.[44]

The farmers apparently required some persuasion because most of their vineyards were dominated by white varietals. Meanwhile, there was a veritable rush to acquire varietal-specific red wines on the part of affluent White consumers. One commentator wryly commented:

> Since 1972 it has been the 'in thing' to rush for an invest [sic] in red wine. And the 'innest thing' is to serve Cabernet – in particular – on all eating occasions. Mass news coverage created the mass hysteria, which resulted in buyers queuing for 'noble reds' as they would normally do for rugby tickets.[45]

If the farmers were to replant their vineyards, they needed to be reasonably confident that they would recoup their investments. Initially, the merchant-manufacturers continued to buy wine from the farmers who bottled their own wines but as the trend intensified, they became less accommodating. In 1973, the SFW declined to buy any more wine from Simonsig unless they ceased bottling their own products.[46] Frans Malan later came to see this as the jolt they needed to strike out independently. Difficult as it was to build a brand from scratch, many farmers felt it was worth the effort because the amount that accrued on each bottle sold was appreciably greater. This refocused attention on the divisive issues surrounding nomenclature and labelling. The independents' claims to distinctiveness hinged on the notion that the grapes were produced and the wine vinified on a clearly defined 'estate'. The problem was that the merchant-manufacturers were already using estate nomenclature even though they sourced their grapes from a wide area. The *Nederburg* range became the flagship of the SFW following the acquisition of the farm in the context of the takeover of Monis Wineries in 1966. Although the implication

[43] Interview with François Naudé, 31 August 2009.

[44] Quoted in Weiss, "Red wine '72: the greatest – if you can get it", *Wynboer*, April 1974, p. 36.

[45] Arnold Helfet, "Wine tasting the lighthearted way", *Wynboer*, February 1975, p. 50 (reprinted from *Cape Times*).

[46] C. W. White, "The creation and development of a South African wine estate, the wines produced and the positioning thereof in the market place", unpublished report, February 2000, p. 16.

was that *Nederburg* wine came from the estate of that name, the grapes were sourced from many different farms.[47] In the case of *Zonnebloem*, the SFW had acquired the right to the trademark and sold a range of wines under the label whereas the farm of that name had ceased producing wine in 1963 and thereafter simply sold their grapes to a cooperative.[48]

In 1969, a handful of farmers established what eventually came to be known as the Cape Estate Wine Producers Association (CEWPA), in an endeavour to promote the shared agenda of the independent producers. The core group included a number of the usual suspects: N. C. Krone, Frans Malan, Spatz Sperling, De Wet Theron, David van Velden and Sydney Back.[49] One of its first interventions was to send a memorandum to government demanding a commission of enquiry to look into wine nomenclature. In this they were supported by the KWV, which had its own longstanding quarrel with the merchant-manufacturers.[50] The Minister of Agriculture agreed to establish an internal commission of enquiry. Predictably, the merchants, who were organized in the Cape Wine and Spirits Institute (CWSI), faced off against the KWV and CEWPA. Eventually, a compromise was reached which led to a distinction between wines that were made, bottled and sold from a single registered estate and those where the wine was made on the estate, but bottled and sold elsewhere.[51] The difference between these types of estate wine was to be reflected on the labels. The CWSI also won the concession that the name of a wine farm could be registered as a brand. This enabled the SFW to protect the *Nederburg* name, although it could not be labelled as estate wine. The *Zonnebloem* brand could also continue without even a link to a specific estate. Despite the concessions to the merchant-manufacturers, the introduction of the WO regulations was claimed as a victory by the independent producers in their quest to promote the authenticity of their product.

The WO framework was predicated on the identification of features unique to each area. The information booklet that was put out by the KWV explained that:

> Within the broad framework of the South African wine-growing regions, there are numerous differences in soil, climate and location. The environmental factors in the Robertson district are, for example, completely different from those obtained in the

47 Van Zyl, *Frans Malan*, p.43.

48 It is not entirely clear when the word estate ceased to appear on Zonnebloem labels, but this seems to have happened around 1969. Venter, "Story", unpublished manuscript, 2010, Distell Archive, pp. 26, 28.

49 The executive posts appear to have moved between them. Malan recalled that he was chairman and Sperling was secretary. But at one point Back was chairman and Braam Van Velden was secretary. See Van Zyl, *Frans Malan*, p. 44; Back, *70 Years*; interview with Braam Van Velden, 5 August 2009.

50 Van Zyl, *Frans Malan*, p. 46.

51 Van Zyl, *KWV*, p. 202.

Table 5.3. *Wine of origin classification: Regions, districts, wards*

Boberg Region	Breede River Valley Region	Coastal Region	Olifants River (Region Only)	Lower Orange (Region Only)	District Only	Ward Only
Tulbagh	Worcester *5 Wards*: Aan die Doorns, Agterkliphoogte, Goudini, Nuy, Slanghoek	Tulbagh			Piquetberg	Cederberg
Paarl	Robertson *9 Wards*: Boesmanrivier, Eilandia, Goree, Hoopsrivier, Le Chasseur, McGregor, Riverside, Scherpenheuvel, Vinkrivier	Swartland *2 Wards*: Groenekloof, Riebeekberg			Klein Karoo	Vaalharts
	Swellendam *1 Ward*: Bonnievale	Paarl *1 Ward*: Franschhoek			Overberg *1 Ward*: Walker Bay	
		Constantia				
		Durbanville				
		Stellenbosch *1 Ward*: Simonsberg				

Source: KWV, *Wines of Origin*, undated.

Stellenbosch district. The result is that the wines from these two districts differ from one another and are peculiar to their particular origin.

The certification system laid out a spatial hierarchy with 5 designated regions, 12 districts, 22 wards and a number of estates that was not fixed (see Table 5.3). The KWV published a booklet outlining the soil, climate, cultivars and style of wines characteristic of each designation, but in a loose and non-prescriptive sense.[52] Producers could apply to have their wine classified according to any of these levels depending on where they sourced their grapes from. The classification was complicated by the fact that Tulbagh and Paarl districts were split between the Boberg and the Coastal Regions in a manner that was never very clearly articulated. A further eccentricity is that two

[52] KWV, *South African Wines of Origin* (Paarl: KWV, undated).

marginal wards, namely the Cederberg and Vaalhaarts, did not belong to any district, while the Piquetberg, Klein Karoo and Overberg districts were not nested in any region.

To qualify as a 'wine of origin', at least 100 per cent of the wine was required to derive from the designated area. Hence a Pinotage that was designated 'Coastal Region Wine of Origin' might include grapes sourced from Paarl and Stellenbosch, but not Worcester. The rationale was that if the producer was drawing on grapes that came only from Stellenbosch, it would be preferable to claim WO Stellenbosch as the place of origin. On the same principle, a wine containing grapes from a single ward might find it advantageous to refer specifically to Franschhoek or the Simonsberg rather than the district designation of Paarl or Stellenbosch. The most complex provisions related to estate wines. As indicated above, estate wines had to be vinified in the cellars of a registered estate, from grapes grown on the same estate, although it was possible for the bottling to take place somewhere else. A producer could request that several farms, which might not even be adjacent, be registered together as a single estate – as happened in the case of Simonsig, which was actually an amalgamation of three separate farms.[53] Equally, there was nothing to stop an estate from buying in grapes, provided that the resulting wines were not labelled as 'estate wines' and were given the appropriate designation, which created some scope for creative marketing.[54] These provisions represented a concession to the independent producers who wanted to trade on the prestige of the 'estate' label, while increasing production beyond what their own vineyards could produce. Such subtle distinctions were no doubt lost on the average consumer.

When the first 14 designations of origin were announced in 1972, it was readily apparent that *terroir* was not the driving principle. Tellingly, the boundaries of the former farming districts were essentially carried over to the new system. Moreover, the regions simply represented larger aggregations of existing districts. The designation of wards did not really catch on, except in Franschhoek (which was initially the only one identified in Paarl District), Wellington (Paarl District), Constantia (Coastal Region) and Durbanville (Coastal Region), and eventually Walker Bay and Elgin (both Overberg District).[55] The 'estate' designation was initially assigned to a mere 14 farms.[56]

[53] The first farm acquired by Frans Malan was De Hoop in 1963, followed by Simonsig (formerly Hillbrow) in 1964. In 1980, Morgenster was added. Van Zyl, *Frans Malan*, p. 58.

[54] James observes that Constantia and Durbanville were wards that were not connected to a district, but it seems clear in the initial regulations that they were districts rather than wards. Timothy John James, "Terroir and law: estates and single vineyards in South Africa's Wine of Origin scheme", submitted in partial fulfillment of the Cape Wine Masters Diploma (October 2000), p. 24.

[55] James, "Terroir and Law", p. 20.

[56] Weiss, "The truth", p. 50.

This quickly rose to 30 estates, of whom no fewer than 19 were located in Stellenbosch, including Alto, whose historic importance has already been noted. By contrast, only De Wetshof was initially listed from Region IV. This confirmed that there remained a de facto division between areas that were seeking to break into quality wine production and those that continued to be dominated by the production of distilling wines. Crucially, there was nothing in the regulations that made it possible for the KWV to insist on maximum yields and cultivars specific to a region, district or ward. And the only *terroir*-related provision with respect to estates was the stipulation that a limited quantity of cultured yeast or bacteria could be added to a wine unless it was 'prepared from grapes harvested on the estate concerned'.[57] Otherwise the farmers were given a free hand in handling the grapes and turning them into wine. In that sense, the WO functioned according to a very different logic to appellations in France, which had demonstrable implications for quality.

Closely related to WO demarcation was the introduction of strict regulations covering labelling, which were intended to convey accurate and consistent details about what was in the bottle. The more detail that was indicated on the label, the greater typicality the purchaser could notionally expect, with vintage and cultivar being the main signifiers. These details were signalled by green and red bands on the labels that were affixed to the neck. The word 'Superior' could be added where a wine had been classified as of exceptional quality – a privilege that was not confined to estate wines.[58] Under the regulations, it was only permissible to mention the cultivar on the bottle if a minimum of 75 per cent of the contents were derived from the grape in question. However, in the case of Cabernet Sauvignon, Cabernet Franc, Pinotage, Shiraz and Riesling the minimum was initially set at 30 per cent, rising to 50 per cent by 1983 and eventually to the norm of 75 per cent. Part of the rationale for a staggered transition was the acute shortage of planting materials for these cultivars.[59]

The management of the WO, together with strict rules on labelling, was handled by the Wine and Spirits Board (WSB) that was ushered into being alongside the WO regulations. The WSB was initially made up of seven members, two of whom were drawn from the KWV, two from the Department of Agricultural Technical Services and two from the CWSI,

[57] Quoted in James" Terroir and Law", p. 22.

[58] A number of Nederburg wines earned the 'Superior' label.

[59] Van Zyl, *KWV*, p. 210. According to Van Zyl, there no target year was set for Riesling and Pinotage, but this seems to have been a temporary concession because later documentation placed these cultivars on the same footing. KWV, *South African Wines of Origin*, p. 6. One significant anomaly was that wine labelled as 'Riesling' was in fact Crouchen Blanc – an anomaly that persisted despite the clear evidence that it was unrelated to Riesling proper.

alongside a non-partisan chair.[60] In 1973, the WSB lacked the capacity to administer the system and the KWV was contracted to perform the work.[61] When it became fully operational, the WSB applied the rules on labelling very strictly. Hence, Frans Malan was taken to court for an offending label that proclaimed a 1978 Superior Estate wine to be '100% Pinotage'. The information was factually correct, and indeed the rule for Superior wines was that where the varietal was specified on the bottle the content needed to be 100 per cent from that cultivar.[62] Nevertheless, the label was deemed to contravene the regulations, despite the wine having been certified. The principle that a single varietal bottling could contain other varietals had apparently been a concession to the merchant-manufacturers, and Simonsig's manoeuvre was interpreted as an attempt to imply that its wine embodied greater integrity.[63] On this occasion Malan had his way, opening the door to other producers to follow suit. But, for the most part, the WSB managed to hold the line and to enforce some of the more arcane provisions of labelling.

Control over Planting Materials

The final piece in the regulatory jigsaw turned on control over what could be planted. One of the traditional strengths of the South African wine industry had been the quality of its viticultural and oenological research. Amerine even claimed that South Africa boasted the 'largest scale of supportive research to volume of wine or acres of grapes than any country than perhaps Germany'.[64] Researchers at UC-Davis and Geisenheim continued to work closely with their counterparts in Stellenbosch. Moreover, Geisenheim continued to train many leading South African winemakers of the future, such as Braam van Velden, Danie De Wet and Nicky Krone, even if others increasingly turned to France and later to California and Australia. Although knowledge flowed freely, there were greater restrictions when it came to mobility of the physical vines. The authorities were keen to regulate the cultivars that entered the country and the way in which they were made available to the farmer. The memories of phylloxera, and the battle against ongoing blight such as downy mildew, were fresh enough to justify maintaining strict quarantine procedures for planting

60 The powers of the WSB were confirmed by the Liquor Products Act of 1989 which increased the size of the Board to 12. James, "Terroir and Law", p. 19.
61 "Address by the Chairman of the KWV, André du Toit, on the Occasion of the 56th Annual General Meeting of Members on Tuesday 4 June 1974", enclosure to *Wynboer* June 1974, p. 3.
62 Van Zyl, *KWV*, p. 203. The 'Superior' category was abolished in 1990 for reasons that are not entirely clear.
63 Interview with Johan Malan, Stellenbosch, 18 April 2007.
64 Amerine, lecture 10, www.youtube.com/watch?v=S-e7zNQ0p3Y minute 37. He commented in particular on the state-of-the-art equipment at Stellenbosch.

material. Almost no new vines had been officially imported since the 1930s, which had apparently led to farmers importing and propagating vines in an unsystematic fashion in the post-war years. An awareness of the potential for diseases to enter under the radar lay behind attempts to tighten up the controls.

The ubiquity of viruses such as leaf-roll was considered to be one of the most pressing challenges facing the industry. However, the viticultural community became deeply divided over the optimal response. At UC-Davis, much of the research had focused on combating viruses, whereas in Europe the breakthrough resided in developing new clones. The practical question was whether South Africa should simply focus on importing the latest European clones rather than becoming bogged down with viruses affecting the existing vines. The influence of Californian research had been reflected in a decision in 1964 to concentrate on the dissemination of 'virus and disease-free material'. Chris Venter notes that:

> This new policy was based exclusively on the scheme proposed by Californian virologists working at the Davis Institute for the improvement of vine-propagation material, and totally ignored the tremendous success achieved in Europe at that stage by methods of mass, type and clonal selection.[65]

Whereas leading researchers at the University of Stellenbosch were in favour of the concentration on virus cleaning, the preference of VORI in Stellenbosch was for importing specific clones from Europe. In 1965, Dr. Hans Ambrosi, a senior viticulturalist at VORI, resigned and returned to Germany over the issue. His close ally was Desiderius Pongracz, a recent Hungarian immigrant and, by all accounts, an irrepressible character. Pongracz, who moved sideways to become Chief Viticultural Advisor at Distillers in 1972, kept up the pressure in favour of importing new varieties, clones and rootstocks over the coming years.[66] Some of the younger farmers who had studied in Geisenheim under Professor Helmut Becker, such as Danie De Wet, were inclined to his position and worked closely with him in the coming years.[67] Pongracz also found a close ally in Dr. Julius Laszlo, whom he helped to defect from Romania in 1975 and who later joined him at Distillers. In 1970, Frans Malan, speaking as the chairman of CEWPA was forthright about what was needed:

> Another bottleneck in our wine industry that I want to single out here is the lack of better varietals and rootstocks. A visit to research institutions overseas convinces one how far behind we are. In the past 30 years there is still not one new wine grape varietal that has been put at the disposal of our farmers. Where our white wines are particularly lacking, we feel that we need to find the solution in the vineyard and not try to fix

[65] Chris Venter, "Pongracz", unpublished manuscript, 2008, Distell Archive.
[66] Venter, "Pongracz", p. 8. [67] Venter, "Pongracz", p. 8.

everything in the cellar. Through research direction overseas, literally thousands of new crossings and selections are available. Hundreds of them are already at an advanced stage of evaluation. I believe that we must on a greater scale and much more quickly be placed in a position to enjoy the advantage of this research already completed. The same goes for rootstocks.[68]

Out of this sometimes fractious debate, a compromise eventually emerged. While much of the emphasis continued to be placed on virus control, the case for accelerated importation of planting material was accepted, albeit under conditions of close monitoring. In 1971, the Department of Agricultural Technical Services formed a Cultivar Committee to manage an approved list of cultivars.[69] Whenever any person or company wished to import planting material, this first had to be approved by the committee, after which a permit to import was issued. Once the material was received, it was sent to the Plant Quarantine Station in Stellenbosch, which fell under the Directorate of Plant and Seed Control of the Department of Agricultural Economics and Marketing. The plants were tested for diseases and remained under quarantine for a period of two years. The caution was justified on the basis that diseases which were not visible on the vines in their European setting often came to light more quickly under South African conditions. If the material was regarded as satisfactory it was passed to VORI, where it was subjected to further trials for a minimum period of three years. VORI tested for viruses and suitability to local conditions on test farms, of which there were 35 in operation by 1985.[70] At this point, the KWV became directly involved. In 1964, the KWV took it upon itself to seek to make high-quality rootstocks and vines available to the farmers. The KWV established mother blocks from the approved materials and then released them to approved nurseries in the various districts. The first visually selected rootstocks were released to the farmers in 1967, followed by the first visually selected vines in 1971 and the first cloned rootstocks in 1972.[71] The system therefore involved a combination of agencies, each of which was responsible for one of the links in the chain.

Although there were sound scientific reasons for maintaining rigorous control, this exacerbated the shortage of varietals that farmers and the merchant-manufacturers were anxious to plant. In 1973, one commentator observed that:

68 Frans Malan: "Jaarverslag van Vereniging van Kaapse Landgoedwynprodsente: rede van F.J. Malan op die Jaarvergadering, 20 Mei 1970", *Wynboer* June 1970, p. 21.

69 Desiderius Pongracz, "Invoer en uittoets van nuwe wyndruifvariëteite", *Wynboer*, November 1970.

70 Eugene Booysen, "Die NIWW: vinger op die pols van ons wynbedryf (2)", *Wynboer*, September 1985, p. 82.

71 D. J. Jacobs (President van die Suid-Afrikaanse Kwekersvereniging), "Plantverbeteringskema bereik groot hoogtes", *Wynboer*, January 1973, p. 27.

And the tragedy, it seems, is that plantings of noble red wine varieties are at present so inadequate that for many years to come South Africa will be hard pressed to supply even the local demand for good bottle-matured red wines, let alone exploit the world demand. Although the wine merchants are now paying as much as R400 a ton for Cabernet Sauvignon, compared with the minimum good wine price of R97 a ton, this variety makes up only 0,61 per cent of the total number of vines and the position with other noble red wine varieties is no better. Furthermore it will take at least eight years before new plantings of these noble varieties will yield marketable bottle-matured wines. And the crunch is that selected planting material is in short supply as well.[72]

In fact, Duimpie Bayly of the SFW observed that the vineyard area under red grapes had declined over the course of the 1960s, so that it accounted for only 21 per cent of the total in 1971.[73] Remarkably, it had contracted further to 15.6 per cent of the surface area under grapes by 1985. There was a precipitous decline in plantings of Cinsault which, in the South African context, had become associated with a reputation for indifferent quality (Table 5.4). The number of Cabernet Sauvignon and Shiraz vines increased significantly between 1958 and 1975 but then contracted, whereas plantings of Pinotage increased steadily. Worryingly, consumer demand for high-quality red wines remained at variance with what existed in the vineyards in the early 1980s. On the side of the white varietals, plantings of Palomino increased significantly between 1975 and then fell back, whereas those of Clairette Blanche and Colombard, which were used for blending and distillation, increased. However, the significant uptake was in the plantings of Chenin Blanc, which skewed the balance in favour of white wines. Chenin established itself as the workhorse grape of the cooperatives, especially in the irrigated districts. Of the noble white varieties, the limited plantings of Sauvignon Blanc decreased after 1975, while Chardonnay, which hardly existed before 1975, increased only marginally. Arguably, the statistics on the hectarage and the total number of vines reveal only so much. As a proxy for quality, it makes some sense to compare the vineyard profile of the irrigated versus the non-irrigated areas *anderkant die berg*. It is significant that most of the Cabernet Sauvignon vines were concentrated in Paarl and Stellenbosch, where the quality agenda enjoyed greater traction (see Table 5.5). This qualifies the overall picture, but it does not alter the reality that the shift towards varietals associated with quality was glacial. Farmers complained that the procedures were so cumbersome that the most desirable cultivars would remain unavailable for the foreseeable future. In the short term the farmers did what they could, both within the letter of the law and well outside of it. Working closely with the Bergkelder, Pongracz

[72] Weiss, "Red wine '72", p. 35. Around 1974, people would queue for red wine at Groot Constantia and were allocated a maximum of six bottles. Interview with Bennie Howard, 17 March 2009.

[73] Quoted in Weiss, "Red wine '72", p. 37.

Table 5.4. *Selected cultivars under vine in selected years (million vines, over a year old)*

Cultivars	1958	1975	1981
Chenin Blanc	24.8	76.4	90.0
Palomino	43.4	63.4	47.5
Semillon	19.9	12.4	8.2
Colombard	0.1	9.5	14.5
Clairette Blanche	4.4	11.0	10.7
Chardonnay	0.0	0.0[a]	0.1
Sauvignon Blanc	0.0[b]	2.8	1.3
Cinsault	54.9	52.0	38.7
Pinotage	0.1	6.7	8.1
Cabernet Sauvignon	0.9	7.5	7.3
Shiraz	0.6	2.8	2.2
Pinot Noir	0.0[c]	0.0[d]	0.4

[a]3,150 vines;
[b]22,871 vines;
[c]18,400 vines;
[d]41,224 vines.
Source: KWV, 'Ontleiding van Wynsoorte', *Wynboer*, various years.

engaged in mass selection of planting material and assisted particular farmers with securing access to it.[74] This enabled a farm like Meerlust to build its reputation as a red-wine producer in Stellenbosch, with the close input of its Italian winemaker Giorgio Dalla Cia, who moved over from Bergkelder in 1978.[75] De Wetshof equally received valuable assistance in securing access to new white cultivars which, in turn, helped Danie de Wet to push the quality envelope around Robertson.

Vertical Integration and Horizontal Solidarity

Estates and Cooperatives on the Move

The passage of the WO legislation, combined with the changing complexion of the wine market, brought out a further recalibration of the relationship between the merchant-manufacturers and the individual producers. CEWPA arose out of an aspiration to strike out independently, to which the companies responded by offering a fresh series of incentives. The SFW had already been producing

[74] Venter, *History of Die Bergkelder*, p. 20.
[75] Interview with Giorgo Dalla Cia, 17 March 2009.

Table 5.5. *Distribution of selected varietals by area (hectare), 1981*

Varietal	Orange River	Olifants River	M'sbury	Montagu	Paarl	Rob'tson	S'bosch	W'cester	Total	% of Total Area
Cabernet Sauvignon	2.82	41.80	140.23	6.95	956.14	60.47	1,127.11	145.27	2,624.79	2.52
Cinsault	6.80	109.73	1,731.26	136.94	3,561.15	809.78	2,707.93	2,941.51	12,005.10	11.56
Pinotage	13.48	49.93	653.34	21.96	851.18	35.31	1,087.50	195.81	2,908.51	2.80
Shiraz	0.03	10.55	45.84	1.52	186.68	18.93	476.81	4.55	746.91	0.72
Chenin Blanc	134.83	1,184.36	5,015.18	532.23	8,337.89	2,472.65	7,509.74	5,126.56	30,313.44	29.21
Chardonnay	0	0	0	0	11.94	7.26	9.15	1.57	29.92	0.02
Sauvignon Blanc	0	3.16	50.21	1.42	125.23	14.35	188.80	8.93	392.10	0.37

Source: KWV, 'Ontleiding van totale stand van wyndruifsoorte soos op 20 November 1981', *Wynboer*, September 1982, p. 4.

cultivar-specific wines under the *Zonnebloem* label. Its strategy was increasingly to purchase the best wines from trusted producers and then to market them under its own brands such as *Nederburg*. In contrast, Distillers responded to the WO and labelling regulations by deepening its links with particular farms. It already enjoyed longstanding relationships with Theuniskraal (Tulbagh) and Alto (Stellenbosch), each of which was registered as an estate under the WO regulations. But in 1974, the sweetheart relationship was extended to as many as 15 producers, including a number that had been formally designated as estates, including De Wetshof in Robertson and Bonfoi, Middelvlei and Uitkyk in Stellenbosch.[76] In order to remain within the rules covering estates, the wine continued to be produced in the cellars of the farms concerned. But, thereafter, the wine was transferred to the cavernous Bergkelder facility in Stellenbosch where the wine was matured in French oak barrels. The latter was something new in the South African context, where it had been customary to use large wooden *stukvats* that imparted little flavour to the wine. By common agreement, it was Laszlo who drove this particular innovation at the Bergkelder.[77] While farmers picked up the pace in planting full-bodied red varietals, most notably Cabernet Sauvignon, Laszlo insisted that ageing in new French oak barrels added another layer of complexity to the wine. Carping from the sidelines, an advertisement for *Nederburg* wines depicted Günter Brözel leaning with intent over a barrel with the caption: 'If you want a really noble Cabernet, don't leave it too long in the cask or you'll end up with a piece of wood to chew.'[78] But in the fine print, Brözel made it clear that he meant that wine should not remain in the barrel longer than two years, which in itself represented a radical shift in winemaking practices. In fact, these ostensible rivals, who became the dominant influences on winemaking practices within Distillers and SFW respectively, were more or less on the same page. After ageing, the wine of Distillers was bottled and sold under the Bergkelder label. The deal was that the farmers were both able to cling on to the estate name and to ride the coattails of Distillers marketing. At the same time, the company secured control over the wine emanating from some of the leading estates.

Not surprisingly, the decision on the part of Distillers to incorporate estate wines into its portfolio exposed cracks within CEWPA. Given that at least half of the vinification process, including malolactic fermentation, took place at the Bergkelder, many members felt that this was against the spirit of the WO regulations governing 'estate wines'.[79] Those who felt especially affronted

[76] Fridjhon, *Penguin Book*, p. 48. [77] Fridjhon, *Penguin Book*, pp. 47–48.

[78] This advertisement appeared repeatedly as part of the SFW's advertising campaign in *Wynboer*. The point was re-iterated during an interview with Brözel, 18 August 2009.

[79] Interview with Danie de Wet, 16 October 2009.

were farmers whose quotas were inadequate and therefore needed to buy in grapes. Jan 'Boland' Coetzee was, in his own words, 'kicked out' of CEWPA when he moved from Kanonkop to set up his own wine farm at Vriesenhof. Needing to buy grapes from his neighbours to become viable meant that he could not pose as an estate wine producer.[80] The internal tensions were never resolved and when members felt that the estate concept had been diluted, many de-listed themselves as estates and ceased to play any further part in CEWPA itself. However, these dynamics took some time to play themselves out.

From the KWV vantage point, it looked as if the companies were imposing a stranglehold over supply at a time when there was a shortage of red wines. When the Bergkelder went a step further and acquired part ownership of a number of the farms, the evidence of vertical integration seemed incontrovertible. Dr. André du Toit took up the matter in his speech to the Annual General Meeting of the KWV in June 1974:

> It is consequently disturbing to detect an entirely new tendency in the liquor industry. While distribution and marketing lie well beyond the influence and control of producers, certain trade interests are apparently concentrating on the acquisition of control, through various means, of certain functions of production which have previously been activities of producers. Indeed, it appears that the principle of vertical integration is being pursued right down to producer level. Considering the closed and tied character of retail outlets, the door is naturally open to total domination should these apparent endeavours succeed.[81]

The fact that producers were striking deals with the companies was a source of irritation. However, the KWV was not beyond learning something from its rivals. Although it was not permitted to sell locally in completion with the merchants, it could market its own version of 'estate wine' overseas. With effect from 1972, it rolled out cultivar-specific wines, under the *Vergenoegd*, *Meerendal and Swartland* labels, that were intended for the export market.[82]

The independent farmers who were not tied to the merchant-manufacturers were under pressure to come up with innovative ways to market their wines, given that they were excluded from the channels controlled by the companies. Most were not particularly wealthy, and a number were swimming in debt. After his family lost everything in the war, Sperling had migrated to South

[80] Interview with Jan 'Boland' Coetzee, 19 April 2007.

[81] "Address by the Chairman of the KWV, Dr. André Du Toit on the Occasion of 56th Annual General Meeting of Members on Tuesday 4 June 1974", enclosure to *Wynboer* June 1974, p. 3.

[82] The KWV began with a *Meerdendal* Shiraz, a *Vergenoegd* Cabernet Sauvignon and a *Swartland* Pinotage ([Anon.], "K.W.V. se new droe rooi wyne" (editorial), *Wynboer*, January 1972, p. 3.

Africa as a penniless immigrant in 1951.[83] Sperling was fortunate enough to secure employment on the Driesprong farm and, when the owner chose to retire, he acquired a bank loan and purchased the farm, which he renamed Delheim. For Sperling and for many others, paying off the debts arising from improvements to cellars, the replanting of vineyards and the purchase of additional land posed a recurring headache. Maintaining a healthy cash flow was a particular challenge, given the lag between making investments and reaping the return. The imperative to get around the difficulties of selling wine from the farm eventually culminated in the inspiration to establish the Stellenbosch Wine Route. The idea was apparently hatched after a holiday in Burgundy taken by Niel Joubert, Frans Malan and their wives. The story goes that Malan was enthused by the opportunity to taste wines at the cellars, and enlisted Sperling, who put in the hard work to develop a plan for a Stellenbosch prototype. The Stellenbosch Wine Route was formally launched in 1971. The rationale was that people would visit the farms and have a chance to become better acquainted with wines that were not as readily available as the big brands. Being on the wine route map also enabled the farmers to sell some of their wine from the farm gate. Initially, there was a singular lack of interest on the part of farmers, which is reflected in the fact that only 1 of 15 private cellars responded to the initial questionnaire. However, the message gradually spread through word of mouth.[84] As the number of members increased, bureaucratic obstacles were placed in the way. According to Sperling, the attempt to get the district road engineer to agree to the erection of signposts was met with the following terse, and faintly surreal, response:

> We cannot allow commercial signboarding on a public road: it distracts the drivers. The next thing the potato farmers will want to establish a route, then the onion farmers. There will be no end to it![85]

There was also an official objection to the route maps that were produced, on the basis that they constituted a form of unauthorized advertising. Furthermore, the regulations stipulated a minimum amount of wine that could be purchased at the farm, namely a dozen bottles. In the early days, the visitors consisted mostly of Stellenbosch University students who drank freely but purchased hardly anything.[86] When Sperling began to serve food to accompany the wine,

[83] Michael 'Spatz Sperling had grown up in southern Germany and after the war and, with the help of his mother's cousin in South Africa, he moved to start a new life. Michael Sperling, *The Memoirs of 'Spatz Sperling'*, 19 July 2005 (unpublished manuscript), pp. 13–14. A version is available online at www.delheim.com/our-story/michael-hans-spatz-sperling/, accessed 16 February 2022.

[84] *Memoirs of 'Spatz Sperling'*, p. 79.

[85] *Memoirs of 'Spatz Sperling'*, p. 80.

[86] Interview with Spatz Sperling, 20 April 2007.

a wealthier clientele began to turn up at the farm and the concept gained some traction.

By 1978, the Stellenbosch Wine Route included 11 estates, but significantly, the Bottelary, Helderberg, Eersterivier and Vlottenberg co-operative wineries had also become members (see Figure 5.2).[87] The success of the initiative spawned replicas in Paarl and Franschhoek and was eventually rolled out across the winelands. The wine routes were important not just for enabling the producers to sell wine for on-site consumption and to take away, but also because it enabled them to create a loyal customer base that did not need to be solicited through the kinds of costly advertising that only the SFW and Distillers could afford. Indeed, part of the appeal to consumers resided precisely in the fact that the wine was somewhat difficult to procure, especially red wine. Many of the leading producers shifted their stock by posting wine to customers in the Transvaal who had visited the farm or knew somebody who had gone on the wine route. In general, the initiative became a remarkable success for three main reasons: it was relatively low-cost because it involved a loose coalition of farmers and cooperatives; it was susceptible to replication while permitting a degree of variation; and it bolstered an association between the wine and the farm where it was produced.

Alongside the wine routes, another innovation that helped promote the profile of wine was the proliferation of a new generation of wine shows. As I have already indicated, festivals that had been initiated in the winelands during the 1950s celebrated the vine as an integral part of Afrikaner culture. The wine shows that took off in the 1970s were sponsored by the KWV and focused on competition as the means to enhance quality and showcase successful innovation. The principle was that the winners in the tasting of young wines from the regional/district shows would compete for prizes in the national wine championship that continued to be part of the annual Western Province Agricultural Show in Goodwood. The Breede River Wine Show, held in the vicinity of Worcester, was the pioneer and the model was quickly replicated elsewhere. At the KWV Annual General Meeting of 1975, André du Toit was especially bullish about the positive spinoffs, especially for the cooperatives, of this addition to the social calendar.

> Our wine growers have already done a great deal to stimulate this new interest in wine to which I have referred. And here I think especially of the regional wine shows established in recent years. The Breede Valley was the first, followed by the Boberg River area. The next is Stellenbosch which will, hopefully, hold its first regional wine

[87] For a profile of the members, see [Anon.], "Die Stellenbosse Wynroete", *Wynboer*, November 1978, pp. 20–31.

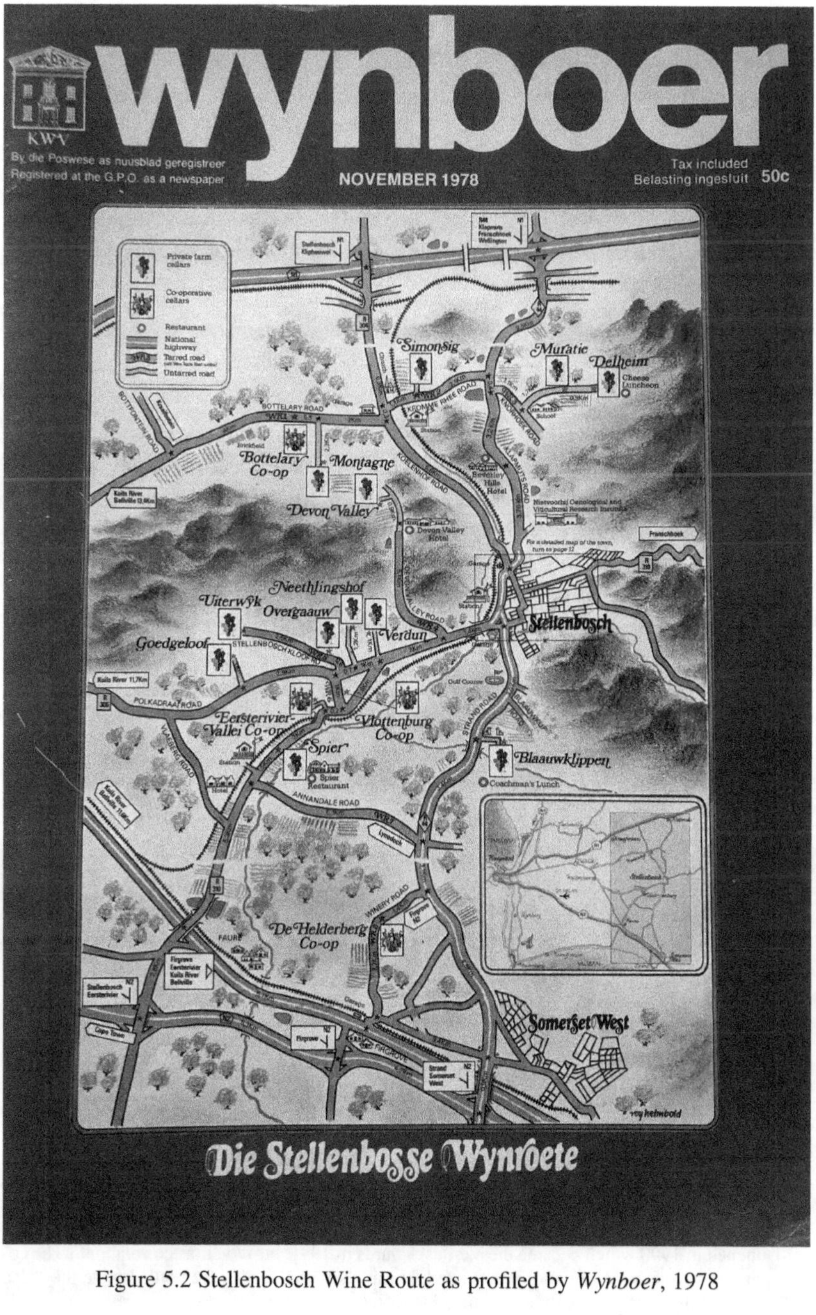

Figure 5.2 Stellenbosch Wine Route as profiled by *Wynboer*, 1978

show this year. These shows have done much to generate interest in regional and area wines and therefore, especially, in wines of origin.[88]

The cooperatives often scored highly with their white wines, whereas the prizes for the red wines tended to be garnered by the independent producers. Du Toit himself had a personal interest in the performance of the cooperatives, given that he became the chairman of the first cooperative merger that very year. The wine shows also supported the KWV's longstanding contention that the future of wine lay in its grounding within the culture of the winelands. In the same speech, Du Toit continued:

> We are progressing, but there is much that remains to be done. The KWV has set itself the task of placing our wine culture – and I speak of culture in the primary sense from vine to glass – on a sound and firm footing here in the Western Cape.

This breathed fresh life into the earlier campaign to hitch Afrikaner nationalism to the vine. Finally, whereas the wine circles were consciously exclusive and elitist, the wine shows were intended to be outward-looking and inclusive. At the same time, they enabled the KWV and the NP to consolidate their strategic alliance in the Cape winelands. The KWV's export wines like *Meerendal* were permitted to compete in the shows and their successes were trumpeted despite the wine not being available for local consumption.[89] One of the practical problems, however, was that the characteristics of the wine, which was tasted when it was very young and before it had been bottled, had often altered by the time it reached the final judging.[90]

Between the early 1970s and the mid-1980s, the wine industry underwent significant transformations. The cooperatives remained the largest producers of wine, accounting for some 84 per cent of the crop and 75 per cent of what was vinified. Even in Stellenbosch, the big six of Welmoed, Eerste Rivier, Vlottenberg, Bottelary, Helderberg and Koelenhof accounted for, by far, the greatest production. Braam van Velden estimated that at their pinnacle they would handle between 6,000 and 12,000 tonnes of grapes each, whereas the SFW and Distillers accounted for only 3,000–4,000 directly.[91] But, while the number of cooperatives remained stable at around 70 (Table 5.6), the number of estate producers had increased to 72. Because numerous aspirants towards quality wine production chose not to adopt the estate designation or dropped out, the ranks of independent producers were considerably greater. Indeed, the

[88] Address by Du Toit to 57th AGM of KWV, 3 June 1975 (supplement), *Wynboer*, June 1975.

[89] Interview with Braam Van Velden, 5 August 2009.

[90] Later on, bottled wines also became part of the wine show before a separate competition was launched in 1990 which became the Veritas Awards in 1991. http://veritas.co.za/about/. The co-operatives were initially under-represented, but as they produced more bottled wine they also competed. Interview with Braam Van Velden, 5 August 2009.

[91] Interview with Braam Van Velden, 5 August 2009.

Table 5.6. *The trajectory of cooperatives and estate wine producers, 1955–1986*

Year	Co-operatives	Estate Wine Producers
1955	41	–
1965	58	–
1973	69	20
1976	70	42
1978	71	45
1983	70	68
1986	70	72

Source: Stellenbosch Farmers' Winery, *Annual Review, 1987*, p. 6.

volume of wine produced by independents as a whole had increased to 25 per cent of the total. Moreover, the push united farmers across the mountain, from Stellenbosch to Robertson and Bonnievale.[92] The independent farmers had clearly made significant inroads, but they still found themselves constrained in various ways. On the one hand, the merchants continued to dominate access to the retail market. This meant that they had to fight a constant battle to expand their market share. On the other hand, the independents became increasingly impatient with the regulatory system that threw up innumerable obstacles. There were three issues that became the focal point for dissatisfaction, namely the restriction on access to cultivars, the certification regulations and the strictures of the quota system. In Chapter 7, I will say more about each of these.

Conclusion

In this chapter, I have submitted the KWV to closer inspection and identified the ambiguity deriving from its formal position as an umbrella-style cooperative and its assumption of state-like functions. I have broken the KWV system down into its constituent parts before reassembling them in a discussion of how merchant-manufacturing companies, cooperatives and aspiring independent producers responded to the system. At the start, many were sceptical as to whether KWV would be able to address the interests of farmers, merchants and consumers in an even-handed manner. The merchant-manufacturers gradually reconciled themselves and even found value in specific regulations that others derided. Hence in 1972, Piet Venter of Distillers stated that:

[92] Lourens Jonker recalled that Weltevrede bottled the first independent wine in the Breede Valley in 1976. Interview, 20 March 2009.

> We live in an era of forward planning and I would be the last person who would advocate that the quota system should be summarily abolished. Our industry has benefited from the quota system thus far. We have enjoyed virtually uninterrupted growth at about 1000 per cent over the past fifty years of the KWV's existence.[93]

The majority of the grape growers were genuinely in favour of the system, given that part of the objective was to prop up producer prices. However, quality producers became more ambivalent with time. Looking back, Jan 'Boland' Coetzee maintained that the entire KWV system was saturated by insider politics and summed up the highs and lows as follows: 'I would say the main stumbling block was the quota system and the exciting parts were the certification system and the wine routes.'[94] As a pithy synopsis of the key findings of this chapter, this serves the purpose rather well.

[93] Piet Venter of Distillers quoted in Weiss, "Red wine '72", p. 38.
[94] Interview with Jan 'Boland' Coetzee, 12 April 2007.

6 Selling Wine to the Many

Competition, Branding and Advertising, 1962–1986

> A 60' film is being produced for non-European audiences. The film portrays a high class restaurant scene in South Africa. A Coloured wine steward is seen being asked by a Frenchman – dining on his own – to recommend a good South African wine. In the background a group of violinists are playing the 'Lieberstein Jingle' as it would have been composed by Beethoven. The theme is only barely recognisable. The steward in the meantime produces the bottle of wine (wrapped in a napkin) and pours some into a glass. The Frenchman takes a sip – everybody is tense and waits in anticipation for his verdict. With a great smile the Frenchman announces that the wine tastes great. Everybody is happy and the violinists now jubilantly play the 'Lieberstein Jingle'. The writer then removes the bottle (Lieberstein) from the napkin and shows it to the audience. Media concentration will be in the Cape Peninsula, Port Elizabeth and Transvaal and will be aimed at Coloureds of all ages and Europeans C & D socio-economic groups.
>
> (1971)[1, 2]

The world of advertising is fantastical, if nothing else. It is also a world in which the messages are often far from being subtle, far less subliminal. Layers of deeper meaning are compressed into a single dimension and bound together with narrative thread. Such is the case with the pitch above, in which global references jostle with a very local perspective on the centrality of race. The fact that the jingle in question is based on a German folk tune represents a hangover from an earlier era when South African producers were at pains to emulate German styles. On the other hand, the fact that the arbiter of good taste is now French neatly captures a shift that was underway in the early 1970s. And although *Lieberstein* itself remained loyal to its sweet white roots the tide was increasingly flowing in the direction of red wine. In South Africa, underperforming products were rarely consigned to the grave – especially when the

[1] Distell Archive, "Martell 1971" file, "Lieberstein, 1970/71".

[2] In this text I refer to 'White', 'Coloured' and 'Black' - categories that are rooted in segregationist and apartheid discourse, but which are impossible to avoid using because they have meaning for the actors themselves. See the 'Note on the Text' on page vi for more detail about the history and use of this term in South Africa.

product in question was invested with so much historical significance – but were kept alive and feeding at lower price points. By 1973, *Lieberstein* had long ceased to be the drink of preference for White South Africans. It now ministered to the thirst of Coloured consumers whose social standing was more or less equivalent to that of poorer White people. Quite why a Frenchman would be ordering *Lieberstein* in a high-class restaurant is anyone's guess. Moreover, it was clearly South Africa's wealthier wine enthusiasts who were likely to be impressed by the opinions of a passing Frenchman. Like many such advertisements, both in a print and film format, this one could be dissected ad infinitum. The layered ambiguities could stand for those that typified the wine industry more generally. It was in the interests of the companies to maximize their sales to all sections of the population. And yet while they often dissented from the racial fundamentalism of the day, they inadvertently reproduced its categories in their own approach to wine marketing.

In this chapter, I am concerned with innovations within the sphere of distribution. This did not merely entail creative marketing strategies, but also some darker machinations to steal a march on the opposition. Although the merchant-manufacturers never managed to achieve anything close to total integration, they aspired to control every aspect of the wine business, from the vine to the glass. This was a worrying prospect for the KWV, which complained to the government that the farmer and the drinker would be the ultimate losers if this was permitted. However, vertical integration was also a contentious issue amongst the liquor companies themselves. The handful of smaller firms complained of market manipulation by the larger players, while the latter accused each other of wanting to establish monopolies. I begin this account, therefore, with the liquor wars of the 1960s and 1970s, before looking in closer detail at the operations of the largest company involved in the production and sale of wine, namely the SFW. I explain in detail how the latter attempted to optimize the sale of its products to different segments of the population through the creation of discrete brands, packaging and advertising. In the process, I seek to offer an answer to the conundrum of why the beer industry prospered after the ending of racial prohibition whereas the wine industry struggled to increase its market share.

Vexatious Monopolies: From Liquor Wars to Market Sharing

In the 1940s and 1950s, the beer and wine industries remained distinct from one another, even if they exhibited certain structural similarities. In each case, the artificially constricted consumer market meant that competition was intense and profit margins tight. The attempt to bypass competitors, or alternatively to replicate their successes, frequently ended up in court. Such was when SFW sued the Castle Wine and Brandy Co. and Henry Collinson in 1942 over the use of the *Ship* brand name.[3] Moreover, companies periodically failed and were bought up by their closest competitors, leading to the consolidation of a small number of major players.[4] There were, however, some old-stagers in the wholesale and retail business, such as Union Wine and E. Snell, who managed to survive by cutting a deal with the manufacturers. Union Wine was acquired by Graham Beck, who had originally made his money in coal, and then joined forces with Douglas Green, a manufacturer that had previously acquired its supplies from the KWV. The new company enjoyed particular success with its dry white wines at the upper end of the market.[5] The Rembrandt Group represented a much bigger fish and was nothing less than global in its ambitions. As we have seen, Rembrandt had made its fortune in tobacco, but subsequently sought to diversify its investments into alcohol.[6] Spirits were the main focus, but Rembrandt also targeted wine through one of its subsidiaries, the Distillers Corporation which it acquired in 1957.[7] In November 1962, the chief executive of Distillers addressed his staff with a rallying cry that was almost Darwinian in its depiction of what was needed to prosper in the liquor market:

> The last but most important factor is that we must now fight and climb in with all weapons at our disposal. The outside world has no sympathy for a man that lies down, but honours and/or respects a man that fights and is successful. We must secure a greater share of the market. We must get [more] income. (my translation)[8]

In effect, this was a declaration of war against the SFW, which dominated the wine sector and owned some of the leading spirits brands. Three years later, Anton Rupert consolidated the group's liquor interests – which included a controlling interest in Consolidated Western Wines Ltd, Roadside Hotels Ltd and shares in P. J. Joubert Ltd and Whitbread – within a new liquor company called Oude Meester Cellars, Distillers and Brewers Corporation Ltd, or Oude

[3] One of the SFW's most successful brands was *Ship Sherry*. Cape Archives, CSC 2/1/1/1430 ref 623 "Interdict and Damages, Stellenbosch Farmers Winery (PTY) Ltd. versus Henry C. Collinson Ltd. (1942); CSC 2/1/1/1430 ref 624 "Interdict and Damages Stellenbosch"; CSC 2/1/1/1430 ref 625 "Interdict, Stellenbosch Farmers Winery (PTY) Ltd. versus E.K. Green and Co. Ltd. (1942)".

[4] Some of the companies that were liquidated were the Standard Wine and Brandy Company, The Lion Wine and Spirit Company and Federal Distillers. Distell Archive "Paarl Perlé Litigation", "Memorandum Stellenbosch Farmers Winery Ltd" dated 15 December 1961.

[5] Fridjhon, *Penguin Book*, pp. 69–70.

[6] Rembrandt also bought shares in Canadian Breweries Ltd in 1969. [Anon.], "Rembrandt expands into liquor".

[7] Anne Mager asserts that Rembrandt owned the KWV. But the latter remained a (super) co-operative performing statutory functions. She also claims that SAB created the Stellenbosch Wine Trust in 1966, whereas the latter was the holding company in which SFW nested. Mager, *Beer*, p. 31. In 1960, SFW controlled 21.9 per cent of the wine trade and 15.1 per cent of the spirits trade. "Memorandum Stellenbosch Farmers Winery Ltd".

[8] Distell archive, Distillers papers, circular letter headed "Ons positie in die drankshandel", dated 8 November 1962.

Meester for short.[9] In the beer sector, South African Breweries (SAB) had similarly established a virtual monopoly through a merger with Union Breweries Ltd, Ohlsson's Cape Breweries and Chandler's Union Breweries in 1956.[10] This meant that there were now three large concerns that held sway in the liquor industry: namely Oude Meester/Distillers, SAB and SFW.[11]

Following de-racialization of the liquor laws, it was anticipated that the consumer market would at least double in size. But nobody was entirely sure how Black consumers would react. One prognosis was that they would naturally prefer sorghum beer to bottled malt beer but might take to wine precisely because of its novelty value. An alternative reading was that because bottled beer was more akin to what Black drinkers were used to, they would shift to the former as they acquired more disposable income. For the liquor companies, the smart thing to do was to straddle beer and wine and to see which way the wind blew. However, the wine companies were in less of a position to carry this off. Rembrandt did seek to enter brewing through franchises from Whitbread and Heineken but was forced to withdraw after struggling to make a dent on SAB's domination of the market.[12] In contrast, SFW remained confined to wine and spirits, where its profitability was a matter for concern. Its profits had fallen from £162,000 in 1957 to £109,000 in 1959, partly because of the unexpected hike in the excise duty the previous year.[13] The company was considered to be under-capitalized, which meant that diversification was a virtual impossibility. Instead, SFW had to look for allies simply to sustain its position in the wine sector. The largest player in the drinks industry by some margin was SAB which turned a profit of £1,114,000 in 1959, making it many times larger than SFW or Distillers. For SAB, diversification into wine was a tempting prospect. On the one hand, an increase in wine sales could realistically be anticipated. On the other hand, this would afford a means to increase the number of wholesale liquor licences at its disposal.[14] The one cause for hesitation was that government might seek to block any such move in the name of preventing vertical integration.

[9] Distell archive, Distillers papers, "Announcement to Shareholders" and "Announcement by Rembrandt Tobacco Corporation", 10 April 1965.

[10] Mager, *Beer*, p. 29. SAB also owned Rhodesian Breweries Ltd. The merger was endorsed by a report of the Board of Trade and Industries in 1958, entitled "Monopolistic conditions in the Liquor Trade and Industry", dated 26 September 1958 (copy in Distell archive).

[11] The nomenclature can be confusing. From this point onwards, I will refer to Distillers when referring to the wine and Rembrandt when referencing the larger group of companies.

[12] Mager, *Beer*, p. 32.

[13] Distell Archive, "Distillers Corporation versus S.A. Breweries", Circular letter by Morgan Bull, chairman of SAB, to SFW shareholders, 24 June 1960.

[14] Mager, *Beer*, p. 32 maintains that the discriminatory Excise duty in favour of wine and against beer was also what led the SAB to move into wine. But the hike in the Excise Duty in 1958 was something that surely reduced much of the advantage.

Table 6.1. *SAB's control of retail trade, 1959*

Category	Total Licensees	No. of Houses Managed by SAB	% of Total	% of Total Beer Trade	No. of SAB Houses Leased/ Sub-leased	% of Total	% of Total Beer Trade
Hotels	1,523	71	4.7	5.3	154	10.1	7.2
Wine and Malt	156	13	8.3	0.2	40	25.6	0.8
Bottle Stores	885	26	3.0	1.0	17	2.0	0.5
All Licensed Outlets	3,944	110	2.8	6.5	211	5.3	8.5

Source: Distell Archive, 'Distillers Corporation versus S.A. Breweries', circular letter by SAB to SFW shareholders, 'The extent of South African Breweries Limited Group's Interests in the Retail Trade".

The 1956 amendment to the Liquor Act had debarred manufacturers and wholesalers from acquiring 'financial interests' in the retail sector and vice versa. This provision had been contested by both the beer and the wine companies. Under Section 166(v) of the Act, all ties were to be terminated by 1962. SAB had attempted to persuade the Malan Commission that this should not be taken to apply to the hotel industry, where they owned many businesses that, in turn, held liquor licences (see Table 6.1). However, the Commission took the view that these amounted to 'financial interests' and were in breach of the law. Not surprisingly, the SAB felt rather ambivalent about the final report of the Malan Commission because it seemed to give with one hand, only to take away with the other. The chairman wrote that:

> We welcome the enlightened thinking reflected in the report in the form of recommendations concerning the broadening of the availability of moderate beverages to all sections of the South African community and the removal of many restrictions upon the sale and purchase of these drinks The report, however, also contains certain other recommendations which appear to impose undue restrictions and possible hardships upon the retail sections of the Liquor Trade, the purposes of which are not clear to us.[15]

The Cape Wholesale Wine Merchants Association felt equally aggrieved by the offending clause and met with the Commission to argue for a change in the wording. Hastings Beck, the secretary, subsequently wrote to the Commission pointing out that it was an unwarranted restraint on business:

> [Since 1958] . . . there have been three liquidations of large producing merchants. The effect of section 166(v) made it impossible for any other producing merchant to acquire

[15] "Distillers Corporation versus", Interim statement by Morgan Bull to members, dated 15 May 1960.

a financial interest in these companies, which may possibly have been a solution in the interests of shareholders, creditors and the industry as a whole. The principle aimed at preventing a further consolidation of retail interests is acknowledged but the effect of the section as it stands, is a grave and prejudicial infringement of producing merchant's rights and cuts directly across the recognised principles of commercial and industrial practice and development.[16]

The SAB and the Association believed that the way forward was to persuade the Minister of Justice, John Vorster, that a further change to the law was imperative. However, a potential complication was that the referendum over whether South Africa should become a republic might culminate in a snap election.[17] Such political uncertainties made it unlikely that the law would be changed any time soon

SAB decided that it was relatively safe to move forward on the basis of a judgement handed down in the Transvaal courts in December 1959. In this particular case, the administrator of the estate of a deceased bottle-store owner by the name of Goldberg purchased shares in P. J. Joubert, which also owned bottle-store and wholesale liquor licences. The point at issue was whether, according to the letter of the law, the estate had directly or indirectly acquired a 'financial interest in the business or undertaking of a producer or manufacturer'. The legal thinking behind the case is puzzling because there was apparently 'nothing in the Act to stop bottle store owners from acquiring interests in producers or manufacturers. The prohibition of the Act is only the other way.'[18] The initial judgement went against the administrator of the estate, but this was overturned on appeal. The court decided that the meaning of 'financial interest' should be interpreted as a proprietary interest, that is, outright ownership. On this basis, the SAB decided to acquire shares in SFW, which was experiencing financial difficulties. Its approach was to make an offer to SFW 'ordinary' shareholders in which their existing shares would be exchanged for SAB shares at a ratio of two to one. This, in effect, allowed SFW shareholders to hold a stake in a larger company, while giving the SAB the controlling stake in SFW. The SAB did not buy the preferential shares, and in that sense did not own the SFW outright. The SAB wrote to SFW shareholders and to its own shareholders to explain the advantages of the arrangement. It also issued W. C. Winshaw and senior managers in SFW with

[16] "Distillers Corporation versus", letter by Hastings Beck, secretary of Cape Wholesale Wine Merchants Association, to Chairman of Liquor Commission, dated 16 June 1959.

[17] "Distillers Corporation versus", Circular letter by SAB to SFW shareholders, W. W. Lance, Company secretary of SAB, to K. E. Wright, c/o Slaughter & May, London, dated 7 September 1960.

[18] "Distillers Corporation versus", legal opinion of Phillip Shock, 21 November 1956, in response to provisions of the Liquor Further Amendment Act, 1956.

contracts that would enable them to continue in their existing roles. It should be noted that the latter were fully supportive of SAB's bid.

The move was, however, interpreted as a threat by Distillers. Somewhat bizarrely, a legal objection was raised by one J. J. Piek, a SFW shareholder, with the aim of having the marriage annulled. It transpired that Piek was working for Rembrandt and had bought his shares after the proposed deal had come to light. Subsequently, Anton Rupert made a series of very public declarations to the effect that he would fight the efforts of SAB to establish a stranglehold over the liquor industry. This took the form of opposing the renewal of SFW liquor licences across the country based on their being in contravention of the Liquor Act. The argument was that if the SAB held shares in SFW, and if the latter owned liquor outlets, this contravened the Act as it stood. Not surprisingly, SAB/SFW reciprocated by raising objections to the renewal of licences that were held by Distillers. Ultimately, the dispute ended up in the Cape Provincial Courts. In the event, the SAB lost the case as well as the subsequent appeal on 23 November 1961.[19] The company was subsequently asked to outline its position by Vorster. In a detailed memorandum, SAB pointed out that it had acted in good faith and that there was nothing in the law to prevent a brewer from acquiring a wine producer or vice versa.[20] The problem arose out of the licensed businesses owned by the SFW.[21] These held wholesale licences for supplying the liquor trade, whereas the SFW owned no retail licences directly. If SAB had purchased the businesses outright, there could have been no objection. However, by acquiring shares in SFW, SAB was deemed to have acquired a financial interest. In its defence against the charge that it was seeking to cement a monopoly, the SAB memorandum pointed out that there were in total 4,200 liquor licences of all descriptions across the country, of which it owned or managed a total of 110.[22]

[19] The judges divided 3 to 2, which was an indication that this was not a straightforward matter. SAB's lawyers had sought to argue that holding shares did not constitute an interest and that even if that was not held to be the case the SAB would only have acquired an interest in the Stellenbosch Wine Trust and not actually in the licensed business of the winery. The lawyers for Distillers maintained that financial interest was not intended to be synonymous with a proprietary interest since such wording could have been used if that had been the intent. They argued that "a person has a financial interest in a business if he is so circumstanced with respect to the business that his financial position is necessarily affected by its fortunes either beneficially or detrimentally".

[20] "Distillers Corporation", "Memorandum of Information submitted to the Honourable the Minister of Justice on Section 166 (v) of the Liquor Act, 1928", 3 April 1962.

[21] These were held at Stellenbosch, Cape Town, Mossel Bay, Port Elizabeth, East London, Durban, Pitermaritzburg, Johannesburg, Pretoria, Bloemfontein, Henneman and Kimberly. Its subsidiary companies held three other wholesale liquor licences.

[22] A separate document claimed that SAB had a controlling interest in about 8 per cent out of 4,000 liquor licences. "Distillers Corporation versus"; "The South African Breweries' Acquisition of Stellenbosch Farmers' Winery", undated.

Moreover, out of some 900 bottle stores, SAB owned or part-owned only 43. Table 6.1 indicates that 15 per cent of beer distribution was controlled by SAB, either through houses managed by the company or through houses leased or sub-leased to tenants. In addition, SAB maintained that it had no means to control the African market because the liquor outlets in the townships would remain under the control of 'special authorities'. Making full use of his ministerial discretion, Vorster subsequently consented to the marriage of SAB and SFW, no doubt accepting the contention that the brewer had the capacity to inject much needed capital into the wine sector. When SFW acquired Monis in 1966, the Minister insisted on a reduction of the SAB stake in SFW. This was, however, a temporary arrangement and Vorster subsequently consented to the complete takeover of SFW by SAB.[23]

The following years witnessed ill-tempered competition between Distillers and the SFW/SAB. Much of the disagreement revolved around control of liquor outlets. Despite the earlier controversy, the introduction of grocers' wine licences had been less than revolutionary in their practical effects. In 1970, the Minister of Justice, Petrus Pelser, reported that a total of 260 applications had been received, but only 17 had actually been approved.[24] In 1971, André Du Toit used his New Year's message to KWV members to complain about the failure to approve many licences to grocers' stores and restaurants:

> Instead of the sale of wine in groceries becoming the general practice, as is the case in most Western countries, the possession of such a licence remains a great exception. Furthermore, with regard to restaurants, the position remains utterly disappointing. While in all fairness it can be accepted that in a wine producing country no stumbling blocks should be placed in the way of restaurants serving wine with food, it appears as though the authorities are in this respect also taking unnecessary strong action and that many restaurants which should be in a position to offer this service to the public, are not doing so.[25]

In effect, the bottle stores remained the most important source of access to alcohol, especially for the White and Coloured segments of the population. At the end of 1978, Rembrandt acquired a major stake in Gilbey's, which meant that the company now had direct access to some of the leading liquor chains – notably Liquorama, Fine Fair and Rebel – which accounted for between 15 and 20 per cent of retail sales. In response, Du Toit made a further appeal to government to 'grant free and unrestricted liquor licences for wine

[23] According to Lothar Barth, a senior manager at SFW, the government acted in recognition of the fact that the SAB had an important role to play in the liquor industry.

[24] Reported in *Wynboer*, November 1970, p. 13.

[25] "New Year's Message from André du Toit (Chairman of the K.W.V.)", *Wynboer*, January 1971.

sales to all grocery shops as a counter to monopolies in the liquor industry'.[26] Michael Fridjhon later observed that while the stake in Gilbey's was formally kept apart from the rest of the company, '[n]o-one who has seriously studied the wine industry in South Africa believes that the relationship is as arm's length as the cosmetics would suggest'.[27] Rembrandt's manoeuvre was matched by SAB's control over other substantial retail chains such as Solly Kramer's.

A second flash point was over brands. *Paarl Perlé* was a lightly petillant white wine modelled on lighter European styles. Following in the footsteps of *Lieberstein* a decade before, *Perlé* wines suddenly captured the imagination of consumers, most of whom would have been White. Monis claimed to have introduced such a product as early as 1963, in the shape of *Capenheimer*, and this was followed by several similar products from two of the independent companies, Douglas Green and Back's Wines. In September 1968, Monis launched *Perlheim Perlé* that was targeted specifically at the Eastern Cape market. The wine was, however, withdrawn in 1971.[28] Meanwhile in January 1970, the Paarl Wine and Brandy Company, a subsidiary of Distillers, proceeded to launch a version of its own, called *Paarl Perlé*. This coexisted with the much less important *Witzenberg Perlé*, which had been introduced in 1968 following the company takeover of the eponymous cooperative. Distillers' figures suggested that while its *Perlé* wines accounted for only 1 per cent of the unfortified wine market in 1971, this had jumped to as much as 28 per cent by 1972. Not surprisingly, the competition wanted a slice of the action. In 1971, there were no fewer than 19 *perlé* wines jostling for attention. In 1970–71, Monis launched its own version of *Paarl Perlé* at a higher price point and with advertising geared to enhancing its 'quality image'.[29] In an attempt to defend its initial advantage, Distillers quickly rebranded its product as *Original Paarl Perlé*. A memorandum enthused about the impact that the product was having across the land:

> Paarl Perlé is acceptable [sic] in all parts of South Africa by all consumers. It has captured the imagination of consumers outside the Western Cape to such a degree that it has become a substitute for other types of beverages. In areas such as Transvaal and O.F.S. where wine was a relatively 'unknown' drink, the Original Paarl Perlé has made the breakthrough and tought [sic] consumers to enjoy this type of liquor. Even in Natal, traditional cane country, wine and specifically Original Paarl Perlé has made an

[26] "Intolerable monopoly: allow wine sales in supermarkets pleads KWV chief", *Star*, 22 November 1978. Rembrandt eventually acquired a 49 per cent stake in Gilbey's.
[27] Fridjhon, *Penguin Book*, p. 62.
[28] Distell Archive, "Further Notes on Monis Paarl Perlé", in "Paarl Perlé Litigation".
[29] "Martell 1971", "Monis Perlé wines advertising, 1970/71".

amazing and unheard impact. The Original Paarl Perlé must be the largest selling wines in bottles (75ml) in South African liquor history.[30]

When Monis copied the success of the green bottle and introduced similar labels, Distillers went to court to defend its brand. The case was settled in such a way that Monis agreed to redesign its labels while continuing to enjoy access to the name. Then, in January 1972, SFW introduced *Selected Paarl Perlé*, which implied that it was a superior product to that of its rival. The two sides had previously agreed not to cast aspersions on each other's brands, and this was interpreted by Distillers as an open violation of that agreement. The case was finally settled out of court in 1978, with SFW agreeing to pay compensation.

The battle over *Paarl Perlé* was as nothing compared to what unfolded in the beer sector. The beer wars have been covered in detail elsewhere,[31] which means that it is possible to offer a more concise overview here. As I have already indicated, the Rembrandt group had attempted to break into brewing, with limited success. In 1972, Louis Luyt, an Afrikaner magnate who had made his money in the fertilizer business, decided to launch his own beer brand. After initial success, an alliance was sealed between Rupert and Luyt to develop a product called *Luyt Lager*. The inevitable battle with SAB was waged in bottle stores, bars, private homes and ultimately in the courts. In 1974, Rembrandt acquired all of Luyt's shares, and under the name of Intercontinental Breweries released a number of novel brands, such as *Colt 45*, onto the market. After a brief honeymoon in which beer drinkers enjoyed genuine choice, heavy losses resulting from price-cutting forced Rembrandt to the negotiating table. The final peace deal went against everything that Rupert had claimed to champion, namely, a liquor trade free of 'vexatious monopolies'. Under the agreement, Rembrandt left the beer market entirely in the hands of SAB. In the wine sector, a new joint company was formed, called Cape Wine and Distillers (CWD), in which the bitter rivalries of the past were formally sublimated. SAB/SFW held 30 per cent of the shares, Rembrandt/Distillers a further 30 per cent and the public 10 per cent. To general surprise, KWV was also cut in on the deal, with an additional slice of 30 per cent. This was remarkable, given the KWV's longstanding opposition to concentration in the industry.[32] According to a later Chief Executive

[30] Distell Archive, "The Perlé wine market", in "Paarl Perlé Litigation".

[31] Michael Fridjhon and Andy Murray, *Conspiracy of Giants: The South African Liquor Industry* (Johannesburg: Divaris Stein Publishers, 1986), pp. 178–184; Mager, *Beer*, ch. 2.

[32] The KWV justified joining CWD on the basis that the two other companies had agreed to sell their liquor outlets within 12 years. This was the basis of the case made to the government. "Address by the Chairman at the Annual Conference of Wine Farmers 27 November 1979", p. 1.

Officer of the SFW, it was Rupert who ensured that the KWV was included because of the likelihood that it would object to any deal it was excluded from, but also out of his own sense of loyalty to the wine farmers.[33] The deal signalled a break with the understanding that the KWV would keep out of the South African liquor market, while introducing a potential conflict of interest between the exercise of its public functions and the pursuit of its private interests. As Michael Fridjhon noted:

> The inevitable conflict of interest of the watchdog of the wine trade enjoying a significant shareholding in a company which would now be handling over 80 per cent of South Africa's wine and spirit sales was all but glossed over in the mad rush to consummate the arrangement.[34]

To all intents and purposes, the peace agreement divvied up the beer, wine and spirits sectors between the former adversaries. The icing on the cake was that they were permitted by the government to tighten their hold over the hotel and retail sectors. In the mid-1980s, the SAB held a commanding interest in 58 hotels from the Southern Sun and Holiday Inn chains, but also controlled 14 grocers' licences through the OK Bazaars supermarket chain.[35]

Rupert appeared to enjoy the last laugh when Rembrandt and the KWV promptly pooled their shares, thereby reducing SAB/SFW to the position of a minority shareholder in CWD.[36] Although SAB retained its shares, it concentrated its energies entirely on its core business, namely, bottled beer. As it turned out, the laugh was on all those whose investments were tied up in wine and spirits. But this is to jump ahead in our story. A final point to be made at this juncture is that although the creation of CWD formally brought an end to open warfare, Distillers and SFW retained their separate identities, management structures and leadership styles. While Distillers continued to be seen as a thoroughly Afrikaner company, in which hierarchies were deeply entrenched, the employees of SFW saw themselves as inhabiting a more convivial and democratic English-speaking business culture in which innovation and sociability went hand in hand.[37] However, there was more than management style at stake because the companies continued to compete vigorously for market share. This is exemplified by the following comment on the battle for

[33] Interview with Frans Stroebel, former Managing Director of SFW, 17 November 2009.

[34] Fridjhon, *Penguin Book*, pp. 13–14.

[35] By the mid-1980s, CWD collectively owned or controlled 212 hotel and liquor outlets, Oude Meester/Gilbey's 57, SAB 159 and Union Wine 131. See table 3 entitled "Producer involvement in retail liquor trade", Fridjhon and Murray, *Conspiracy*, p. 394.

[36] Fridjhon, *Penguin Book*, p. 14.

[37] Those who worked for SFW recalled that it was always good fun, which helped to build an esprit de corps that long survived retirements. Interview with Francis Naughton, 24 March 2009.

command of the sparkling wine market in an SFW memorandum dating from 1982/83:

> Now that the 5th Avenue [Cold Duck] blend has been rectified, the only weakness GMX [Grand Mousseux], 5th Avenue and Nederburg have, is that they're competitively out-maneuvered each festive season by price-cutting from their major competitors. The year-end is too important a period for all sparkling wine sales for this to be allowed: any losses suffered at this time cannot be recouped during the rest of the fiscal year.[38]

The competitors in question included Gilbey's and Bellingham, but also Distillers whose *Here XVII* and *Fleur du Cap* were making inroads into the Johannesburg and Pretoria markets. Little love was lost between companies that continued to regard each other in adversarial terms despite coming under the same umbrella. The competition between them was only somewhat mitigated by the fact that whereas SFW focused more on wine, Oude Meester/Distillers concentrated more on spirits. In 1982/83, the latter accounted for 63.3 per cent market of the spirits market, while SFW only controlled 24.9 per cent.[39]

In Search of the Elusive Wine Drinker

Once the liquor laws had been de-racialized with effect from 15 August 1962, the companies readied themselves for an uptake in sales. As Mager indicates, however, there was no sudden surge,[40] but then neither was there the orgy of drunkenness that the opponents of the amendment had predicted. Nevertheless, there remained considerable optimism about the medium-term prospects for the liquor industry. While Mager has mapped out the subsequent trajectory of the beer market, my interest here is in tracking the parallel history of wine. The industry understood that 'non-white' consumers would not necessarily flock to the products of the vine once these became open to them. It was necessary to turn wine into an object of desire. This required some carefully tailored advertising, which presupposed some prior knowledge of what the public identified with. This is where market research came in. The SFW, in particular, sought to build wine brands around each of the imagined clusters of consumers. This meant that considerable attention was paid to images, developing

[38] The change to the blend in *5th Avenue Cold Duck* was described as "disastrous". Over a 12 month period from 1982/83 to 1983/84, SFW wines on the Reef (Johannesburg) and Pretoria plummeted from 62.5 to 56.5 per cent of market share, although SFW still commanded 61.8 per cent of the overall market. Distell Archive "Sparkling Wine Overview 1984/85" in "Brand Plans 1984".

[39] Distill Archive, "Brandy", Table III, in "Brand Plans 1984".

[40] Mager, *Beer*, p. 20.

attractive (or merely functional) bottles and labels, and chiselling away at particular price points.

Although all the players were in favour of unfettered distribution to the entire population, they found it difficult to escape racial framings. The merchant-manufacturing companies and the KWV imagined a market for alcohol that would continue to be segmented according to race, with gender, age, and region adding additional layers of nuance. Within the marketing strategies for wine, there was a constant tension between two ways of making sense of consumption patterns. On the one hand, it was an article of faith that consumers travelled along a sensory continuum from sweeter white wines to semi-sweet wines and eventually to red wines, with many women tending to stop at the boundary between *rosé* and red wines. Hence, selling wines to Black consumers would inevitably have to start with sweeter styles and follow this natural progression. The possibility that Black consumers might actually prefer to drink red wines was not seriously entertained. On the other hand, the wine companies believed that the various population groups also had different proclivities, which made them susceptible to alternative kinds of messages. While Coloured consumers were considered to be intensely loyal to the same brands over time – and logically, therefore, did not move very far across the spectrum – White consumers were considered to be adventurous and yet also more fickle. The wine companies were never too sure whether Black consumers were more akin to White or Coloured consumers. One article in *Wynboer* in 1974 commented that, 'The fickle drinking habits of the Bantu have always been the bane of many a liquor marketing man. Just what the next rage will be is a question few can answer.'[41] The author attributed this pattern to trendsetters who were likely to champion brands that were considered prestigious, and he specifically cited the fate of *Paarl Perlé*, which lost its lustre in the shebeens once it dropped into the same price bracket as cheaper beers. But others were inclined to the view that Black consumers were rather loyal. The records of the SFW suggest that the company fluctuated between these positions. While Black consumers in the Eastern Cape were considered to exhibit some of the particularities of Cape Coloured consumers, their urban cousins on the Rand were considered more likely to follow White drinking habits and to be susceptible to the vagaries of fashion. But it would be fair to say that the companies never really felt that they had got to the bottom of what made Black consumers prefer one product over another. This contributed to the closing of what became a dangerous vicious circle. Because the companies suspected that Black consumers were not naturally wine drinkers, very little wine advertising was designed specifically for them. When sales were

[41] [Anon.], "Shebeens", *Wynboer*, July 1974, p. 8.

disappointing, this merely seemed to confirm the initial suspicion rather than provoking a change in strategy.

I will develop this argument in greater detail with specific reference to the SFW, but first it is worth saying something more about what we know about consumption patterns in the immediate aftermath of the amendment to the Liquor Act. One of the multiple ironies is that while the laws were being deracialized, the collection of market information reinscribed racial categories. In 1965, the National Bureau of Educational and Social Research published a series of reports on alcohol consumption based on surveys carried out across the country. The signifier was race, with separate reports being commissioned to address the consumption habits of designated groups: White, 'Bantus', Coloured (in the Cape and Natal), and Indians. The report on White consumption came to a number of conclusions that would certainly have interested the liquor industry. The survey revealed that as many as 31.8 per cent of White women abstained from alcohol as against 18.6 per cent of men. Of those who drank, women expressed a clear preference for wine (46.9 per cent) over beer (24.4 per cent) and spirits (28.7 per cent), whereas men preferred beer (40.9 per cent), followed by spirits (37.4 per cent) and only then wine (21.7 per cent).[42] A rather surprising finding was that White Afrikaans speakers of both sexes actually ranked wine (37.6 per cent) almost on a par with beer (38.3 per cent) and well ahead of spirits (24.1 per cent), whereas English speakers drank more spirits (39.5 per cent) than wine (31.4 per cent) or beer (29.1 per cent). It also found that this pattern held up regardless of income level. The report established that there was a clear preference for beer in the under-24 age category at 64.2 per cent, which dropped to 24.1 per cent in the 40–59 category and 21.9 per cent in the over-60 cohort, at which point spirits became the drink of preference. The report confirmed that White people drank more wine as they got older but there was much less variation than for beer, with a range from 25 per cent in the youngest cohort to 35 per cent in the oldest. The message was that there was much that could be done to increase wine consumption, especially amongst women, English-speaking men and the youth.

The report on Coloured consumption also confounded what might have been predicted on the basis of successive parliamentary debates and commissions of enquiry. The report found that 38.8 per cent of Coloured people were teetotallers, a figure that reached 56.2 per cent for women. Of those who drank, wine was favoured by 78.5 per cent of urban and 87.3 per cent of the rural Coloured population, with spirits in a distant second place (12 per cent and 2.7 per cent, respectively) and bottled beer in third place (6.9 per cent urban and

[42] J. D. Venter, *Die Drinkpatroon van die Blankes in Suid-Afrika* (Pretoria: Departement van Onderwys en Wetenskap, 1964), table 5.2, p. 61.

0.9 per cent rural).[43] This confirmed that Coloured consumers were the one section of the population who exhibited an overwhelming preference for wine. This pattern was further confirmed by a survey of the liquor industry in 1972, which revealed that Coloured consumption accounted for 46 per cent of the market for unfortified wine.[44] The report on Black consumption was equally revealing. It found that amongst the rural Black population, 73.2 per cent drank 'Bantu beer' as against 24.4 per cent for 'strong drink' (spirits), and only 6.5 per cent wine and 2.9 per cent for bottled beer. In the urban areas, the percentage who drank 'Bantu beer' rose to 87.7 per cent, while wine dropped to 2.2 per cent, and 'strong drink' and bottled beer to 0.3 per cent.[45] This supported the perception that there was a vast untapped market for both wine and bottled beer in urban centres. For beer and wine producers alike, there was an incentive to prise open the market for their various products. The Black market was, by far, the largest and the one that the liquor companies lined up in their sights. In 1970, the same survey found that while unfortified wine accounted for only 19.1 per cent of the liquor consumed by Black people, they already accounted for 31 per cent of the wine market by value. This was less than the Coloured, but more than the White population (22.5 per cent).[46] The report also claimed that unfortified wine was 'fast becoming popular among Africans'.[47] There were, however, some differences in the strategies pursued by the companies. In the case of beer, there was very little differentiation between the products based on quality or price. By contrast, the wine market was in the process of becoming much more variegated according to both price and quality.

To understand the complexities of the wine market, I turn now to a detailed examination of the operations of SFW, which remained the largest producer of wine. It was also the one company that sought to cover the complete spectrum of price points. In what follows, I will address each of the bands in turn, and will dwell on some of the products in greater detail. I will pursue this detailed analysis, taking two snapshot years separated by just over a decade, namely 1970/71 and 1981/82. Over this period, a significant development occurred in the SFW's marketing strategies. In 1970/71, the SFW's approach to marketing started from each of the products, of which there were relatively few, and then divided them according to race, gender and income group (from A to D) (Table 6.2). A decade later, the products were banded first according to price –

43 J. D. Venter, *Die Drinkpatroon Van die Kleurlinge in Kaapland en Natal* (Pretoria: Departement van Onderwys en Wetenskap, 1965), table 5.4, p. 43.

44 J. L. Rushburne and H. Hamman, *A Survey of the Liquor Industry in South Africa*, No. 7, July 1972 (Johannesburg: Statsinfom, 1972), p. 44.

45 J. D. Miles, *Die Drinkpatroon Van Die Bantoes in Suid-Afrika* (Pretoria: Departement van Onderwys en Wetenskap, 1964), table 6.1, p. 84. The 'Bantu beer' was the mainstay of the beer-halls.

46 Rushburne and Hamman, *Survey*, p. 44.

47 Rushburne and Hamman, *Survey*, p. 42.

Table 6.2. *Marketing of SFW wines, 1970–1971*

Product	Price Point	Intended Market	Advertising Channels	Promotions
Grand Mousseux (sparkling)	MP	White consumers of both genders, but with aspiration to break into Afrikaner market	Press, cinema	"Miss Champagne"
Monis Perlé	MP	White consumers, 18–35 years, B + C income groups; Coloured consumers	Press, cinema	
Zonnebloem range (4 wines)	HP	White males, A + B income groups	Press	
Lanzerac range (5 wines)	MP	White consumers, 18–35 Years, B + C income groups	Magazines, merchandising	
Nederburg range (4 wines)	HP	English and Afrikaner males, A + B income groups	Press	
Tasheimer	HP	White lower A + B and upper C income groups	Magazines, merchandising	
Lieberstein	LP	White consumers, C + D income groups; Coloured consumers	Press, cinema, merchandising	
Zonnheimer	LP	All groups, especially Western Cape	Press	
Virginia	LP	Cape Coloured consumers, Black consumers	Cinema, bus-shelters	
Golden Mustang	LP	Black consumers, especially Transkei	Bus shelters, merchandising	
Tassenberg	LP	White consumers, including Portuguese + Italian immigrants	Cinema	

Source: Distell Archives, 'Martell, 1971'.

high-priced (HP) through medium-priced (MP) to standard-priced (SP) – and a brand plan outlined the approach appropriate for each according to target groups, which were further broken up according to race, gender, age cohort and region (Table 6.3). This reflected the increasing complexity of selling wine to a highly stratified population, but it also revealed the extent to which the SFW was trapped within categories of its own making.

The SFW and the Wine Market

Distillers differed from the SFW in that it focused on the middle to upper tiers and abstained from the lower end of the wine market. Its earliest success was with white wines targeted at White consumers, most notably *Grünberger*

Table 6.3. *Market share of wine products, 1981–1984*

Price Point	1981/82	1982/83	1983/84
Total HP	100.0	100.0	100.0
SFW share of HP	34.6	33.6	31.4
Distillers share of HP	25.4	23.6	23.1
Gilbey's share of HP	7.8	6.4	5.0
Others' share of HP	32.2	36.4	40.5
	1982	*1983*	*1984*
Total MP	100.00	100.00	100.0
SFW share of MP	37.7	44.5	42.8
Distillers share of MP	40.9	39.7	39.9
Gilbey's share of MP	9.5	3.8	10.6
Union Wine share of MP	4.7	7.6	6.0
Others' share of MP	7.1	4.4	0.7
	1982	*1983*	*1984*
Total SP still	100.0	100.00	100.0
SFW share of SP	61.8	61.8	64.0
	1982	*1983*	*1984*
Total SP Perlé	100.0	100.0	100.0
SFW share of SP Perlé	2.0	2.0	–
Distillers share of SP Perlé	98.0	98.0	100.0
	1981/82	**1982/83**	**1983/84**
Total sparkling	100.0		
SFW share of sparkling	63.6	62.8	61.8
Distillers share of sparking	12.7	11.9	11.0
Gilbey's share of sparkling	16.9	18.5	18.6
All other including imported	3.8	6.8	8.6

Source: Distell Archive, 'Brand Plans, 1984' 'HP Wine Overview 1984–85'.

Stein, which dates to 1941 and whose sales remained respectable in the early 1980s. As we have already seen, the company had subsequently attempted to corner the market for *perlé* wines. When White consumers began to warm to red wines in the early 1970s, Distillers enjoyed considerable success with its *Fleur du Cap* and *Stellenryck* ranges. The former built a solid reputation as a well-crafted set of wines made from grapes drawn from many different farms, and it still accounted for 7.7 per cent of sales in 1981/82.[48] Through its Bergkelder subsidiary, Distillers also established close relationships with particular farms, which amounted to no fewer than 15 in 1974.[49] After the

[48] According to Michael Fridjhon, it was pitched at the middle range of the high-priced wines (HPs) with the intention of making it affordable. *Penguin Book*, p. 47.

[49] The farms attached to Bergkelder in 1986 were Alto, Allesverloren, Bonfoi, De Wetshof, Goede Hoop, Hazendal, Jacobsdal, Koopmanskloof, L'Ormarins, Le Bonheur, Meerlust, Meerendal, Middelvlei, Mont Blois, Rietvallei, Theuniskraal, Uitkyk and Zandvliet.

completion of the Bergkelder maturation cellar in Stellenbosch in 1968, the first of its kind in the southern hemisphere, the company exercised much greater control over the wine that came from its associated farmers.[50] The Bergkelder range capitalized on the estate concept, with the farm and cultivars clearly indicated on the labels.

For SFW, the objective was to have a foot firmly planted in all tiers of the wine market. In part, this enabled the company to spread its bets. It also enabled SFW to track changing tastes as wine novices began at the cheaper end of the spectrum and became accustomed to spending larger sums of money. SFW did not merely develop its brands, but assiduously cultivated its image as the purveyor of value-for-money products. A series of newspaper advertisements in the mid-1970s sought to build trust in the SFW by featuring particular individuals in the company and the role they played in advancing the cause of quality.[51] The hope was that trust would travel from one brand to the next, which is why the occasional glitch with a particular product – for example with *La Vie* and *5th Avenue Cold Duck* at different moments – was viewed with such consternation. The SFW attempted to stay two steps ahead of consumers and one step ahead of the competition. It experimented with innovations in packaging and bottling that were designed to reinforce brand images and create a consumer buzz. The bag-in-the box – which was pioneered in Australia but popularized in South Africa – as well as the jug and the screwcap, were amongst the most significant developments of the 1970s where the SFW was very much in the vanguard.[52] In the 1980s, it also enjoyed considerable success with flavoured wines.

Some cooperatives aspired to break their dependence on the SFW and to exploit many of the same openings. Perhaps the most enterprising was the Swartland Co-operative. In 1978, it despatched some of its production to the wine companies, notably the Clairette Blanche, Colombard and Semillon, but it also bottled sweet and dry Chenin Blanc under its own label.[53] In 1981, it ceased selling to the merchant-manufacturers altogether, although it continued to produce for the KWV export ranges. Its intention was to retreat from the production of distilling wine while developing its own range of drinking wines in a variety of formats, including the standard 750 ml bottle and the 5-litre

[50] The cellar, which covered one acre of space cut into the Papagaasiberg mountain, was consciously modeled on those in France and Germany. The project began in 1974 with West German advisors. Distell archive, Distillers papers, Press release, 25 February 1974.

[51] One of these focused on Francis 'Duimpie' Bayly and his role in blending SFW wines. The advertisement, which is to be found in the Distell Archive (SFW publicity files), was published in a supplement to the *Financial Mail* on 26 August 1977.

[52] The Australian innovation that was pioneered by Angove's was reported in the industry magazine in 1966. [Anon.] "A bag of wine please: Australian innovation has advantages for both domestic and export trade", *Wine, Spirit and Malt*, February 1966, p. 15.

[53] Simon Rappoport, "Swartland: land of bread and wine", *Wynboer*, July 1978, pp. 16–19.

bag-in-the-box. As it turned to producing red varietals such as Cabernet Sauvignon and Shiraz, the Swartland Co-operative also embraced barrel maturation. It was able to take advantage of the existence (at that time) of independent retailers such as Solly Kramer and the Rebel Group, who ensured access to consumers across the country without having to pass through the channels controlled by SFW.[54] Its success was reflected in a membership base which expanded from 83 to 102 farmers between 1978 and 1991, by which time there was also a waiting list to join.[55]

Room at the Top: High-Priced Wine

In the 1970s, there was a level of excitement surrounding wine that had not been witnessed since the halcyon days of *Lieberstein*. A stratum of more affluent Black consumers counted for something in numerical terms. The Coloured elite of Cape Town was sizeable but was also largely Muslim. Amongst more affluent White consumers there was considerable spending power, even if this was adversely affected by the accumulating economic difficulties in the 1980s. Alongside the proliferation of wine circles, a highly significant development was the initiation of the Nederburg Auction in March 1975. The idea seemingly originated with Lothar Barth, the German Managing Director of the SFW, who believed that an annual event like that of Kloster Eberbach would enable the industry to showcase its best wines.[56] With time, the auction garnered considerable publicity at home, and increasingly abroad. The estate producers benefited most from the perceived exclusivity of wines that commanded a greater financial premium.

The Wine of Origin (WO) system enabled wine lovers to experiment both with grapes and with the different styles. However, the same legislation also provided the wine companies with a readymade marketing platform. The SFW, for example, was quick to introduce a series of 'area wines' that foregrounded the district of origin and the grape varietal. The advertising was couched in quasi-educational language, alerting consumers to the specific attributes of the various districts. The aim was to differentiate an upper tier of wines that bore the hallmarks of place – although the word 'terroir' was strikingly absent – and that set them apart from products that were blended from grapes drawn from many different locations. Although white wines continued to dominate, the trend was increasingly towards red wines. By 1984, red wines accounted for

54 S. P. Brown, "An evaluation of the marketing strategies of good wine from selected co-operatives", unpublished paper, Durban, 1991, pp. 14, 44–50.

55 Brown, "An evaluation", p. 51.

56 Peter Garrett, "The Nederburg wine auction", *International Journal of Wine Marketing* 6 (1) 1994.

18.5 per cent of the overall HP market for red and this was continuing to increase year on year.[57] These wines were increasingly aged in oak barrels, were more expensive and, given the shortage of the necessary planting materials, were in short supply. This meant that there was often a rush to corner red wines that were regarded as market leaders. The pecking order was in constant flux. In the late 1970s, *Alto Cabernet Sauvignon*, which belonged to the Bergkelder stable, attracted the highest prices at the Nederburg Auction, but a decade later the mantle of exclusivity had passed to a wine such as *Meerlust Rubicon*, which was made in an identifiably Bordeaux style.

Whereas an estate producer could cultivate a small circle of adherents, the SFW needed to ensure that even its HP wines sold in sufficient quantities. This necessarily meant blending the wine from various producers even when they did originate from a single district. The message was that the SFW was in a position to produce wines of the highest quality because they could select the premium grapes. The other recurring theme was that it was perfectly possible to purchase quality wines at reasonable prices. The SFW was conscious that drinkers felt intimidated by the impenetrable language of wine aficionados. A series of advertisements sought to puncture cherished myths about wine and to challenge the perceived snobbery that attached to the product. One such feature, entitled 'Some Home Truths about Wine Myths', pointed out that drinking red wine at room temperature was based on European conditions and was often ill-suited to the South African climate. The equally cherished notion that white wines should be consigned to an ice bucket was dismissed on the basis that it killed the bouquet and resulted in a wine that tasted like 'mildly-flavoured iced water'.[58] The message, which echoed many of the themes of the KWV's own public information campaigns, was that drinking wine should not be regarded as something excessively complicated or out of the ordinary. The one exception was, of course, sparkling wine which, borrowing from the Champagne script, was advertised as a drink befitting special occasions.

At the top end, the merchant-manufacturers were chasing a relatively small number of consumers. Whereas SAB narrowed the product range, the wine sector underwent a proliferation of brands. In 1970/71, the wines that were unequivocally aimed at the upper end were limited in number: that is, the *Nederburg* range, which consisted of three white wines and a Cabernet Sauvignon, and the *Zonnebloem* range which comprised another four. Ten years later, the SFW supported 10 ranges at the HP level, many of which contained many varietal-specific products. The SFW was the dominant force in the HP market and was keen to defend its exalted position. In 1982/83, Distillers accounted for 23.6 per cent of the sales, with most coming through

[57] Distell Archive, "Brand Marketing Plan 1984/85: Chateau Libertas".
[58] Distell Archive (SFW publicity files), "Some home truths about some wine myths".

sales of *Fleur du Cap* and *Grünberger*. Gilbey's accounted for a further 6.4 per cent through the *Bertrams* and *Twee Jongegezellen* labels. Other smaller companies – Bellingham, Boschendal, Douglas Green – and independent producers accounted for a further 36.4 per cent. This was an indication that there was stiff competition for market share at the top end (see Table 6.3). Bellingham alone sustained 13 brands, and SFW had cause to worry about the positive press they were receiving from wine critics. Although the volume from independent producers was small and they did not advertise to any great extent, the demand for wines from specific estates was growing year on year as wealthier consumers tired of generic blends. At the end of 1986, Christine Rudman who had just joined the SFW observed that 'the co-ops, dynamic estates like Simonsig and house brands are where the major market growth is coming from'.[59] The SFW therefore needed to actively defend its position within the HP market, as it lost market share in the early 1980s (see Table 6.3).

The SFW response was to substantially increase advertising in the White market, mostly through pitches in glossy magazines such as *Scope*, *Personality* and others geared to the business community.[60] In 1981/82, SFW controlled 34.6 per cent of the HP market and spent 36.2 per cent of the advertising. Two years later, its market share had fallen to 31.4 per cent, whereas its share of the advertising spend had risen to 39.7 per cent (Table 6.4). A particular concern was that while the Johannesburg Reef and Pretoria accounted for 41.8 per cent of all HP sales, SFW's market share had fallen from 30.1 per cent to 26.9 per cent, whereas Bellingham wines were in the ascendancy. Although SFW maintained seven main ranges in the HP bracket, it was only *Nederburg* wines that were performing well, and even these struggled. As the brand plan for 1984 acknowledged:

> The market has changed a great deal since the 70s. Consumers have a greater quality perception than ever before, and also a greater sense of adventure in their HP wine drinking needs. Innovation and wine quality are therefore the two prime requisites for success in the market, and SFW has some weaknesses in this regard. It also has a serious problem in the Reef/Pretoria area. Competitive companies appear to be much more successful at building market share through the below-the-line support and sales attention than SFW.

In 1984, the bid to 'retain Nederburg's dominant position' included plans for the launch of a range of Special Wines 'that would create excitement' and a decision to increase the advertising budget had trailed its share of the HP market. The company recognized that the Black market was potentially

[59] Distell Archive, SFW pricing correspondence, Memorandum from Christine Rudman to Mr. D. Coleman, 10 December 1986.

[60] Magazine advertisements accounted for 39.7 per cent of all advertising expenditure at the top end in 1983/84. *Nederburg* was also advertised through television and cinema, but this was not the case with *Zonnebloem*.

Table 6.4. *Advertising and market shares for HP wines*

Brand	1981/82 Advertising Share	1981/82 Market Share	1982/83 Advertising Share	1982/83 Market Share	1983/84 Advertising Share	1983/84 Market Share
Nederburg	15.5	21.0	11.5	21.5	12.6	20.2
Zonnebloem	5.7	5.3	4.6	4.3	4.3	3.8
Oude Libertas	3.0	2.5	4.6	2.5	3.5	2.2
Lanzerac Rose	3.2	0.8	3.0	1.0	2.0	1.0
Tasheimer	4.8	2.4	4.2	2.3	3.4	1.9
La Gratitude	1.7	0.6	1.9	0.7	1.1	0.4
Chateau Libertas	1.8	1.0	1.4	1.1	1.4	1.2
La Vie	–	–	–	–	7.1	0.1
Graca	–	–	–	–	3.8	0.2
Other SFW	0.5	1.0	–	0.2	0.5	0.4
TOTAL SFW	36.2	34.6	21.2	33.6	39.7	31.4
TOTAL DISTILLERS	26.8	25.4	32.2	23.6	27.1	23.1
TOTAL GILBEY'S	14.0	7.8	11.5	6.4	9.1	5.0
Bellingham	12.4	8.8	8.5	9.9	7.2	9.9
Boschendal	0.7	1.9	0.3	2.1	1.1	3.3
Douglas Green	4.8	5.8	13.0	7.6	9.7	7.7
All Other	5.1	15.7	3.3	16.8	6.1	19.6
TOTAL	100.0	100.0	100.0	100.0	100.0	100.0

Source: 'Brand Marketing Plans', Distell Archives.

important, especially in the Transvaal. Tellingly, however, this was couched in the rather hackneyed language of emulation. Hence the 1984 plan noted that: 'A very small percentage of blacks are drinking *Nederburg*, all from the higher income and social groups who realise it will do their image good to drink wine at certain functions or public gatherings.' But the company decided not to dedicate any resources to advertising HP wines to Black consumers, preferring instead to rely on below-the-line promotions which cost less. The strategy was:

> To create a demand for Nederburg wines in the black market in a soft sell high image way. A proposal is being put together for a Life Style Club for the higher income and social groups in the Transvaal black areas. In addition, Nederburg must be seen at all top social events in these areas.[61]

Only Distillers made an effort to advertise directly to Black consumers, but the sums spent were small. Indeed, the overall amounts spent on the Black market by the wine firms in 1983/84 were minuscule: that is, R17,000 in print, R27,000 in cinema and R39,000 in television advertising at a time when the total spend for the industry was R3,829,000.[62]

The back-up to *Nederburg* was still *Zonnebloem*, which had been a key weapon in the SFW armoury for decades. In 1970/71, SFW records suggest that the *Zonnebloem* range had become popular amongst affluent White males, especially 'top businessmen'.[63] However, by 1984 the SFW conceded that 'Zonnebloem has got a bit left behind'. The marketing strategy was to introduce some new wine styles into the range, while paying for double-page and full-colour magazine and newspaper advertisements with an orientation towards 'males, Afrikaans speakers, high income, and Transvaal bias'. No consideration was given to promoting this range to anyone other than a White audience. The SFW recognized that many of its other established brands were languishing. The *Oude Libertas* range was described as 'sitting in no-man's land', given that it could not compete with the cooperative wines on price or with the leading brands and estate wines on image. In this case, the SFW hoped to revitalize the brand and launch a print advertisement campaign. Similarly, *Tasheimer* was thought to be suffering from the backlash against Chenin Blanc wines. *Chateau Libertas* was considered important because of its historic association with SFW, but also redeemable through changes to packaging, fresh advertising and an orientation towards Pinotage. In the case of *La Gratitude*, one proposal was to consider killing off the *grande dame* – who had been going since 1936 – although this was not acted upon.[64]

[61] Distell Archive, "Brand Plans, 1984: La Vie, 1984/85".
[62] Distell Archive, "Brand Plans, 1984: HP Wine Overview 1984/85". [63] "Martell, 1971".
[64] Van der Merwe, *Magic*, p.48.

La Vie was launched in September 1983 as an 'off-dry' white wine that was designed to appeal to the 'unsophisticated palate' and 'modern fun-loving people'. The SFW was of the view that it would have 'potential among young, modern, free spending black consumers' and an effort was made to increase its appeal through disco promotions. But, as with *Nederburg*, it was decided that 'the budget does not permit a separate plan for the secondary market of urban Blacks and Coloureds, so we have to rely on spillover'.[65] Two years later, the product had to be withdrawn. Although *La Vie* had flopped, the SFW decided to launch one more brand onto the market in September 1983. *Graça* was presented as a 'light, off-dry wine ... inspired by the warmth and charm of Portuguese wines'.[66] It was pitched at the bottom end of the HP bracket and was aimed mostly at younger drinkers. It sold in a distinctive bottle, and the advertising was directed at 'current beer drinkers who are occasional beer drinkers', playing on its supposedly 'cheeky' character. This wine was also pitched at the restaurant trade, and a particular association with seafood was emphasized.[67] In 1989, a survey of white wine drinking found that *Graça* lagged well behind *Nederburg Stein*, *Grünberger Stein* and *Bellingham Grand Cru*. An internal memorandum noted that the brand depended on 'a few people drinking a lot and that this seemed to be borne out by direct observation!'[68] Although most of the wine in the HP range was targeted at young White males, *Lanzerac Rosé* was a product specifically directed at White women. The wine was advertised through women's magazines, with a sales push in advance of Valentine's Day and Mother's Day.

Although sparkling wines were treated as a category in their own right, it makes sense to consider them within the HP category. In the early 1970s, *Grand Mousseux* held the largest share of the market. The sponsorship of a 'Miss Champagne' campaign on university campuses was a clear indication that 'GMX' was also aimed at a younger age bracket. In 1981/82, the SFW still commanded a 69.1 per cent share of the market. But the SFW faced mounting competition from other companies as well as from independent producers like Simonsig which had pioneered the production of sparkling wine in a *champenois* style. The Reef and Pretoria was the region with the highest growth, and this was also where 'GMX' faced the fiercest competition. It was packaged to look like champagne and came in three formats according to the level of sweetness. At a time when imports accounted for a very small share of the

65 "Brand Plans, 1984: HP Wine Overview 1984/85".

66 It was intended as a South African take on vinho verde. The Portuguese connection was pushed to the point that the labels had to be changed in 1983 for fear of misleading consumers. Van der Merwe, *Magic*, p. 39.

67 Distell Archive, "Brand Plans, 1984: Graça".

68 Distell Archive, loose SFW papers, Memorandum from J. H. Gibson, to B. Glass and D. Conradie (28 August 1989).

market, the branding message was that 'Grand Mousseux is South Africa's only traditional "champagne."' The product was advertised through television and print, with a particular focus on bridal magazines. *Nederburg* sparkling wines were aimed at a notionally more sophisticated audience. Finally, whereas 'GMX' advertising was targeted at predominantly male consumers, *5th Avenue Cold Duck*, 'a pink "champagne" which is modern, young, off-beat', was directed more at younger women. Predictably, it was ever so sweet.

The Bulging Middle: The Centrality of MP Wines

In some respects, the MP sector was the most important of all because there was a realistic possibility of expanding the volume of sales to all population groups. The profit margins were also higher than for SP wines. The SFW explicitly positioned itself as the champion of South Africa's equivalent of good *vin ordinaire*. The attempt to beef up the middle is reflected in the fact that of the 10 wines that the SFW sought to market in 1984, only *Tassenberg* had been on the books in 1970/71. A significant turning point came in 1973, when the SFW introduced the *Autumn Harvest* range at the lower to middle end of the MP cluster. The range was eventually extended to no fewer than eight wines. The labels were intended to be appealing to the eye as well as easy to understand. They simply depicted a Cape Dutch farmhouse and the specific varietal, with a distinguishing colour for each. The wine was bottled with a screwcap, and in 1979 it also became available in a bag-in-the-box format. The Transvaal was, by far, the most important destination. Part of the marketing strategy was to encourage more White women to embrace white wine. The anticipated market was 55 per cent female and 55 per cent English-speaking. The chosen theme was 'a healthy outdoor appeal … to fun-loving sociable people'. The print advertisements depicted happy couples engaged in friendly banter around a table or indulging in romantic picnics in woods and along gently flowing streams (see Figure 6.1). Noticeably absent were images of groups of women drinking together. By the early 1980s, television slots were given precedence in the SFW campaign strategy.

The addition of a *Crackling Perlé* to the range in 1976 was an attempt to extend the appeal to a Black consumer market. For both segments, *Autumn Harvest* was regarded as a way to lead consumers into a more compete appreciation of wine. The 1984 brand plan stated that:

> The brand will communicate with both major race groups, depicting Autumn Harvest as the best tasting, highest quality convenience wine which fits their informal lifestyles … Autumn Harvest offers both intrinsic and extrinsic quality re-assurance and as such should encourage a greater understanding of natural wine leading to an overall increase in the per capita consumption of natural wine.[69]

[69] Distell Archive, "Brand Plans, 1984: Autumn Harvest".

Figure 6.1 SFW advertisement for Autumn Harvest Crackling
Source: Distell Archive.

The brand was a substantial success, accounting for around a third of the market for MP wines in the early 1980s. The difficulty that the SFW faced was that its rivals sought to undercut *Autumn Harvest* on price. As the brand plan noted:

> The MP wine market has become a complex market with the inflow of the 'rats and mice' brands. Furthermore, with the excellent harvest that we have had for the last few years, we can expect even more Co-ops to enter the market at very competitive prices. This situation forced S.F.W. to change their strategy, firstly with Kellerprinz.[70]

The document observed that the range was suffering 'serious image problems in the Eastern Cape and Transvaal'. In the former case, Distillers' *Castelo Ginger Fizz* had made significant inroads. This was part of the attempt by rival companies to attract new consumers by introducing flavoured wines. The SFW responded by introducing its own variant of ginger *perlé*, called *Spark*, but its impact was marginal – at only 5 per cent of the market in the early 1980s.

The SFW sought to protect itself against what it depicted as 'concocted wines' through more innovative packaging and more aggressive marketing. In the case of *Crackling*, this included shebeen tastings and live disco shows. The latter was seen as particularly important for reaching urban and rural consumers alike. The plan also included greater expenditure on television, newspaper, radio and cinema advertisements that were designed to support the image of *Autumn Harvest* as a wine that was both affordable and of superior quality. The message of conviviality that had been created for White consumers was now repackaged for a Black audience. But the 'emotional' messages delivered up for the urban and rural Black communities also had a somewhat different emphasis. Urban Black men – and women too – were expected to identify with the message that *Crackling* 'reflects the sociable way of life I enjoy. I would be happy to drink it anywhere with friends'. In the rural eastern Cape, part of the pitch was to the pleasure of drinking with friends, but the product was also supposed to enable the drinker to 'escape from the tedium of daily life'.

Convincing White men that there was nothing effeminate about drinking wine posed a particular challenge, not least because beer had been packaged as quintessentially male. A dimension of SFW strategy was to promote red wines as a suitable product for men. In the 1970s, the *Kellerprinz* range was constructed around images of male bonding around 'the typical lifestyle of braaivleis, boerewors and biltong'.[71] In order to reinforce this cognitive association, a Kellerprinz Braai Competition was launched by the SFW. The wine, which was directed to those 'who generally do not have sophisticated wine-drinking habits', was made available in both a box and jug format. Again, there was some attempt to make inroads into the Black market:

[70] Distell Archive, "Brand Plans, 1984: Kellerprinz". [71] "Brand Plans, 1984: Kellerprinz".

The Braai is the brand's property and ad hoc regional braai promotions will still be held. The Fun Braai concept is extremely successful in the Transvaal and should be extended to other regions. Specific shebeen promotions in the black areas will be held, and for support here a number of trade objects will be produced.[72]

The greatest competition came from Gilbey's *Valley* wines which were also sold by the jug and had found willing customers in the shebeen trade since the late 1970s. The company also expressed plans for regional promotions, including a Winelands marathon, a drama festival in the Western Cape and promotions for butchers in Pretoria.

Tassenberg was the other product within the MP range that was considered as strategically important. It was a red wine pitched at the lower end of the MP range and was made mostly from Cinsault grapes, although the exact blend differed from one year to the next. By the early 1980s, it enjoyed a reputation out of all proportion to its relatively modest sales figures. As time went on, 'Good old Tassies' thrived from a nostalgia amongst those who had once been students.[73] The product remained especially popular with the student body and the Portuguese community, and many SFW staff swore by its quality. It was positioned as 'an outdoor, macho lifestyle brand that reflects the brand's unpretentious and unique personality'. Finally, *Roma White* was a dry wine that originated in the Monis portfolio. It was sold largely to Portuguese living in the Transvaal who apparently deployed it as a mixer with Coca-Cola. It was rebranded in 1989 and then eventually killed off.

Standard-Priced Wines

Finally, we come to those wines that were pitched at the bottom of the market. Many of these had a venerable track record, most notably *Lieberstein* and *Oom Tas*. Although the profit margins were extremely tight, the SFW counted on what it considered a loyal customer base, especially amongst Coloured drinkers in the Western Cape. Its aim was to hold onto the latter while making inroads into the much larger Black market. The SFW considered that Coloured drinkers manifested a dogged attachment to specific brands and associated styles, which meant that radical innovation was not considered necessary or even desirable. The SFW had learned from its chastening experience with *Oom Tas*, a dark-hued dry white wine that had established a loyal constituency in the rural Cape (it was not marketed in other provinces) soon after its introduction in 1952. At one point in the 1960s, the SFW unwisely decided to correct a printing error on the label, which erased something that looked like the number

[72] "Brand Plans, 1984: Kellerprinz".

[73] Braam Van Velden recalled that, as a student, the price of a whole bottle of Tassenberg was the same as that of a glass of brandy and Coke. Interview, 5 August 2009.

Figure 6.2 Oom Tas Label (with the '7' located towards the right below clouds and above hill)
Source: Distell Archive.

'7' (see Figure 6.2). The latter was thought to mark the halfway mark in the bottle, which was of considerable importance for weekend drinkers who would typically buy a bottle together to share. The change to the label provoked such an uproar – allegedly including fist fights amongst drinking companions – that SFW was forced to reinstate the old labels for fear of losing its most loyal customers. *Oom Tas* was crucial to SFW because it was second only to *Virginia* as the most widely consumed white wine. SFW learned that what was in the bottle also counted a great deal. The lore within the SFW was that even a slight change to a given blend would be detected by Coloured consumers who would trust their palates and vote with their feet.

Virginia itself accounted for 28.4 per cent of the SP market in 1981/82. In 1970/71, the marketing for *Virginia* was conducted through cinema advertisements and posters appended to bus shelters. The advertising jingle 'The Wine for Men Who Enjoy Being Men' needed little deconstruction, nor did the poster advertisements that depicted images of bulging biceps. Later in the 1970s, the SFW attempted to consolidate its hold on the Coloured market through sponsorship of football in the Cape. The SFW was in no doubt about the intended market: 'Virginia is positioned as a wine for heavy consumers of

Table 6.5. *Racial distribution of low-priced wine market (percentages)*

Wine Type	White Consumers	Black Consumers	Coloured Consumers	% Share of Total LP
White semi-sweet	10	20	70	64.5
White dry	90	5	5	2.2
Golden semi-sweet	5	75	20	11.5
Golden dry	–	10	90	9.5
Rose	85	5	10	2.3
Red	80	15	5	4.5
Perlé	75	20	5	5.5
Total	10	25	65	100

Source: [Anon.], 'Suid-Afrika se landswyne onder die soeklig: n ontleding in al sy komponente', *Wynboer*, February 1977, table 3, p. 33.

alcoholic beverages, including spirits and beer.' Football promotions continued to be used to promote Virginia as 'a natural and masculine' wine during the 1980s. By this point, the market share of *Lieberstein* had dwindled to 8.1 per cent. Although some working-class White drinkers continued to patronize it, it had come to viewed as primarily a wine for middle-aged Coloured men in the Cape and Black consumers in the Cape, the Transvaal and South-West Africa (Namibia). The remaining products were geared to even more specific niches. In the early 1980s, SFW still sold one cheaper *perlé* wine, *Perlino Perlé*, which only accounted for 15.9 per cent of sales in that sector of the market. It was restricted to Natal and South-West Africa. *Zonnheimer* was targeted at poorer Black and Coloured people in the Western and North-Western Cape and was not advertised at all. The same was true of *Golden Mustang*. In 1970/71, the latter had been directed at Black consumers in the Eastern Cape, but 10 years later the intended market had shifted to Coloured populations in the Orange Free State and the Cape. Finally, *Royal King* was a sweet white sold to Coloured and Black people in the North-Western Cape. As Table 6.5 demonstrates, the LP end of the entire market was explicitly divided up according to designated racial segments. As much as 75 per cent of the 'golden semi-sweet' wines were consumed by Black people, but only 10 per cent of the 'golden dry' (principally *Oom Tas*), for which the other 90 per cent was accounted for by Coloured drinkers. What the industry was probably insufficiently alert to was the fact that Black consumers were more oriented to red wines at the LP level than their Coloured counterparts were.

Within the SP bracket, the SFW had a firm grip on the market. In the company's view it was aided somewhat by the difficult economic conditions of the early 1980s. One memorandum noted that: 'The positive trend in the market may be attributed to the current state of the economy, forcing many consumers to trade down to SP wines from more expensive drinks.'[74] It was also helped by the fact that its principal competitors displayed little interest in plumbing the cheaper end of the market. However, a serious concern for the SFW was that the cooperatives began to offload wine that they could not otherwise find a market for. This became a contentious issue in the 1980s, as I will demonstrate in greater detail in the next chapter. According to Lothar Barth of the SFW, the dumping of bulk wine in the market at below the good wine price set by the KWV – in large plastic containers (*swartvarkies*) or bag-minus-the box (*papsak*) – damaged the image of the entire industry.[75]

Racial Imaginings and the Market for Wine

In 1972, the survey of the liquor industry predicted that between 1970 and 1976 the sales of unfortified wine would grow by an annual average of 17 per cent and that its share of the liquor market would increase from 25.9 per cent to 37.1 per cent of sales over the same period.[76] This projection was based on the anticipated uptake from Black consumers whose rising income would enable them to make the transition away from 'Bantu beer' as they sought 'to imitate European drinking habits'. The report went on to predict that:

> In view of the large share of Africans in the total market for unfortified wines (31,0% of the total by value in 1970 and worth R16,8 m), expansion of this group market must considerably increase, not only the national total of wine sales, but also the proportion, therein, of 'inexpensive' class wines.[77]

Amongst White consumers, the survey reported 'no less than a revolution in European drinking habits.'[78] More favourable taxes by comparison with bottled beer and spirits, could be expected to enlarge the market for middle-tier wines. In addition, it noted that the effects of the 1964 revision to the Liquor Act were likely to have an important effect:

> A subsidiary factor will be the availability of unfortified wine from grocers, which will increase the convenience of shopping for wine and remove the stigma undoubtedly attached by many women to the open purchase of liquor in bottle stores . . .[79]

On the other hand, the survey noted that the Coloured segment of the market appeared to have reached saturation point.

[74] Distell Archive, "Brand Plans, 1984: The SP Wine Market".

[75] Selling at below the minimum price was technically illegal. Lothar Barth, "Wine plan needed to rejuvenate static SA market", *Liquor Store Monthly*. In fact, Barth also had second thoughts about the bag-in-the-box and the image it helped to create. Lothar Barth, "Problems Persist", both in "50 Years in the SA Liquor Industry – 1940 to 1990", *Liquor Store Monthly* (possibly 1991).

[76] Rushburne and Hamman, *Survey*, p. 40.

[77] Rushburne and Hamman, *Survey*, p. 45.

[78] Rushburne and Hamman, *Survey*, p. 46.

[79] Rushburne and Hamman, *Survey*, pp. 45–46.

Table 6.6. *Wine and beer consumption per capita (in litres), 1970–1985*

Year	Natural Wine	Sparkling Wine	Fortified Wine	Total	Beer
1970	8.75	0.09	2.59	11.43	13.72
1975	7.27	0.11	2.80	10.18	19.09
1976	7.05	0.10	2.74	9.89	20.21
1977	6.43	0.11	2.47	9.01	19.47
1978	6.35	0.11	2.21	8.67	20.13
1979	6.60	0.11	1.95	8.74	22.90
1980	7.12	0.12	1.86	9.09	29.62
1981	7.66	0.14	1.84	9.64	33.87
1982	7.60	0.14	1.64	9.38	37.97
1983	7.99	0.14	1.47	9.60	39.31
1984	8.27	0.16	1.47	9.90	41.16
1985	8.35	0.16	1.41	9.92	41.18

Source: Distell Archives, *Stellenbosch Farmers' Winery Annual Review*, 1987

As predictions go, the survey was well wide of the mark. As Table 6.5 reveals, the pattern was actually a decline in the per capita consumption of natural (table) wine, followed by a slow increase in the 1980s. In the case of sparkling wine, consumption per capita was static in the 1970s, and then increased marginally in the first half of the 1980s. The steady decline in the consumption of fortified wines continued unabated. If the three products of the vine are taken together, there was a reduction of per capita consumption from 11.43 litres per capita in 1970 to 9.92 litres per capita in 1985 (see Table 6.6). Over the same period, the per capita consumption of beer rose sharply from 13.72 litres to 41.18 litres per capita. Measured in terms of crude volume, the consumption of natural wine grew slowly over the 1970s, and only began to register significant growth in the first half of the 1980s. In 1970, South Africans consumed 160,285 million litres of natural wine as against 279,126 million litres in 1986, amounting to an increase of 57.4 per cent (Table 6.7). Over the same time period, the consumption of beer increased more than fivefold. Moreover, a ranking of liquor brands by market share in 1986 revealed that the three SAB beer brands came top, while *Autumn Harvest* stumbled over the line at fifteenth place, with a turnover equivalent to a mere 4 per cent for that of Castle Lager.[80] *Kellerprinz*, *Oom Tas* and *Virginia* followed close behind, but cumulatively their impact on the liquor market was still very small.[81]

80 *Castle Lager* alone captured 27.5 of the alcohol turnover whereas *Autumn Harvest* accounted for 0.8 per cent in 1986. Data on turnover for top 25 alcohol brands from Distell Archive, "Stellenbosch Farmers' Winery Annual Review, 1987".

81 "Stellenbosch Farmers' Winery Annual Review, 1987".

Table 6.7. *Wine and beer consumption, 1970–1985 (million gross litres)*

Year	Natural Wine	Fortified Wine	Sparkling Wine	Beer
1970	160,285	53,568	2,011	259,098
1975	185,944	71,710	2,736	488,286
1976	184,035	71,586	2,626	527,537
1977	171,943	66,018	2,829	521,391
1978	173,276	60,329	2,973	550,762
1979	186,392	55,108	2,989	642,296
1980	206,651	53,953	3,525	860,358
1981	228,779	54,853	4,260	1,011,757
1982	233,517	50,345	4,260	1,166,537
1983	251,553	46,453	4,351	1,242,079
1984	268,837	47,875	5,212	1,337,710
1985	279,126	47,009	5,456	1,376,725

Source: Distell Archives, *Stellenbosch Farmers' Winery Annual Review*, 1987.

Clearly, the wine companies had failed to make the kind of inroads into the Black market that SAB had achieved with beer. Moreover, they seemed to have lost ground in the Coloured segment of the market. A KWV survey of Coloured adults in 1987 found that 51 per cent of Coloured men and only 24 per cent of women drank alcohol, in comparison with figures of 82 per cent for White men and 71 per cent of White women. But in a remarkable reversal, beer had overtaken wine as the drink of preference:

> Unlike Whites, where the frequency of drinking beer and wine is on a par, beer, amongst Coloureds dominates. On average, beer is consumed 5,8 times per month and wine 4,1 times per month. Flavoured wine is the next most frequently drunk alcoholic beverage (2,4) followed by brandy at 1,7 times, rum at 1,6 times then champagne at 0,7 times per month.[82]

This raises the fundamental question of why beer and wine followed such divergent trajectories. There are a number of possible reasons why wine sales were so disappointing, but I will focus on three: the nature of the product, the marketing message and the mode of advertising. As far as the product itself is concerned, some in the industry fell back on the comforting explanation that Black people were simply not natural wine drinkers. But as had been noted many times before – from Louis Leipoldt to the Malan Commission – there was a ready market for wine in Lourenço Marques. There was no intrinsic reason why the same should not have been true of South Africa. The reasons

[82] Distell Archive, "Market Research", "KWV Research Project – Coloured Adults", 21 October 1987.

surely resided elsewhere. It is significant that after establishing a beer monopoly, SAB relied on only three brands, namely *Castle*, *Lion* and *Carling Black Label*, although *Amstel* was later added as a premium brand.[83] Given the very restricted choice, it was relatively simple to build brand identities. *Black Label* was targeted particularly at Black consumers and traded on the (false) perception that it contained a greater alcoholic content. The SAB was also remarkably adept at encouraging White consumers to express a strong attachment to either *Lion* or *Castle* as rival brands. In the wine industry, by contrast, there was a bewildering array of brands and labels that many consumers found confusing. Moreover, there was a belief in the industry that Black South Africans associated wine with the structures of oppression.[84] Wine also had an unfortunate association with chronic alcoholism in the rural Western Cape, not least because of the link to the dop system. Wine was, consequently, a much harder sell for people who had not grown up drinking it. By contrast, neither beer nor spirits carried the same burden of negative associations.

The second reason is that the wine companies struggled to find a set of marketing messages that would appeal directly to Black consumers. In the case of beer, SAB advertising pushed the association between beer and conviviality amongst men. In particular, it sought to build on the idea of bonding around sport. The sports in question differed – rugby and cricket in the case of White consumers and football in the case of Black and Coloured ones – but the message was comparable. In the case of *Black Label*, 'America's Lusty, Lively Beer', the masculine theme was linked to its foreign provenance. The notion that by drinking Black Label one might find oneself in communion with an international community of beer drinkers was echoed in advertising for spirits. One *Bols Brandy* advertisement from 1974 played on the simultaneity of time, with three pictures juxtaposed: in the first two, drinkers in Europe and South America are shown enjoying their *Bols* around a table, and in the third larger picture four well-dressed Black men savour their own drink over a game of draughts. The caption reads 'All Over the World Friendships Form Around Bols Brandy'.[85] The glossy advertising for *Mainstay*, a cane spirit, typically involved scantily clad men and women – increasingly Black and White together – frollicking at exotic beach locations. In the case of wine, the use of names that sounded German was part of an attempt to invoke European associations, but the other imagery was very much rooted in local motifs, most notably Cape Dutch homesteads, from which the images of slavery were hard

[83] Amstel was brewed under licence from Heineken. Mager, *Beer*, p. 58.

[84] Bennie Howard, formerly of the SFW publicity department, expressed this view in conversation. It was also mentioned in an interview with Francois Naudé, 31 August 2009.

[85] The advertisement is contained in a folder in the Distell Archives entitled "Bols Brandy Superstar Show (1980)".

to erase, and the Cape fold mountains. To drink wine was to be reminded of the fact that one was cut off from the rest of the world and mired in a past that never seemed to move on. The theme of conviviality was central to wine advertising, but with the important difference that the industry tried to ensnare female drinkers while seeking to reassure male drinkers. Although this worked well in the case of *Autumn Harvest*, it translated less effectively to the Black market. For the wine companies, the Black female consumer scarcely existed as a category.

While the marketing for *Virginia* made a very explicit appeal to Coloured masculinity through the association with football, it is noteworthy that the wine industry failed to develop advertising messages that were explicitly geared to Black consumers. In the years immediately after legalization, there were some clumsy efforts in this direction. The KWV initially took up the challenge with a series of promotional advertisements. However, these essentially recycled themes and images that had initially been crafted for a White audience, most especially the claim that drinking wine with food was a marker of civilization and distinction. A series of advertisements depicted African middle class nuclear families who put their children to bed and settled down to a meal together or with their equally respectable friends (see Figure 6.3). The scenarios that were depicted must have felt distinctly implausible. The wine companies themselves introduced brands that they thought would appeal to Black drinkers on the basis of an appeal to masculine themes, in effect extrapolating from some of their marketing to Coloured men. In 1969, Monis put out *Samson Special* advertisements that depicted a woman feeling the biceps of a man holding a glass of wine – one with a Coloured subject and another with a Black one. A large poster depicted a bodybuilder in a similarly unsubtle attempt to associate wine with masculinity. The brand did not survive. In 1970/71, the SFW was marketing *Golden Mustang*, a sweet white wine, to Black consumers, using cowboy imagery which was very similar to the deployment in advertisements for *Black Label* beer and *Marlboro* cigarettes. The notion that Black South Africans were obsessed with virility, and quite possibly cowboys, explains the alarmed tones in which a Distillers employee reported overhearing an SFW counterpart remarking that he intended to spread the word that their product would render the drinker impotent.[86] Over time, the effort to market wine to Black consumers became more tokenistic. Insofar as they were targeted at all, it was by introducing Black models into contrived social settings that had been previously developed to sell wine to White and Coloured consumers. The Lieberstein advertisements aimed at Black consumers are a clear case in point, even down to the implausible accordion (Figure 6.4).

[86] Distill Archive, "Graça", in "Brand Plans 1982".

Figure 6.3 KWV advertisement aimed at Black elite
Source: Distell Archive.

Figure 6.4 Lieberstein advertisement for a Black audience
Source: Distell Archive.

This brings us to a third reason, namely the way in which the marketing messages were disseminated. As I have indicated, in the case of SFW there was almost no targeted advertising for Black consumers. The SFW preferred to engage in 'below-the-line' promotions. In the early 1960s, SAB had sought to increase the market for beer through sponsorship of the Cold Castle festival. This model was then copied by wine and spirit companies. E. K. Green introduced *Jazzman* brandy and the Castle Wine and Brandy Company introduced a Jazzking of the Year Award to promote *Golden Castle*, a sweet white wine. In 1967, the award was lifted by the drummer Early Mabuza, and the following year he was runner-up to the saxophonist Winston 'Mankunkunku' Ngozi (Figure 6.5).[87] After a promising start, the attempt to sell wine through jazz withered. In the 1970s, the association between alcohol and music continued, but it was spirits that constituted the principal focus. In 1972, the local megastar was Richard Jon Smith, a Coloured performer who was described in the *Sunday Times* as an 'ad man's dream'. SFW made Smith the centrepiece of its brandy promotion through a 'Bols Show' that was held in townships around Johannesburg.[88] His agent could have been speaking for the wine industry itself when he commented that:

> When you deal with the Black market you cannot rely on the conventional advertising and promotional methods of Press and radio. I believe the best way to reach Blacks is through live entertainment. They don't normally get much live entertainment, but when it is made available, it never fails to draw the crowds.

The fact that the SFW chose to market *Bols* through jazz, and not wine, indicates that there was a conscious strategy to separate the marketing for wine and spirits. The belief was that small-scale promotions, in which wine was given free to customers was all that was effectively required. In the case of the lesser brands, such as *Golden Mustang*, even the promotions were abandoned. At the bottom end of the market, the assumption was that Black consumers would find their way to wine if it was cheap and sweet enough. This mindset persisted despite the fact that by 1977 Black people accounted for 25 per cent of the LP wine market.[89] At the MP and HP levels, the thinking was that because Black consumers were inclined to mimic their White counterparts, it was less important to advertise directly than to ensure that wine was served at influential occasions. Across the board, this meant that Black South Africans were left to discover wine of their own accord rather than being

[87] A copy of the promotional record is in the Distell Archive, but see http://electricjive.blogspot.co.uk/2011/03/jazz-royalty-swinging-bittersweet.html.

[88] Smith was also deployed by BP and Coca-Cola. [Anon.], "Superstar Richard: He's an ad man's dream", *Sunday Times*, 26 August 1972.

[89] [Anon.], "Suid-Afrika se landswyne onder die soeklig: 'n ontleding in al sy komponente", *Wynboer*, February 1977, table 3, p. 33.

Figure 6.5 Advertisement for 'Golden Castle Jazzking of the Year'
Source: Distell Archive.

directly courted by the industry. By contrast, the SAB invested large sums of money in bringing images of the good life steeped in beer to Black consumers of all kinds – and it evidently reaped the awards.

The breakdown of the White and Coloured consumer markets into discrete segments suggested that the SFW had a fine-grained understanding of its customer base. By contrast, the only serious distinction amongst Black consumers was between urban drinkers on the Rand and predominantly rural consumers in the Eastern Cape. To redress the problem of imperfect information flows, the industry began to listen more closely to the shebeen owners in the latter half of the 1970s. A feature article in *Wynboer* magazine in 1978 dealt specifically with the topic of wine and shebeens and noted that the latter remained more popular than beer halls because they provided a space where men could drink in the company of women. Following in the footsteps of a 1974 article, it identified no fewer than five different types of shebeen according to what was on offer and the clientele they attracted.[90] At one end were the 'high class shebeens' where food was available for purchase and which were characterized by 'dim lights and soft jazz emitting from an expensive hi-fi'. Next came the 'middle-class shebeens' which lacked the 'luxurious trappings'; then the small shebeens which obtained their supplies from municipal bottle stores and shebeen kings; and then again the 'Black beer shebeens'. At the extreme end of the spectrum were the 'drinking dens' where all manner of concoctions were served and criminality was rife. The implication was that the wine industry needed to pay greater attention to the first three types of shebeen, where there was potential to expand the market for wine. However, the author of the article noted that this would require an educational campaign to inform Black people of the manifold benefits of wine.

An additional nuance in the article was the observation that Africans were, above all, social drinkers who typically shared what they bought:

> The Blacks were never, not even to this day, partial to the colonialistic habit of sundowner drinking. Drinking alone in front of the family or even with the wife has never been a happy circumstance among them. Unlike custom in Western civilization, the Black knows no set hours in which it is sociable to consume alcohol. By nature he is a sociable person and indeed a social drinker. He is inclined to want to drink in large groups sharing his liquor with easy-going gregarious company.[91]

This meant that it was important to make available wine of a high quality that could be sold in more substantial quantities. Moreover, this article invoked the mantra that Africans were likely to prefer sweeter styles, much as Afrikaners had in the past:

[90] [Anon.], "Wine and shebeens in Soweto", *Wynboer*, October 1978, p. 14.
[91] "Wine and shebeens", p. 12.

In the case of wine the Black man has discovered his appetite improves after a few glasses and in doing so he remains sober. Another reason is the wine can be bought in larger containers at cheaper prices. According to one shebeen, the Black man realizes that by buying one large container of wine, he can drink for longer and enjoy the product . . . It would appear as though the Black man gives preference to the elegance of certain containers and many of them choose a certain wine because it is presented in a beautiful container. What taste does the Black man go for in natural wine? The answer is undoubtedly late vintage and stein wines. Why? For most of them the change to these types of wines is quite acceptable from the sweet fortified wines. They say that the drier products are too 'acid' to their taste, which is completely understandable.[92]

Curiously, however, the photographs that accompanied the article depicted shebeen drinkers partaking of a dry red wine called *Valley Select*. Bellingham had spotted a gap in the market and was pushing it in the shebeen trade with some success. This was not cheap wine, but part of its appeal resided in the fact that it was sold in the jug format. An article in *Wynboer* observed that *Valley Select* had become the highest selling wine in the medium- and high-price categories combined, accounting for 12.8 per cent of sales, placing it just ahead of *Autumn Harvest*. This was surely proof that there was a real possibility to sell red wine to Black consumers at somewhat higher price points. But the momentum was not maintained, the fashion for that product passed and the opportunity was missed. The reassessment of shebeens was reflected in the strategies of SFW as it rolled out its wine plan in 1979.[93] The SFW made more of an effort to promote its wine, especially once shebeens became eligible to function as licensed premises with effect from 1980.[94] In 1982 the SFW donated money to the National Taverners' Association, which was the vehicle for the shebeen owners. The SFW even seems to have assisted with their application for liquor licences, which was a highly bureaucratic ordeal.[95] A photograph album in the Distell Archives reveals the effort then being invested by the SFW in cultivating the licensed shebeen owners. The problem is that the timing of this awakening was unfortunate.

Although the sales figures for wine improved in the 1980s, there was too much bulk wine chasing a dearth of consumers. The SFW was being ruthlessly undercut by the cooperatives who offloaded bulk wine in minimalist packaging at below

92 "Wine and shebeens", p. 16.

93 The wine plan was intended to take wine to the country at large. Seventy members were recruited and trained on the sales side and a further seventy were recruited for outreach activities, including house-to-house visits along the lines of a Tupperware party. Bennie Howard quoted in Johannes Richter, "SWB-Wynplan herdenk na 40 jaar", *Wineland*, September 2019, p. 30.

94 Fridjhon and Murray, *Conspiracy*, pp. 294–295.

95 Distell Archive, "SFW sponsors NTA", *eSpontini* (official organ of the National Taverners Association distributed to shebeens/stokvels/runners through the country). There were 108 licensed shebeens in the country in 1986, which was still a small fraction of the total.

the minimum price. The KWV, which was privy to every transaction, was surely in the know. But it pretended not to see anything that did not enter the distilling pool. The net consequence, as Frans Stroebel recalled, was that the SFW was forced to more or less abandon marketing at the lower end of the market:

> I blame the KWV who has had certain powers to do certain things and they didn't do it. Wine's image has been declining seriously because of products that was allowed to sell in this country … I don't know what the English for it is – *papsakke*, it is just this plastic without the box. Those type of products was allowed despite the fact that we fought it. So what happens is the guys come with that product on the market against a boxed wine … the reason why these guys also then could do it was they undermined the minimum wine price … I am controlled and here comes a guy and he undermines me on my price. It was co-ops. Now when that happened our market went down. You try to compete, [but] there is no profit in it. So what do you do? You start saying it's not worth our while to market that, so that the marketing behind wine declined from a serious figure to I think in the end about 6 or 7 per cent of our marketing budget. And SFW climbed out of that market and just tapped it.[96]

The SFW also responded to the evidence that younger Coloured consumers were turning their backs on wine by introducing new products like *Hunter's Gold* that contained some wine but were essentially mixers. More importantly, the SFW shifted the balance of its operations from wine to spirits, given that wine was responsible for 70 per cent of its turnover but accounted for only 30 per cent of its profits.[97] In the process, the SFW thrust itself into a highly contested market in which its main competitors, namely Distillers and Gilbey's, enjoyed a headstart. Inevitably, wine was reduced to the status of a poor relation. The SFW retained an emotional attachment to wine, but now saw its long-term profitability as residing elsewhere in the liquor trade.

Conclusion

In this chapter, I have considered two aspects of what unfolded after the liberalization of the liquor laws in the early 1960s. The first was an intensification of the struggle for control of the alcohol sector, which culminated in an SAB monopoly over beer and a division of the greater part of the wine and spirits sector between the SFW, Distillers and the KWV. The second was the development of new products, buttressed by marketing and advertising plans, that targeted different population groups along racial lines. The SFW was the largest player in the wine sector, and I have dissected its strategies in close detail. The SFW had a large sales team and was renowned for its professionalism and *esprit de corps*, especially under the leadership of Ronnie Melck

[96] Interview with Stroebel, 17 November 2009.
[97] Interview with Stroebel, 17 November 2009.

(1979–1990). However, it was faced with a difficult choice between building the wine business and focusing resources on the spirits side of the operation where the returns were higher. The pressures heaped upon the company intensified as cooperatives began offloading cheap wine onto the market in the most basic containers. In the end, the creative marketing of wines to Black South African consumers became a casualty of a race to the bottom, the underlying causes of which resided in the KWV system itself.

7 A Perfect Storm

Deregulation and Restructuring in the Wine Industry, 1985–2000

> This is an incredible system. No farm without a quota may produce any grapes for wine. If it has a quota, it is permitted to produce an historically fixed quantity of grapes, *regardless of type or quality*. There is no differentiation between table wine and distilling wine in the quota, despite the clear demarcations in the market place.[1]
>
> (John Platter, 1984)

As we have already seen, the wine industry after 1940 was as highly regulated as anywhere in Europe, and in several respects more so. Producers were instructed as to the varietals they were permitted to plant; where they could plant them; where they could make the wine and in what volume; the minimum price they could expect to receive; and the information that could be conveyed on the bottles. The governance structure of the industry had important ramifications for the next swing of the pendulum during the 1990s, when two elements came into play. On the one hand, wine farmers came to regard the KWV system as an obstacle, and increasingly fashioned ways to challenge and subvert its operations. On the other, the sudden transformation in the political landscape, culminating in the rise to power of the African National Congress (ANC) in 1994, transformed the political landscape. Having been closely tied to the National Party (NP), it was a daunting prospect for the KWV to find common ground with a government that expressed no great love for White farmers. Moreover, the unexpected enthusiasm that the new regime displayed for market-oriented reforms – putting economic growth ahead of redistribution – meant that the best the KWV could hope for was a negotiated transition of its own. Within a matter of years, the wine industry had been converted into one of the least regulated in the world although, as we will see in the next chapter, regulation returned in alternative guises. In this chapter, I seek to explain why the KWV system became untenable, and then to chart the very particular way in which it was dismantled.

[1] John Platter, "A barrel of trouble", in "Liquor, a Survey", supplement to *Financial Mail*, 26 October 1984, p. 7.

Declaring a Surplus: The Return of an Old Foe

Of all the functions performed by the KWV, the most important was the alignment of output with demand. The quota system, price control and surplus removal were all devised with that imperative in mind. In the mid-1960s, at precisely the moment when mergers were taking place amongst the merchant-manufacturers, there was a shortage of wine that necessitated importation and the implementation of a purchasing quota for merchants. In the early 1970s, there was a specific shortage of red wine that reflected the delay between changing consumer tastes and what stood in the vineyards. The KWV's response in 1964 was to persuade the Minister of Agriculture to increase the production quota by 50 per cent, and in 1970 it was increased by a further 60 per cent.[2] The net result, as we saw in Chapter 5, was that the size of the wine crush spiralled upwards. In their annual reports to members, KWV chairmen repeatedly insisted that production and demand remained broadly in alignment and that any mismatch simply reflected inevitable time-lags.[3] By the mid-1980s, however, serious doubts began to be expressed about whether the KWV genuinely had the situation under control.

It was common knowledge that wine sales were trailing far behind those of beer despite the removal of the excise duty on unfortified wine. Given that beer still managed to beat wine on price, the question was why the article was so expensive. Part of the KWV's answer was, as ever, that there were prohibitive markups in the sphere of distribution. Hence André du Toit, in his chairman's speech of 1977, noted that because the money paid to the producer accounted for only a quarter of the final selling price, it was only the state (through taxes), the wholesalers and retailers (through pricing) that actually had the wherewithal to bring the price down.[4] But an article in the *Sunday Times* in 1984 expressed a widely held opinion that high minimum prices were at fault, rendering the product more expensive than it might otherwise have been.[5] The author noted that the prices incentivized farmers to churn out greater volumes than the market could absorb, which then required the KWV to sell distilled alcohol at a financial loss. He pointed out that the KWV had sold brandy to Poland at a loss of R1.5 million in order to reduce the size of the spirits lake.

[2] [Anon.], "KWV: sprong deur verlede... die toekoms in", *Wynboer* Mei 1991, p. 17. The farmers were able to apply for conditional or conditional additional quotas.

[3] For example, "Address by the Chairman at the Annual Conference of Wine Farmers, 27 November 1979". These speeches were always published in the pages of *Wynboer*.

[4] "Address by the Chairman of the KWV, Dr. André du Toit at the Fifty-Ninth Annual General Meeting of Members on Tuesday 7 June 1977 at Paarl", *Wynboer*, July 1977.

[5] David Carte, "KWV give-aways in bid to drain the lake", *Sunday Times*, 15 July 1984. The article claimed that the brandy in question cost the KWV 81 cents a litre, but it received only 20 cents a litre. The KWV meanwhile announced it had made a record profit of 12 million in 1983. [Anon.], "KWV's 1983 profit tops 12 million", *Farmer's Weekly*, 22 June 1984.

The article concluded by observing that the incoming KWV chairman, Pietman Hugo, who had come to office on a platform of reform, would have his work cut out since 'most of his electorate is outside the quality wine-growing areas and is happy with protection'.[6] The differences in the yields that farmers could expect differed markedly. In locations like Stellenbosch, the farmers could expect 6 or 7 tonnes of grapes per hectare, whereas in the irrigated areas it was more like 30 tonnes, and sometimes much higher.[7] It stood to reason that even if the minimum price for good wine was double that of distilling wine, the farmer in the irrigated area would enjoy a much greater financial return. It was in their interest to maximize output, safe in the knowledge that the KWV was required by law to purchase the product. In response to such criticisms, Hugo noted at the start of 1985 that the wine companies sometimes paid up to four times the minimum price for wines in the High-Price (HP) bracket. He also maintained that while prices had been raised for the second year in succession, the increase of 9.9 per cent for good wine and 4.5 per cent for distilling wine was below the combined effect of inflation and rising production costs, which amounted to an average annual increase of between 13 and 14 per cent.[8] The message was that the KWV was well aware of the problem and was addressing it by encouraging farmers to embrace cultivars that were conducive to the making of wine of higher quality.

As indicated in Table 7.1, the percentage of wine that was declared as surplus – that is, wine that was consigned to the distilling pool and for which there remained no domestic demand as brandy – reached a peak of 51 per cent in 1984. Although the surplus fell back again, in most years more than a third of what was classified as distilling wine could not be absorbed by the domestic market. The KWV could deploy the surplus to produce more brandy for export, and it actively sought to export more grape juice, but the market remained constrained by ongoing consumer boycotts. An open township revolt and the declaration of a State of Emergency in 1985–1986 were hardly conducive to the worldwide distribution of South African products. As a result, the KWV was reduced to stockpiling brandy, that is, when it could not find obliging Polish buyers. Moreover, on several occasions the official surplus declaration, which was based on predicted demand in a given year, was based

6 Hugo was MP for Ceres from 1979–1987. He was a somewhat unlikely reformer given his own history as a farmer producing for a co-operative winery and his role as chairman of the Slanghoek Co-operative. However, he had also worked in banking and publishing and was also a cattle breeder. See feature articles in *Wynboer* June 1994, pp. 21–22. One of Hugo's claims to fame was initiating the Breede River Valley "Young Wine Show" which created the model for wine shows in other districts. [Anon.], "Pietman Hugo: KWV gets an A-team' leader", *Management*, August 1984, p. 12.

7 Interview with Giorgio Dalla Cia, Stellenbosch, 17 March 2009.

8 [Anon.], "Wine industry: paying for growth", *Financial Mail*, 25 January 1984, p. 1.

Table 7.1. *Distilling pool and declared surplus, 1970–1988*

Year	Distilling Wine Pool, Hectolitres at 10% Alcohol by Volume	Declared Surplus as % of Distilling Wine Pool Supplies
1970	2,217,760	20.0
1975	3,365,569	22.0
1976	3,723,569	23.5
1977	3,021,850	23.0
1978	3,683,949	28.5
1979	4,040,571	27.3
1980	4,523,394	39.1
1981	4,187,374	38.5
1982	4,504,645	29.5
1983	4,923,966	45.8
1984	4,679,790	51.0
1985	4,107,219	42.6
1986	3,165,627	39.3
1987	3,964,229	33.6
1988	–	31.9

Source: KWV, *Statistics Survey Nr 12: 1988*, table 2.4.6, p. 11.

on a significant underestimate.[9] The size of the declared surplus was the tip of the iceberg. Of the wine that was sold for drinking purposes, there was an excess that was effectively dumped on the market. This had a depressing effect on the wine market in general. In 1979, 12 per cent of all wine sales were HP, 30 per cent MP and 58 per cent SP. In 1984, the relative proportions had changed to 12 per cent, 47 per cent and 41 per cent. But, by 1991, the trend had reversed: while 12 per cent were still bracketed as HP, MP wines stood at only 32 per cent and SP wines were back up to 56 per cent.[10] Moreover, while some wine avoided being consigned to the distilling pool, it was clearly entering the market through illicit channels and so undermined the entire system of statutory control.

This failure of the KWV to take the industry firmly in hand was widely commented upon during the 1980s. The estate wine producers, who were not really affected by minimum pricing, felt that there was a demand for their product and that they could survive perfectly well without the bureaucratic web spun by the KWV. The largest wine companies, who were co-shareholders in Cape Wine and Distillers (CWD) along with the KWV, were

9 Van Zyl, *KWV*, p. 252.

10 Lothar Barth, "Free market principles will determine the industry's future", in "50 years in the SA liquor industry – 1940–1990", *Liquor Store Monthly* (possibly 1991).

more directly affected. Distillers was close to the NP, which made it less willing to be overtly critical of the system, whereas SFW felt less constrained. In several speeches and interviews, Lothar Barth, who rose to became chairman, maintained that the KWV was failing to fulfil its statutory responsibilities and was tacitly encouraging the proliferation of bulk wines.[11] Much of the blame was attached to the cooperatives that were accused of offloading the most basic wine on the market in ways that seemed to defy the legislation on minimum pricing. The fact that they were exempt from income taxes only compounded a sense of grievance on the part of the merchant-manufacturers who were not permitted to crush more than a small proportion of the total production, and were required to purchase from the cooperatives.[12] The latter, on the other hand, believed that at a time of economic recession it was the duty of the KWV to stand up for the interests of the ordinary grape-grower. Because they represented the vast majority in almost all the wine districts – namely, 4,465 growers in the early 1990s[13] – the KWV felt compelled to listen. This accounts for the delicate balancing act attempted by Pietman Hugo. While his package of reforms included the promotion of noble cultivars and a freeing up of the quota system, it also included a pledge to listen closely to the farmers across the wine districts. For critics of the KWV, pandering to the majority meant that it was unable to adopt the difficult decisions that the management admitted were necessary. As late as June 1994, and in his last annual address to KWV members, Hugo continued to insist that 'the minimum price system and the pooling of the surplus product remains a safe bulwark for stability and basic certainty in the wine industry'.[14] However, a minority of wine producers openly dissented and were prepared to embrace a world without any form of price control. It is to some of these that I now turn.

Subverting the Quota System

As the quote from John Platter at the beginning of the chapter makes clear, it was difficult to discuss the future of the wine industry without addressing the quota system. It was the handiest instrument at the KWV's disposal and the most controversial. Many farmers who aspired to make their living from wine were forced to persist with mixed farming because their quotas were inadequate. Some were allocated more generous quotas than others for no reason other than their previous record of production. Moreover, the system

[11] Barth, "Free market".
[12] The companies were not permitted to crush more than 4 per cent of the harvest directly and were therefore required to buy from the co-operatives. Brown, "An evaluation", p. 14.
[13] Brown, "An evaluation", pp. 16, 24.
[14] [Anon.], "Minimumprys bly sê Hugo by sy lasste Algemene Jaarvergadering", *Wynboer*, June 1994, p. 23.

effectively meant that wine farming was confined to existing districts that elected directors to the KWV, and ruled out the possibility of producing wine in areas that might actually be better suited to the vine. The KWV continued to subscribe to the position that it had to be strict for fear of unleashing a flood of unwanted wine. But as early as 1974, Duimpie Bayly of the SFW made a case for doing away with quotas where red wine was concerned:

> When all is said and done, however, we find that the better red wine varieties which are sought after today have their own built-in quota. Many of us feel that with the awakening interest both locally and abroad in South Africa red wines a serious effort should be made to exempt these noble wine varieties from quota restrictions within certain well-defined localities. Under the legislation providing for names of origin this should be a comparatively easy matter to arrange.[15]

It was apparent, however, that there would be resistance from districts *anderkant die berg* if special privileges were granted to red wine producers in Stellenbosch, Paarl or Durbanville. Hence the quota system was retained, and because of the heavy yields typical of the districts that produced mostly white wines for distillation, this inevitably had a knock-on effect on the quotas that were available to all farmers. Moreover, the existing system created an incentive to increase yields simply in order to stand still.[16] The KWV was not unaware of these realities and introduced a series of reforms that were intended to remove the worst rigidities. Hence, Hugo announced the initial concession early in his tenure: where a fixed quota was allocated to a particular farm it could be transferred to another farm regardless of who the owner was, provided that it was located within the same district.[17] Although this was a start, it was regarded by many farmers as insufficient.

Typically, it was outsiders who drove the wheels of change. When it comes to the quota system, one such individual occupies a special place in the recent history of Cape wine. Tim Hamilton Russell had studied geology at Oxford University – where he developed a particular interest in climatology[18] – and lived periods of his life abroad, where he had developed a taste for the best French wine. He went on to enjoy a highly successful career at the helm of J. Walter Thompson, the international advertising firm which had its South African headquarters in Sandton (Johannesburg) and derived some of its business from SFW. Looking forward to an early retirement, Hamilton

[15] Quoted in Weiss, "Red wine'72", p. 38.

[16] The logic of the argument is that as the surplus increased this eventually fed back into the minimum price and forced the farmers to produce more in the hope of receiving some of the *agterskot* that came after the end of the year. Fridjhon and Murray, *Conspiracy*, p. 145.

[17] The concession did not apply to conditional quotas and it was permitted up to a maximum of 3,000 hl. at 10 per cent alcohol by volume. Naturally, the KWV had to give its consent. KWV, *Quota*.

[18] Interview with Tim Hamilton Russell, Hermanus, 29 August 2006.

Russell decided to satisfy a lifelong passion and to try his hand at wine. 'Advertising keeps me stimulated. Farming keeps me sane,' he once commented.[19] He was firmly of the opinion that most South African wines were being produced in places that were far too hot to be conducive to optimal quality. His quest, therefore, was to locate a site in a cool climate zone where the grapes would benefit from cooling sea breezes. His search began at Cape Agulhas, from where he made his way along the coast, taking temperature readings and advice from soil scientists.[20] Eventually, he happened upon the Hemel-en-Aarde Valley, in close proximity to the holiday town of Hermanus where he also owned a home. The valley had the singular advantage of benefiting from the cooling properties of the ocean, while being protected from the south-easterly winds by the hills. There were few vines in evidence, but there were visual reminders of a time when grapes had been used to make wine for distillation, including old barrels, presses and stills.[21]

Hamilton Russell set about purchasing two farms in December 1974 and then applied to the KWV for a quota. The KWV turned him down on the basis it was not intending to issue fresh quotas at that time, but he was given an assurance that his application would receive serious consideration if the situation changed. By this point, he had already taken the risk of planting vines on the farm called Braemar, where he also constructed a cellar. Fortunately for Hamilton Russell, the second farm had a small conditional quota attached to it.[22] He then resorted to the subterfuge of pretending that the wines were being made from the farm with the quota, whereas the grapes were mostly coming from Braemar.[23] This was, of course, strictly illegal. Remarkably, he appears to have pulled the wool over the eyes of the KWV inspectors by claiming that the vines on the farm without the quota were being used for experimental purposes. By leaving the grapes on the vines in the first five rows and dropping other bunches on the ground, he was able to convince the inspectors that everything was above board.[24] But at this point, he ran into fresh complications. Under the regulations, it was only possible to put the varietals on the labels if the wine had been certified by the Wine and Spirits Board (WSB). The catch was that if he requested certification, his farms would have been inspected and his subterfuge exposed. He therefore had to resort to

[19] [Anon.], "Burgundy-on-sea: the most southerly vineyard in South Africa", *Finance Week*, 25 February–3 March 1982, p. 297.

[20] Interview with Hamilton Russell, 29 August 2006.

[21] J. E. Mace, "Venture into wine country... Walker Bay", *Wynboer*, June 1975, pp. 12–17.

[22] Interview with Hamilton Russell, 29 August 2006. There was a limited amount of wine being produced in the valley. A nearby farm had Cabernet Sauvignon under vine. Interview with Kevin Grant, 19 August 2019.

[23] Fridjhon, *Penguin Book*, pp. 231–232. These were located on the farm that now belongs to Bouchard Finlayson. Interview with Hamilton Russell, 29 August 2006.

[24] Fridjhon, *Penguin Book*, p. 232. Interview with Hamilton Russell, 29 August 2006.

other inventive ways of getting around the problem. By 1983, he was selling wines under generic names: Grand Vin Blanc (actually Sauvignon Blanc), Premier Vin Blanc (Chardonnay), Grand Vin Noir (Pinot Noir) and Grand Cru Noir (a blend of Cabernet Sauvignon and Merlot).[25] But he also smuggled coded lettering onto the labels to signal to those in the know what they were actually drinking. Simon Rappoport, a wine writer for *Wynboer*, was let in on the secret at a tasting. His favourite turned out to be the Grand Vin Noir 'with a cryptic P3 superimposed in pink on the neck-label to indicate that it is a 1983 pinot noir. The wine's identity was only revealed after the tasting . . .'[26] As Hamilton Russell wines repeatedly came out on top in blind tastings, they attracted greater attention, and inevitably the secret came out. In 1985, he was fined for having dared to place the varietals that went into his blends on the label.

Hamilton Russell made use of his advertising connections to sustain media interest in his searing critique of the entire KWV system which he regarded as being anchored in the structures of Afrikaner power and a 'millstone' around the neck of the minority of farmers interested in pursuing quality.[27] In particular, he kept up a critique of the quota system on the basis that: '[T]he current quota system precludes the opening of many cool high potential viticultural areas. Quotas should be reassigned on merit.'[28] Michael Fridjhon plausibly maintains that he ultimately caused enough embarrassment to bring about a change to the law.[29] As we have seen, the KWV had already been proposing modifications, but the stand-off with Hamilton Russell led it to go further down the road towards freeing up quotas. With effect from the 1986 harvest, it became possible for farmers to sell their quota allocations to other farmers within the same or an adjacent district. This enabled Hamilton Russell to regularize his farming operations by buying quota from farmers in Elgin. However, his efforts to persuade the WSB that he should be allowed to use the term 'estate' fell on stony ground. The changes to the law were important because they enabled other farmers who were seeking to produce wine under their own labels to expand their operations. Finally, and perhaps most importantly, the reforms intensified doubts about whether the entire system was necessary in any case. In successive years, further concessions were made, including the right to consolidate quotas between farms, the possibility of offsetting overproduction on one farm against beneath-quota production on

[25] At this point, he had not fixed on Chardonnay and Pinot Noir.
[26] From a feature called "Choices" in the private papers of Tim Hamilton Russell.
[27] Interview with Hamilton Russell, 29 August 2006.
[28] [Anon.], "The thoughts of Tim Hamilton-Russell", *The Wine Press*, 9 September 1984.
[29] Fridjhon, *Penguin Book*, p. 234.

another, and the exemption of certified export wine from the scheme.[30] When the system was abolished altogether in 1992, not many farmers shed a tear.

The change to the quota regulations did not signal the end of the battles between Hamilton Russell and the KWV. Hamilton Russell went a step further by publicly criticizing the labour practices of some farmers in the industry. Along with Simon Barlow, John Platter and Peter Younghusband, he initiated the Winelands Commitment. This was essentially a charter to support the implementation of fair labour practices, but it also went further in calling for the end of apartheid and the Group Areas Act.[31] When Hamilton Russell granted an interview to the *Daily Telegraph* in 1989, in which he described labour conditions as 'morally indefensible', the KWV was livid. It reacted somewhat petulantly by boycotting the Diners Club Winemaker of the Year luncheon that had been organized in honour of Peter Finlayson, Hamilton Russell's then winemaker.[32] The ongoing battle with the WSB, which was allegedly being encouraged by the KWV to take a hard line, continued for many years more. In 1991, in a high-profile case, Hamilton Russell was taken to court for using references to banned French names, for example 'Chablis-style Chardonnay', in its newsletters and publicity material. Hamilton Russell was found guilty on two charges and fined R500 or three months' imprisonment. His defence was that it was ludicrous that he was not allowed even to mention Finlayson's visits to Burgundy in his newsletter when all the offending information was factually true. He also claimed, possibly with some merit, that he was being victimized because of his criticism of the way the wine industry was governed.[33] In subsequent correspondence with the government official who had brought the case against him, he also pointed to a number of other producers who were invoking French names, including, by this point, Peter Finlayson who had left to create a new joint enterprise next door with Mike Clark and Paul Bouchard, under the hybrid name of Bouchard-Finlayson.[34] Despite the legal setback, the case was also productive in its own way. Hitherto, Hamilton Russell had attempted without success to persuade the KWV to support a relaxation of the stance on nomenclature. He had also written to the Minister of Agriculture, 'Kraai' Van Niekerk, to demand a

30 Van Zyl, *KWV*, pp. 269–270.

31 Apparently, 23 farmers were originally approached to join the group, but no others signed up. [Anon.], "Cape Crusader", *Wine*, March 1990, p. 52. The Commitment had seven cardinal principles (copy in my possession).

32 Graham Lizamore, "Wine industry in ferment over Cape farmer's attack", *The Argus*, 10 November 1989, p. 8.

33 "Wine boss fined over use of French names for wines", translation of article from *Die Burger*, 14 December 1991 (in Hamilton Russell's personal papers). Finlayson made repeated visits to Prosper Maufoux, a *négociant* in Burgundy and this had been mentioned in the newsletters.

34 Tim Hamilton Russell to Andries Tromp, 9 December 1991 (papers of Tim Hamilton Russell). The letter pointed to the claim to the Burgundian origins of Paul Bouchard.

less rigid interpretation of the Liquor Products Act (No. 60) of 1989, and with a similar outcome. But in March 1992, he was invited to join a 'French names working group' which was to investigate whether the kind of terminology he had been using might in fact be admissible in European countries. And the following year, the WSB advised the Minister of Agriculture that it was time to repeal four government notices that had been intended to reinforce the terms of the Crayfish agreement of 1935. This did not revoke the ban on using French appellations per se, but it did remove some of the restrictions on what could be put on labels and in advertising materials. None of this would have happened were it not for the willingness of Tim Hamilton Russell to flirt with illegality in the interests of effecting change. There was one other respect in which he did this, and it is to this that I now turn.

The Chardonnay Scandal

As I indicated in Chapter 5, there was broad agreement that there was an urgent need to diversify and improve the planting material that was made available to farmers. With the creation of the Wine of Origin (WO) framework, and the emergence of the estate producers, there was a demand for cultivars that were considered to be more conducive to quality. In its own self-image, the KWV had taken a proactive lead in making improved planting material freely available. In 1970, Gewurztraminer, Cabernet Sauvignon, an improved Pinor Noir clone and Sylvaner had all passed the necessary tests and had been handed over to the KWV for multiplication. However, the system was slow to respond to shifting consumer preferences that were tilting towards French cultivars and red wines. Danie De Wet, who was a key protagonist in the events that ensued, attributed the tardiness of the KWV and the Directorate of Plant and Quality control, to a certain degree of arrogance and an ongoing obsession with all things German. He recalled how at one point in the mid-1970s the KWV made a great fanfare of the release of three German varietals – Riesling, Burger and Bukettraube – at a time when farmers were looking for a different set of cultivars altogether.[35] By 1986, the planting material that was currently available contained many of the most desirable cultivars, including Sauvignon Blanc, Chardonnay and Cabernet Franc, but in minuscule quantities. Almost a quarter of the vines that the KWV advertised as being available for purchase in 1986 consisted of Colombard, followed by Chenin Blanc and 'Cape Riesling', which turned out to be Crouchen Blanc and not Riesling at all

[35] He knew not of a single farmer who actually planted Burger in South Africa. Interview with Danie de Wet, 16 October 2009.

Table 7.2. *Select list of planting materials available to farmers, March 1986 (in bundles)*

Varietal	Total Bundles Available
Colombard	6,362
Chenin (SA clone)	4,300
Cape Riesling	3,642
Chenin (Montpellier clone)	2,322
Harslevelu	1,600
Cabernet Sauvignon	1,260
Muscat d'Alexandrie	1,150
Bukettraube	903
Sauvignon Blanc	400
Pinot Noir	300
Merlot	231
Chardonnay	100
Shiraz	35
GRAND TOTAL of Bundles Available	28,138

Note: A bundle consisted of 2,000 eyes.
Source: "KWV Plantverbeteringskema: bekendstelling van materiaal beskikbaar 1986", *Wynboer*, March 1986, pp. 60–61.

(see Table 7.2).[36] This suggested strongly that even when the system was consciously embracing French varietals, it was more responsive to the needs of the farmers producing bulk wines from heavy-bearing vines. An additional problem was that not all of what was released was considered by the farmers to be up to scratch. The Pinot Noir was a Swiss clone that was used for making sparkling wine and was considered to be less suitable for still wine. Moreover, the Chardonnay was known to be severely virused, despite having negotiated all the quarantine hurdles. In 1984, Pietman Hugo acknowledged the shortage of in-demand cultivars, but offered a reassurance that the problem was being taken in hand. Within a matter of months, however, a scandal broke which revealed the extent to which farmers had lost faith in the system.

In the early 1980s, rumours were rife that a number of organizations and individuals were involved in illegally importing vines. It subsequently came to light that the authorities had been alerted to such a possibility in 1982 when the Viticultural and Oenological Research Unit (VORI) wrote to the Department of Agriculture and Fisheries stating that it was 'aware that a considerable amount of material has entered the country illegally and some of the material

[36] The prominence of Harslevelu in the list is somewhat surprising. Dr. Laszlo noted at a tasting that it was a very ordinary grape that was used in blending to make tokaji. [Anon.], "The wine wenches taste Harslevelu", *Wynboer*, July 1985, pp. 56–58.

may be particularly interesting clones of existing cultivars'.[37] What brought matters to a head was the expression of doubt by the WSB about the purity of what had been ostensibly planted as Chardonnay. When inspectors visited farms where Chardonnay was known to exist, these doubts were confirmed. It turned out that the Chardonnay in question was nothing of the sort, but rather a lesser grape known as Auxerrois. The latter was not on the list of approved cultivars and therefore had to be uprooted at financial cost to many farmers. Many had acquired their vines from plant breeders who were officially approved by the KWV, and who were left with large numbers of vines that they could no longer sell. The farmers had good reason to believe that they were acquiring genuine Chardonnay and demanded action. The question that arose was how these vines had entered the system in the first place, and how it was that they had apparently been disseminated through the very structures that were supposed to guarantee authenticity. John Platter, who had inadvertently planted Auxerrois at Delaire (Stellenbosch), pointed out that the credibility of the entire WO system was under threat:

> The South African wine industry faces an acutely embarrassing crisis. Officials have now stated what many have suspected – that at least one clone of "chardonnay" vines widely planted in Cape vineyards may not be chardonnay at all but a similar variety named auxerrois. If so, a question hangs over the identity of all wines classified as chardonnay by the Wine and Spirit Board. Though no absolute verifiable confirmation yet exists, this is stunning news. The dilemma calls for firm action immediately. Otherwise the entire Wine of Origin system will fall into disrepute.[38]

Frans Malan demanded that farmers who had tried to steal a march should face the full rigour of the law. The ensuing public controversy meant that the issue could no longer be avoided, and the government duly appointed a one-man commission of enquiry under Justice Klopper to investigate. The enquiry revealed that there had been illegal importation of vines dating as far back as the early 1970s. The main perpetrators were Rhodes Fruit Farms (RFF), which was part of Anglo-American group, Distillers, and many of the leading lights of the wine revolution. The latter included Danie De Wet, N. C. Krone, Sydney Back, Jan 'Boland' Coetzee, Nico Myburgh and, somewhat ironically, Frans Malan himself. Moreover, it became clear that the perpetrators had gone to elaborate lengths to evade the law. Whereas some of the material had been sent

[37] Republic of South Africa, Report of the Commission of Enquiry into the Cultivar Purity and Illegal Importation of Certain Vine Propagating Material (Pretoria: Government Printer, September 1986), p. 30 [hereinafter Klopper Commission].

[38] John Platter, "The Chardonnay furore", *Platter's Wine Times*, July 1985. See also his evidence to Klopper Commission where he indicated he had two hectares that were planted in 1983, p. 20.

through the mail,[39] RFF had gone to the trouble of flying its consignments into Swaziland and then transporting them by road.

Almost all the perpetrators admitted their guilt, but they also pleaded that the system was so cumbersome that they had been left with very little option other than to flout the law. This point was made explicit in a written submission by Distillers, the lead culprit, which stated that:

> People such as Dr J. Laszlo and Messrs Danie De Wet and the late D.P. Pongracz took the only course available to them in their efforts to meet their responsibility to the South African vinicultural industry, and they decided to obtain, in a very responsible manner, the world's best plant material from the world's best known vinicultural institutions. By taking this step they did the South African vinicultural industry a great service and made it possible for the industry one day to be reckoned amongst those of the great wine farming countries of the world. In their actions they never attempted to enrich themselves, but they made it possible for farmers who are associated with the Distillers Corporation either as estate producers or grape suppliers to have some of the best plant material in the world, stemming from the premium international cultivars, in their vineyards today.[40]

Klopper took the point and while he confirmed the apparent guilt of several individuals, he also accepted that there were mitigating circumstances: the long delays in acquiring good planting material had indeed held the industry back, and the fact that the perpetrators had come clean spoke in their favour. The Commission did, however, make a scapegoat of Peter Finlayson, whom it described as an unreliable witness. It is tempting to see this as yet another salvo in the war between Hamilton Russell and the wine establishment. Perhaps the most damning revelation was that the KWV and government agencies had been well aware of the illicit imports, but had preferred not to act. In the final event, Klopper advised against initiating legal proceedings on the remarkable grounds that this would cause 'embarrassment to the Government and on the other hand have a negative effect on unity in the wine industry'.[41] In the final event, nobody was held to account for what had been serious infringements of the law. For some this was simple common sense, but there was also a feeling outside the industry that the wine farmers were being treated according to a different set of standards to everyone else. Some of the perpetrators took pride in having broken the system – which they were 'fucking fed up with' – wide open.[42]

[39] Jan 'Boland' Coetzee recalled that he had sent cuttings from Burgundy, that were disguised as a box of chocolates, for collection from the KWV offices. This clearly provided a source of some personal satisfaction. Interview, 12 April 2007.

[40] Klopper Commission, p. 67. [41] Klopper Commission, p. 31.

[42] Interview with Coetzee, 12 April 2007. Coetzee placed a framed picture from the front cover of *Die Burger* on the wall of his tasting room identifying him as a vine smuggler. The twentieth anniversary of the scandal was also marked in 2006.

The Chardonnay scandal illustrates a number of important points that are central to the argument in this book.[43] Firstly, it underlines the role of international connections and the desire of producers to be more in step with international trends. Two of the key protagonists were Hungarians with a good sense of the global wine scene, namely Desiderius Pongracz and Julius Laszlo. In the former case, Klopper was unable to establish any guilt, but Pongracz was certainly of the view that there was a need to acquire better planting material at any cost. Laszlo similarly believed that the country needed to update its vineyards. Equally striking is that most of the protagonists were individuals who had spent periods studying in Europe, especially at Geisenheim and, to a lesser extent, Weinsberg. Indeed, there is a striking correspondence between the Geisenheim connection and implication in smuggling: Danie De Wet, Peter Finlayson, Achim Von Arnim and N. C. Krone were all products of the venerable German institution. Moreover, most of the cultivars that were smuggled were of German origin, including Rhine Riesling and Weisser Riesling, and others that were less known. But the fact that the Colmar clone of 'Chardonnay' was located at the eye of the storm also underlines the shift towards France, which happened to be one that Laszlo was very much in favour of. Indeed, it was Laszlo who appears to have been behind RFF's decision to import vines from France in 1977, that is, before he took up employment with the Bergkelder. It was seemingly Finlayson who took delivery of the material and had it transported to South Africa. The initial plantings by Hamilton Russell in Walker Bay had been with approved planting materials that turned out to be virused, which made it necessary to find a better alternative.[44] The smuggled cuttings were few in number and needed to be painstakingly reproduced, which took some years. Some were given to De Wet who, in turn, had them multiplied by professional plant breeders in Wellington.[45] Through these breeders, many of whom were also handling officially sanctioned material,[46] many other farmers acquired what they imagined to be authenticated Chardonnay. De Wet also handed on some of the material to other farmers directly. Frans Malan had apparently been the recipient of one such delivery, but when the vines were mature, he came to the conclusion that they were not real Chardonnay – a suspicion that was

[43] This episode has also been examined in detail in Gavin Williams, "Importing Chardonnay: A South African political farce", American Association of Wine Economists, Working Paper No. 141, September 2013.

[44] The Chardonnay suffered from leafroll. Interview with Hamilton Russell 29 August 2006.

[45] Klopper Commission, pp. 19, 22–24.

[46] This was ascertained by comparing the list of nurserymen who were listed as the people from whom planting materials could be acquired with the list of those nurserymen who had lost financially by being stuck with Auxerrois which had originally been passed to them by Danie De Wet. [Anon.], "KWV Plantverbeteringskema: bekendstelling van materiaal beskikbaar 1986", *Wynboer*, March 1986, pp. 60–61; Klopper Commission, p. 20.

confirmed by Professor Chris Orffer of Stellenbosch University.[47] It was at that point that Malan publicly blew the whistle by alerting the press.

The final point to note here is the interweaving of public and private interests. Bergkelder clearly encouraged the specific estates with which it was dealing to plant the illegal vines. Anton Rupert had apparently ensured that his own farm of l'Ormarins was one of the beneficiaries. But other independent producers, like Sydney Back and Frans Malan, had imported some of their own material independently. Government bodies certainly had wind of what was happening, as did the KWV itself, but apparently nobody wanted to be the first to broach such a sensitive issue at a time when the industry was already in the doldrums. The Directorate of Plant and Seed Control (DPSC) received much of the criticism but defended itself on the basis that it had no say in what was actually imported: its function was simply to implement quarantine. The Cultivar Committee handled applications to import cultivars, but it did not have a proactive remit. The DPSC also noted that some of the individuals who sat on the Cultivar Committee were the very people who were implicated in the scandal.[48] It also observed that 'the KWV and VORI were only too well aware of many illegal imports', but had failed to act.[49] In effect, what Klopper revealed was utter confusion as to who ultimately held responsibility. If ever there was an indictment of the KWV system, the Chardonnay fiasco was it.

Although there was general agreement that quarantine was necessary – as underlined by the problems encountered by downy mildew on imported vines – there was also a consensus that there was a need to streamline the process of regulation with minimal delay. For many farmers, this was best accompanied by a more market-driven approach to the industry more broadly. In the years that followed, a leaner version of the system enabled the worst bottlenecks to be avoided. Braam Van Velden noted that a system of open quarantine permitted planting material to be propagated much more expeditiously than before.[50] He recalled that Overgaaauw, which had been making port-style wines since the 1940s, was the first farm to be allowed to import vines under the reformed dispensation. It imported six cuttings of Touriga Nacional, two of which were sent to Plant Quarantine, two to Nietvoorbij, while the final two were left with the farm under open quarantine. By the time the planting material had been cleared by the authorities, they already had 2,000 Touriga vines under production. These changes to the quarantine system faciliated the significant new plantings that occurred during the 1990s.

[47] Interview with François Malan, 25 July 2009.

[48] It referred specifically to Dr. Piet Venter, the Production Director of Bergkelder. Klopper Commission, p. 75.

[49] Klopper Commission, p. 75.

[50] Interview with Braam van Velden, 5 August 2009.

The Unravelling of Regulation

Although the KWV survived the Chardonnay scandal, its credibility had been severely dented. Within a decade, virtually the entire regulatory edifice was dismantled. The reasons owe a great deal to the changing political landscape in South Africa, especially following the 1994 elections that brought the ANC to power. But it also reflected dynamics that were internal to the wine industry.

One significant development was the beginning of a culture shift within the KWV itself. Lourens Jonker was elected as one of the two KWV directors for Robertson in 1981. As an estate producer, he faced 'a fierce fight' against a rival candidate who represented the interests of cooperative producers in the district. Because there were only 9 or 10 independent producers in the Robertson District and no fewer than 11 cooperatives, he was elected against the numerical odds. Jonker recalled that the area had always been associated with distilling wine, but that some farmers had begun to plant varietals that were more conducive to the production of drinking wine. By the 1990s, the ranks of independent producers were growing. More broadly, the shift in the balance of power was reflected in the fact that more good wine producers were elected to the KWV. Hence, while there was fierce infighting between the directors, the balance had shifted somewhat towards the good wine producers. As Jonker put it:

> There has always been a sort of a fight between the directors from the other side of the mountain and this side of the mountain, pitting the distilling wine against the good wine people. But they were in the majority, so the distilling wine people couldn't win.[51]

Jonker was elected vice-chairman of the KWV in 1991, and in 1994 he succeeded Pietman Hugo. Jonker was amongst those arguing strongly that the quota system had outlived its usefulness. In 1990, there was a vigorous debate within the KWV, in which Jonker argued that rolling out additional quotas, including for new producing areas like Hermanus, was more likely to exacerbate overproduction because under the law farmers were required to plant vines within three years of being granted a conditional quota. This argument prevailed and, in Jonker's words, 'We never looked back from that day onwards.' Although farmers who had only recently purchased properties with a view to selling the quotas were furious, the decision to completely ditch one of the fundamental planks of regulation was accepted without demur by most KWV members. The cooperatives were now vested with greater powers to control production by their members, but to all intents and purposes the curbs on production had been abandoned.[52]

[51] Interview with Lourens Jonker, 20 March 2009.
[52] National Agricultural Marketing Council, The Impact of Deregulation on the South African Wine Industry, NAMC Section 7 Committee Report (Pretoria: NAMC, 2002), p. 19.

The ending of the quota system, which took effect from 1992, inevitably forced the KWV to rethink some of its other commitments. If there was an upsurge in new plantings, accompanied by a significant increase in output, the KWV would find itself bound by a statutory obligation to absorb the surplus. At the same time, there was mounting evidence that the government was about to jettison the orthodoxies of a generation and embrace deregulation for the agricultural sector. In 1992, Kraai van Niekerk appointed a committee of enquiry under the chairmanship of Professor W. E. Kassier, the head of the National Agricultural Marketing Council (NAMC), to investigate the impact of control boards operating under the Marketing Act of 1968, on both farmers and consumers.[53] The report concluded that the system of regulation was not achieving the desired ends and was essentially unsustainable.[54] But it was also candid about what it regarded as 'arrogance, self-righteousness and self-imposed omniscience' on the part of what it called 'organized agriculture' acting in defence of the status quo.[55] The wine industry eventually fell outside its remit because it was governed by separate legislation, but it was alluded to and many of the observations – for example, about price controls – were easily extrapolated.[56] A number of the most important recommendations had a particular resonance, most notably that there should be a 'moratorium on the creation of private monopolies through the privatization of the public monopolies'; that control boards should be permitted to deregulate, but only in such a way as 'these measures serve to open access to all existing and potential players and increase transparency'; and that a further moratorium be placed on the practice where 'private organisations exercise de facto statutory powers'.[57] The KWV was not a public monopoly, but neither was it a private organization. It was formally a cooperative, but it was exercising statutory functions much like the agricultural control boards.

Whereas the KWV had always set the minimum price in consultation with the Minister, Van Niekerk decided to engage in a wider consultation that would include the merchant-manufacturers. According to Frans Stroebel of SFW, it was a retiring KWV director who had let slip that if one cooperative sold wine to another, it was deemed to lie outside the minimum pricing

[53] There were no fewer than 21 agricultural marketing schemes in operation in 1992. Department of Agriculture, Report of the Committee of Inquiry into the Marketing Act (Pretoria: National Department of Agriculture, 1992), p. 36. Van Niekerk served as Minister of Agriculture from 1991 to 1996 within a unity government. He had previously been involved with a co-operative in the Northern Cape and was unsympathetic to vested interests in the winelands proper. Interview, 23 October 2009.

[54] Report of the Committee of Inquiry into the Marketing Act, p. 26.

[55] Report of the Committee of Inquiry into the Marketing Act, p. 75.

[56] Initially, it was not so clear that the wine sector would be kept out of the enquiry and the KWV was kept on tenterhooks.

[57] Report of the Committee of Inquiry into the Marketing Act, pp. 75–76.

provisions.[58] It transpired that cooperatives were purchasing each other's wine, which they then offloaded onto the market with the most rudimentary packaging and at prices well below the equivalent for SFW products – and crucially also, below the designated minimum price. The SFW had responded to this inside information by setting up the Western Cape Co-operative and coming to its own sweetheart deals with a number of existing cooperatives. In a manner reminiscent of the vine-smuggling saga, all this remained below the radar until a moment around 1993, when Van Niekerk invited representatives of the firms to a meeting to discuss the price for the upcoming year – a unique event in itself. Stroebel recalls that he remained silent during the deliberations until the Minister was prompted to ask why he was so uncharacteristically silent.[59] His sardonic reply was that the minimum wine price no longer concerned SFW because they had now joined everyone else in undermining it. He went on to reveal how this was possible within the formal letter of the law. The Minister then asked the KWV representative for confirmation that this was indeed correct, which he did. Van Nierkerk's response was to declare a freeze on the minimum wine price for the coming year as well as his intention to bring the entire system to an end, which followed in short order in 1994. For SFW and for many farmers, the KWV had been failing, for some years, to discharge its functions in an equitable manner. Moreover, the race to the bottom had contributed to a further deterioration in the image of wine as a product, which the KWV had done so much to champion in earlier decades.

As the NP and the ANC negotiated a political transition, the KWV realized that nesting within the cooperative sector did not provide adequate protection from a potentially hostile government. In particular, the worry was that if an incoming administration decided that the KWV was akin to a parastatal, it might seek to take over the board.[60] In 1994, the year Nelson Mandela was elected to power, Jonker began the process of converting the KWV into a private company. This involved holding meetings all over the country to explain the proposal, which revealed resistance from some farmers, Meanwhile, Michael Fridjhon, who had been brought in to advise the new Minister of Agriculture, Derek Hanekom, alerted the government to the fact that the KWV had accumulated assets in the performance of its statutory functions. While the KWV sought to curry favour with Mandela, who was invited to some of its public functions, Hanekom adopted a hard line. This was interpreted as a possible prelude to a takeover of the KWV.[61]

[58] Interview with Stroebel, 17 November 2009. The revelation came around 1996/7. The KWV director was apparently trying to protect the long-term interests of his own co-operative.

[59] Interview with Stroebel, 17 November 2009.

[60] Interview with Jonker, 20 March 2009.

[61] Interview with Jonker, 20 March 2009.

In 1996, the KWV announced its intention to apply to the courts in the Western Cape for a change in its status from a cooperative to a company. The government contested the application and requested time to consider a future regulatory framework and assess how assets of the KWV that were accumulated in the performance of its statutory functions should be dealt with. A bitter wrangle ensued, with the KWV insisting that all the assets belonged to its members. The Minister secured approval from the court to launch an enquiry into the wine industry, which was chaired (once again) by Professor Kassier. The committee weighed up the advantages and disadvantages of retaining some form of statutory control and came down firmly against the status quo and in favour of deregulation on the basis that there should be no exception for the wine industry.[62] On the specific issue of surplus removal, the preference of the KWV was for the retention of this function, but in the event that this was not possible it 'would prefer regulation through the market with a minimum of State interference with respect to surplus removal functions'.[63] It specifically opposed bringing wine under the provisions of the 1996 Marketing of Agricultural Products Act on the basis that wine shared greater similarities with the manufacturing sector. The committee recommended that the Wine and Spirits Act (No 47) of 1970 be repealed in its entirety by the time the KWV was converted to a private company. It also recommended that certain residual functions be devolved to a new body that represented the interests of the industry as a whole.

At the Kassier Committee hearings, it was apparent that the KWV did not see eye to eye with the Cape Wine and Spirits Institute (CWSI), which represented the collective interests of the merchant-manufacturers. The latter feared that if the KWV was allowed to become a private company, deploying its accumulated assets, it would compete directly with them on the domestic market.[64] This apprehension existed despite the fact that KWV was a joint shareholder in CWD, alongside SFW and Distillers. In the Kassier Report, the CWSI placed on record a minority position, which was that KWV assets had been accumulated in the performance of its statutory functions, assets 'which could then be freely used to compete unfairly with other participants in the wine and spirits trade'.[65]An independent audit commissioned by Hanekom concluded that some of the KWV assets were indeed acquired through the

[62] Republic of South Africa, Report of the Committee to Investigate Regulation of the Wine and Distillation Committee, 1 February 1997 (Pretoria: Ministry for Agriculture and Land Affairs, 1997), pp. 33–34 [Kassier Committee].

[63] Report of the Committee to Investigate [Kassier Committee], p. 31.

[64] Interview with Riaan Kruger, former executive director of CWSI, 2 December 2009.

[65] Report of the Committee to Investigate [Kassier Committee], p. ix. The assets consisted partly in the form of vast quantities of stockpiled brandy.

performance of public functions.[66] However, a report to the Registrar of Co-operatives in 1997 found that '[t]he fact that the co-operative performed a statutory function did not contribute to their reserves and therefore no assets could be acquired with such funds'.[67] A follow-up enquiry credited the KWV with having 'contributed substantially to certain of the industry's successes' and delivered stability. But it also indicated that the KWV had refused to hand over documents relating to its financial affairs. It further noted that the KWV was both a regulator and a commercial participant and that it had received produce 'for no consideration under certain circumstances and resulting profits (and losses) from dealing with this surplus'.[68] The report was critical of its predecessor but did not resolve whether the financial assets in question belonged to the state. The impasse ultimately led to an out-of-court settlement. Jonker recalls that while the KWV felt that it was on solid ground, its legal team advised coming to a negotiated settlement.

> We were in the process of winning this court case, and then this senior lawyer came to me and said 'Listen come and sit down and let's talk about this. You are going to win this battle, but you are going to lose the war because the government is always there. They can come up with new Acts and they are in the process of changing that co-operative law in any case.' So we had to ok.[69]

The CWSI eventually dropped its own objections when the KWV pledged itself to a commitment not to enter the domestic market for wine, which it rescinded in 2000.

As for the ANC government, it brokered a profoundly political deal in which the disputed assets were recycled to stitch together a working consensus. This has been unpicked in all its bewildering complexity by Gavin Williams.[70] In 1997, the KWV was permitted to establish a private company, KWV Group, with many of the shares residing in the hands of the members of KWV Co-operative, until the latter was eventually bought out in 2002.[71] At the same time, a formal agreement was reached between the KWV and the Minister after a representative was appointed by both sides to hammer out

66 Thabo Kobokoane, "Punch-drunk KWV could be forced to settle with Hanekom", *Sunday Times/ Business Times*, undated.

67 D. G. Steyn, Appointed Inspector, "Confidential Preliminary Report to the Registrar of Co-operatives: Assets of the KWV", 31 January 1997. I am grateful to Riaan Kruger for a copy of this report and others referenced below.

68 "Investigation into the Affairs of the Ko-operatiewe Wynbouwersvereniging van Suid-Afrika Beperk in terms of Section 13 of the Co-operatives Act Number 91 of 1981", combined report of Inspectors, July 1997.

69 Interview with Jonker, 20 March 2009.

70 Gavin Williams, "Black economic empowerment in the South African wine industry", *Journal of Agrarian Change*, 5 (4) 2005.

71 The new company was called KWV Ltd, in which VINPRO held a minor stake. Williams, "Black economic", p. 486.

the details. The deal was regarded as a bitter pill, as Lourens Jonker himself indicated:

> Hell, I put this to the Board but up to now I wasn't very happy about this whole agreement because I said 'why would they pick on KWV; what about all the other big co-operatives in South Africa? But now the government they picked on KWV to make an example of them'. It was so unfortunate.[72]

The KWV agreed to transfer part of the assets, valued at R369 million, to a South African Wine Industry Trust (SAWIT) by means of 40 quarterly payments.[73] SAWIT was, in turn, subdivided into two non-profit companies – the Wine Industry Business Support Committee (BUSCO) and the Wine Industry Development Company (DEVCO). BUSCO was charged with backing the bodies that looked after the industry, most notably SAWIS, VINPRO (providing services to the farmers) and Wines of South Africa (WOSA). DEVCO, on the other hand, was supposed to support 'previously disadvantaged' groups – a linguistic recoding of the term 'non-whites' in the post-apartheid era – in entering the wine industry and to promote the upliftment of farm workers. SAWIT began to work closely with the Black Association for the Wine and Spirits Industry (BAWSI), a broad church that claimed to represent the interests of Black businessmen and farmworkers alike. In 2004 a deal was clinched, with the backing of the government, in which a consortium consisting of SAWIT, BAWSI and a number of Black entrepreneurs purchased a 25 per cent stake in KWV. As Williams indicates, SAWIT's own resources had come from the KWV in the first place, but in addition the KWV loaned part of the money to members of the consortium for them to be able to purchase the shares.[74] All of this frantic recycling of assets was necessary to make the sums add up as well as to enable the new managers of the KWV to make their peace with the ANC. Although the deal notionally empowered farmworkers, it was essentially cut between Black and White businessmen, who acquired most of the shares, and the government. White farmers remained members of individual cooperatives, but after 2002 they were formally detached from the KWV. As the association made the transition to a private company, Charles Kohler's creation was formally brought to an end. The years that followed were difficult ones for the KWV, which was beset by a succession of takeover bids, claims of asset-stripping and internal schisms.[75] The one asset that the KWV did control was the immense quantities of high-quality brandies that had been made from

[72] Interview with Jonker, 20 March 2009.

[73] "Agreement Entered into between the Minister for Agriculture and KWV (Proprietary) Limited", 17 December 1998, p. 9.

[74] Williams, "Black economic", p. 498.

[75] Danie De Wet was the 6th Chairman of the KWV, but was apparently squeezed out. He referred to the interest of new investors in the company as 'asset-stripping'. Interview, 16 October 2009.

the wine surplus and which were stockpiled in Paarl. But it could no longer acquire wine at minimal cost, and it was over-stretched as a business. Perhaps inevitably, ownership of the KWV passed to a succession of external investors.[76]

Struggles over Distribution: A Partial Refrain

At the turn of the 1990s, the wine and spirits industry was struggling to remain profitable in the context of a severe economic crisis. On the one hand, the competition between the main players on the domestic market remained as intense as ever. Despite the fact that SFW and Rembrandt/Distillers had been part of CWD since 1979, they remained at arm's length. Formally, it was Rembrandt that provided the management direction because it held the majority (60 per cent) of the shares together with the KWV. But on a day-to-day basis, the companies remained distinct. In 1988, CWD was formally subdivided into two companies separately listed as SFW and Distillers Corporation. However, Anton Rupert apparently continued to take an interest in the SFW and was instrumental in the transfer of Frans Stroebel from Rembrandt in the capacity of managing director in 1989.[77] Despite the fact that Rembrandt owned 49 per cent of Gilbey's, this equally made little difference to the way that the company functioned. Management control remained with the United Distillers (UD), which held the majority of the shares. Gilbey's also had a track record of opposing the hegemonic pretensions of the CWSI. As the SFW's own profits increasingly came to hinge on selling spirits rather than marketing wine, it sought to move further into the space already occupied by Distillers and Gilbey's. Summing up this rather confused picture of linked shareholding and competing strategies, Frans Stroebel recalled that:

> There was nobody from Rembrandt that ever shared with me what's going on. And there was a Rembrandt guy actually sitting in as a non-Director on the Distillers Board as well as on the SFW board as a sort of shareholders' representative. And he was aware of all the facts and figures, but he was for instance not sitting on any Board meetings of Gilbey's.[78]

[76] In 2011, Hosken Consolidated Investments acquired a majority shareholding, and then in 2016 the latter sold out to Vasari.

[77] Dave Marlow served as executive chairman from 1988 to 1991. He was regarded as a 'Rembrandt appointee'. [Anon.], "Stellenbosch Farmers' Winery: stating as they are?", *Financial Mail*, 11 October 1991. After he left SFW, he became a director of Rembrandt. He briefly overlapped with Frans Stroebel. The latter had previously been a senior member of South Africa's delegation at United Nations. He later served as private secretary to Pik Botha, the country's Foreign Minister. In 1988, he joined Rembrandt. He was close to Rupert and was sent to head SFW at a difficult time. He had no previous experience in the liquor industry, but Rupert apparently considered that he had the leadership credentials that were needed. Van der Merwe, *Magic*; Interview with Stroebel, 17 November 2009.

[78] Interview with Stroebel, 17 November 2009.

Much of the day-to-day competition between the companies revolved around imported spirits for which they held competing franchises. Hence Gilbey's distributed *Smirnoff* vodka and *J&B* whisky; Distillers sold *Johnnie Walker*; and SFW controlled the *Bell's* and *Haig* whisky brands. The battle for market share between them was intense, even though the products in question all originated with UD, and then, after further mergers in 1997, with the global liquor giant Diageo.

At the same time, SFW and Distillers both had a complicated relationship with the KWV. The SFW relationship with the KWV was especially fraught and turned on three specific bones of contention. SFW continued to resist annual increases in the minimum prices for wine, especially when these were above inflation. Secondly, and relatedly, SFW was frustrated by the manner in which the KWV attempted to regulate not just prices, but also the content of wine-based products. In the 1980s, SFW had become aware of a backlash amongst younger Coloured drinkers,[79] in part because of the association of wine with alcoholism and rural immiseration. Their response was to introduce flavoured wines, following a change to the law in 1984. The SFW hoped to open a new line of products, which might have some of the fashionable appeal of beer. However, the KWV insisted that 98 per cent of the content had to consist of wine.[80] It was also empowered to regulate the alcohol and sugar content of all wine-based products. At a minimum of 7 per cent alcohol, flavoured wines had a far higher alcohol content than beer, which rendered them less attractive for social drinking.[81] The products that were launched by SFW briefly flourished. At one point, in 1985, *Esprit* was the world's largest selling flavoured wine outside of the United States, while this category in general accounted for more than 10 per cent of the natural wine market.[82] But the fashion proved short-lived. In the 1990s, SFW turned to the production of ciders, notably *Hunter's Gold* and *Savanna*, which proved extremely popular with younger drinkers precisely because of the lower alcohol content. The KWV was deeply concerned that the latest trend would be detrimental to the interests of the farmers and sought to persuade the SFW to market products that were wine-based. In return for the KWV agreeing to free up its controls over alcohol levels, SFW introduced new products such as *Crown* that were based on grape concentrate, but with an alcohol content closer to beer. On this aspect of KWV regulation, the SFW eventually had its way.

[79] In this text I refer to 'White', 'Coloured' and 'Black' - categories that are rooted in segregationist and apartheid discourse, but which are impossible to avoid using because they have meaning for the actors themselves. See the 'Note on the Text' on page vi for more detail about the history and use of this term in South Africa.

[80] Van der Merwe, *Magic*, p. 35.

[81] Interview with Stroebel, 17 November 2009.

[82] Van der Merwe, *Magic*, p. 35.

Thirdly, SFW was resentful of the manner in which the KWV sought to intervene in the spirits market. SFW took exception to the fact that its most successful spirits product, *Mainstay*, was hobbled by the artificially high price they paid for cane spirit. This was itself a consequence of the way the KWV used its political leverage to force the cane producers to align their prices. As Stroebel noted, the threat that if they failed to match price rises for wine spirit, the KWV would ask government to increase the level of duty instead.[83] SFW and Distillers realized that the only way they could remain profitable was to break the alliance between the cane producers and the KWV. SFW informed the cane producers that they were dropping the prices they were prepared to pay for spirit from R10 to around R2.50 a litre. The producers were, however, assured that they would be able to sell a lot more of their spirit as a result:

> Of course, they complained like hell etcetera, and I said 'wait a minute, you are going to lose a little bit, but you are not losing anything because I will now buy all my vodkas and all my gins which used to be wine spirits I will now . . .' And the KWV side, of course, they were furious. They basically accused me, that I was now taking the bread from the farmer's table by doing that. But at that stage I was bleeding like hell from opposition companies who could buy at that price – R2.50, 2.75 – while I had to pay something like R10.[84]

On this occasion, SFW and Distillers closed ranks and agreed to purchase cane spirit at the same price. The threat that the merchant-manufacturers wielded was that of building their own cane distilleries. At the point when the cane producers gave way, Stroebel recalls that the chairman of their association commented with evident regret that 'you have just broken down one of the most stable monopolies in this country'.[85] The principal loser was, of course, the KWV, which was already struggling to dispose of the annual surplus of distilling wine. The threat of SFW and Distillers to opt out of buying wine spirit inevitably meant that the oversupply would increase, placing even greater pressure on the KWV.

Although the merchant-manufacturers had scored unprecedented victories against the KWV, a much more formidable adversary was drawing up alongside. Not long after it was launched, there were hints that Diageo intended to play a more active role in the South African liquor market, in effect entering the home terrain of SAB Miller (hitherto SAB). In particular, a rumour circulated to the effect that it intended to channel all its products through Gilbey's, building on the company's well-developed sales infrastructure. Although Rembrandt would still hold its financial stake in the company, Distillers and SFW discovered that the international spirits brands at their

83 Interview with Stroebel, 17 November 2009.
84 Interview with Stroebel, 17 November 2009.
85 Interview with Stroebel, 17 November 2009.

disposal were to be taken away from them. They were able to secure some financial compensation, but the challenge of developing alternative products from scratch was a daunting one, especially because the Diageo brands had always been the most profitable part of their operations. Given the lack of any interest by SAB Miller in becoming more deeply invested in CWD, the threat to their very survival now brought the SFW and Distillers closer together. Active negotiations began over a full merger of the old adversaries in 1999. These came to fruition the following year when the new company, Distell, was constituted without objections from the Competition Commission. The merging companies reassured the public that there was no immediate plan on the part of SAB to sell its stake.[86] The KWV retained its own stake (through its former deal with Distillers) until 2009, when it finally withdrew.

The merger was driven by an appreciation that it was self-defeating for SFW and Distillers to continue their rivalry when much larger international players were circling. A subsequent document defending the merger noted that:

> Well-resourced MNEs are constantly seeking new and profitable markets, especially emerging markets. The threat of entry by global firms and their actual entries have increased the contestability of all regional markets such as South Africa. Furthermore, new benchmarks for production and marketing success have been set, particularly those arising from the many mergers with and between MNEs. The increasing global competition is an ongoing trend, which must also affect and involve local firms. Against this backdrop, Distell's merger rationale can be seen in perspective and the necessity therefore can be understood.[87]

The merger did, however, face concerted opposition. Michael Fridjhon proposed that it be considered by the Competition Commission in the light of the Competition Act of 1998.[88] When the Commission confirmed that the merger was not 'notifiable' because ultimate control of the companies had not altered, Bulmers and Seagrams took the matter to court. Against the claim that the merger was detrimental to competition, Distell maintained that it was essentially a response to greater competition within liquor markets across the globe: the pooling of resources and the rationalization of management structures would help the company protect its local interests, while enabling the company to become a global player in its own right. Although its domestic and international sales and profits were disappointing in the early years, Distell weathered the storm.[89] By 2018 the company seemed to have turned the

[86] A subsidiary of SAB held a 30 per stake in both SFW and Distillers. After the merger, and the acquisition of SAB Miller by Anheuser-Busch in 2016, its shares were finally disposed of.

[87] "Distell: Report on Competition, January 2002", unpublished report, Distell Archive, p. 19.

[88] Michael Fridjhon, "Monopoly: a tired vintage", *Business Day*, 20 April 2000.

[89] Charlotte Matthews, "Lower profit and static turnover from Distell", *Business Day*, 21 August 2001.

corner, based in part on its development of the market for 'ready-to-drink' (RTD) beverages and in part on growing sales in other parts of Africa. SAB had been the first alcohol company to internationalize its operations, and now Distell sought to go down the same route. But what was unclear was whether wine had any place in the new scheme of things.

Conclusion

In this chapter, I have followed through in some detail the precise manner in which the KWV system unravelled. The shift in the political balance of power in the early 1990s was clearly a factor because the KWV could no longer count on the friendly consideration of the government. But the inner contradictions had already been exposed in the 1980s, as farmers operating outside of the cooperative system became increasingly disillusioned with the quota system and with the minutiae of certification. The multiple battles fought by Tim Hamilton Russell brought the underlying issues into sharp relief. At the same time, the merchant-manufacturers kicked against the anomalies arising from minimum pricing. But in many ways, it was the Chardonnay scandal which implicated prominent farmers and the companies alike in the illegal importation of cultivars, which exposed the failings of the KWV system as a whole.

While the KWV management accepted that much of the criticism was justified, pushing through reform was difficult when elected directors favoured the retention of the status quo. Consequently, the KWV stood accused of perpetuating the mass production of cheap wine. Much of it leaked onto the market at below the minimum price, while the remainder was destined for distillation. Because the farmers were only paid for the distilling wine that was not declared part of the surplus, the KWV accumulated a stockpile of brandy at minimal cost to itself. The KWV system became a veritable house of cards because the grape farmers were being protected from the full force of the market at the same time as the KWV was accumulating substantial assets. Those who were caught in the middle – independent farmers, wine companies and consumers – bore the inevitable consequences. The arrival of the ANC government, and the fundamental questioning of the premises of statutory control, created considerable uncertainty for the KWV. Fearing a takeover, the KWV began the process of converting itself into a private company, which focused attention on who owned the assets. In the end, a convoluted deal was struck which enabled a minority of the assets to be recycled in support of the Black Economic Empowerment (BEE) agenda of the government and the rest to be used to finance the initial support for core services to the industry. This freed the KWV to go its separate way as a private company.

8 The Renaissance of South African Wine

Innovation, Sustainability and Empowerment since the 1990s

> Things are not perfect – far from it – but, against considerable odds, South Africa is a qualified modern success story. Nothing exemplifies that success like the Cape wine industry. In 1993, South Africa exported 24.5 m litres of wine. By the end of 2013, that figure has risen to 525.7 m litres. Too many of those litres are exported in bulk ... but South African wine enjoys a reputation that was unimaginable at the end of the apartheid era, exporting its wines to 140 countries worldwide. It has also launched praiseworthy initiatives that cover sustainability, traceability and better labour practices. Again, these are not perfect, but they show that South Africa is keen to overcome its past ... A combination of old vines (especially for whites), diverse soils, investment, hard work and pure winemaking talent have transformed South African wine. The speed of change in the Cape is truly remarkable.[1]
>
> (Tim Atkin, wine judge and critic, 2014)

The end of international isolation, combined with the winding up of the cumbersome KWV system, created an entirely new mix of possibilities in the 1990s, but also some challenges. On the one hand, the safety net, on which the growers had come to depend, was whisked away. This left the majority at the mercy of an unpredictable market, in a context where there was no longer any entity that was required to absorb the surplus or indeed to buy the grapes. A worst-case scenario was that producer prices would plummet in the midst of chronic overproduction, forcing many farmers out of business altogether – and with severe consequences for workers as well. On the other hand, the ending of international sanctions and deregulation of the industry created an opportunity for those aspiring to export wines of higher quality. At the same time, a narrowing of income differentials across the racial divide might also have been expected to stimulate the domestic market. A decade before the KWV system imploded, John Platter contemplated what a world without regulation might look like. He acknowledged that 'the fresh air of free market principles

[1] Tim Atkin, *South Africa 2014: Special Report* (author, 2014), p. 5.

might be painful at first', but anticipated that a 'revamping from quantity to quality' would be accompanied by an influx of new entrants.[2]

The second scenario comes closest to capturing the eventual outcome, but the strengths did not necessarily lie in the places that might have been predicted. Ironically, much of the success that Tim Atkin applauded was based on a reconfiguration of some existing elements. A gradual awakening to the specificity of South African growing conditions led producers to distance themselves from the New World tag. Moreover, some of the cultivars that had been stigmatized because of their association with a mass-produced product turned out to be capable of producing wines of considerable finesse. And yet, the pursuit of transformation through continuity also came with its downsides. While wine critics pointed to a marked improvement in quality, the persistence of acute social inequalities was undeniable. Coloured, and increasingly Black, farmworkers continued to provide poorly remunerated labour, while viticulture, oenology and farm ownership remained overwhelmingly White.[3] At the same time, a heavy dose of irony resides in the fact that an industry that had welcomed an end to suffocating controls found itself subjected to systems of self-regulation and certification that were taxing in their own way.

The downsides of going global were not unique to South Africa, but what was unusual was the need to simultaneously navigate global and local transitions. In this chapter, I will assess how these dual transitions were managed at an industry level, amongst cooperatives, merchant-manufacturers and private cellars. In the first section, I deal with the conjuncture between an imperative to become more globally competitive while meeting new environmental standards and aligning with the government's BEE agenda. While this material does not always make for the most riveting reading, it is essential for understanding the new landscape of wine governance once the KWV system was wound up. In the second section, I weigh up the success with which industry restructured itself from the 1990s to the recent past. And in the third, I briefly examine the record of empowerment initiatives in the industry.

From Recurring Nightmares to Industry Visions

In the second half of the 1990s, there was a keen appreciation that, while dismantling the KWV system was long overdue, a series of structural challenges required strategic intervention at the level of the industry as a whole. It was

[2] This was early speculation on the part of John Platter, in "A barrel of trouble", p. 7.

[3] In this text I refer to 'White', 'Coloured' and 'Black' - categories that are rooted in segregationist and apartheid discourse, but which are impossible to avoid using because they have meaning for the actors themselves. See the 'Note on the Text' on page vi for more detail about the history and use of this term in South Africa.

fortunate that deregulation did not lead to a complete unravelling of key industry functions. The fundamental viticultural and oenological research that had been carried out in Nietvoorbij continued after the latter was absorbed by the Agricultural Research Council (ARC). South African Wine Industry Information and Systems (SAWIS), which was headquartered in Paarl, was tasked with collecting and making available statistics on plantings, harvests, cultivars and exports, and with disseminating relevant information relating to legislation and certification.[4] The certification of Wines of Origin (WO) resided with the Wine and Spirits Board (WSB), which retained oversight for seals and the labelling of the wines. In 2003, VINPRO was re-created on a cooperative basis and later as a non-profit company providing outreach services to producers. It also assumed responsibility for publishing *Wineland*, the industry magazine that filled the gap that opened when *Wynboer* folded. It also played an advocacy role in alliance with the South African Liquor Brandowners' Association (SALBA). Finally, Wines of South Africa (WOSA) assumed the key responsibility for promoting the reputation of South African wines abroad. These essential services, which had been performed by the KWV, came to be supported by a series of levies under the Marketing of Agricultural Products Act of 1996.

Industry spokesmen routinely complained that European farmers benefited from subsidies (which they most certainly did), whereas their Australian counterparts enjoyed support in export promotion. However, the willingness of the ANC government to lend the wine industry a helping hand was distinctly moot after 1994. It had limited sympathy for White farmers, and it had no desire to reintroduce state intervention through the backdoor. However, the ANC did have a clear political interest in advancing its BEE agenda. The administration of Thabo Mbeki (1999–2008) signalled its willingness to support a package that would combine an agenda for modernization of the wine industry with the promotion of social transformation within the winelands. While most farmers accepted that change was unavoidable, and indeed desirable, many were also concerned that an overly vigorous pursuit of BEE would imperil their own efforts to make much needed investments in the vineyards and cellars. In the two decades after the millennium, the principal players endeavoured to find a way of becoming globally competitive while incorporating as much of the empowerment agenda as they could either stomach, or pay for. The balance shifted several times over the years, as I will now elucidate in greater detail.

In 1999, the Wine Industry Network for Expertise and Technology (WINETECH) was established as an association dedicated to advancing quality. It was predicated on the view that South Africa had lagged behind the rest of the world and needed a conscious strategy to close the gap. WINETECH

[4] Many of its personnel had previously worked on the quota side of KWV operations.

represented the Cape Wine and Spirits Institute (CWSI), CEWPA, the Co-operative Wine Cellars Committee, the Independent Wine Growers' Association and the National Research Foundation (NRF). That same year, WINETECH served notice of plans to launch *Vision 2020* as a long-term plan for the wine and brandy industries. The programme, which was jointly financed by the Department of Trade and Industry (DTI) and SAWIT, entailed a two-year evaluation of the current state of the industry, followed by a further two years of strategizing. *Vision 2020* was a balancing act, with the techno-cratic vision of being 'innovation-driven and globally competitive' and the producer 'of great quality and uniquely South African products' weighing in the scales against a more socially inflected commitment to 'reflecting good citizenship and social responsibility' and the aspiration to be 'a leader in viable socio-economic transformation and the development of human capital'.[5] In 2002, the South African Wine and Brandy Company (SAWB) was established, with a mandate to implement the new strategy. The management team included a representative of the wholesalers, wine farmers and cooperatives, but with the addition of a representative for labour. This was deemed essential, despite the lack of any obvious contenders for the seat at the table. At various moments, the Confederation of South African Trade Unions (COSATU) and the Food and Allied Workers' Union (FAWU) had attempted to speak on the behalf of farmworkers, but they had failed to establish a membership base in the winelands.[6] The labour representative ended up being Nosey Pieterse of the Black Association for the Wine and Spirits Industry (BAWSI). Pieterse was not a trade unionist but the marketing director of a Black empowerment company, and had formerly been an industrial relations manager at the KWV.[7] According to Gavin Williams, BAWSI never conceived of itself as a trade union, but rather as a broad coalition of labour, business, NGOs, community organizations and interested individuals.[8] Its claim to represent workers resided in the fact that the Plaaswerkersvereniging, which was not a conventional trade union either, was one of its affiliates.[9] BAWSI was nevertheless invited on the pragmatic grounds that it was 'currently the most representative

[5] This summary is derived from SAWB, "A strategic plan for the South African wine industry" (draft 2, July 2003), no page given, http://pmg-assets.s3-website-eu-west-1.amazonaws.com/docs/2003/appendices/030610sawbdraft.htm, accessed 14 March 2022.

[6] Williams, "Black economic", pp. 496–497.

[7] Andries du Toit, Sandra Kruger and Stefano Ponte, "Deracializing exploitation? 'Black Economic Empowerment' in the South African wine industry", *Journal of Agrarian Change* 8 (1), 2008, p. 15.

[8] This was how Pieterse himself described BAWSI. Williams, "Black economic", p. 489. One of the leading figures in BAWSI who served on various committees was Ockie Bosman who had come to prominence through the Rural Foundation in the 1980s.

[9] Du Toit et al. go as far as to refer to dub it a "phantom organization". See Du Toit, Kruger and Ponte, "Deracializing", p. 15.

association consolidating the perspective of black persons and organisations in the wine industry'.[10]

The formulation of *Vision 2020* overlapped with the Mbeki government's Strategic Plan for South African Agriculture in which the grand vision was 'to generate equitable access and participation in a globally competitive, profitable and sustainable agricultural sector contributing to a better life for all'. The SAWB was subsequently requested to formulate a Wine Industry Strategy Plan (WIP), with a view to aligning *Vision 2020* and the government's own Strategic Plan. The resulting document helpfully laid out the principles underpinning the two documents and sketched a roadmap for the future. It was explicit about the failure of *Vision 2020* to elaborate a strategy that went beyond rendering South Africa competitive within a global marketplace:

> The operating rule in implementation will be that any action plans to further one of these objectives may not be at the expense of the achievement of any of the other objectives. It is in this respect that the Vision 2020 strategy *seems to err in its cautious approach to the empowerment, equity and participation objective while comprehensively focusing on global competitiveness and sustainable environmental systems.* Therefore, it is now necessary to establish the appropriate set of considerations and strategies around this objective and related strategies in the wine industry.[11] [my emphasis]

The strategic goals of WIP were (i) 'to generate equitable access and participation within the wine value chain' (ii) 'to enable environmentally sustainable production systems'; and (iii) 'to promote socially responsible consumption of the produce of the vine'. The invocation of value chains, which became increasingly prominent in strategy documents, was significant because it created the impression of a win–win dynamic for actors engaged in each link in the chain. The reference to environmental sustainability and the need to avoid compounding the scourge of alcoholism flagged larger societal issues that could not be reduced to the imperative of penetrating markets, or even spreading the socioeconomic benefits more equitably. The four broad goals were then projected onto six specific strategies.

The question was whether the government would find enough in the WIP document to dovetail with its own policy of promoting economic growth with redistribution. Gavin Williams has suggested that there was at least some government reticence until SAWB was able to strike a deal with SAWIT and agree on a set of industry scorecards that aligned the wine sector with the objectives of the agrarian variants of Broad-Based Black Economic Empowerment (B-BBEE), namely WineBEE and AgriBEE.[12] Du Toit et al. identify a discursive shift from around 2003:

[10] SAWB, "Strategic plan". [11] SAWB, "Strategic plan".

[12] WineBEE, the Wine Industry Transformation Charter, was launched for the wine sector in 2007, but quickly ran aground. It was then folded into the more generic AgriBEE which ran

Previously, the emphasis had been on worker rights and land and agrarian reform on the one hand, and growth and competitiveness on the other hand. The BEE nomenclature was wholeheartedly adopted by both old and new wine industry players. Although access to land and land reform remained part of the debate, the focus had now shifted firmly towards BEE.[13]

The manner in which KWV enabled 25.1 per cent of its shares to be acquired by a coalition of White investors, BEE companies, BAWSI, and an employees' association took some of the pressure off the wine sector as whole.

In 2014, there was one further attempt to articulate a strategic vision. Surveys were conducted with industry players to prepare the ground for what was launched as the Wine Industry Strategic Exercise (WISE). The latter was envisioned as a joint initiative between VINPRO, WOSA, SAWIS, WINETECH and SALBA.[14] It also included representatives of Distell and the producer cellars (that is, the former cooperatives) on the 'task team'. The notable omissions this time around were the KWV, CEWPA and representatives of the farmworkers. WISE evidently built upon WIP because its six work streams (also described as pillars for growth)[15] were a light retouch of the latter's six strategies. WISE identified 10 projects that were supposed to feed into the work streams, each of which was to be led by one of the core organizations.[16] The documentation also referred to 11 specific targets to be achieved by the end of 2025. Only two dealt explicitly with empowerment issues: namely, the aspiration to boost Black ownership of land and water resources from 2.5 to 20 per cent and to increase employment from 270,000 to 375,000 by 2025. The swing of the pendulum back towards a more business-oriented framing points to a combination of fatigue and frustration with BEE.[17] The emphasis was now explicitly placed upon rendering South African wine and spirits more competitive on the basis of 'market and value-chain driven' logics, alongside the application of relevant research and new technologies. As part of the former, the aim was to check the drift towards the export of wine in containers, and to ensure that future growth was built on quality bottled wines. The re-statement of the importance of research was significant because there was a growing apprehension that South Africa's research capacity was being stripped through a lack of public funding and the haemorrhaging of

from 2008. Agatha Herman, *Practising Empowerment in Post-Apartheid South Africa: Wine, Ethics and Development* (London and New York: Routledge, 2018), pp. 38–43.

13 Du Toit, Kruger and Ponte, "Deracializing", p. 18.

14 SALBA was formerly the Cape Wine and Spirits Institute (CWSI). Its membership included all the largest liquor producers.

15 Rico Basson, "The SA Wine Industry Strategic Exercise (WISE)", Cellar Conference, 6 August 2014, https://vinpro.co.za/Media/Default/Downloads/06_RBasson_SA_wine_industry_strategic_exercise.pdf, accessed 14 March 2022.

16 For details, see www.winesouthafrica.info/wise-information/#projects, accessed 14 March 2022.

17 Herman, *Practising*, pp. 38–43.

leading researchers to institutions in Australia and North America.[18] The dire implications of climate change was also a large part of what pushed research back up the list of priorities.[19] The focus on tourism built on many years of highlighting the importance of wine to the Western Cape economy and that of the country as a whole.[20] Moreover, it could easily be made to tally with the pledge to generate more jobs in the winelands. At the time of writing, it remains to be seen how many of the objectives for 2025 will be realized.

While the language of empowerment became less conspicuous at an industry level, a discourse of environmental sustainability gained greater traction. This reflected global trends as well as concerns amongst local conservationists that the unique ecosystems of the Western Cape were under threat from a combination of climate change and the heavy demands on water made by alien species of trees. *Vitis vinifera* was hardly native and, under conditions of monoculture, could be seen as a potential enemy of biodiversity. And while wine farmers had long been constructing their own dams to harness water more efficiently, the vine was clearly not water neutral either.[21] When the Cape Floral Region was added to the UNESCO World Heritage list in 2004, this brought the underlying issues into sharper relief because most of the country's vineyards were located within the Floral Region and some bordered onto the eight designated protected areas.[22] Hence the industry needed to find a way of presenting viticulture as environmentally defensible. Two interconnected initiatives sought to address issues of sustainability and establish certifiable

[18] Interview with Jan 'Boland' Coetzee, 12 April 2017. Danie de Wet also expressed concern about the loss of the gene pool because of the lack of a co-ordinated effort to collect material from the oldest vineyards. Nietvoorbij has a vineyard which hosts all the cultivars that had been trialled at some point or other. The failure to adequately maintain the vineyard because of funding constraints became a source of regret to many. Interview, 16 October 2009.

[19] See N. Vink, A. Deloire, V. Bonnardot and J. Ewert, "Terroir, climate change, and the future of South Africa's wine industry", paper for the pre-AARES conference workshop on The World's Wine Markets by 2030: Terroir, Climate Change, R&D and Globalization, Adelaide, 9 February 2010.

[20] Conningarth Economists, Final Report – Macro-Economic Impact of the Wine Industry on the South African Economy (Also with Reference to the Impacts on the Western Cape) (Pretoria: Conningarth Economists, 2015).

[21] There have been many studies that seek to measure the water footprint of wine, and there has been some speculation on how this might be affected by climate change. For example, see Lee Hannah, Patrick R. Roehrdanz, Makihiko Ikegami, Anderson V. Shepard, M. Rebecca Shaw, Gary Tabor, Lu Zhi, Pablo A. Marquet, and Robert J. Hijmans, "Climate change, wine and conservation", *PNAS* 110 (17) 2013.

[22] https://whc.unesco.org/en/list/1007/, accessed 18 February 2022. The documents submitted to UNESCO, referred to agriculture broadly and noted its greater impact in low-lying areas. Although vineyards were not planted in the higher mountains, there was a potential impact on indigenous vegetation at lower elevations. Section 1.5 "Factors affecting the Cape Floral Region and the protected areas", no pages given, in Republic of South Africa, Nomination of the Cape Floral Region for Inclusion on the World Heritage List (Pretoria: Government of the Republic of South Africa, 2003).

standards. The first of these was the Integrated Production of Wine (IPW) scheme, which was launched as a voluntary initiative in 1998, with the aim of aligning South Africa with international standards, including the guidelines of the International Organization of Vine and Wine (OIV).[23] The process of implementing IPW accreditation resided with WSB. IPW and WSB subsequently teamed up with WOSA to launch Sustainable Wine South Africa (SWSA). With effect from 2010, all producers who wished to bottle wine for export were required to be formally accredited. In the same year, a new set of wine seals was introduced for those that were deemed to be compliant.[24] In addition to the information on the wine labels relating to place of origin, cultivar and vintage, an 'Integrity and Sustainability' seal signalled that a producer met with IPW sustainability standards. The list of criteria included safeguarding the health and safety of workers, the implementation of measures to minimize the use of chemicals, and action to increase biodiversity on the farms. The points system was remarkably detailed and, indeed, was something the KWV might have conjured up. In the vineyards, points are awarded for a wide range of criteria, including suitability of the terrain, the selection of appropriate cultivars and rootstocks, the efficiency of pruning and trellising practices, canopy management, the efficiency of water use in irrigation, and the judicious use of herbicides and pesticides.[25] In the cellar, points are awarded for energy efficiency, reducing carbon emissions, adhering to advised SO^2 levels, managing wastewater, disposing of solid waste, dealing with breakages during bottling and even controlling ambient noise.[26] Compliance is audited every three years. Despite the complexity of the system, no fewer than 95 per cent of producers were reportedly compliant by 2022, which was reflected in the ubiquity of the Integrity and Sustainability seals adorning South African wine bottles.

The second initiative was the Biodiversity and Wine Initiative (BWI) which was launched in 2004, with funding from the World Wide Fund-South Africa (WWF-SA),[27] WOSA, WINETECH, Rand Merchant Bank (RMB) Fund and Critical Ecosystem Partnership Fund. Crucially, this also entailed a partnership with the Botanical Society of South Africa.[28] The objective was to assist

[23] www.ipw.co.za/, accessed 18 February 2022.

[24] The expectation was that the old seals would ultimately be phased out as compliance became the industry norm. In the short term, a producer could apply for the existing WO seal or for a joint WO/IPW seal.

[25] IPW, "Manual for Farms", dated June 2020, www.ipw.co.za/content/manuals/MANUAL%20Farm%20FINAL%20June%202020.pdf, accessed 11 March 2022.

[26] IPW, "Manual for Wineries and Bottling Facilities", dated June 2020, www.ipw.co.za/content/manuals/IPW%20Manual%20Cellar%20June%202020%20FINAL.pdf, accessed 11 March 2022.

[27] WWF-SA had co-funded the UNESCO World Heritage bid.

[28] "Biodiversity and Wine Initiative (BWI): Stewardship within an Industry Context", dated December 2009, www.sanbi.org/wp-content/uploads/2018/04/2-stewardship-wine-industry-bwi.pdf, accessed 17 February 2022.

farmers in setting aside land for conservation and incentivize entering into stewardship arrangements with CapeNature. The BWI ensured that biodiversity standards were worked into the IPW environmental guidelines after 2005. Participating farms could become ordinary members or champions. In the case of the former, much of the focus was placed on stripping out alien vegetation to permit the re-introduction of the indigenous fynbos, which made minimal demands on water and were conducive to the return of insect life. Champions were required to set aside as much as 10 per cent of their land for conservation in perpetuity. Both these statuses were carefully audited.[29] Allocating land for conservancy was really only an option for the producer cellars, whose members could pool land,[30] and the very largest estates like Paul Cluver that could allocate tracts without encroaching on the core vineyard area. The main claim to success of this programme, which formally ended in 2016, was that 144,000 hectares were set aside as conservation land within the Cape Floral Kingdom, in excess of the 94,545 then under vines.[31] This helped justify the larger claim that the futures of the vine and indigenous species of flora were thoroughly compatible.

In addition to the IPW and BWI, there was a push in the direction of organic and biodynamic winemaking. There was no organization that was driving either of these trends, even if Biodynamic and Organic Wines of South Africa (BWSA) emerged as a loose association of like-minded producers. Although a couple of farms had begun to embrace organic principles by 2005, some were allegedly 'greenwashing', or making dubious claims to being 'organic but uncertified'.[32] There was also scepticism amongst the public, who initially looked upon organic wines as being of lesser quality.[33] On the other side, there was at least a system of international certification that producers could turn to, even if there were different bodies carrying out the audits for the European Union and North American markets. In 2019, five different international bodies offered accreditation for organic wines, while Demeter accredited biodynamic wines. Although the industry had a long way to go to catch up with a country like France when it came to farming organically, there

[29] Biodiversity members and Champions were also entitled to add additional stickers to their wines bearing the words "Nature Friendly". "CEPF Final Project Completion Report", dated December 2006, www.cepf.net/sites/default/files/final_sawbc_bwi.pdf, p. 2.

[30] These accounted for most of the land under conservation. François Anton Bezuidenhout, "South African producer/co-operative Wineries", submitted in partial fulfilment of the Diploma of Cape Wine Master, 2014, p. 63.

[31] www.wosa.co.za/swsa/en/Biodiversity/, accessed 18 February 2002. The champions remain because the stewardship agreement was written into the title deeds. Interview with Paul Cluver Snr., 20 August 2019.

[32] Interview with Johan Reyneke, 14 August 2019. Amongst the pioneers were Reyneke (Stellenbosch), Avondale (Paarl) and Klein Constantia (Constantia).

[33] Interview with Reyneke, 14 August 2019, and with Billy Hughes, 23 August 2019.

was a sense of pride in the fact that the country was well ahead of the curve when it came to embracing biodiversity.

Finally, there were two further initiatives that were intended to reinforce ethical standards within the industry. The first was the Wine and Agricultural Ethical Trade Association (WIETA). It was primarily concerned with the promotion of responsible labour practices across the industry. Its voluntary code covered 10 principles, including a ban on child labour, freedom of association, the right to a living wage, and security of housing and tenure.[34] The regular audit included interviews with a cross-section of the workforce to verify the claims made by applicants. As of 2012, WIETA introduced a separate seal for wineries that were approved. Covering the vintages between 2015 and 2019, a total of 689 specific wines earned the seal. This represented a relatively small selection of the total wine produced and included a disproportionate number from the Distell stable as well as from the producer cellars. In 2019, 6 bottlers, 35 cellars, 5 exporters, 2 individuals and 1,028 'producers' had been successfully audited,[35] although judging from the use of SAWIS identifiers a small number of these were involved with other products like cheese.

The second initiative was Fairtrade, which took off in Europe and North America in the 1980s as part of a push to deploy consumer power in the interests of a more equitable system of global trade. In 1997, Fairtrade Labelling Organizations (FLO) was established to provide a bridge between the various national organizations and to create a common set of standards and systems of certification. One applied to small-scale farmers, who were to receive a guarantee of minimum prices and a financial premium, while a second applied to 'hired labour'. In 2004, a set of specific indicators for the wine industry in South Africa was hammered out with stakeholders in the industry. While Fairtrade would work with smaller farmers, its approach to the accreditation of commercial farms was based on their compliance with more stringent requirements.[36] In effect, B-BBEE requirements were folded into criteria for Fairtrade accreditation, with a focus on worker ownership, participation in management, employment equity and skills development.[37] The mechanism that was widely used for providing workers with equity was a grant under the Land Reform and Agricultural Development (LRAD) programme that was intended to facilitate the transfer of land ownership to

[34] http://wieta.org.za/, accessed 14 March 2022.

[35] http://wieta.org.za/wine-buyers/, accessed 14 March 2022.

[36] For a discussion of this process from an insider, see Sandra Kruger, "A case-study of Fairtrade labelling and worker empowerment on two wine and fruit farms in the Western Cape", unpublished MPhil. thesis, University of the Western Cape, 2008, pp. 16–19.

[37] Herman, *Practising*, p. 117.

Black South African hands.[38] In essence, the workers combined their LRAD grant with a financial contribution of their own to become 'co-owner and employee' of a farm.[39] This, in turn, meant that they would qualify for the Fairtrade premium which was supposed to be spent on social benefits such as housing and leisure facilities. Agatha Herman indicates that problems arose once producers had met the initial B-BBEE requirements, in part because continuing compliance became complicated when the workers sold their shares.[40] In 2010, Fairtrade was once more de-linked from B-BBEE, after which farms that aspired to increase exports were more likely to combine Fairtrade and organic accreditation than make explicit reference to B-BBEE. Between 2003 and 2008, the number of farms producing wine and/or fruit under the Fairtrade label increased 10-fold to 50 farms.[41] The attraction was that it facilitated access to large supermarket chains, particularly in the United Kingdom,[42] and to the state alcohol monopolies in Scandinavia. Fairtrade wine also began to receive greater recognition on the domestic market. At the time of writing, South Africa is the world's biggest producer of Fairtrade wines, accounting for two-thirds of the total sales.[43]

The bewildering array of certification procedures was something that producers learned to live with. A discernible pattern is that wineries that opted for one initiative would embrace at least one other. Hence independent and producer cellars embraced empowerment initiatives and became organic, as in the case of Reyneke, or they embraced environmental sustainability alongside empowerment, as in the case of Paul Cluver. The most natural synergy lay in being both organic and environmentally sustainable. But all this imposed a considerable financial and bureaucratic burden on smaller producers. Many cellars found themselves locked into a perpetual cycle of applications, audits and certification procedures that came close to matching the complex bureaucratic web spun by the KWV. Certification was formally voluntary, but there was considerable pressure from international supermarkets and Nordic government buyers to subscribe to their version of global ethical standards. South

38 Equity schemes were one of the four types of projects that were formally supported.

39 Republic of South Africa, "Land Distribution for Agricultural Development", www.nda.agric.za/docs/Policy/redistribution.htm, accessed 14 March 2022.

40 Herman, *Practising*, pp. 118–121. If the workers contributed some money, they were entitled to an additional sum. William G. Moseley, "Fair trade wine: South Africa's post-apartheid vineyards and the global economy", *Globalizations* 5 (2) 2008, p. 298.

41 Kruger, "Case-study", p. 11.

42 As of 2005, UK accounted for 36.5 per cent of all exports, followed by the Netherlands on 16.8 per cent. Germany, Netherlands and Canada had a higher proportion of wines imported in bulk than the UK. Stefano Ponte and Joachim Ewert, "Which way is 'up' in upgrading? Trajectories of change in the value chain for South African Wine", *World Development* 37 (10) 2009, table 4, p. 1642.

43 www.fairtrade.org.uk/Farmers-and-Workers/Wine, accessed 14 March 2022. In 2002, there were 24 accredited producers.

African producers were typically small by comparison with their international competitors, which meant that their bargaining power was correspondingly attenuated.[44] I will return to some of these issues in the next chapter. I will now proceed to an analysis of the success with which the wine industry embraced the opportunities that followed from deregulation and the end to international consumer boycotts.

Going Global: The Economic Transition Writ Large

In 2002, the National Agricultural Marketing Council (NAMC) commissioned an expert committee to evaluate the impact of deregulation. The report commented favourably on the reorientation of the vineyards towards noble cultivars and the heightened emphasis placed on maximizing quality.[45] It also commented on the rapid increase in the total number of cellars from 260 in 1996 to 355 in 2001.[46] An earlier report had commented on a number of high-profile investments from inside and outside South Africa, such as those of Anne Cointreau-Huchon through the acquisition of the Morgenhof estate in Stellenbosch, and the joint venture of Anthonij Rupert and Baron Benjamin de Rothchild in the Rupert & Rothchild winery near Paarl.[47] The NAMC assessment was more guarded, observing that there was little evidence of significant corporate investment and that most of the funding originated from within South Africa.[48] But its overall message was, nevertheless, upbeat. The trends that were captured in the report became even clearer over the next decade (Table 8.1). In what follows, I will separate out four domains within which to track the trajectories of change: two relating to production – represented by investments in the cellars and the vineyards – and two others relating to distribution in the shape of exports and domestic consumption.[49]

To start with the cooperatives, a radical restructuring was inevitable once the KWV system was dismantled. With the demise of the distilling pool and minimum pricing, the cooperatives could only realistically survive by developing their own product ranges for drinking wine. The Swartland Co-operative, which was one of the largest, with 102 members, had already reduced its distilling wine component to 20 per cent of the total production by 1991, and was selling most of its wine in bottles or as bag-in-the-box.[50] Others

[44] On the ways in which power imbalances are accentuated by the focus on managing sustainability, see Stefano Ponte, "The hidden costs of environment upgrading in global value chains", *Review of International Political Economy*, 29 (3), September 2022.

[45] NAMC, *Impact*, p. 56. [46] NAMC, *Impact*, p. 25.

[47] Wesgro, *The Wine Industry in the Western Cape* (Cape Town: Wesgro, 2000), p. 21.

[48] NAMC, *Impact*, p. 56.

[49] For an early mixed assessment, see Ponte and Ewert, "Which way".

[50] Brown, "An evaluation", p. 50.

Table 8.1. *Number of cellars crushing grapes, 2000–2020*

Producer Type	2000	2008	2020
Producer cellars/co-operatives	69	58	45
Private cellars	277	504	457
Producing wholesalers	9	23	27
Total	355	585	529

Source: SAWIS, *SA Wine Industry Statistics*, various years (Paarl: SAWIS).

endeavoured to follow suit, but generating sufficient funds to make the necessary investments in the cellars was a struggle. In 1990, the Drakenstein Co-operative, which was one of the oldest, collapsed.[51] A couple more threatened to succumb after 1998 and were taken over.[52] As Joachim Ewert indicates, the dominant pattern was one of mergers and conversion into private companies.[53] In 1996, for example, four of the Stellenbosch cooperatives merged to form Stellenbosch Vineyards. Many were rebranded as 'producer cellars', in which limited elements of the cooperative framework were retained alongside a structure based on shareholding rather than membership. The Mamreweg Co-operative, for example, was divided into three in 1996: a holding company to handle the financial assets; a limited liability company, Darling Cellars Pty Ltd, to control the production and marketing of the wine; and the producer cooperative which supplied most of the grapes.[54] Commonly, the production and marketing sides of the operation were separated in order to channel greater energy into developing viable brands for the domestic and overseas markets. The larger producer cellars were henceforth able to exploit their production capacity to the full, using grapes sourced from beyond their former members. The most revealing statistic is that the total number of producer cellars declined from a total of 69 in 2000 to 45 in 2020. The only region where there was an increase after 2008 was in Worcester, while by far the largest number were located in neighbouring Breedekloof (see Table 8.2). While some of the producer cellars thrived, others continued to struggle. Simonsvlei began by converting itself into a producer cellar in 1996, and in 2003 it abandoned the cooperative model entirely and took to buying grapes purely on a contract basis. At the end of 2019, it was forced to file for business rescue.

Turning to private cellars, the numbers rose rapidly from 277 at the turn of the millennium to 504 in 2008. Some of the new entrants were farms that had

[51] Brown, "An evaluation", p. 18.

[52] The large Citrusdal Cooperative in the Olifants River area, which had 185 members, was purchased by Charles Back in 2007. James, *Wines*, p. 191.

[53] Joachim Winfried Ewert, "A force for good? Markets, cellars and labour in the South African wine industry after apartheid", *Review of African Political Economy* 39 (132), 2012, p. 233.

[54] Interview with Riaan De Waal, 23 January 2015.

Table 8.2. *Number of producer cellars (former cooperatives), 2008–2020*

Region	2008	2010	2012	2014	2016	2018	2020
Northern Cape	4	3	3	3	3	2	2
Olifants River	3	3	3	3	3	3	3
Swartland	4	4	2	2	2	2	1
Klein Karoo	6	4	4	4	4	4	4
Paarl	8	8	7	7	6	6	7
Robertson	10	11	10	9	9	9	8
Stellenbosch	2	2	2	2	2	2	2
Worcester	5	8	8	8	8	8	8
Breedekloof	16	11	11	11	11	11	10
Cape South Coast	–	–	–	–	0	0	0
TOTAL	**58**	**54**	**50**	**49**	**48**	**47**	**45**

Sources: SAWIS, "'Wine Industry Structure in 2018" (Paarl: SAWIS) and "SA Wine Industry 2020 Statistics" (Paarl: SAWIS), p. 7.

been reliant on selling their grapes and opted to construct their own cellars. Others represented new investments in farms that might otherwise have been dedicated to fruit and other farming activities. Many of the high-profile investments came from those who had made their fortunes on the Johannesburg Stock Exchange, in banking or in the 'tech' industries. The remarkable speed with which cathedrals to Bacchus sprang up across the winelands – in the shape of ultra-modernist, glass-fronted cellars and tasting rooms looking out over sculpted vineyards[55] – was an indicator of the heightened cachet attached to wine. For well-heeled investors, the entry into wine production was a lifestyle choice as much as anything else – which entailed making a small fortune, so the standing joke would have it, by sinking a large one. An example was the impressive Tokara winery at the top of the Helshoogte pass linking Stellenbosch and Franschhoek, which was opened by G. T. Ferreira of RMB in 2000 (Figure 8.1). Ferreira invested heavily in the venture and made no secret of the fact that Tokara would be unprofitable for many years to come. Some high-profile investments emanated from other parts of the wine-producing world. An example is the arrival in Stellenbosch of Michel Laroche, of Chablis fame, who purchased L'Avenir in 2005, from where he set out to explore the potential of Pinotage alongside Chenin Blanc.[56] Another example from Stellenbosch is the founding of Glenelly by May-Eliane de

[55] Prime examples would be Tokara and Delaire on opposite sides of the R310 pass, and the Ernie Els winery in Stellenbosch. Others blended Cape Dutch buildings with contemporary architecture, such as Rustenberg.

[56] Laroche was one of the creators of the Advini stable which subsequently acquired stakes in Le Bonheur and in Ken Forrester Vineyards. James, *Wines*, p. 141.

Figure 8.1 Tokara cellar/vineyards with Delaire on hillside, Stellenbosch
Source: Kwally Nugent.

Lencquesaing, the erstwhile owner of the esteemed Bordeaux property of Pichon-Longueville Comtesse de Lalande. In 2004, her team planted grapes on a former fruit farm bordering onto Rustenberg, and went on to construct a state-of-the-art cellar.[57] For those of more modest means, who typically had been engaged in the industry for generations, it was a matter of graduating to a higher league. By far the largest concentration of private cellars was in Stellenbosch, where the numbers remained broadly stable over the following decade.

Everywhere, the downstream consequences of the global financial crisis of 2008 took its toll. The banks were reputedly reluctant to lend and there was speculation about the dire consequences that would follow if the bubble were truly to burst.[58] After 2012, marginal and over-extended wineries went out of business or turned to other activities such as olive production. The falling number of private cellars was striking around Paarl and nothing short of attritional in Worcester (Table 8.3). Cape South Coast was the one region that bucked the trend.[59] This reflected the attraction of quality producers to cool climate areas. At the time of writing, this region accounted for many of the country's most esteemed wines. As of 2020, the number of independent

[57] The owner is a greatly revered figure in the wine world and was winner of the *Decanter* "Wine Woman of the Year Award" in 1994.

[58] Interview with Simon Barlow, 30 August 2006.

[59] At the time of writing, the Cape South Coast embraces Cape Agulhas, Elgin, Overberg, Plettenberg Bay, Swellendam and Walker Bay.

Table 8.3. *Number of private cellars, 2008–2020*

Region	2008	2010	2012	2014	2016	2018	2020
Northern Cape	10	9	10	10	14	11	11
Olifants River	15	11	14	12	12	12	11
Swartland	34	33	33	29	31	28	27
Klein Karoo	16	22	25	25	22	19	15
Paarl	152	128	128	119	120	109	113
Robertson	52	53	54	54	43	37	36
Stellenbosch	170	172	178	170	172	168	161
Worcester	42	49	52	49	13	12	10
Breedekloof	13	16	15	17	19	17	16
Cape South Coast	–	–	–	–	47	55	57
TOTAL	**504**	**493**	**509**	**485**	**493**	**468**	**457**

Sources: SAWIS, "Wine Industry Structure in 2018" (Paarl: SAWIS) and "SA Wine Industry 2020 Statistics" (Paarl: SAWIS), p. 7.

wineries had come down substantially to 457 cellars – a figure that was substantially lower than in 2008 and yet still far higher than in 2000. This reflected the transformational impact that was wrought by renewed access to overseas markets.

Finally, and on the same point, what is striking is the increase in the number of producing wholesalers (the current preferred term for merchant-manufacturers). In 2000 there were only 9 of these, whereas by 2010 this had mushroomed to no fewer than 26, a figure which remained steady at 27 in 2020.[60] The list included some established names like Distell, which still owned the Nederburg, Durbanville Hills and Drostdy Hof brands, and DGB, which retained the Bellingham and Boschendal labels. Distell, which owed 27 per cent of its revenues to wine, still accounted for 26 per cent of the wine sales by value around 2020, although the sale of four of its wine farms signalled an intention to scale back parts of its operation.[61] On the other side, there were also a number of new players that identified an opportunity for increasing sales to the European market. The secret lay in commanding sufficient volume, and this was achieved by buying grapes from producers who lacked the capacity or the inclination to sustain their own brands. As the cooperatives were restructured, there were many growers looking for alternative outlets for their best grapes. The new entrants included Constellation

[60] Vink et al., "South Africa", table 14.2, p. 402; SAWIS, *Wine Industry Statistics*, Nr. 43, 2018 p. 6.

[61] In 2017, Le Bonheur and Stellenzicht were sold, and in 2020 Alto and Plaisir de Merle followed. However, these farms had only contributed around 4 per cent of the grapes that Distell used.

Table 8.4. *Vineyard area and production of wine, 1996–2018*

Year	Areas under Vine (Excl. Sultanas), in Hectares	Total Production of Wine (Million Litres)[a]	Total Number of Wine Cellars
1996	85,176	845.0	260
1997	87,301	811.4	295
1998	89,935	770.3	315
1999	92,601	796.8	337
2000	93,656	694.9	355
2001	94,412	665.1	388
2002	96,233	718.9	428
2003	98,605	885.3	505
2004	100,207	927.9	561
2005	101,607	840.6	581
2006	102,146	939.8	576
2007	101,957	978.3	560
2008	101,325	1,016.5	585
2009	101,259	998.6	604
2010	101,016	932.7	573
2011	100,568	972.6	582
2012	100,093	1,056.8	582
2013	99,680	1,103.2	564
2014	99,464	1,146.0	559
2015	106,017	1,123.1	566
2016	95,775	1,053.1	568
2017	94,545	1,143.1	546
2018	93,021	944.8	542
2019	92,067	934.5	533
2020	92,005	1,038.5	529

[a]Includes wine for brandy and for distilling, but excludes grape juice concentrate/grape juice.
Sources: SAWIS, *Status of Wine-Grape Vines as of December 2017* (Paarl: SAWIS, 2018), p. 3; SAWIS, *South African Wine Industry Statistics*, various years.

Brands, which acquired the Kumala and Flagstone brands in 2006–2007; Origin Wines, which added three South African wines to its international portfolio; and Brand Phoenix, which sourced grapes from producer cellars to support its First Cape brand. These three came to occupy much of the shelf-space in British supermarkets.[62]

Turning to the vineyards, Table 8.4 indicates that there was a steady expansion of the area under vines over the decade between 1996 and 2006, followed by an equally clear contraction thereafter. In the end, the total area under vines reverted to roughly what it had been in 2000. The total production of wine decreased between 1996 and 2001, but then began climbing steadily until

[62] Ponte and Ewert, "Which way", p. 1643.

Table 8.5. *Change in vineyard area by selected wine grape, 2000–2020 (hectares)*

White Cultivars	2000	2008	2020
Chenin Blanc	22,567	18,852	17,148
Colombard	11,432	11,877	10,507
Sauvignon Blanc	5,346	9,155	9,831
Chardonnay	6,067	8,255	6,587
Muscat d'Alexandrie/Hanepoot	4,047	2,167	1,560
Semillon	1,029	1,153	1,064
Muscat de Frontignan	773	689	859
Viognier	50	892	730
Other White	n/a	4,295	2,754
Total White	*n/a*	*56,825*	*50,967*
Red Cultivars			
Cabernet Sauvignon	8,824	12,697	9,920
Shiraz	3,631	9,907	9,151
Pinotage	6,501	6,088	6,637
Merlot	4,888	6,614	5,387
Ruby Cabernet	2,050	2,381	1,943
Cinsault	3,533	2,241	1,701
Pinot Noir	487	727	1,198
Cabernet Franc	488	979	788
Other Red	n/a	2,866	4,313
Total Red	*n/a*	*44,500*	*41,038*
TOTAL	**93,656**	**101,325**	**92,005**

Sources: SAWIS, *Status of Wine-Growing Vines as of 31 December 2018* (Paarl: SAWIS, 2019), figure 5, p. 7; "SA Wine Industry 2020 Statistics" (Paarl: SAWIS), p. 12.

2008. This reflected the delayed impact of new plantings using virus-free materials. Thereafter a plateau was reached at historically unprecedented levels of production, with annual variations generally reflecting the recurrence of drought. As revealing is the increased prominence of the so-called noble cultivars, alongside a further shift away from white towards red grapes (Table 8.5).[63] These two trends are clearly related, given that the bulk of the distilling wine from the cooperatives had historically derived from high-yielding white cultivars. The producer cellars made a concerted effort to transform their vineyard profile. The Robertson Winery, which was supplied by 35 growers with vineyards covering more than 1,900 hectares, encouraged

[63] Pinotage was conventionally counted alongside the other so-called 'noble varietals': Chardonnay, Sauvignon Blanc, Cabernet Sauvignon, Merlot, Shiraz and Pinot Noir. At the start of the millennium, these all came to sit within the top 10 most planted grapes, with the exception of Pinot Noir and Pinotage.

farmers to replant more red cultivars like Cabernet Sauvignon, Shiraz and Merlot.[64] Again, farms that supplied Darling Cellars transitioned from producing 70 per cent white to 70 per cent red varietals between 2001 and 2006.[65] Darling Cellars bought grapes from former members but also signed contracts with other farmers, and made a particular effort to source grapes from some of the steeper slopes of Groenekloof. It also endeavoured to persuade farmers to protect their old bush vines, which it believed had the potential to sustain wines of the highest quality.[66] The independent producers similarly replanted their vineyards in anticipation of shifting demand. Overseas reconnaissance by the Malan family led to the conclusion that Simonsig was spread too thinly.[67] In 1980, 72 per cent of the vineyard area of Simonsig consisted of white varietals, but by 2000 this had fallen to 57.4 per cent as Pinotage and Cabernet Sauvignon were planted and became the dominant grapes overall.[68]

Amongst the white varietals there was a steady decline in plantings of Chenin Blanc, although it remained the largest single grape overall in 2020. The largest plantings of Chenin were in Breedekloof, Olifants River, Swartland and Paarl. Its reputation in locations like the Swartland soared as producers switched their focus to maximizing quality. At the start of the millennium, wineries invested heavily in planting Chardonnay, but when consumer interest waned, many were forced to strip the vines out again.[69] In 2018, the largest Chardonnay vineyard area was in Robertson, where Danie de Wet had begun the love affair with this cultivar. Plantings of Sauvignon Blanc remained on a slow upward trajectory, with the greatest concentration of vines in Stellenbosch, and a secondary hub in Robertson where the Springfield estate demonstrated its potential. It also received a new lease of life in Constantia and in the hills above Noordhoek (on the Atlantic coast) where Cape Point Vineyards established the first vineyards in 1996.[70] Semillon held its own, but Palomino virtually disappeared. Viognier was amongst the lesser white varietals which won loyal adherents, with the greatest plantings in Paarl.

[64] James, *Wines*, p. 250. [65] Interview with De Waal, 23 January 2015.

[66] In some cases, they were too late. In one case, the winemaker arrived at a farm which had coveted 75-year old Cabernet Sauvignon bush vines, only to find they were in the process of being bulldozed. Interview with De Waal, 23 January 2015.

[67] Interview with François Malan, 25 July 2009.

[68] C. W. White, "The creation and development of a South African wine estate, the wines produced and the positioning thereof in the market place", unpublished report, February 2000", pp. 55, 73.

[69] Danie de Wet cited the rise and fall in the fashion for Chardonnay and the rise of Sauvignon Blanc as examples of the unhealthy influence of wine writers who, he felt, drove wine fashions. He conceded, however, that over-oaking may have had something to do with the manner in which consumers fell out of love. Interview with Danie de Wet, 16 October 2009.

[70] Interview with Riandri Visser, 22 August 2019.

Amongst the red cultivars, similar adjustments took place. As with Chardonnay, plantings of Cabernet Sauvignon were substantial in the early period but fell back again in the decade after 2008 as the market became saturated. However, it remained the third most planted grape and the most planted red overall, with concentrations in Stellenbosch, Paarl and the Swartland. There was a surge in interest in Shiraz after 2000, but this again flattened out over the next decade. Like Cabernet, it is widely planted in Stellenbosch, Paarl and the Swartland. Initial interest in Merlot declined, although it remained important for the production of Bordeaux-style blends that were a particular feature of Stellenbosch. The area dedicated to Cinsault suffered from the same image problem as Chenin Blanc and continued to be associated with producer cellars. The vineyard area contracted despite the increasingly positive reviews that the minimalist versions of the single varietal wines received.[71] Pinotage experienced a revival of fortunes and was the sixth most planted varietal in 2018. This was inspired in part by the efforts of the Pinotage Association to advertise the virtues of the country's very own gift to the vine and to offer practical advice on planting.[72] In the case of Pinot Noir, there was a steady expansion from a low base, with the cooler climes of the Cape South Coast, notably Elgin and the Hemel-en-Aarde Valley, leading the way. In terms of the vineyard area, it narrowed the gap with Cinsault, the red grape that had once held sway. To a surprising extent, Pinot Noir was also present in the warmer climes of Paarl, Stellenbosch and Robertson. Significantly, it was the only cultivar for which private cellars accounted for the bulk of production. What the SAWIS statistics only hint at is the experimentation with a much larger range of minor red varietals. Cabernet Franc is reflected in the statistics, but several other southern European varietals began to show up in the vineyards. This included Petit Verdot, Malbec, Mourvèdre, Carignan, Tinta Barocca and Touriga Nacional. Although some of these had long been used for blending and fortification, a handful of farms began to bottle single varietal versions. What is striking about the proliferation of cultivars is that a good many of them, especially the Italian ones, were originally introduced by A. I. Perold, although they did not find favour at that time. This changed in part because of a greater receptivity to Italian food and wine styles.[73]

[71] Cinsault had traditionally been used in blends, often alongside Cabernet Sauvignon. Once Merlot became available, it tended to replace Cinsault. The revelation that Cinsault could stand on its own was a belated one. Yvonne le Riche, "Revolutionising Cinsaut", dissertation submitted to the Cape Wine Academy in partial fulfilment of the Diploma of Cape Wine Master, 2015, p. 20.

[72] Pinotage Association, *Guidelines for Pinotage Vineyards* (Stellenbosch: Pinotage Association, 2005).

[73] Barbera, Catararrato, Aglianico, Dolcetto Nero, Inzolia (both red and white), Nebbiolo, Perricone, Teroldego, Trebbiano were all introduced from Italy, seemingly by Perold. Van Zyl, *Prof. C.J. Theron*, pp. 19–20. Altygedacht in Durbanville has a long history of working

Ultimately, a successful transition hinged on the ability of the industry to expand the overall market for products of the vine. In the early 1990s, there was an awareness that South Africa had a lot of catching up to do when it came to competing in the export market. Hans Stroebel made an analogy with the return of South Africa to international rugby and the chastening revelation of how much the country had been left behind:

> It was the same in the wine industry. We were only looking at the local component, the local taste, the local way of handling it. And it was only after '94 when we had the opportunity to go and work in the top wineries of the world and then bring our people [that it changed] . . . So it's a question at that stage of the insulation [sic]; it had a serious impact on the competitiveness of our wines.[74]

The shock of being found wanting was something that rugby administrators and wine producers found equally chastening. In either case, the conscious strategy was one of learning from the international competition to hopefully beat it. The SAA Wine Shield, which pitted the best of South Africa against Australia in 1995, did not end well: Australia won 8 of the 11 categories while South Africa boasted only 3 category winners (open dry white, Riesling and dessert wine).[75] The competition occasioned some controversy because some considered it ill-advised to embark on such a competition before South Africa was ready. Michael Fridjhon and John Platter, on the other hand, felt it was necessary for wineries to get a sense of where they really were positioned in terms of global quality standards.[76]

One approach to making up lost ground, which harked back to the study tours of a bygone era, was to beat a path to other regions of the wine-producing world in search of valuable lessons. François Malan of Simonsig described his brother Pieter as travelling 'in the slipstream of Mandela'.[77] He himself participated in visits both to the Napa Valley and Australia. France was an obvious attraction, given the push towards particular red cultivars. However, language continued to be perceived as a barrier, while many believed that Australia provided a model of a New World country that had successfully

with Barbera and markets a single varietal wine. Nebbiolo has been bottled by Steenberg since the 1990s. Vermentino, the white cultivar associated with Sardinia, is a recent introduction and is now being produced at Voor Paardeberg by Ayama. Bosman Family Vineyards is the first to market a single-varietal Nero d'Avola. Portuguese red grapes were adopted much earlier because they were used to produce South African grapes. But the range of Portuguese cultivars used for still wine has also expanded.

74 Interview with Frans Stroebel, 17 November 2009.

75 Chris Shanahan, "Australia and South Africa wines go head to head in South African Airways Wine Shield", 26 November 1995, https://chrisshanahan.com/articles/1995/australia-and-south-african-wines-go-head-to-head-in-south-african-airways-wine-shield/, accessed 1 May 2022.

76 Interview with Philip Van Zyl, editor of *Platter's South African Wine Guide*, 21 February 2009. Platter, Fridjhon and Gyles Webb of Thelema were the three South African judges.

77 Interview with François Malan, 25 July 2009.

broken into European markets. What became apparent very quickly, though, was that the structure of the industries in the two countries was fundamentally different. Whereas Australian production was dominated by a handful of large players, who could command substantial advertising and promotional budgets and sustain high volumes, the South African landscape was dominated by a plethora of small producers. In many ways, New Zealand would have offered a more appropriate model; because it was a comparative latecomer, its wines had managed to nest amongst the higher price points, and it produced some of the varietals, notably Pinot Noir and Sauvignon Blanc, that were of particular interest to South African producers. With time, the producers of premium South African wines sought to distance themselves from the New World tag, in part because they were not seeking to produce the 'fruit bombs' that had drawn such attention to Australia wines.[78] But, equally, the scale of production was such that it made more sense to focus on wines that gave expression to the particularities of terroir (see Chapter 9). A second option was to engage in joint ventures with foreign partners who brought a combination of much needed capital, know-how and contacts. An example was Vilafonté, which developed into a partnership between Zelma Long and Phil Freese of Long Vineyards in California and Mike Ratcliffe of Warwick in Stellenbosch.[79] A third option, for those who could afford it, was to buy in external expertise in the hope that some of the magic would rub off. By the 1990s, flying consultants such as Michel Rolland were selling their expertise across the world.[80] Adding some South African projects to the portfolio posed few barriers, provided the price was right.[81] Distell led the way when it enlisted Paul Pontallier from Chateau Margaux to advise on the direction of their then flagship estate, Plaisir de Merle.[82]

By far the most encouraging development was the surge in wine exports (Table 8.6). Between 1997 and 2007, exports of all wine more than quadrupled in volume. In 2008, exports accounted for more than half of total production for the first time, a feat that was bettered in 2013 when all previous records were broken. In most years, exports hovered just shy of half of total production. Although still wines accounted for most of the growth, there was also a

[78] Interview with Anthony Hamilton Russell, 25 August 2006.

[79] James, *Wines*, pp. 203–204. The Ratcliffe family sold Warwick to an American investment firm in 2018. In February 2022, Ratcliffe bought his partners out of Vilafonté.

[80] Rolland was profiled unsympathetically in a documentary that critiqued globalization, and the standardization of production, in the wine industry. Jonathan Nossiter, *Mondovino* (Pathé, 2004).

[81] Remhoogte (Stellenbosch) was one farm that bought in the advice of Rolland before the latter withdrew in 2008. James, *Wines*, p. 155.

[82] Interview with Stroebel, 17 November 2009. The late Pontallier and Zelma Long were two of the judges in the 1995 SAA Wine Shield alongside Robert Joseph, the founder of *Wine International* magazine and chair of the International Wine Challenge (IWC).

Table 8.6. *Export volumes and domestic consumption, 1996–2018 (litres)*

Year	Natural/Still Wine	Fortified Wine	Sparkling and MCC Wine	Total Litres	Export of All Wine as % of Total Production	Domestic Consumption of Still, Fortified and Sparkling Wine[a]	Per Capita Consumption, of Still, Fortified and Sparkling Wine (Litres)	Market Share, Still Wine
1997	107,972,398	1,265,296	805,048	110,042,742	20.1	366,891,229	8.90	15.9
1998	115,782,195	1,116,766	524,676	117,423,637	21.6	349,743,967	8.30	15.7
1999	126,263,186	695,535	809,619	127,768,340	21.4	355,710,576	8.26	15.5
2000	139,800,022	471,513	685,237	140,956,772	26.1	357,188,173	8.00	17.0
2001	175,978,105	548,388	779,299	177,305,792	33.4	363,721,168	8.02	17.4
2002	215,511,730	520,936	1,360,842	217,393,508	38.3	364,687,939	7.86	17.3
2003	236,374,075	525,789	1,564,707	238,464,571	33.5	326,416,227	6.97	15.2
2004	265,761,884	413,393	1,552,885	267,728,162	38.4	329,171,792	6.95	15.5
2005	279,128,314	406,982	1,537,824	281,073,120	44.7	323,577,865	6.75	14.9
2006	269,166,416	486,547	2,018,235	271,671,198	38.3	325,554,423	6.72	14.5
2007	309,337,583	405,696	2,796,366	312,539,645	42.8	343,140,741	6.99	14.6
2008	407,299,650	423,207	3,971,972	411,694,829	53.9	343,251,491	6.90	14.5
2009	389,023,730	282,791	6,285,376	395,591,897	49.1	325,725,845	6.46	13.9
2010	370,909,346	401,700	7,212,677	378,523,723	48.5	333,192,800	6.51	14.0
2011	350,414,988	348,858	6,649,735	357,413,581	43.0	341,070,966	6.56	14.0
2012	408,910,701	2,274,425	8,032,172	417,217,298	47.9	350,459,924	6.64	14.0
2013	517,404,596	282,980	7,897,830	525,584,956	57.4	356,552,253	6.65	14.1
2014	414,834,333	348,954	7,473,395	422,656,682	44.1	383,623,386	7.04	14.9
2015	412,444,375	310,819	7,623,111	420,018,305	43.4	414,494,898	7.49	16.0
2016	424,088,450	385,543	3,866,705	428,360,376	47.7	427,112,420	7.60	16.2
2017	444,010,922	315,303	4,059,269	448,398,546	48.8	439,329,897	7.70	16.3
2018	414,992,259	351,157	4,819,937	420,163,353	51.0	421,054,526	7.27	15.4
2019	316,663,992	174,149	2,944,739	319,782,880	38.2	390,494,129	6.64	14.2
2020	314,333,283	221,005	3,417,893	317,972,181	35.4	313,801,781	5.26	13.7

[a]*Note*: Up until 2000 – and thereafter excluded – the figure includes grape-based liquor and alcoholic fruit beverage component.

Sources: Export figures up to 2006 from SAWIS, *SA Wine Industry Statistics, 2012 and South African Wine Industry Directory, 2009–2010* (Paarl: Wineland, 2009), p. 493. From 2007 onwards, figures from SAWIS, *SA Wine Industry Statistics, 2018*. Consumption figures after 2000 from SAWIS, *SA Wine Industry 2020 Statistics*.

surge in sparkling wine exports until 2015, which reflected the positive relationship between quality and price for Méthode Cap Classique (MCC) wines.[83] Whereas Germany had once topped the list of bulk importers, it had been overtaken by the UK. The increase in exports was undoubtedly a significant achievement given the low base from which the country was starting. It served to stave off the catastrophe that would have unfolded if producers had continued to be restricted to the domestic market. However, the downside was that much of the expansion was accounted for by an increase in bulk exports that created less added value. Indeed, in 2018 no less than 60.5 per cent by volume of wine exported was in bulk rather than in a packaged format, and this was especially true of white wine.[84] The chairman of VINPRO, Anton Smuts, claimed that 14 per cent of bulk white wine exports was being sold cheaper than water itself, at a time when 80 per cent of producers were operating at below sustainable profit levels. He also pointed to the reality that bulk wine was mostly uncertified.[85] One of the structural limitations that shaped this pattern was the very high cost of packaging. In 2006, Distell estimated that South African bottling and packaging cost €1 more per case than in Europe. This possibly reflected limited competition in the domestic market where a single glass company, Consol, accounted for 75 per cent of the business.[86] Between 2008 and 2018, the cost of packaging is estimated to have risen by 146 per cent, at a time when the overall average production costs for wine increased by 52 per cent.[87] Given that as much as a quarter of the cost of a bottle of wine was accounted for by the bottle/packaging, there was a financial incentive for overseas buyers to ship their wines in bulk and to bottle them on the other side. This evidently undermined the efforts of industry spokesmen to use certification as a means of demonstrating adherence to the highest environmental and ethical standards and to ensure that as much as possible of the added value remained within the country.

The demonstrable success on the export front was counterbalanced by the reality that domestic consumption declined during the first decade after 1996. The emigration of upwards of half a million White people was blamed for

[83] MCC wines were made with the same grapes and in the same style as Champagne, but cost around a third of the price for a product that was often of comparable quality. Graham Beck's MCC wines enjoyed considerable success in UK supermarkets like M&S and in specialist wine shops in the UK.

[84] SAWIS, *Wine Industry Statistics*, Nr. 43, 2018, table 8.2., p. 22.

[85] Arabella Mileham, "South Africa must 'wake up' and stop selling bulk wine cheaper than water, Vinpro boss says", *The Drinks Business*, 17 January 2019, www.thedrinksbusiness.com/2019/01/south-africa-must-wake-up-and-stop-selling-bulk-wine-cheaper-than-water-vinpro-says/, accessed 17 February 2022.

[86] Interview with Anthony Hamilton Russell, 25 August 2006.

[87] Conningarth Economists, Final Report, p. 3.

Table 8.7. *Per capita consumption of wine (over age of 15 years) in select producing and non-producing countries, 2018 (litres)*

Wine-Producing		Minor and Non-producing	
Portugal	62.1	Belgium	31.5
France	50.2	Namibia	27.7
Italy	43.7	Netherlands	24.7
Austria	31.3	Ireland	22.6
Australia	30.0	United Kingdom	22.6
Spain	26.4	Cape Verde	18.2
Argentina	24.9	Iceland	16.7
New Zealand	24.3	Canada	15.7
Greece	21.9	United States	12.4
Chile	15.8	Finland	12.3
South Africa	10.6	Guinea-Bissau	8.2

Source: OIV Statistics, presented at https://twitter.com/capewinereview/status/1455259692108820483/photo/1.

some of this shrinkage, but there was also a limit to what the local market would bear.[88] Between 2011 and 2018, consumption for all wine products edged upwards again, as did the per capita consumption of still wine and the market share of wine. Government bans on wine sales during the COVID-19 pandemic threw a spanner in the works in 2020 and 2021, when domestic sales may have been 15 per cent lower than anticipated.[89] The overall trend is significant because the adult per capita consumption of beer, which had dominated consumer preferences since the mid-1960s, contracted from 87.119 litres in 2000 to 77.81 litres in 2018. The only other alcoholic product for which consumption was growing was spirits other than brandy and whisky. However, the reality is that per capita consumption of all wine was still lower in 2018 than it had been in 2000. These figures do, however, need to be placed in some kind of international perspective. European producing countries experienced a marked contraction in domestic consumption in the second half of the twentieth century (Table 8.7). In France, for example, per capita consumption of wine averaged 126 litres between 1890 and 1914 but plummeted to an average of 53 litres between 1990 and 2014.[90] Over the same period, per capita consumption fell more slowly in Argentina, from 46 to 34

[88] The estimates vary wildly, given that the official statistics miss many who have left, but also some who have returned. Anthony Hamilton Russell made the point that there was no evidence that White people who remained were drinking any less. Interview 25 August 2006.

[89] Tracy Davids, Nick Vink and Kandas Cloete, "COVID-19 and the South African wine industry", *Agrekon* 61 (2) 2022, p. 50.

[90] Anderson and Pinilla, "Global overview", table 2.3, p. 43.

litres, and in Chile from 24 to 14 litres. In Australia and New Zealand, where the real take-off of the wine sector came late, there was a significant rise in domestic consumption, from 5 to 23 litres and from 1 to 18 litres, respectively. Like Australia, South Africa drank an average of 5 litres from 1890 to 1914, but this had only increased to 8 litres in the 1990–2014 period. But whereas Australian wine consumption was on a downwards trajectory, that of South Africa was bending the other way, if only ever so slightly.

Finally, it is important to return to the issue of quality. Since the 1970s, South Africans had sold relatively little drinking wine overseas and had, equally, imbibed very little wine that originated from other parts of the world. One of the greatest challenges facing the industry was, therefore, that of aligning with global tastes. Although the industry was keen to establish an identity of its own, it was also at pains to eradicate certain signature features that singled out South African wines, and usually not in a good way. In 2007, Tim Atkin contrasted the improving quality of white wines with the disappointing character of the reds:

South African reds are easy to spot in blind tastings: apart from the clumsy use of oak (a common fault), they often combine high levels of alcohol with a green, under-ripe tinge and a whiff of burnt rubber ... (O)n current performance South Africa is the least exciting red-wine producing country in the New World.[91]

This reference to burnt rubber touched a raw nerve, but it was just the hint of the storm that was about to be unleashed. In April 2008, a British wine writer, Jane MacQuitty, penned a scathing assessment of South African wines in *The Times*:

A recent tasting of the five-star wines and runners-up in the 2008 John Platter Guide, widely regarded as the Cape's crème de la crème, proved to be a cruddy, stomach-heaving and palate-crippling disappointment.[92]

This dismissive comment provoked expressions of outrage in South Africa, but she was not alone in some of her critique. In a contemporaneous documentary, the fate of South African wines at the International Wine Challenge was profiled.[93] The judge who spoke to the camera was none other than Atkin, who again lamented the under-performance of South African red wines.

[91] Tim Atkin, "South African wines worth fighting for", *The Guardian* 7 January 2007, www.theguardian.com/lifeandstyle/2007/jan/07/foodanddrink1, accessed 17 February 2022.

[92] Jane MacQuitty, "South Africa is struggling", *Times*, 9 April 2008, www.thetimes.co.uk/article/south-africa-is-struggling-3djt8bcd0jb, accessed 24 March 2022.

[93] "Wine: Disc 3, The Future" (director Nick Angel) (Oxford Film and Television for BBC director, 2009). South African wines fared much better at the 2009 Decanter World Wine Awards when they won 23 gold medals, 130 silver medals, 246 bronze medals, and 131 commended certificates.

But, within a decade, the picture looked markedly different. South African wines had begun to score highly at international competitions and favourable comparisons were made with hallowed regions of the wine world, such as the Rhône and Bordeaux. There were a couple of factors at work here. Firstly, the overall quality of the wine certainly improved as plantings of better clones came into full bearing and producers made a conscious effort to keep yields within acceptable bounds. Secondly, there was a greater alertness to the 'burnt rubber' signature and a conscious effort was made to address it. At first the industry was unclear as to the underlying cause, although it seemed more pronounced in certain varietals than others. One suggestion was that farmers tended to harvest before the grapes had reached full phenolic ripeness.[94] Many producers then went to the opposite extreme, producing highly alcoholic wines that were fruit-heavy and lacked finesse. Eventually, wineries found a way to strike the right balance. Another suggestion was that virused vines might struggle to produce grapes that were universally ripe, a feature that would have receded as the vineyards were replanted with unvirused clones.[95]A very different response was to observe that a more pleasant variant was an overtone of dark chocolate. On the basis that New Zealand Pinot Noir was highly regarded despite tasting very different to Burgundy, and despite exhibiting its own signature aromas and taste, some producers embraced novelty. Diemersfontein in Wellington enjoyed overnight success with its Pinotage and sparked a number of copycat 'chocolate wines'. For members of the Pinotage Association who were seeking to elevate the image of the cultivar, this was perhaps a double-edged sword. It suddenly made Pinotage 'sexy', but it potentially detracted from the campaign to elevate it to the equivalent of a noble cultivar. Over time, many critics, including MacQuitty herself, fundamentally revised their opinion about South African red wines. Tim Atkin came to champion the virtues of all the country's wines and established himself as the most influential foreign critic.[96] At this point, I will turn to assess the reverse side to the success story, which is the uneven record of empowerment initiatives within the wine industry.

Social Transformation in the Wine Industry

B-BBEE was supposed to drive a transformation in the patterns of ownership to the benefit of 'previously disadvantaged' peoples. Businesses that had a

[94] That this was common practice to reduce the alcohol content (and to increase yields) is clear from the KWV's own documents.

[95] There has even been a suggestion that tar poles used for trellising might have been at fault. Jamie Goode, "Recalling the burnt rubber controversy – what was the cause?", 3 August 2021, https://winemag.co.za/wine/opinion/jamie-goode-recalling-the-burnt-rubber-controversy-what-was-the-cause/, accessed 12 March 2022.

[96] Atkin produced an annual Special Report that was closely read and cited by South African producers.

turnover of less than R50 million (roughly £4.4 million in 2004) were formally exempted. However, even those that fell beneath the threshold were required to apply for a license to produce alcohol, which had to be renewed periodically, and this required compliance with the scorecard.[97] There were seven weighted measures in 2004: namely ownership (20 points); management control (10); employment equity (15); skills development (15); preferential procurement (20); enterprise development (15); and socioeconomic development (5).[98] The scale of the manufacturing wholesalers and the producer cellars evidently meant that they could not avoid taking action. Distell responded by giving employees shares in the company and focusing on training and skills development. KWV similarly focused on training workers. Some of the larger entities also embraced the need to make workers part-owners of an offshoot enterprise. As early as 1999, Distell entered a deal with a group of BEE investors to acquire a farm in Papkuilsfontein near Darling. A trust for workers owned more than a third of the shares in the business, which was originally known as Tukulu but was later rebranded as Earthbound. The latter achieved certification as an organic producer and, in line with Distell's BEE pitch, much of the emphasis was placed on skills training and housing for workers.

A report from 2011 which presented incomplete data on private and producer cellars identified 62 'direct empowerment' programmes. Of these, 17 involved the provision of equity ownership in the cellars and 20 in the vineyards. A further nine were housing projects, two entailed initiatives through management, and bringing up the rear was a single profit-sharing scheme. Under the 'human resources' heading, nine initiatives focused on skills and training, seven involved mentoring and one promised greater equality in employment. A further 61 programmes met B-BBEE criteria through outsourcing and procurement, but this impacted farmworkers in a more indirect way. On these figures, ownership of equity and/or housing were clearly the preferred routes to empowerment on the farms.[99] The same report noted that 62 per cent of the producer cellars were engaged in BEE projects of one kind or another.[100] When it came to individual farms, the most common route to compliance was to transfer equity to workers through a designated trust fund. The farms contributed, some of the resources typically derived from LRAD grants. Although individual workers received a relatively small sum of money,

[97] Interview with Anthony Hamilton Russell, 25 August 2006.

[98] This was revised in 2012 to impart added weight to management control and to emphasize socio-economic development. Herman, *Practising*, p. 14.

[99] Department of Agriculture, Forestry and Fisheries, *A Profile of the South African Wine Market Value Chain* (Arcadia: Directorate Marketing, 2011), p. 116.

[100] *A Profile*, p.115.

they were able to pool the resources to become joint shareholders in the business.[101]

Broadly, there were three main variants of empowerment deals.[102] Under the first, the workers acquired a farm and a brand of their own, or at least substantial part-ownership in a new venture. The profits were then used to support improved housing, social amenities and education initiatives. An early example is the creation of Thandi wines in Elgin. As early as 1996, Paul Cluver and the South African Forestry Company Limited (SAFCOL) had initiated the Lebanon Fruit Farm Trust (LFFT) to cater to workers from both companies and residents of Lebanon village. Cluver and SAFCOL contributed 200 hectares of land which gave each of them a one-third stake, while the remainder of the shares were divided between a trust for those who had received a government grant (147 households) and a second trust set up for members of the Lebanon community (250 members).[103] Half of the Cluver shares were sold to the SFW in 1998, while SAFCOL subsequently withdrew from the deal.[104] When Thandi Wines was established as a distinct brand in 2000, LFFT held two-thirds of the shares and Vinfruco, a company involved in the marketing of wine, the remaining third. Sandra Kruger's analysis would suggest that the relative success of Thandi rested on four pillars. Firstly, it did not confine itself to making wine but also engaged in the export of fresh fruit, thereby creating a second income stream. Secondly, Thandi secured Fairtrade accreditation, which made the workers eligible for a premium that could be channelled into collective benefits. Thirdly, Thandi was able to generate larger volumes after two other empowerment farms became shareholders and agreed to supply the needed grapes. And, finally, Thandi enjoyed privileged access to local and international marketing channels after Vinfruco and Stellenbosch Vineyards created the Company of Wine People in 2005. Because LFFT controlled two-thirds of the shares, this ensured that the profits from the increased sales of wine came back to the trust. Another case is the creation of the Fair Valley Association that was established for farmworkers at Fairview around 1997.[105] With the assistance of a land grant, the Association acquired its own farm and Fair Valley was launched as a distinct brand. Like Thandi, Fair Valley wines acquired Fairtrade accreditation, which assisted with gaining access to overseas markets. A third example is the creation of a Bouwland Partnership in 2003, on the joint initiative of Beyers Truter and Jan Hendriks. Truter had been the winemaker at Kanonkop before

[101] Moseley, "Fair trade", p. 298.

[102] WOSA listed 46 'Empowerment Projects' that covers the spectrum. See www.wosa.co.za/Sustainability/Socially-Sustainable/BEE/Empowerment-Projects/, accessed 27 February 2022.

[103] Kruger, "Case-study", p. 102. Here I draw extensively on this highly informative thesis.

[104] Kruger, "Case-study", p. 89.

[105] Herman, *Practising*, p. 49.

moving on to establish Beyerskloof, while Hendriks had also worked there and was the founder of the Stellenbosch Farm Workers Association. The intended beneficiaries were 39 families from Kanonkop, Beyerskloof and Bouwland. Land for the Bouwland Estate was purchased with support from LRAD and other sources, and a separate brand was established. While the trust that was created for the workers owned 74 per cent of Bouwland Estate, Truter owned the other 26 per cent.

In the second variant on empowerment, workers became part-owners of an existing business. Hence, at Bosman Family Vineyards, the deal entailed the Adama Appollo Workers Trust acquiring a minority stake in the business. The company was certified as BEE-compliant in 2008 and went on to acquire Fairtrade certification.[106] A much publicized example is Solms-Delta in the Drakenstein Valley. Mark Solms went on record countless times to say that he felt unable to make wine in good conscience without tackling the legacies of chronic poverty, low self-esteem and endemic alcoholism amongst farmworkers.[107] Solms secured the assistance of a friend and businessman/philanthropist, Richard Astor, who purchased the neighbouring farm. Together they mortgaged these properties and purchased a third farm, Deltameer, a portion of which was then transferred to the workers through the Wijn de Caab Trust. At the same time, shares in the Solms-Delta wine business were divided three ways between Solms, Astor and the Trust. The workers therefore became owners of a portion of the land and part-owners of the overall business. Over the years, the workers came to benefit from purpose-built housing and better access to schooling in a manner that made Solms-Delta a model. A particular innovation was the opening of a museum at the tasting room that was operated by the former employees. Following commissioned archaeological research, the museum peeled back layers of history at the adjoining farms. Whereas most producers skirted over the history of slavery, the Solms-Delta Museum listed the names of all the slaves who were known to have worked there and where they originated from. As part of an effort to instil a sense of community whilst tackling the realities of alcohol abuse, there was also an ambitious effort to resuscitate musical traditions, which were showcased at an annual harvest festival. For many, Solms-Delta offered a glimpse of what empowerment could look like when handled imaginatively.[108]

A third variant was one in which the structures of ownership did not change, but profits from distinct labels were channelled into achieving practical social

[106] Herman, *Practising*, p. 118.
[107] Interview with Mark Solms, 14 November 2019. This is also the subject of the documentary, "Wine: The Future".
[108] During interviews, the positive image was broadly vindicated by the owner/workers. Group interview with selection of Solms-Delta farmworker/owners, 9 December 2011.

improvements. Johan Reyneke recalls that he started out as a farm worker. When he wanted to move into farming, he sought to convince his co-workers to apply for a joint loan. After struggling to persuade the banks to lend to the group, he raised the money to acquire a farm in his own name. He offered his co-workers a choice between a stake in the business or assistance with the acquisition of their own houses. Most expressed a strong preference for off-farm housing and education rather than waiting for a slow and uncertain financial return in the business.[109] Reyneke took on the onerous financial responsibility of securing bonds for the houses that the families themselves selected, all of which were in nearby towns. He also introduced a second brand, Cornerstone, the profits from which went towards supporting the workers' welfare.

Herman helpfully distinguishes between the principles of empowerment and social development.[110] She demonstrates that many initiatives served to improve the material conditions of farm workers and their families. This was particularly true of Fairtrade affiliates, because the premium could be used to upgrade housing and social amenities.[111] However, she argues that this did not necessarily mean that workers were empowered in the sense of being able to set the agenda. During interviews, several farmers claimed, without wanting to be too specific, that there were many questionable empowerment schemes afoot. The bigger the business and the more complex the value chain, the less likely it was that ordinary workers would be able to make their voices heard. But even where the business was much smaller, a strong element of paternalism persisted. Typically, farmers had a seat on the trusts that managed the assets and set the priorities. They often justified their continuing intervention on the basis that the workers lacked the knowledge to make the most informed business decisions. The structural issue here was that while workers/shareholders often wanted to see immediate improvements in their income and living conditions, the farmers were mindful of the need to plough profits back into the business. Conversely, farmers who wanted to step back also faced a moral dilemma. Hence Reyneke was disappointed to discover that half of the workers sold their houses and used the proceeds to buy consumer goods. He had entered a crippling debt to pay the bonds, but ultimately had to accept that the owners had the right to choose.[112] The underlying problem was that so little money was being made from the production of wine that many of the hopes that were placed in empowerment deals were simply unrealistic. The frustration that many of the former workers experienced often led to a dissipation in the initial enthusiasm. This was shared for different reasons by the farmers, who felt let down by different tiers of the governmental system. It was

[109] Herman, *Practising*, p. 69. [110] Herman, *Practising*, pp. 86–114.
[111] Herman, *Practising*, pp. 89–102. [112] Interview with Reyneke, 14 August 2019.

often difficult to improve access to housing on the farms because these were zoned as agricultural rather than residential areas. When Reyneke wanted to buy a second farm for the workers and was turned down by the banks and the industry body which talked most about empowerment, he turned to the government. He recalls a meeting with a senior ANC figure who informed him that the only possible deal was one in which government would provide the money and take ownership of the land, while an ANC cadre would move into the manor house.[113]

The wider context was one in which the ANC government had itself become sceptical about whether an equity approach to land reform was yielding the desired results. At Solms-Delta, the business struggled to manage its debts alongside its ongoing commitments to the workforce. In 2016 the Department of Rural Development and Land Reform acquired a 50 per cent equity stake in Solms-Delta through the National Empowerment Fund as part of its revised approach to land reform. Solms and Astor disposed of their shares in the belief that the Trust would own 50 per cent of the business and 50 per cent of the land. But the terms of this kind of bailout were that ownership would pass to government, thereby converting the workers into tenants. This was the complete opposite of what empowerment was supposed to embody. To compound matters, a failure to release the funds in a timely manner led to a downward spiral.[114] Solms-Delta was placed under business rescue, which involved the sale of the remaining stocks of wine and an end to winemaking at the farm, leaving the workers without any income.[115] The Solms-Delta implosion, more than any other, underlines fundamental contradictions at the heart of the empowerment agenda: on the one hand, the difficulties of effecting fundamental change at the level of a farm, and on the other the incoherence of the government approach to land reform. Given the emerging difficulties with transferring an ownership stake to the workers, many trusts chose to prioritize education for the children of farm workers. While the expectation was that some would graduate to more managerial and technical roles, it was frankly acknowledged that pursuing an alternative career might be the best option for the next generation.[116]

[113] Interview with Reyneke, 14 August 2019.

[114] Tamlyn Currin, "Liquidation looms for showcase Cape estate", dated 6 September 2018, www.jancisrobinson.com/articles/liquidation-looms-for-showcase-cape-estate, accessed 22 February 2022.

[115] Bulelwa Payi, "Solms-Delta workers left hungry as land deal sours", *Weekend Argus*, 5 September 2021, www.pressreader.com/south-africa/weekend-argus-sunday-edition/20210905/281801402071277, accessed 26 February 2022.

[116] The Land of Hope Trust, which was intended to benefit workers from Radford Dale, was one that placed the emphasis on education. John Platter, who chaired the Trust, contrasted this initiative with others that were dubious. See www.landofhope.co.za/about-us, accessed 27 February 2022.

A sense of disillusionment was felt even more forcefully by those who were excluded from any empowerment deal and experienced a deterioration in their job security. The ANC government intervened formally to bolster the rights of farmworkers by granting rights to land and guarantees of a minimum wage, and yet the consequences were the opposite of those that were intended. The Extension of Security of Tenure Act (No. 62 of 1997, amended in 2018) was supposed to grant long-term security of tenure to farm workers (dubbed 'occupiers of land'), to extend their fundamental rights and to regulate evictions.[117] Where farmworkers had lived on a farm before 1997 with consent that was later revoked, they were to be classified as 'occupiers' provided they had remained continuously on the land. Crucially, workers who had lived on the land for a period of one year were presumed to have been on the land with consent. Some farmers took pre-emptive action by relocating their workers, who had often lived on the farm for generations and where they had enjoyed access to schooling and leisure facilities.[118] The more socially responsible employers built improved housing off-site, took care of the utility bills and arranged regular transport to and from the farm. The more cynical ones applied pressure to workers to leave 'voluntarily', by cutting off water or electricity.[119] At the same time, the rising costs of labour led many farmers to reduce the number of people they maintained on the permanent payroll. Whereas workers had hitherto been paid during peak and fallow periods within the farming cycle, owners increasingly preferred to recruit at peak times only. A particular bottleneck was during harvesting when the window of opportunity for bringing in the grapes at optimum ripeness was narrow. Typically, a farm might retain the services of a few of its permanent workers, on better terms than before, but then resort to labour brokers to furnish the remainder as and when they were required.[120] The system of recruitment varied from formal contracts to ad hoc arrangements according to which brokers would drive through rural townships and scoop up day workers from the roadside. This meant that many Coloured workers who had moved off the farms no longer had a guarantee that they would be employed at all – especially when brokers favoured townships where recent arrivals from the Eastern Cape were located. The cumulative outcome was the worst of both worlds: that is, the ending of paternalism removed the basic safety nets, while a short-term approach to labour recruitment was associated with systematic casualization and job insecurity.

[117] Extension of Security of Tenure Act (No. 62 of 1977), Article 3 "Consent to Reside on Land".

[118] It also has to be acknowledged that many farm workers preferred to live off farm when offered the option of their own houses.

[119] Human Rights Watch, *Ripe with Abuse: Human Rights Conditions in South Africa's Fruits and Wine Industries* (New York: Human Rights Watch, 2011), p. 10.

[120] Ewert and du Toit, "Deepening divide", p. 317.

Some of the worst abuses happened on marginal farms which had only ever supplied grapes to the cooperatives. In a controversial report, Human Rights Watch (HRW) documented the poor conditions experienced by farmworkers and claimed to have found examples where the dop system still persisted.[121] The prevailing wisdom amongst wine farmers was that such abuse was confined to more remote farming districts that were not predominantly wine-producing.[122] To some extent, this is confirmed by the research conducted by BAWSI across 65 farms, involving interactions with 700 workers, which was released at around the same time.[123] The BAWSI report was generally critical and pointed the finger at specific farms, but its data also suggested that there were markedly different practices. In the so-called 'Winelands' (Stellenbosch and Franschhoek), all 8 farms paid above the minimum wage while in Drakenstein (Paarl, Wellington and Klein Drakenstein) and Breede River (Robertson and Worcester), 10 farms paid above and 5 paid below, and along the West Coast (including Swartland, Malmesbury, Riebeeck-West and Vredendal), 11 paid at above the minimum wage and 16 paid less. In the 'Winelands', more than half of the workforce still lived on farms, while in Drakenstein/ Breede River and the West Coast the reverse was the case.

Whereas workers living on farms had hitherto been excluded from collective action, the changing patterns of labour deployment made it easier to mobilize. In 2012–2013, farmworkers embarked on a series of unprecedented strikes that threw some of the underlying tensions into sharp relief. The dispute began in De Doorns, which was largely a fruit growing area where migrant workers faced precarious conditions, and spread more widely. The strikes quickly became politicized as the ANC government and the Democratic Alliance (DA), which controlled the Western Cape, scored political points and various trade-union constellations jostled for the right to represent farmworkers.[124] Although the epicentre of the strike was fruit farms *anderkant die berg*, farmers across the winelands were acutely aware that labour unrest could spread and become mixed up with a larger range of social grievances. In Stellenbosch, there was a fear that recent arrivals who

121 Human Rights Watch, *Ripe*, pp. 66–68.

122 VINPRO maintained that only a third of the 60 farms covered in the HRW report were actually wine farms. Cassie du Plessis, "Farm labourer rights furore", *Wineland*, 1 October 2011.

123 BAWSI, *Farmworker Voices: Reflections of Worker Conditions on South African Farms* (Western Cape Sample Study) (Paarl: BAWSI, 2011).

124 [Anon.] "Farm workers union Csaawu should be saved", *Mail and Guardian*, 17 November 2014, https://mg.co.za/article/2014-11-17-farm-workers-union-csaawu-should-be-saved; and Joylean M. Baro, "A colonial hangover: big profits, massive exploitation in the Cape winelands", *Equal Times*, 1 July 2015, www.equaltimes.org/colonial-hangover-big-profits?lang=en#.XOsGhtNKgdU, accessed 26 February 2022.

could not find housing would resort to occupying land that was not under vines.[125]

The record of nearly two decades of BEE was therefore mixed. However, it is important to recognize that while the wine industry remained overwhelmingly White in terms of ownership of vineyards and cellars, and control over distribution channels, some significant changes did occur. These were often based not on the transformation agenda of central government or the goodwill of the farmers, but on the initiative taken by those who wished to break into wine. Some members of a newly rich Black elite invested in wine farms as prestige ventures whilst remaining distanced from the practical aspects of production. An example is the senior ANC politician and businessman, Tokyo Sexwale, who purchased Bloemendal in Durbanville and briefly acquired a stake in Constantia Uitsig.[126]Although such individuals were beneficiaries of BEE on the larger stage, it would be stretching a point to suggest that their wine acquisitions were instances of empowerment in the wine industry. More significant is the unprecedented emergence of Black-owned wine businesses that were involved in the production and sale of wine. In 2020, WOSA listed 60 'black-owned brands' in wine.[127] Many of these were the product of ownership deals with workers, but others represented entirely independent initiatives. An example is that of M'hudi in Stellenbosch, which was the first Black, family-owned farm. Malmesy Rangaka, a clinical psychologist, and her husband Diale ('Oupa'), a retired academic, deployed their own resources to purchase an ailing fruit farm in Stellenbosch in 2003.[128] The Rangakas had no relevant experience and no functioning cellar, and relied for some time on the assistance of neighbouring Villiera. The breakthrough came when M'hudi secured a contract to supply Marks & Spencer (M&S) in the United Kingdom, which already had a standing agreement with Villiera. Although M&S did not agree to take their entire range, the contract came to account for half of the farm's exports and provided a secondary route into Woolworths in South Africa. Membership of the South African Black Vintners

[125] Kayamandi township in Stellenbosch began to encroach onto farmland. Tensions came to a head in 2019, when squatters crossed the boundary that separated the township from the Louisenhof farm and proceeded to erect their own dwellings. The murder of the owner shortly afterwards fostered a heightened sense of anxiety.

[126] Tokyo Sexwale, a former ANC prisoner on Robben Island and Minister of Human Settlements. He led a consortium which took a 50 per cent stake in Constantia Uitsig in 2006. In 2013, the farm was sold to new owners. Shanaaz Eggington, "Sexwale's prize farm for sale", *Sunday Times*, 21 July 2013, www.pressreader.com/south-africa/sunday-times-1107/20130721/281672547552710, accessed 26 February 2022.

[127] www.wosa.co.za/Sustainability/Socially-Sustainable/BEE/Black-owned-Brands/, accessed 25 February 2022. The South African Black Vintners Alliance (SABVA) only had 10 members in 2008, and it is not clear whether this has increased since then.

[128] Their struggle to build the M'hudi brand is profiled in the television documentary, "Wine: The Future".

Alliance (SABVA), which enjoys the backing of BEE advocates, was instrumental in securing access to the American market. In more recent times, Herman observes, M'hudi pursued a familiar strategy of sourcing grapes to maximize production, whilst seeking to diversify its markets.[129] Another successful example is the founding of Aslina Wines by Ntsiki Biyela, the country's first Black woman winemaker, who left Stellekaya to establish her own export-oriented brand in 2016. Although these cases stand out because they are comparatively rare, the emergence of Black businesses was fundamental to changing the public perception of wine. I will return to these themes in Chapter 9. Here, it remains to note that the summation by Tim Atkins, with which this chapter began, captures the broadly positive outcome of South African efforts to simultaneously modernize the industry whilst embracing issues of empowerment and environmental sustainability.

[129] Herman, *Practising*, pp. 59–62.

9 Terroirs, Brands and Competition

The Emerging Landscape of South African Wine

> I think in a sense we looked at ourselves and said who are we now? Since 1992, we are part of the bigger world and accept the fact. We had to redefine ourselves. So immediately, we said your range is too big and so we cut down on all these unimportant varieties and said let's do world class varieties . . . the Chardonnays, the Cabernets. So we took out a lot of these old vineyards. It was definitely more market driven then for exports, while in the 80s we were driven by local consumption . . . But now there is an explosion that was also brought about . . . by the markets opening for us. Everybody started to want their own farm with their own label.[1]
>
> (François Malan, Simonsig, 2009)

This personal reflection conveys a sense of how established producers experienced the new landscape of wine as it revealed itself in the 1990s. Palpable excitement at the prospect of going global was tempered by the realization that wineries needed to engage in critical reflection and invest in restructuring their operations. In the first section of this chapter, I address the belated turn to a discourse of terroir while emphasizing its varied regional inflections. In the second, I compare some of the approaches to branding and the relationship with certification and labelling. In the final section, I address the tension between competition and cooperation and suggest some reasons why the estate concept floundered whereas the wine routes and associations dedicated to particular cultivars fared rather well.

Terroir at Last: Wine against the Elements

One of the most striking discursive transformations in the wine world since the turn of the millennium has been the popularization of a discourse of terroir – and South Africa is certainly no exception. Today, it features prominently on winery websites and a disquisition on the topic – typically with a gesture in the direction of a bottle containing a cross-section of soil deriving from an area of vineyard – is an integral part of the tasting-room experience. The turn to terroir

[1] Interview with François Malan, Stellenbosch, 25 July 2009.

is striking given the fact that the KWV, merchant-manufacturers and individual producers had previously displayed scant interest in the concept despite their receptiveness to a range of other European influences.

In France, the bundle of associations has been in constant flux, while always turning on an essentialist credo that there something was transmitted from the land/soil to other domains – whether that be individual temperament, artistic disposition or sensory experience. When it came to food and wine, the connotations were not always assumed to be positive.[2] Hence a *goût du terroir* might signal something rustic – quite literally earthiness – and not necessarily desirable. The concept gained further traction in the nineteenth century through its association with emerging branches of science, notably geology and chemistry. The notion that the composition of the soil imparted a particular character to the grapes, and that this could be detected on the palate, was what ultimately cloaked terroir in the mantle of scientific verity. As early as 1801, Jean-Antoine-Claude Chaptal and his co-authors distinguished between *goût du terroir* being 'the dissolution or evaporation of a part of the mineral or metallic substances that comprise the soil of certain vineyards' and a *goût articifielle du terroir*, which was an undesirable taste that was attributable to the surrounding flora and fertilizers.[3] But reception of the concept was also influenced by considerations that were as much political. Some of the appeal lay in a celebration of local specificity, which was in part a response to the centralizing tendencies of the French state. An appeal to terroir also became a weapon of the vigneron against the *négociant* as well as a form of defence against competition from other wine regions. In Burgundy, an insistence that human agency had shaped the viticultural landscape, including the very soils themselves, implied that the human and the natural elements could not be distinguished.[4] By logical implication, the terroirs and climats of Burgundy were never replicable.

To producers in other regions of the world, much of this discourse seemed self-serving and indeed a defensive response to the threat of greater international competition in the wake of the Judgement of Paris in 1976. French proponents of terroir became fond of the assertion that New World wines were made in the cellar, as well as the assertion that globalization represented an existential threat to wines that offered a true expression of

[2] On this point, see Thomas Parker, *Tasting French Terroir: The History of an Idea* (Oakland: University of California Press, 2015).

[3] Jean-Antoine-Claude Chaptal, François Rozier, Antoine Augustin Parmentier and Louis d'Ussieux, *Traité théoretique et pratique sur la culture de la vigne* (1801), cited in Parker, *Tasting French Terroir*, p. 140.

[4] Demossier, *Burgundy*.

terroir.[5] An insistence on the fundamental importance of the soil is one that many New World producers and commentators have been inclined to question. John Gladstones observes that soils and geology have tended to be the focus of attention where climate differences are small. Conversely, 'climate is the main terroir factor where climate is most limiting, or where topography provides a locally wide range of climates.'[6] The logical implication is that in other locations, climate might feature rather more prominently in a no less coherent understanding of terroir. From a Californian vantage point, Mark Matthews argues that terroir carries almost no explanatory value for wine scientists who rarely deploy the term, and least of all in the expansive French sense.[7] He points out that soils do not transmit taste to the grapes in any straightforward fashion, and that these are actually much more influenced by aerial influences such as the sun and water.[8] Conversely, a wider definition of terroir could be summed up simply as 'the environment' and risks becoming so general as to serve very little purpose. Over time, however, producers in the so-called New World have warmed to terroir as a concept that is sufficiently malleable to suit their own purposes. Since it is patently untenable to maintain that only France possesses terroir, producers in places like New Zealand or Oregon have announced their own distinct terroirs as affording the optimal expression of particular cultivars.[9] Moreover, climate-change scenarios raise questions about whether hallowed regions like Bordeaux might become too hot to produce premium wines, underlining the point that soil is not the only element in the equation.

In South Africa, terroir has generally been taken to refer to the natural elements exclusively, for which there are obvious historical reasons. Farmers have historically performed very little of the physical labour in the vineyards, and they have not been inclined to treat farmworkers as the bearers of a glorious vinous patrimony. In deciding what natural elements might determine the character of a wine, soil has also received less influence than climate. In 1823, William Bird referred to Cape wines as being 'racy, or tasting of the soil', echoing one meaning of a *goût du terroir*.[10] He went on to observe that this defect was not present in the wines of Constantia, but noted that there was

5 This position comes across clearly in the Jonathan Nossiter's film *Mondovino*. In practical terms, the battle played out in the efforts to block Robert Mondavi from establishing a foothold in southern France at Aniane. This is covered in the film. See also Olivier Torrès, *The Wine Wars: The Mondavi Affair, Globalisation and "Terroir"* (Houndmills: Palgrave Macmillan, 2006).

6 John Gladstones, *Wine, Terroir and Climate Change* (Mile End: Wakefield Press, 2011), p. 77.

7 Mark A. Matthews, *Terroir and Other Myths of Winegrowing* (Oakland: University of California Press, 2015), pp. 198–199.

8 Matthews, *Terroir*, pp. 52, 175–185.

9 For New Zealand, see the documentary film, David Nash and Samuel Mark-Brown (dirs.) *A Seat at the Table: New Zealand's Wine Story* (Republic Films and Studio Nash, 2019).

10 Bird, *State*, p. 41.

a lack of consensus over whether the problem might have been 'overcome by the sweetness of the grape, or that this wine will only grow on one spot, free from imparting such taste'.[11] In other words, the issue was whether it was the Muscat grapes or the Constantia soils that were key to avoiding the unpleasant taste. Bird went on to cite a Constantia farmer, Sebastiaan Van Reenen, who claimed that the quality did not appear to be affected by whether the vines were grown on white sand, clay or gravel. Instead, he considered that it was 'the hill' that made all the difference.[12] Presumably, what he meant was that the slopes provided the vineyards with just the right amount of sunshine and shielded the vines during the hottest part of the day. Two hundred years later, wine producers in Constantia were routinely claiming this feature of the topography as part of their own unique terroir.

Over the twentieth century, the composition of the soils was routinely invoked, but it was only ever one element. A. I. Perold spent much of his time trialling favoured varietals that might thrive in particular types of soils under particular climatic conditions. But this was more a work of trial and error than the application of a soil-based concept of terroir. In the 1980s, when many independent producers aspired to develop their own wines, they were typically driven by two (non-exclusive) considerations. The first was the imperative of securing access to better cultivars, which was considered to be the primary determinant of overall quality. The second was the possibility of shifting to cool climate zones once the rigidities of the quota system were abandoned. The first was evidently not driven by a concern with terroir, even if farmers believed that specific cultivars would be more suited to the particular land they were planting on. The second was compatible with a conception of terroir, but one in which temperature and exposure to sunlight were the leading elements. Even now, there are producers working in cooler areas who regard climatic factors as the primary determinant of quality. De Rust farm in Elgin had long been involved in fruit exports and was originally selected by SFW to supply grapes because its high elevation and cooler temperatures seemed to correlate with better quality. Ernst Le Roux, who joined the SFW in 1971, applied the Winkler scale to growing conditions at the Cape in a thesis submitted to the University of Stellenbosch.[13] Elgin was presumably excluded

[11] Bird, *State*, p. 110.

[12] Van Reenen inherited a farm called Witteboom, that shared a hedge with Groot Constantia. He renamed the farm High Constantia. Most of the farm is residential accommodation today.

[13] The scale had been designed by A. J. Winkler and Maynard Amerine at the University of California–Davis. It established a classification based on the number of growing degree days when the temperature rose above 10°C. They devised a scale running from I to IV, with I having the coolest temperature profile. Le Roux concluded that of the 36 wine-growing areas in the Cape, nowhere corresponded to Region I and only Constantia and Durbanville met the profile for Region II. Stellenbosch and Darling fell into Region III and Robertson and Malmesbury into Region IV. E. G. Le Roux, "n Klimaatstreekindeling van die suid-wes Kaaplandse

because it was not a wine-producing area at the time, but Le Roux seems to have concluded at a later stage that it mapped onto Region I/II which exhibited the optimal temperatures for producing quality wine.[14] To this day, Paul Cluver Sr is inclined to emphasize the singularity of the climate in Elgin, which he notes has roughly the same sunshine hours as Beaune, and substantial degree differences with Stellenbosch.[15] His take on soil, on the other hand, is a straightforward one: 'There's loads of bullshit on soil. You can manipulate soil, but you can't manipulate climate. That is a sort of wine-speak, but there is not very much science behind it.'[16]

The appropriation of terroir has been shaped in significant ways by the parallel evolution of the Wine of Origin (WO) system. Significantly, this has taken on board the importance of terroir in the narrower sense of soil, climate and topography.[17] The WO framework has been popular because it has been adaptable to the interests of producers at the local level. The initial framing made broad allusions to soil types, but these was not accorded any overriding significance.[18] Indeed, the designation of origin was defined by the location of the cellar rather than the siting of the vineyards.[19] Regions were delineated very broadly, while the districts were defined by administrative boundaries. Again, the wards were often demarcated according to arbitrary expedients such as positioning on either side of a road. Over time, however, the WO became more finely tuned as new regions, districts and wards were carved out.[20] The most recent addition to the districts was the creation in 2017 of 'Wine of Origin Cape Town', embracing 30 wineries across the four wards of Constantia, Durbanville, Philadelphia and Hout Bay. Moreover, within the

wynbougebiede", unpublished Masters thesis, University of Stellenbosch, 1974, pp. 84, 88–89, 102–103. Le Roux went on to head Nederburg which was part of the SFW stable.

14 Interview with Paul Cluver Snr., 20 August 2019.

15 Interview with Cluver, 20 August 2019. However, one study that compared temperature readings at De Rust and Nietvoorbij between 2003 and 2005 revealed that between January and April, the mean hourly temperature difference was only around one degree. By contrast, Elim was three degrees cooler than Nietvoorbij. Meryl Weaver, "The emergence of vine cultivation in cooler-climate viticulture areas in South Africa with specific reference to Elgin and Elim", submitted to the Cape Wine Academy in partial fulfilment of the Diploma of Cape Wine Master, 2006, pp. 4–8.

16 Interview with Cluver, 20 August 2019.

17 The OIV definition is much broader. "Wine of Origin Scheme", www.wosa.co.za/The-Industry/Wines-Of-Origin/Wine-Of-Origin-Scheme/, accessed 9 March 2022. Although WOSA does not refer explicitly to the wider OIV definition, it is implied.

18 Hence, an information brochure produced by the KWV stated that the red soils of Constantia are of granitic origin while some low-lying vineyards and those in the valleys were located on sandy soils of Table Mountain sandstone origin. More or less the same formulation was used for Durbanville. *Wines of Origin.*

19 Interview with Neil Ellis, 29 October 2009.

20 The regions were Stellenbosch, Paarl, Robertson, Swartland, Breedekloof, Olifants River, Worcester, Northern Cape, Little Karoo and Cape South Coast. Within a district, farms could remain unallocated to a specific ward.

existing districts there has been pressure to establish additional wards. The late chairman of the demarcation committee, 'Duimpie' Bayly, explained that the initiative always had to come from the producers themselves and was evaluated according to criteria that are typically associated with terroir, notably the identification of distinct soil types, aspect and climate.[21] Inevitably, there have been controversies as subdivisions potentially create winners as well as losers.[22] But the general consensus seems to be that there is abundant potential for building a sense of identity around more granular territorial units.

Some of the ways in which producers relate understandings of terroir to the WO system can be illustrated through a comparison of Stellenbosch, the Swartland and the Hemel-en-Aarde Valley. Stellenbosch is an appropriate place to start because it is the one WO district where a sustained effort has been made to identify 'natural terroir units' (NTUs) based on 'relatively homogeneous topography, climate, geological substrate and soil'.[23] Carey et al. explain that Stellenbosch contains no fewer than 1,389 NTUs, of which 778 were under vines in 2001. But only 302 covered an area of greater than 25 hectares. The authors conclude from this that many of the NTUs are too small to be 'economically or practically viable'.[24] The data, which confirms the impression of a fractured natural landscape, present an interesting conundrum for those wineries seeking to make terroir-based wines. A large farm is likely to have a mix of terroirs to play with, but a smaller unit is unlikely to have enough of any one NTU to make a high degree of specificity financially attractive.

In the initial WO demarcation, Stellenbosch was defined as a district, but it only had a single ward, Simonsberg, nesting within it, whereas Robertson had no fewer than nine. In more recent times, the inclination has been to make a virtue out of variety. By 2019, Stellenbosch consisted of seven wards: Banghoek, Bottelary, Devon Valley, Jonkershoek Valley, Papegaaiberg, Polkadraai Hills and Simonsberg-Stellenbosch. In 2020, Vlottenberg was constituted as a separate ward, while an application to create a Helderberg ward was also submitted.[25] Given that some of the leading producers clustered around the Helderberg mountain, stretching towards Somerset West, it is

21 Interview with Duimpie Bayly, 15 August 2019.

22 Hence Darling Cellars ceased to be able to use the Swartland name once Darling was designated as a separate district. Some producers have also been concerned about farms being split in two by ward boundaries.

23 Victoria A. Carey, D. Saayman, E. Archer, G. Barbeau and M. Wallace, "Viticultural terroirs in Stellenbosch, South Africa, I: the identification of Natural Terroir Units", *Journal International des Sciences de la Vigne et du Vin* 42(4), 2008, p. 169.

24 Carey et al., "Viticultural terroirs", p. 182.

25 "Notice of applications for Vlottenberg and Helderberg, Information and Call for Comments", dated 4 February 2020, *Wine Law* 1, 2020 (Wine and Spirits Board, 2020), www.sawis.co.za/winelaw/download/87_New_demarcations.pdf, accessed 8 March 2020.

perhaps surprising that an application took so long to materialize. Ironically, the Simonsberg Hills, which account for the country's most highly regarded Cabernet Sauvignon and Bordeaux-style blends,[26] remained subdivided between Simonsberg-Stellenbosch and Banghoek, with the neighbouring farms of Tokara and Delaire falling one either side of the road that constitutes the dividing line. In addition, Simonsberg-Paarl, on the other side of the mountain, has remained within the Paarl district. Here, the WO system related to the logic of terroir in an uneven way. The case for a new ward was typically based on claims about terroir that had to be documented in detail. But producers who might be thought to share a common terroir continued to plant a multiplicity of grapes and, in the case of Simonsberg, they continued to straddle districts and wards. Not everyone was convinced that Stellenbosch was playing to its strengths. Hence Michael Fridjhon mused about whether a certain eclecticism, combined with the lack of a shared vision, threatened the reputation of Stellenbosch.[27] Some producers also believed that a multiplication of wards would only make sense if consumers understood and bought into the concept of terroir-based wines. Overseas consumers are likely to have heard of Stellenbosch, but to be baffled by references to strange-sounding places like Polkadraai.

For SAWIS, the statistical district of Swartland includes WO Swartland and the smaller WO Darling. In 2020, greater Swartland had the fourth-largest vineyard area, with 12,344 hectares under vine grapes, representing 13.42 per cent of the total.[28] WO Swartland was designated as a single district under the original demarcation and contained a single ward, namely Riebeeksberg. It also remained geographically the largest district even once Darling had been hived off. Although there were established wineries in the past, most notably Allesverloren, the Swartland was historically associated with growers who sold their grapes to the local cooperative. Understandings of the terroirs of the Swartland have largely been shaped by the particularities of climate. The district is characterized by much lower rainfall than in somewhere like Stellenbosch, but at the same time the vineyards located on the slopes benefit from cooling breezes coming off the Atlantic Ocean. Charles Back of Fairview in Paarl was amongst the first to recognize the potential of the area after an epiphany involving Sauvignon Blanc grapes that were then being delivered to the Swartland Co-operative. Back purchased the Klein Amoskuil farm near Malmesbury with a view to making wine from Swartland grapes. The

[26] This includes Kanonkop, Rustenburg and Thelema, but also more boutique operations such as Camberley.

[27] Michael Fridjhon, "Stellenbosch – in need of an urgent re-think?", Winemag.co.za, 28 August 2019, https://winemag.co.za/wine/opinion/michael-fridjhon-stellenbosch-in-need-of-an-urgent-re-think/.

[28] "SA Wine Industry Statistics 2020", table 5.2.

subsequent impetus emanated from a younger cohort of winemakers led by Eben Sadie, Back's former winemaker. When Sadie struck out independently, he was instrumental in encouraging several of his peers who were making wine elsewhere, to shift their focus to the Swartland. Amongst his close associates was Adi Badenhorst, who left his own job as the winemaker at Rustenberg to purchase a farm with a small cellar.[29] These individuals saw an opportunity to put the Swartland firmly on the wine map. Whereas innovators of a previous generation had imagined the reinvention of South African wine in the image of Bordeaux and Burgundy, the Swartland producers displayed a greater affinity with southern France, Spain, Portugal and Italy, where a number had gained experience. Sadie himself spent around a decade in Priorat (Catalunya) before returning to the Cape. Their approach was to isolate cultivars that could extract the most typicality from distinct soil types in very specific locations – somewhat in the spirit of Perold.[30]

The self-styled Young Turks were also mindful of the need to hone an image for the Swartland. This inspired the launch of the Swartland Revolution, an annual event with an attitude that focused attention on wine and food from the area. At the same time, the revolutionaries hammered out the terms of an association of like-minded producers. Whereas the WO system had never been prescriptive, the Swartland Independent Producers (SIP) introduced strict rules for its members. To qualify for the Swartland Independent badge of approval, the wine was required to be certified as 'Wine of Origin Swartland'.[31] Logically, the wine needed to be entirely 'vinified, matured and bottled in the Swartland' from grapes grown there.[32] A commitment to minimal intervention was embodied in the stipulation that the wine should have 'no inoculated yeast or yeast supplement; will not be acidified; has no added tannin; will not be chemically fined; [and] will not undergo any technological process (reverse osmosis) which will alter the constitution of the wine'. Perhaps the most remarkable prescriptive element was the identification of certain approved varietals that were considered 'suited to expressing Swartland conditions' (read terroir). The list comprised red varietals typical of the Southern Rhône, namely Syrah/Shiraz, Grenache, Mourvèdre, Carignan and Cinsault, but also Tinta Barocca and Pinotage, which had a track record in the Swartland. Shiraz became a priority for a good number of producers who had participated in harvests in the northern Rhône and had come to better appreciate the influence of different soil types (schist and granite) on the

[29] Interview with Eben Sadie, 21 August 2019, and Adi Badenhorst, 11 February 2015.

[30] Interview with Eben Sadie, 21 August 2019.

[31] The distinctive logo is used by the members, but does not adorn the bottles.

[32] Swartland Independent Producers, "The core elements of a regional wine", https://swartlandindependent.co.za/values/, accessed 22 July 2023.

character of the wine.[33] Ironically, the list of white varietals excluded Sauvignon Blanc, which had caught Back's eye in the first place. The reason was that it made heavy demands on water, which was an especially scarce commodity in the Swartland.[34] The approved list for white cultivars again contained a number that were associated with the Rhône, namely Marsanne, Rousanne, Viognier, Clairette Blanche and Grenache Blanc, but it also extended to Chenin Blanc, Palomino, Semillon, Muscat d'Alexandrie, Muscat d'Frontignan, Colombard and Verdelho.

In contrast with Stellenbosch, most SIP members owned relatively few vines. They therefore needed to cement close relationships with grape farmers who had once supplied the cooperatives or the SFW. They actively sought out grapes derived from gnarled old bush vines that have been a distinctive feature of dryland farming across the Swartland. Paying well above the market price for the best grapes was considered necessary to establish a lasting relationship and to avoid being left high and dry.[35] Another insurance policy was to lease the land along with the grapes over a period of some years. However, the winemakers also sought to influence what was newly planted. Hence David and Nadia Sadie encouraged the farmers they worked with to plant vines on a range of different soils, yielding different iterations of Grenache which could then be blended to create single-varietal bottlings.[36] What is noteworthy is that the Swartland revolutionaries managed to restore the reputation of Chenin Blanc and Cinsault. The latter, in particular, began to emerge in a much lighter style that was unrecognizable from the *dikvoet* (literally thick-footed) Hermitage of old. Many SIP members could not afford to buy expensive cellaring equipment that were such a feature of Stellenbosch, and some positively revelled in being 'low-tech'. Adi Badenhorst, for example, was more than content to use open fermenters and preferred to purchase an old wooden stukvat rather than invest in expensive stainless-steel tanks.[37]

This was always intended to be a perpetual revolution, and experimentation proceeded apace based on understandings of what was likely to work best in the light of climate change prognoses. In 2019, Eben Sadie was experimenting with a number of cultivars from Italy, Portugal and even Greece (notably Assyrtiko) in the belief that revered French varietals were not necessarily the

[33] Interview with David Sadie, 21 August 2019.

[34] The upside of the varietal is that it is much more wind resistant, which is a serious concern at Noordhoek which is battered by the southeasterly winds, but is not a concern in the Swartland. Interview with Riandri Visser, 22 August 2019.

[35] Jancis Robinson, "Young guns of Cape need ammunition", 11 April 2015, www.jancisrobinson.com/articles/young-guns-of-cape-need-ammunition, accessed 8 March 2022.

[36] They also preferred an older clone to one of the newly imported ones. Interview with David Sadie, 21 August 2019.

[37] Interview with Badenhorst, 11 February 2015.

most appropriate for South African conditions.[38] The search was on for cultivars that were better adapted to cope with the underlying water deficit and recurring drought. David Sadie indicated that their own focus shifted from Shiraz to Grenache for the simple reason that the vines required half as much water.[39] Under SIP rules, members can propose additions to the approved cultivar list, based on the intrinsic merits of the grape and sensory evidence that experimental plantings are able to yield high-quality wines under local conditions. In 2019, Tempranillo/Tinto Roriz was under active consideration.[40] As the reputation and prices of Swartland wines soared, the maverick image inevitably began to wear a little thin. The leaders of the SIP therefore terminated the 'Swartland Revolution' and decided to align more closely with the Swartland Wine and Olive Route. In sum, the story of terroir in the Swartland was one in which climate, reckoned in terms of both temperature and rainfall, established the fundamental terms of engagement. The rest was about the intrinsic characteristics of the cultivars and their ability to generate different taste profiles when planted in the diverse soil types of the district.

The case of the Hemel-en-Aarde Valley, which was assigned to the Cape South Coast region under the WO, reveals a different set of permutations again. Since the pioneering efforts of Tim Hamilton Russell in the 1980s, the valley cemented a reputation as the source of the country's best Pinot Noir and Chardonnay – even if this was increasingly challenged by producers pushing further down the east coast. The area is minuscule in comparison with the Swartland and Stellenbosch, with its closest equivalent being Constantia. Over time, producers in the valley became more alert to the differences that soil types could make to the character of particular clones. There is a variation in the soil composition as one ascends the hill from Hermanus, with Bokkeveld shale yielding to Cape granite and Table Mountain sandstone. It is generally agreed that the same clones planted on different sections of the slope yield distinct styles of wine, as they do in Burgundy.[41] But wineries are also alert to temperature variations and the effects of differential exposure to sunshine at points along the slope.[42] Whereas the Swartland revolutionaries found it convenient to mould themselves to the external borders of the district, the producers of the Hemel-en-Aarde internalized a fragmented sense of geology

[38] Interview with Eben Sadie, 21 August 2019.

[39] Interview with David Sadie, 21 August 2019.

[40] Interview with Eben Sadie, 21 August 2019. Interestingly, there appear to have been small plantings of Tempranillo in the Swartland dating to 1950. Marius Malan, "Is the Swartland the new South African wine hub?", submitted in partial fulfilment of the Diploma of Cape Wine Master, 2014, p. 29.

[41] Interview with Kevin Grant, 19 August 2019, and with Bevan and Gordon Newton Johnson, 20 August 2019.

[42] At times of the year, there is apparently around a 4 degree Celsius temperature differential with Stellenbosch. Interview with Bevan and Gordon Newton Johnson, 20 August 2019.

and projected it back onto the WO. When Walker Bay was reclassified from a ward to a district in 2004, some argued that the differences along the slope were pronounced enough to warrant the creation of distinct wards. After some haggling over nomenclature, two wards were consecrated in 2006, namely Hemel-en-Aarde Valley and Upper Hemel-en-Aarde Valley. Three years later, Hemel-en-Aarde Ridge was added. For critics, this subdivision of an already very small appellation was nothing short of perverse. But for the cellars in question, the importance of seemingly small variations was integral to their own sense of what terroir meant. Although they competed for trophies, the producers also managed to pull together and advertise the uniqueness of what the valley had to offer. The Hemel-en-Aarde Wine Growers Association holds an annual Pinot Noir celebration, to which guests from Burgundy have been invited, while the Hermanus Wine and Food festival provides a focus for all the producers in the valley.[43]

Brands, Images and Prices

For those producers who embraced the concept of terroir, this became an essential part of how they went about marketing their wines. However, many others concentrated on building brands that drew on the WO system but paid very little attention to terroir.

As South African wine producers re-entered the global marketplace, they were presented with three major challenges. The first was that they were in danger of being caught in no-man's land. On the one hand, with the exception of some former cooperatives, they were too small to benefit from economies of scale. On the other, whereas consumers associated Argentina with Malbec, Australia with Shiraz and California with Cabernet Sauvignon, there was nothing that made South Africa distinctive, with the problematic exception of Pinotage. Indeed, the cultivar mix became more fragmented as farmers experimented freely. The second was to decide how far to go in aligning with the various industry strategies that were outlined in Chapter 8. And thirdly, there was a need to ensure that as much of the value that was realized in the sale of a bottle of wine accrued to the cellars, rather than to middlemen. For the more established wineries, it was a matter of becoming embedded at higher price points. For the rest, it was a matter of breaking even in a context where overall production costs were lower than other major producers except for Chile.[44]

43 Interview with Newton Johnsons, 20 August 2019.

44 South African farms had abundant access to cheap labour and the cost of land was relatively cheap. At one point, a report commissioned by WOSA appeared to suggest the opposite. Interview with Anthony Hamilton Russell, 25 August 2006.

Given that Cape wineries were typically small, the objective for many was to push for greater volume, but without compromising overall quality. This balance could be achieved in the vineyards by managing yields and planting the best clones available. It was also possible to invest in equipment that enabled grapes to be processed more efficaciously and for the process of bottling and labelling to be expedited. However, the most serious constraint was typically a dearth of high-quality grapes to work with. One response was to focus on quality in the best vineyards, whilst permitting higher yields from secondary ones.[45] But this only made sense if the winery had enough vines in the ground in the first place. For most cellars, the optimal solution was to buy in grapes, in the process throwing a lifeline to many ordinary grape-growers. This, in turn, had implications for the crafting of brand identities. One strategy was to build an expansive portfolio of wines, made up of red, white and sparkling wines aimed at a number of price points. The objective was to entice consumers to pay more for the premium ranges while simultaneously appealing to those who were looking for value at the intermediate and standard levels. Introducing new product lines, such as single-varietal bottlings of hitherto unfamiliar cultivars, fostered a sense of novelty. The risk, as the experience with Chardonnay underlined, is that fashions can come and go all too quickly. Replanting vines is a costly business and not something that can be done repeatedly. Spreading the bets across an entire portfolio, and periodically introducing a new line or two, served as a means of squaring the circle. The producer cellars were the first to embrace this strategy once they had abandoned the focus on distilling wines. Amongst the independent producers, a pioneer was Charles Back who created a highly successful brand around Fairview Wines in Paarl. Back elected to deregister Fairview as an estate in the belief that this would enable him to access better grapes and in greater quantities.[46] To this end, he acquired additional vineyards in Paarl, Stellenbosch, Darling and the Swartland, and bought in other grapes from along the west coast.[47] As indicated above, Back also acquired his own farm near Malmesbury to guarantee access to Swartland grapes. He later constructed another cellar and tasting room for a second Spice Route label.[48] This drew on grapes from the farm as well as from others across the Swartland. This meant that the bottles could legitimately be labelled 'Wine of Origin Swartland'. Like SIP members, Back experimented with varietals that went well beyond the list of so-called noble cultivars, including Grenache, Carignan and Mourvèdre. Based on healthy volumes, the separate Fairview and Spice Route labels

[45] Interview with Braam Van Velden, 5 August 2009.

[46] James, "Terroir and law", p. 35.

[47] James, *Wines*, p. 191.

[48] Tim Atkin, "The Swartland Revolution", dated 8 August 2013, https://timatkin.com/the-swartland-revolution/, accessed 8 March 2022. James, *Wines*, pp. 244–245.

managed to claim shelf space in supermarkets as well as specialist wine shops across Europe and North America.

A very different version of the same model was pursued with considerable success by Van Loveren in Robertson. The latter was a family-run business, which only began making its own wine in the 1990s. It was unusual in that the Retief family owned abundant land and operated on a scale that was more akin to a cooperative. Although most independent producers targeted the export market, Van Loveren looked inwards when it launched its *Four Cousins* 'naturally sweet' wine in 2000. By December 2007, the product was allegedly outselling the 2-litre bottle of Coca-Cola at the Pick 'n Pay supermarket in SOWETO's newest and largest Maponya shopping mall.[49] Phillip Retief recalled that the product was not initially targeted at Black consumers and was not pitched at the lower price points. The winery was acting on the perception that while consumers in general talked dry, they actually drank sweet.[50] The wine, which included a generous dollop of grape syrup, was low in alcohol and was sold in a larger 1.5-litre format. The image of the eponymous four cousins on the label was uncomplicated and created a sense of trust and familiarity around the brand. The take-off began not in the townships but amongst university students around Cape Town. It then spread across the Western Cape, before finally catching on in Johannesburg and other urban centres. The success of *Four Cousins* briefly conferred a premium on Van Loveren, but the product was quickly copied by others, including Distell and producer cellars. However, the winery avoided engaging in a race to the bottom and opted to remain visible at higher price points. According to Retief, *Four Cousins* rubbed shoulders with a handful of products that were a focus of middle-class aspirational consumption, such as Hennessy brandy and Johnny Walker whisky.[51] Van Loveren also made a successful pitch in other African countries where the *Four Cousins* began to sell well. By 2018, Van Loveren had risen to become the third largest producer of wine – behind Distell and the KWV, but ahead of DGB and a producer cellar like Robertson Winery.[52] Remarkably, it juggled with no fewer than 11 ranges. Alongside its cheaper products and empowerment labels, it marketed the *Zandvliet* estate range, a single vineyard range, and a 'Retief Reserve'.

The alternative approach was to build a brand around a reputation for exclusivity. At a time when many new players were entering the field, there was a danger of producers undercutting each other. The strategy was therefore

[49] Lynn Foxcroft, "Growing the consumption of wine amongst emerging market consumers in South Africa", submitted in partial fulfilment of Cape Wine Masters Diploma, 2009, p. 41.

[50] Interview with Phillip Retief, 19 August 2019. [51] Interview with Retief, 19 August 2019.

[52] Van Loveren accounted for 2.4 per cent of the volume produced. Wesgro, "Sector: Wine", March 2017, p. 11.

to differentiate the premium wines from the rest of the pack by targeting higher price points. Many of those producers that had been around since at least the 1980s had acquired a reputation for consistent quality. Such was the case with Meerlust, which had achieved a quality breakthrough in the 1970s. Their flagship wine remained *Rubicon*, a Bordeaux-blend that was only released onto the market under that label in the best years. Meerlust also produced a Pinot Noir, a Merlot, a Cabernet Sauvignon, a Chardonnay and a red blend in the years when Rubicon was not marketed. The winery consciously avoided any temptation to proliferate new product lines. Kanonkop, which many wine critics regarded as the most consistent producer over several decades, was even more tightly focused. As early as 1981, the decision was taken to abandon the 'everything-to-everybody' approach and cull the production of Chenin Blanc, Rhine Riesling and Pinot Noir.[53] Johann Krige was clear that the integrity of the Kanonkop brand rested on projecting an image of consistency based on a limited range of red wines that had a proven track record and were trusted by consumers.[54] The range consisted of a Cabernet Sauvignon, a Pinotage and *Paul Sauer*, a Bordeaux blend. There was no longer even a nod in the direction of white wines. Kanonkop later added a 'Black Label' Pinotage at a higher price point which was consistent with the overall strategy. Faced with constraints of the farm size, the Kriges eventually bought in some of their grapes. This enabled them to launch a second 'Kadette' range, consisting of a red blend and a Pinotage pitched at a lower price point, and a Pinotage Rosé. In this way, Kanonkop managed to retain a reputation for producing wines of the very highest quality, whilst hoisting its sales in the middle bracket. Similarly, Hamilton Russell Vineyards homed in on Pinot Noir and Chardonnay and built their image around a local appropriation of Burgundian styles of winemaking in the Hemel-en-Aarde Valley. When they acquired additional farms for the production of high-end Pinotage and Sauvignon Blanc, the wines were vinified in separate cellars and bottled under the *Ashbourne* and *Southern Right* names respectively.[55] This clear separation avoided infringing on the integrity of the Hamilton Russell brand, whilst growing the overall business with external partners.

As the discussion of terroir might lead one to expect, the responses of producers played out somewhat differently across the various districts. In the Hemel-en-Aarde Valley, producers tended to restrict their plantings to Pinot Noir and Chardonnay. In contrast, the majority of producers in Stellenbosch tended to aim for a broader palette of wines. Although Stellenbosch was

[53] Beyers Truter was the winemaker at the time. [Anon.], "SA Legend Johann Krige", www.wosa.co.za/WOSA-News/Blogs/Cape-Chatter/SA-Wine-Legend-Johann-Krige/, accessed 22 May 2022.
[54] Interview with Johann Krige, 11 August 2009.
[55] Interview with Anthony Hamilton Russell, 25 August 2006.

renowned for its red wines, even the leading wineries tended to include a significant number of white varietals in their offerings. Hence Rustenburg marketed two premium wines, a Bordeaux blend (*Peter Barlow*) and a Chardonnay (*Five Soldiers*), alongside a longer list of red and white wines made mostly from the noble cultivars. Simonsig's profile was broadly comparable, but with the addition of a number of sparkling wines. Because Stellenbosch was relatively warm, even at higher elevations, some producers acquired vineyards in cool climate areas that were better suited to white wines. Hence, the cellars of Thelema Mountain Vineyards in the Helshoogte crushed grapes from their vineyards in Elgin to sustain a separate Sutherland range. In Robertson, where the initial shift to quality wines was associated with white wines, producers like Springfield came to market a range of white and reds based on the same range of noble cultivars.

Turning to the second challenge, the proliferation of industry strategies presented opportunities as well as operational challenges. Wines that qualified for the Fairtrade label achieved instant recognition and shelf space, although that meant they were destined for lower price points. Wineries that demonstrated a commitment to environmental sustainability were unlikely to gain much from affixing an additional sticker to the bottle, although it could provide helpful publicity on websites and other marketing materials. The most difficult choice was whether to embrace farming organically because it came at some cost, at least in the short run, without necessarily adding to the brand image. A point that is repeatedly made is that the soils of the Cape are shallow, very impoverished in organic matter, and retain water much less effectively than their counterparts in other regions of the wine world.[56] A key consideration is that soils that are organically more complex lose less water from run-off, while the use of cover crops helps to reduce evaporation. At the same time, organic producers maintain that the use of herbicides and pesticides creates sterile soils that are more prone to water loss. Hence many farmers understood the logic of protecting the organic matter in the soil and harnessing water more efficiently. However, the decision to go organic has been a slow, and sometimes painful, learning process. Johan Reyneke, who is one of the pioneers, came to his decision to farm differently after his vineyards in Stellenbosch were afflicted by a multitude of pests. His well-intentioned efforts to plant grains in order to build biomass led to plummeting yields within a matter of three years. With the assistance of a microbiologist, he came to appreciate that it was necessary not just to rebuild the organic matter, but also to be alert to the nitrogen content of the soil. He switched to planting legumes as well as grasses that attract beneficial predators, thereby obviating the need for spraying pesticides and herbicides.

[56] Interviews with Eben Sadie, 21 August 2019 and Cluver, 20 August 2019.

He also introduced Nguni cattle, whose manure served as a substitute for chemical fertilizer. Consequently, his yields improved greatly. Other wineries such as Ataraxia in the Hemel-en-Aarde Valley have similarly come to realize the benefits of operating with a 'living-soil' philosophy.[57] It is in the interests of organic farmers to widen the circle because one's ability to pursue the chosen path depends on the practices of one's neighbours. Reyneke described having some rows of vines excluded from certification because those who were conducting the audit found traces of chemicals that had been blown across from the next-door farm. Fortunately, five of the neighbouring farms converted to farming organically after some initial scepticism. Reyneke also noted that informal study groups have been created to enable farmers to exchange knowledge in a context where much of the wisdom comes from trial and error.

Although most farmers have not gone as far as even thinking about becoming biodynamic, the number of farmers who embraced principles of organic agriculture has certainly increased. In 2019, BWSA reported that 16 wineries claimed some form of accreditation as organic producers, while 4 others had stopped making wine, withdrawn or allowed their certification to lapse. It also listed three biodynamic producers, one of whose registrations had also lapsed.[58] By 2022, there were 25 wineries that were accredited as fully organic by one of the four certification agencies. This appeared to confirm the impression that interest has taken off.[59] However, whereas Reyneke felt the need to continue seeking accreditation in order to uphold the integrity of the organic label, others refrained from doing so. Although producers in the Swartland were clearly embracing organic methods, possibly only one of the SIP members was accredited in 2019.[60] Equally, the pronounced emphasis on the importance of soil did not translate into accreditation for any farms in the Hemel-en-Aarde Valley. Again, Riandri Visser at Cape Point Vineyards highlighted a conscious effort to minimize spraying while making greater use of horse manure – but without seeking any organic certification.[61] Because they have not gone through any formal procedure, producers often allude to organic practices on their websites whilst avoiding explicit use of the 'O' word. There are several reasons for an ongoing reticence over certification. It can be intrusive, bureaucratic and extremely expensive. In the words of Johan Reyneke:

57 Interview with Grant, 19 August 2019.

58 Biodynamic Organic Wine South Africa, https://biodynamicorganicwine.co.za/biodynamic-producers/, accessed 22 May 22. In 2022, only Reyneke and Elgin Ridge were certified by Demeter as biodynamic producers.

59 Reyneke estimates that there are between 30 and 40 organic producers and between 5 and 10 biodynamic producers, but without necessarily being certified. Interview, 14 August 2019.

60 Org de Rac in Piketberg was accredited as organic, but was not a member of the Swartland Independent. Nativo appears to be accredited by the EU and NOP.

61 Interview with Riandri Visser, 22 August 2019.

> Trust me, I dislike it . . . It takes a lot of my time, a lot of admin, and it costs me a lot of money. South Africa doesn't have organic standards, or biodynamic ones for that matter. So now I have to certify depending on where in the world I export to. So if I export to Europe, I have to pay for EU certification. If I export to America and Canada, I have to apply for NOP certification. If I want to meet biodynamic status, not only do I have to pay for certification, but I have to pay a percentage on turnover to use the logo. These are fundamentally wrong.[62]

Another reason is that those who aspire towards making high-end wines wish to avoid being seen to make populist gestures so as to boost sales. But more fundamentally, there seems to be little evidence that being an organic producer adds very much to the image of the brand.

Finally, when it came to sheer profitability, there were a few additional options available to producers. For most cellars, securing a contract to supply a supermarket chain, whether in South Africa or overseas, was a boon. But the margins were inevitably tight and there was no guarantee that a contract would be renewed from one year to the next. The larger producers fought for supermarket space with their second brands while channelling their premium wines to specialist wine retailers at higher price points. The leading wineries subscribed to the view that the Cape's best wines were under-priced. Hamilton Russell Vineyards were amongst the first to ratchet their prices up, for which there were many good arguments. One was quite simply that producing premium wines came at an additional cost that had to be passed on. But the thinking was also that higher prices helped foster an aura of exclusivity that more affluent consumers were willing to pay for. Other producers in the Hemel-en-Aarde replicated this model, as did the main players in Stellenbosch. After 2010, driving prices up also became the preferred business strategy in the Swartland where the products of Sadie Family Wines and Mullineux & Leeu fetched prices that would hitherto have been unimaginable. This was justified in part by modest volumes and in part by consistently glowing reviews in the international wine press.

When it comes to branding, particular mention should be made of producers who marketed wines while owning relatively few vines, or even none at all. Although this often referred to as a négociant model, the individuals typically aspired to ownership of some vines. A pioneer was Neil Ellis, who began purchasing grapes in the 1980s. He was amongst those who campaigned successfully for a revision of the WO regulations to enable grapes to be moved across boundaries and for the place of origin to be linked to the vineyards rather than the cellars. By 2009, Neil Ellis Wines had reached a point where a third of the grapes came from its own vineyards, a third from long-term grower contracts and a third from spot-buying for lesser labels.[63] For Black and

[62] Interview with Reyneke, 14 August 2019.

[63] Interview with Ellis, 29 October 2009.

Coloured winemakers seeking to break into the industry,[64] the approach was attractive because it dispensed with the need to raise large sums of money to purchase an entire vineyard. Interestingly, many of the new wine brands were established by collectives of women, including Seven Sisters, Women in Wine, and Ses'fikile.[65] Typically, their ambition was to reach a point where they would own some of their own vines, much as new entrants in the Swartland had managed to do. In contrast, others were content to purchase wines from trusted producers and marketed them under their own labels, using cultural symbols and/or name recognition to gain wider appeal.[66] House of Mandela was founded by a daughter of Nelson Mandela by his first wife, along with her daughter. The company created a wine portfolio alongside a range of fashion items, drawing unashamedly on the Mandela name and Xhosa cultural imagery. The wines were sourced from across the Western Cape, largely from the producer cellars, and some of them qualified to be marketed as Fairtrade wines, enabling them to reach both an export and a domestic market.[67] Another case was the establishment of the Bayede! brand, under the patronage of King Goodwill Zwelithini, which formally qualified as a BEE-registered company. The latter similarly marketed a wide range of products, including olive oils, coffee, craft beer and spirits, alongside its wines. The wine bottles, which were adorned with Zulu beadwork and a label indicating that they were sold 'by appointment' to the king, made explicit references to Zulu history and the continuing relevance of the monarchy. Van Loveren in Robertson provided at least some of the wine that entered the bottle.

Collective Action Problems

At this point, I turn to consider the working out of a structural tension between the imperative to pull together and the desire to remain one step ahead of the pack. At one level, career trajectories were such that those who worked closely together at one point might find themselves in competition at another. A well-established pattern was one in which a winemaker who helped to

[64] In this text I refer to 'White', 'Coloured' and 'Black' - categories that are rooted in segregationist and apartheid discourse, but which are impossible to avoid using because they have meaning for the actors themselves. See the 'Note on the Text' on page vi for more detail about the history and use of this term in South Africa.

[65] On Seven Sisters, see Herman, *Practising*, pp. 64–67.

[66] This would include Ses'fikile (2006), whose owner, Nondumiso Pikashe, identified tavern owners in the townships as amongst her most ardent supporters. Mary-Anne Gontsana, "Sesfikile, the women's winery", 14 July 2015, www.groundup.org.za/article/sesfikile-womens-winery_3116/, accessed 25 February 2022.

[67] [Anon.], "House of Mandela Wines: Q&A with Tukwini Mandela!", 8 November 2018, https://thesophisticatedlife.com/blog/house-of-mandela-wines/, accessed 25 February 2002.

cement the reputation of a cellar moved on, often to join a rival, but sometimes with a view to setting up his/her own winery. Hence Kanonkop launched the independent careers of Jan 'Boland' Coetzee and Beyers Truter, while Meerlust was the making of the reputation of Giorgio Dalla Cia. Many partings were highly amicable but when the former winemaker set up a cellar in the proximity, this could be a source of some friction. Moreover, some of the differences of approach reflected generational shifts. Many of the innovators of the 1970s and 1980s had been shaped by their studies in Germany and participating in harvests in Bordeaux, Burgundy and California. Even when they passed on the winemaking duties to their children, the latter were often informed by a different set of international influences. In general, the generation of winemakers that cut its teeth in the new millennium was much more likely to be shaped by its encounters with southern France, Spain, Italy and New Zealand.[68] These creative tensions were regarded by many as a healthy development, but they also underlined the extent to which the industry spoke with many different voices.

All Shall Win Prizes: The Scoring Game

Whereas wineries had once resorted to physical mailing lists to render themselves more visible, the big change came with the possibility of creating relatively light-touch websites. Typically, these contained basic information concerning the vineyards and cellar, the core team and its range of products. Some offered an abridged account of the history of the farm. Increasingly, wineries outlined their philosophical approach, complete with references to terroir, and their concrete commitments to empowerment initiatives and environmental sustainability. However, the obvious problem with relying on a website was that it required consumers to make the click in the first place. Securing a favourable mention in one of the wine magazines or wine blogs was more likely to make that happen. To get noticed, it was considered important to score highly in one competition or another.

After 1994, South African producers entered a growing number of national and international competitions. A medal meant that stickers could be affixed to the wine bottles in the hope of impressing shoppers browsing the shelves or merely visiting the websites of retailers. In South Africa itself there were no fewer than 12 general competitions, of which the Veritas, the Old Mutual and Michelangelo awards were the most prestigious. And there were another 11 that concerned specific cultivars, sparkling and fortified wines, of which

[68] In addition, South African wineries received interns from other parts of the world in greater numbers.

the Pinotage ABSA Top 10 is the best known.[69] On the international level, those competitions that mattered most were the International Wine and Spirits Competition and the Decanter World Wine Awards. Scoring well in the latter had the additional advantage that the results would be covered in *Decanter* magazine and might confer further free publicity in a subsequent feature article. Despite the costs involved, wineries tend to enter successive competitions in the hope of garnering a medal or two along the way. The bewildering array of stickers that came to adorn wine bottles diminished much of the intended effect and a number of the leading wineries chose to be selective, or indeed to enter no competitions at all, so as to maintain the aura of exclusivity.[70]

In fact, the statistical chances of receiving a competition medal were rather good, as the *Platter Guide's* listings indicated. Wines that performed highly in one competition might not receive anything at a different one. Several possible reasons are commonly adduced for this. One is that wine judges may not be entirely consistent in their judgements, for which there is now a body of evidence relating to international competitions.[71] A more likely one is that when wines are lined up in a blind tasting, the result will often depend on what they are standing next to. Hence a lighter style of red wine might suffer from being placed alongside one of the so-called 'fruit bombs'. The third and more likely reason is that the aim of tasting in competitions is to establish which wines should progress to the next round. The scores tend to be awarded at the end of the process once their place in the rank order has been decided. This is very different to the methodology of *Platter* in which the tasters endeavour to understand what the winery is seeking to achieve before tasting the wine sighted, and then they might taste the same wine several times over before awarding a score. In this format, there was equal place for the 'shrinking violet' as well as the 'fruit bomb'.[72]

In South Africa, *Platter* came to be regarded as the most reliable guide to quality – even if Tim Atkin's annual *Special Report* gained traction. Such was the mystique surrounding scoring that John Platter attempted to retreat from the star system when he was still the editor. He pointed to some obvious anomalies, such as when the 1994 Stellenzicht Syrah scored more highly than the 1990 Penfold Grange in the 1995 SAA Wine Shield, but received only a

[69] This information is based on what the South African Wine Index had on their website in 2019. The listings were subsequently removed.

[70] Interviews with Johann Krige, 17 August 2009 and Kevin Grant, 19 August 2019.

[71] Robert J. Hogdson, "An examination of judge reliability at a major U.S. wine competition", *Journal of Wine Economics* 3 (2) 2008; Robert H. Ashton, "Reliability and consensus of experience wine judges: expertise within and between?", *Journal of Wine Economics* 7 (1) 2012.

[72] Interview with Philip Van Zyl, editor of *Platter's Wine Guide*, 21 February 2009.

silver medal in the Veritas competition.[73] He therefore sought to replace the system of absolute scores with a very simple symbol of either two bunches or a single bunch, with the latter not necessarily indicating that it was inferior wine, but signalling that it might be idiosyncratic in its own way and so attractive for all that.[74] However, neither the wineries nor the consumers were happy with the new system, and when Platter stepped down the new editorial team were left with little option than to revert to a five-star scoring system, albeit with some added features that indicated criteria such as value for money. Hence, the pattern was set according to which cellars would either sell out in almost no time if they received four-and-a-half or five stars or be left with stock if they scored less than four. The great advantage was that there seemed to be no obvious way for producers to game the system because there was no preferred style that the designated tasters were expected to look for. This avoided a South African version of the Parker effect.[75]

The buzz that was generated by wine journalists and critics tended to focus not merely on the wines that performed well, but also on the winemakers who were seen as leading innovation. But keeping a secret for any length of time was difficult in a context where news travelled fast. Cellars typically recruited young winemakers, while the better-endowed producers added specialist viticulturalists as well. The wineries vied to recruit the most exciting talent, and often allowed some latitude to experiment as a means of retaining their services. But as one of them explained (off the record), winemakers also socialized amongst themselves – typically around the weekend braai and/or or surfing – and actively exchanged information in a way that the farm owners were scarcely aware of. Consequently, few secrets survived very long. At the same time, established winemakers shared much of their know-how and philosophy through participation in the Cape Winemakers Guild, which was founded in 1982 and whose individual membership was by invitation only.

Estates, Cultivars and Routes

As we have already seen, the CEWPA was a loose coalition of producers whose shared interests resided in promoting the concept of 'estate wine' as an indicator of superior quality. However, CEWPA was hobbled by the compromises that were struck in the early years. Producers who were linked to the

[73] Interview with Philip Van Zyl, editor of *Platter's Wine Guide*, Stellenbosch, 21 February 2009, http://winecellarplus.co.za/2017/03/09/1994-stellenzicht-inside-story/, accessed 1 March 2022.

[74] Interview with Van Zyl, 21 February 2009.

[75] The world's most influential wine taster, Robert Parker, famously developed a 100-point scoring system. He was known to favour a certain style of wine, and it is widely believed that producers in Bordeaux, whose prices came to depend on his scores, modified their styles to maximize their scores.

former Bergkelder and SFW had managed to secure exemptions from the principle that an 'estate wine' needed to be grown, made and bottled on a designated estate. The regulations had also been crafted to take account of a subdivision of older farms that led to a situation where the cellar and the farming units (defined as 'away-lying land') might not be contiguous. Over time, there was a proliferation of exemptions that devalued the integrity of the concept. As of 2000 there were 92 designated estates, but of these 13 were permitted to conduct post-fermentation processes elsewhere, 26 were allowed to bottle off the estate, while another 13 were authorized to farm separate pieces of land as an estate.[76]According to Braam van Velden, the then chairman of CEWPA, the concept became diluted when around half of the estates were operating according to some exemption or another.[77] Looking back, Danie de Wet was less inclined to blame Bergkelder than farmers who lacked the inclination or the capacity to handle their own products.[78] In the minds of the general public, there was understandable confusion: some esteemed producers were assumed to be producers of estate wine when they were not, and there was a lack of clarity about second wines made from bought-in grapes when these were labelled in a manner that ostensibly linked them with an estate.[79] Weighing the benefits against the disadvantages, a significant number of estates elected to deregister. Rustenberg and Fairview did so in 1998 to develop their second labels, and Villiera followed suit the following year. By this point, attendance at CEWPA meetings had plummeted, causing one leader to sum up the attitude as 'could not give a damn'.[80]

Within CEWPA, there was some disagreement about how the association could extricate itself from the impasse. Most of the younger members apparently favoured a tightening up of the regulations, even if that meant that estates with 'away-lying land' would lose out.[81] The secretary, who had played a leading role in drafting the regulations, took the opposite view. In 2003, CEWPA successfully prevailed upon the WSB to reconsider the regulations governing estates. After extensive consultations, a decision was taken to terminate the controversial exemptions. Henceforth an 'estate wine' could only be labelled as such if the grapes derived from the estate itself, or from a neighbouring farm that was managed as part of the same unit, and if the

[76] James, "Terroir and law", pp. 28, 58–59.

[77] Quoted in Karin Theron, "Changes on origin terrain: more freedom for use of estate names – but 'estate wine' is another matter", *Wineland* 1 November 2003. Interview with Braam Van Velden, 5 August 2009. Van Velden's own estate, Overgauuw, was permitted to bottle elsewhere.

[78] As a matter of pride, he went his own way and bottled his own wines in 1992. Interview with Danie de Wet, 16 October 2009.

[79] James, "Terroir and law", p. 37.

[80] Don Tooth quoted in James, "Terroir and law", p. 33.

[81] Interview with Ellis, 29 October 2009.

vinification and bottling took place on the estate. The announcement prompted further defections by existing estates, who believed that tighter rules would not work in their favour. Some that had been associated with Bergkelder continued to hold out based on historic rights, and as late as 2009 there was talk of legal action to resolve the logjam.[82] By this point, the leadership of CEWPA was also in dispute with its secretary. Danie De Wet, a former chairman, recalled that he had not been invited to a meeting in the past three or four years.[83] In effect, CEWPA withered on the vine and most producers who continued to deploy the estate label were members in name only or not at all. In 2013, 11 cellars came together to form Premium Independent Wineries of South Africa (PIWOSA).[84] Stripped of the 'estate' baggage, they were free to promote themselves as producers who were making premium wine from the very best grapes. The rules required evidence of ethical winemaking under one or other of the accreditation schemes. Some of the producers who had previously been active in CEWPA were conspicuously absent from PIWOSA, as were most of those who had deregistered and gone their own way. However, a number of their winemakers belonged to the Winemakers Guild. At the time of writing, it remains to be seen whether PIWOSA will escape the internal tensions that bedevilled CEWPA.

A rather more successful effort at pulling together involved a focus on particular cultivars. The Pinotage Association was founded in 1995. Fronted by Beyers Truter, its core members consisted of enthusiasts and friends, many of whom had often been working with the cultivar for decades. The Association sponsored research in the hope that more famers would embrace it.[85] Pinotage was initially a hard sell, especially outside South Africa, and the association recognized that it was necessary to raise the bar on quality, through better clones and vinification methods, and to banish stubborn myths about its taste profile. The ABSA Pinotage Top 10 played an important role by recognizing the leading exemplars of modern Pinotage through an annual competition. Significantly, the Pinotage Association inspired parallel initiatives, such as the Chenin Blanc Association which was founded in 2000. More recently still, a Stellenbosch Cabernet Collective was established in 2018 with a view to

[82] Interview with Jan 'Boland' Coetzee, 19 April 2007.

[83] Interview with Danie de Wet, 16 October 2009.

[84] As of 2022, the members of PIWOSA were De Grendel, The Drift, Glenelly, Jordan, Journey's End, Ken Forrester, Klein Constantia, Paul Cluver, Raats, Radford Dale and Springfield. On the social responsibility ticket, PIWOSA sponsored the Women in Wine Initiative to promote the education of previously disadvantaged women in different fields related to wine. See https://piwosa.com/, accessed 1 March 2022.

[85] Hence, it established an experimental vineyard at the Stellenbosch Institute of Advanced Study (StIAS).

reinforcing the impression that many of the country's best expressions of the grape emanated from Stellenbosch.

Every bit as important were the wine routes which drew attention to the clustering of wineries, but also provided a practical means for producers to work together. In Chapter 5, I pointed to the transformative effect of the Stellenbosch Wine Route when it was launched in 1971. Fifty years later, there were no fewer than five Stellenbosch wine routes: Bottelary Hills, Greater Simonsberg, Helderberg, Stellenbosch Valley and Stellenbosch Berg. In addition, there were 21 other wine routes, including 2 that included olive oil tastings and one each for the Orange River and for Kwazulu-Natal. Many farms on the various wine routes established restaurants that were intended to bring in additional customers and maximize returns. Charles Back was also one of the first to grasp the business logic of selling the wine farm experience to visitors who were likely to remain loyal to a brand they could visualize. His tasting room and restaurant in Paarl provided a model for many wineries. Back subsequently purchased the neighbouring farm to Fairview, where he opened another tasting room and a whole complex dedicated not merely to Spice Route wines, but also to the tasting of cheese, chocolate, craft beer and much else besides.[86]

The routes mapped broadly onto the WO system. Hence the Greater Simonsberg wine route curled around the Simonsberg Mountain, straddling more than one WO ward, and yet it did not include the opposite side of the mountain.[87] In principle, there was a shared interest in attracting visitors to follow the route, especially those who were signed up by tour companies that tended to stick to the map. However, many visitors used their own cars and could therefore be tempted to go off-*piste*. Tasting rooms would typically direct visitors towards other farms with whom they enjoyed a friendly relationship. But given that they would only make one stop for lunch, there was inevitably some stiff competition. In Stellenbosch, there were significant asymmetries that affected the experience of smaller wineries. It was estimated that the average voyager on the Stellenbosch route only visited 3.5 farms in a day in 1999, a figure that is likely to have remained fairly constant.[88] No fewer than 27 per cent of winery visits on the Stellenbosch wine routes were accounted for by Spier which built a hotel, tasting room and restaurant, and laid on pony rides for children.[89] This amounted to significantly more than the

86 Interview with Charles Back, 15 August 2019.

87 Kanonkop was designated as WO Simonsberg-Stellenbosch, while Delaire was WO Banghoek.

88 Figures are from Imre Joseph Demhardt, "Wine tourism at the 'Fairest Cape': post-apartheid trends in the Western Cape Province and Stellenbosch (South Africa)", in C. Michael Hunt (ed.), *Wine, Food and Tourism Marketing* (New York: Haworth Hospitality Press, 2004), p. 122.

89 Demhardt, "Wine tourism", pp. 124–125.

next four producers combined, namely Delheim, SFW, Simonsig and Vergelegen. However, Stellenbosch embodied its own dynamics, given that there were so many wineries jostling for attention. On the Paarl wine route, it seems likely that Fairview similarly dominated the footfall which, in this case, came down to a smaller concentration of wineries. Along the other wine routes, there tended to be a more balanced distribution in the context of fewer visitors overall. In the districts where the cooperatives had historically dominated and the number of private cellars was far fewer, the challenge for tourists was sometimes to locate enough wineries to visit in a day.

Over time, the routes became more diverse in their offerings. Many wineries had endeavoured to diversify beyond wine, turning to the production of olives whose labour demands could be dovetailed with those of wine. The standard winery visit increasingly included olive oil and cheese tastings, and often involved opportunities to walk and cycle in conservation areas.[90] The final point to make is that whereas much of the dynamism along the wine routes was driven by foreign tourists, it was also sustained by substantial numbers of South African visitors. And whereas those who took to the routes had once been almost exclusively White, the wineries were attracting a much more diverse group of visitors by 2020. However, because most of the Black and Coloured wine producers do not own their own vineyards and tasting rooms, they were also less visible as participants along the wine routes.

Conclusion

In Chapter 8, I identified transformations that unfolded at the level of the wine industry as a whole, most notably the considerable success with developing an export market. In this chapter, I have brought the focus back to the efforts of individual producers to play to their strengths once they had come to appreciate that the Australian model was in many ways a misleading one. It is striking that whereas terroir was never embedded within the initial WO framework, there has been a marked uptake in the concept amongst the producers of premium wines. But as the comparison of Stellenbosch, the Swartland and the Hemel-en-Aarde Valley also illustrates, producers have related to terroir in distinct ways. The relative significance attributed to climate and soil is one clear difference, while the mechanism for matching cultivars to location exhibits another. Interestingly, while many wineries have embraced the importance of striving for environmental sustainability, relatively few have gone down the organic route.

[90] Johan Bruwer, "South African wine routes: some perspectives on the wine tourism industry's structural dimensions and wine tourism product", *Tourism Management* 24, 2003.

This has led me to a closer consideration of the logics surrounding cooperation and competition. I have demonstrated that while the leading wineries opted to cultivate a reputation for exclusivity, others used the flexibility of the WO system to create a broader product range, typically on the basis of grapes bought in from more distant locations. This enabled them to increase volume without compromising on quality. While some producers have attempted to raise their profile by being present in as many wine competitions as possible, in the hope of winning prizes and garnering some positive publicity, others have preferred to rely on the *Platter Guide* and the international wine press to raise their profile. On the other side, it is striking how producers have also found reasons to collaborate. The activism reflected in the Pinotage Association is a case in point. The WO system has itself provided a mechanism through which producers have been able to forge a sense of common identity based on locality. The Hemel-en-Aarde is a prime example, where a collective ethos within the valley coexists with a desire to explore the distinct attributes of the specific wards. But it is also reflected in the success of the many wine routes that have drawn attention to the specific attributes of a given place. No less important is the way in which age cohorts have underpinned a sense of common purpose, from those who cut their teeth in the 1970s and 1980s to the young winemakers who are bound by a shared interest in experimentation today. What is different about the current cohort is that it is no longer exclusively White.

Conclusion

The Mutual Entanglement of Race and the Vine

The broad swathe of history that is covered in this study is bracketed by two shocks that illustrate some of the ways in which global and local processes became closely intertwined. The first was the coming ashore of phylloxera in the 1880s, after having already devastated large swathes of vineyards across Europe. The second was the arrival of the COVID-19 pandemic in 2020 that led the government not merely to ban alcohol sales on four successive occasions, but also to block the export of South African wines for a total of three weeks.[1] Each of these neatly encapsulates some of the key thematic concerns of this book.

The rebuilding of the industry in the wake of phylloxera highlighted the contribution of something rather new – namely a fully elaborated wine science – both to understanding and warding off the various afflictions of the vine and of the wine itself. The COVID pandemic unexpectedly elicited a reprise of a temperance agenda that had peaked a century before. The contention was that the country had a drinking problem and that alcohol-related injuries threatened to overwhelm the health services at a time of national crisis. Much as vine diseases never really went away, most notably in the shape of stubbornly persistent viruses, temperance demonstrated its capacity to bounce back after a long period of dormancy. It is probably no exaggeration to say that for A. I. Perold and Louis Leipoldt, vine diseases and temperance extremism represented equivalent existential threats. The solution in either case turned out to be the exercise of regulation in a moderated form. The experience of dealing with phylloxera, fungal diseases and viruses underpinned the case for maintaining strict quarantine controls. These had to be balanced against the desire of producers to secure timely access to rootstocks and cultivars. Equally, the best defence against prohibition was deemed to be a form of liquor control that accentuated the benefits of moderate consumption. There was a certain symmetry in these preferred responses to diseases and temperance, in that while the

[1] For details, see Davids, Vink and Cloete, “COVID-19”, pp. 44–45, 48.

first involved regulating aspects of wine production, the second managed the terrain on which consumption took place.

In each case, technical issues very easily assumed a political form, leading to instances where the intended cure was at least as troubling as the ailment. By the 1980s, an excess of caution surrounding the importation of cultivars meant that the country was saddled with vines that were heavily virused and cultivars that were out of step with what farmers and consumers wanted. Again, the industry was burdened with a form of racialized prohibition that debarred most of the population from drinking wine and brandy between 1928 and 1962. All of this came to pass because the KWV needed to satisfy its own constituency – the majority of farmers dependent on the sale of grapes and the production of distilling wine – whilst cutting deals with the party in power. It was only with the political earthquake of the early 1990s that grape growers and wine producers were forced to make very rapid adjustments.

As the reader may have already noticed, I have come close to a framing in terms of three fields that were alluded to in the Introduction. As indicated there, I chose not to apply the model that has been fully elaborated by Xabier Itçaina, Antoine Roger and Andy Smith.[2] But it retains heuristic value to make sense of the four main periods of innovation that I return to here.

(1) c. 1890–1920. As I have already indicated, advances in wine science played a catalytic role in the remaking of the South African industry in the aftermath of phylloxera, as they did everywhere. Conscious choices were made about the selection of rootstocks and cultivars that were best suited to South African conditions. The rootstocks were entirely new to the Cape, while the vineyards were replanted with a combination of some established and other less familiar cultivars. Many of the decisions were informed by European evidence but modified in the light of trials in the field. The business of selection and replanting coincided with the establishment of Elsenburg College and the Faculty of Agriculture of the University of Stellenbosch as centres of research and training across the viticultural and oenological sciences. From having solicited external expertise in the later nineteenth century, the focus shifted to building local capacity and home-grown talent. This was the period when A. I. Perold made his mark, often mediating and interpreting between the European and South African wine worlds, whilst helping to fashion Afrikaans as a language of scientific enquiry.

While wine science was cloaked in a new aura of authority, aspiring farmers weighed up the risks and returns on planting vines after a period of price volatility. Until the First World War, there were some paying alternatives in the Breede Valley, whereas in Constantia, Stellenbosch, Paarl and the

[2] Itçaina, Roger and Smith, *Varietals*.

Drakenstein the vine was considered to be the only realistic option. With the collapse of these alternatives, the inclination of ordinary farmers living *anderkant die berg* was to plant vines. At the same time, there was acute tension between the merchants and the farmers, especially after the formation of the KWV in 1918. Having borne the costs of replanting, the farmers needed more remunerative prices. Initially, the KWV sought to negotiate a single set of prices with the merchants while removing the overall surplus from the market. It was only when the KWV proved unable to sustain a lasting deal and discipline its members that it turned to the government. In 1924, the KWV received devolved authority to regulate all wine that was destined for distillation. This removed much of the element of risk and emboldened farmers to plant more vines. This was especially the case *anderkant die berg* where access to irrigation after the construction of the Brandvlei Dam in 1922 fundamentally altered the economics of grape production. This, in turn, made disposal of the resulting surplus an even greater imperative.

What the wine farmers wanted was for 'light wines' to be made more freely available to the totality of the population. However, the Women's Christian Temperance Union (WCTU) and its collaborators in the South African Temperance Alliance (SATA) lobbied hard for even more restrictive alcohol legislation. Their ultimate objective was outright prohibition, but the first step was to push for the termination of alcohol sales to 'non-whites' and the introduction of Local Option provisions for White people. Although the temperance movement did not have everything its own way, it could point to the 1928 Liquor Act as a victory. Henceforth, all Black South Africans were debarred from purchasing wine and brandy, while the liquor licensing laws were ratcheted up for White, Cape Coloured and Asian consumers.[3] Inevitably, this further depressed the potential for growth of the domestic market for wine. This outcome demonstrates that the balance of political forces was evenly poised, with neither the KWV nor SATA managing to achieve its most preferred outcome.

(2) 1921–1939. In the second period of innovation, a minority embraced the production of higher-quality wines that were not subjected to price control. Ironically, a return to some elements of imperial preference during the Great Depression made wine production for the British market suddenly more attractive. The merchants P. B. Burgoyne & Co. galvanized aspiring producers of quality wines to raise their standards and reorient their vineyards towards premium cultivars. As the European tour of Frank Myburgh, Manie Malan and André Simon in 1932 demonstrates, there was remarkable optimism surrounding the export of still and fortified wines. Although much was made of

[3] In this text I refer to 'White', 'Coloured' and 'Black' - categories that are rooted in segregationist and apartheid discourse, but which are impossible to avoid using because they have meaning for the actors themselves. See the 'Note on the Text' on page vi for more detail about the history and use of this term in South Africa.

how scientific winemaking was propelling innovation, it was arguably more a case of eliminating the major faults than capitalizing on particular breakthroughs. The desire of quality producers to escape the constraints of a dormant domestic market was what led farmers like Manie Malan to take up the challenge. Unfortunately for them, the KWV restricted the access of wine merchants to wine spirit and competed with independent producers on the British market. When war broke out in 1939, the period of optimism came to a definitive end. Whereas quality producers in Constantia and Stellenbosch wished to be left free to find their own market, the failure of the KWV to address the reality of overproduction culminated in an extension of its powers to cover 'good wine' in 1940. This was resisted by the quality producers and merchants, who feared systematic discrimination in favour of the producers of the most basic wine. It ultimately came down to a political decision on the part of the Smuts government at a moment of national crisis. His administration agreed to extend regulation to cover 'good wine' despite the indifferent track record of the KWV. In part, Smuts wanted to mollify the distilling wine farmers and in part he wanted to dodge the burden of asserting direct state control.

(3) 1950s to mid-1960s. Although the KWV was empowered to act across a broad front, it took some years for the regulatory pieces to be assembled. Minimum pricing came in early, but it took more time to roll out the quota system because the KWV wanted to avoid antagonizing farmers in the outlying districts and improved market conditions made intervention less urgent. The breathing space coincided with a sustained period of innovation, which resulted from a conjuncture between favourable economic circumstances and developments in oenology. On the one hand, the greater purchasing power of White consumers in the 1950s translated into an uptake of interest in white wines. On the other, there was a more nuanced understanding of how the temperature of the must during fermentation affected the bouquet of the wine. Technological improvements in the shape of temperature-controlled stainless-steel tanks made it possible, for the first time, to produce white wine of a much higher and more reliable quality, and on a truly industrial scale. The KWV continued to accuse the merchants of price gouging and pursuing a strategy of vertical integration that was inimical to the interest of the farmers. But there is no doubt that it was the firms, most notably SFW and Distillers, that actively pursued improved standards of production in close collaboration with the farmers they worked with. But the costs of installing new equipment also provided a spur to the resurgence of the cooperatives, which established new cellars with concessionary loans. This had important long-term consequences because it converted many more farmers into grape growers and further narrowed the ranks of independent producers. Nevertheless, the Lieberstein revolution represented a moment of high optimism as White consumers, both male and female, became the focus of targeted advertising and emerged as committed wine drinkers for the first time. This boom continued well into the

1960s, when the deracialization of the liquor laws promised to unlock a more capacious domestic market.

(4) Late 1960s–mid-1970s. In short order, there was a parallel development with respect to red wines, the sudden fashion for which caught almost everybody by surprise. Much of the initiative was taken by independent producers, most of whom belonged to CEWPA, who aspired to bottle and sell their own products. It was out of a desire to connect with the discerning wine drinker that Spatz Sperling, Frans Malan and others pioneered the establishment of the Stellenbosch Wine Route, which proved so successful that the cooperatives also came on board. The initial response of the firms was to sever their links, but they subsequently realized that there was more to be gained from making concessions. Following the construction of the Bergkelder, Distillers was able to offer access to its maturation facilities as well as its marketing channels for farmers who agreed to remain part of its stable. Crucially, the introduction of the WO system made it possible to market wines with reference to geographical origin. No less importantly, the firms were also able to secure exceptions to the rules governing estate wines, rendering it possible for estate producers to make use of the Bergkelder label. At the same time, the firms made the first concerted efforts to target the potentially vast Black consumer market. It is here that some legacies of racial readings of consumption were most starkly apparent. Companies like SFW pitched some products at segments of the Black market, but ultimately failed to invest sufficient resources to compete with what SAB was rolling out for beer. Because SAB owned SFW, some of the glitter should have rubbed off, but in reality SFW was detached from its parent company and reaped none of the benefits of association. Whereas beer sales soared, wine sales turned out to be disappointing.

In the scientific field, particular innovations contributed to the marked improvement of red wines. A greater understanding of the benefits of malolactic fermentation was part of what lay behind the success of the Bergkelder. Equally, the ageing of red wines in small oak barrels was credited with the improved quality of red wines on a farm like Meerlust. However, the scientific community also became divided in the late 1960s over what needed to be done to bring the vineyards up to scratch. Although the approval and release of cultivars was a carefully managed process, it did not prevent viruses from revealing themselves. Whereas researchers and students had traditionally spent time in Geisenheim, collaborations with the University of California–Davis and French institutions became more important. The disagreement about whether it was preferable to concentrate on eradicating viruses or to import new European clones was eventually resolved through a compromise. But it was not one that made the planting materials available any quicker. This ultimately led all the major players to subvert the system by smuggling vines from Europe, which came to a head in the Chardonnay scandal of 1986.

Table C.1. *Area in hectares under vines (wine only) and total wine production (thousand hl.), 1961–2020*

Year	1961	1975	1981	2000	2020
Area under Vines	57,869	109,526	103,773	93,656	92,005
Total Wine Production	3,186	6,939	7,595	6,945	10,385

Source: KWV Annual Vineyards statistics; *Statistics Survey* No. 12, 1988.

Meanwhile, other problems were accumulating within the bureaucratic field. Whereas there was initially a period of wine shortage, this changed as more vines were planted. The KWV solution to overproduction was the quota system that eventually set a production limit on each farm, based on historic levels. In theory, the system would be flexible enough to allow production levels to increase in line with demand, but in practice it created multiple distortions. Fundamentally, the quota system did not prevent a substantial increase in new plantings. On the contrary, the vineyard area expanded greatly during the height of regulation, as Table C.1 demonstrates. What the system did ensure, however, was that vines could not be planted in the cool-climate zones like the Hemel-en-Aarde Valley, which were more likely to be conducive to superior quality. Moreover, the relatively narrow gap between the minimum prices prescribed for distilling and drinking wine meant that grape producers and smaller farmers had no financial incentive to pursue quality. Inevitably, the declared surplus went up, which obliged the KWV to resort to ever more ingenious strategies of draining the distilling wine lake. By the 1980s, the regulatory system began to come apart at the seams as cooperatives offloaded wine in basic containers at below the minimum price. This killed the market for standard-priced wines and led firms like the SFW to begin diversifying in the direction of spirits. Once advertising budgets were slashed, targeting the Black consumer market through advertising was effectively abandoned altogether.

(5) Mid-1990s–the present. The fifth period of innovation began in the mid-1990s and continued in a discontinuous fashion through to roughly 2008 when the global financial crisis struck. The abrupt end of the KWV system, and renewed access to global markets, facilitated a shift towards quality production on the part of private cellars. The relentless drive towards experimentation with cultivars and the probing of new sites of production was tempered only by the tight profit margins. Deprived of the safety net that surplus disposal had afforded, the cooperatives variously folded, were bought out or reconstituted themselves as producer cellars. While SFW and Distillers (and then Distell after the full merger) turned to spirits and RTD products, a whole host of export-oriented firms sought to create economies of scale based on cutting deals with producer cellars and grape growers.

After 2012, the area under vine plummeted, but the average farm size increased, and overall production levels bounced back to pre-crisis levels. Meanwhile, independent producers either turned to creating terroir-based wines pitched at much higher price points or set about establishing distinctive brands based on some combination of grapes that came from their own farms and others that were sourced from further afield. The spectrum included boutique wineries that sourced their grapes from growers who in a bygone era would have supplied the cooperatives. At the same time, all the actors were required to simultaneously adjust to the requirements of B-BBEE and the increasingly stringent ethical and sustainability guarantees that overseas buyers (such as supermarket chains) demanded. In the second decade of the millennium, fresh challenges emerged in the shape of a recurrence of drought that underlined the urgency of responding proactively to climate change. Innovation has increasingly focused on more effective water management, the removal of alien plant species and experimentation with southern European cultivars that are considered to be less water-dependent and more resistant to drought. In the process, climatological science has become an increasingly visible accompaniment to viticulture and oenology in the scientific armoury.

It is worth pondering what industry leaders of an earlier era might have made of these long-term trends. In the second decade of the twentieth century, C. W. H. Kohler had concluded that equitable outcomes would be impossible without a measure of regulation. But after the 1990s, deregulation benefited many growers who sold their best grapes to producers of quality wines, most notably in the Swartland. The fact that so much of this wine found an overseas market demonstrated the enormous potential that lay in pursuing an export strategy, a point that Cuthbert Burgoyne and André Simon would no doubt have appreciated.[4] Nor was there an inexorable drive towards monopoly. There was fierce competition amongst new entrants in the new millennium but, if anything, the wine sector was less monopolistic than it had been in the 1970s. However, it is undeniable that overseas supermarket chains were able to drive extremely hard bargains, which kept smaller producers teetering on the margins of unprofitability. If Kohler mostly got it wrong, Perold was certainly vindicated in his view that there were many European cultivars that would do well in South Africa, provided they were planted in the right places and accorded the appropriate degree of care and attention. Spatz Sperling, Frans Malan and their colleagues were equally justified in thinking that independent producers would benefit from bottling and marketing their own wine.

[4] There is evidence to suggest that exports have historically been the driver of production. Nick Vink, Willem H. Boshoff, Johan Fourie and Rossouw van Jaarsveld, "Wine cycles in South Africa", *Journal of Wine Economics* 13 (2), 2018.

And, finally, Hamilton Russell was certainly proved correct about the quality dividend that would follow from planting premium cultivars like Pinot Noir and Chardonnay in cool climate zones.

Going global has clearly had a transformative effect on the wine industry. But within South Africa, one historic legacy continues to cast a long shadow, and that is race in its many (dis)guises. South Africa was unique in the modern world for its reliance on slavery and the forms of quasi-bonded labour that followed emancipation. Consequently, the wine sector became heavily dependent on Coloured manual labour, while farmworkers consumed much of the cheap wine that resulted. The vicious circle of alcoholism in the Cape winelands reproduced a host of other social ills and contributed greatly to the negative image associated with wine to this day. By stark contrast, restrictive liquor legislation prevented Black South Africans from acquiring a taste for wine, unlike in the neighbouring Portuguese colonies. Black politicians in the ANC and their White counterparts in the South African Party (SAP), National Party (NP) and United Party (UP) agreed on very little in the first half of the twentieth century, but they generally subscribed to the view that alcohol posed a threat to the moral fibre and well-being of the majority of the population. Theophilus Schreiner, D. F. Malan and Julius Malema make for unlikely bedfellows, but they each construed wine through the prism of race.

There are some signs that wine is gathering interest amongst Black consumers, as the recent successes of the Soweto Wine Festival and the *Four Cousins* brand attest to. Fledgling Black wine businesses were the most heavily affected by the COVID restrictions, but this may prove to be a temporary setback. Moreover, it seems likely that a new crop of young Black and Coloured winemakers will be amongst those driving innovation in the years to come. The message that one does not need to be White and bearded to make wine – or indeed to be able to judge and comment with confidence on the merits of what is in the glass – is one that is steadily gaining traction. Over the coming decades, this is likely to make a significant contribution to erasing both the negative image and the mystique surrounding wine. Normalizing wine is surely the key to increasing its appreciation and repositioning it as something other than just another form of cheap alcohol. A real breakthrough is only likely to happen when wine is democratized at every level – from the structures of production and channels of distribution to the simple pleasures of consumption. But much will also depend on how wealth is distributed in the coming decades. Putting it simply, wine will only really become the drink of the many when the multitude of ordinary South Africans can actually afford to buy it.

Bibliography

Primary Sources

Official Documents

Parliamentary Debates and Select Committees

Unie Van Suid-Afrika, *Verslag van die Gekose Komitee oor die Kontrole oor Wyn en Spiritualieë Wysigingswetsontwerp* (Cape Town: Cape Times, 1940) [SC 7-'40].

Unie Van Suid-Afrika, *Debatte Van Die Volksraad* (Cape Town: Cape Times, Parliamentary Printers), various years.

Union of South Africa, *Debates of the House of Assembly* (Cape Town: Cape Times, Parliamentary Printers), various years.

Commissions of Enquiry and Reports

Cape Colony, *Report of the Select Committee Appointed to Consider the Wine Trade Papers* (Cape Town, 1860).

Cape of Good Hope, *Report of the Select Committee Appointed to Consider and Report on the State of the Wine Trade* (Cape Town, 1865).

Cape Government Notice No. 783, "Report on the Cape Vines", 9 June 1880.

Cape of Good Hope, *Preliminary Report of the Phylloxera Commission 1893, Quarantine Regulations, with Proceedings, Minutes of Evidence and Appendix* (Cape Town, 1893).

Report by C. H. Kohler to Chairman of the Government Liquor Commission, 1931, reprinted in Wine and Spirit, May 1932 [Report by C. H. Kohler to Liquor Commission].

Union of South Africa, *Commission of Enquiry Regarding* [*the*] *Cape Coloured Population on the Union* (1937).

Union of South Africa, *Report of the Wine Commission* (Pretoria: Government Printer, 1937) [U.G. No. 25, 1937].

Union of South Africa, *Report of the Cape Coloured Liquor Commission of Inquiry* (Pretoria: Government Printer, 1945) [U.G. No. 33, 1945].

Union of South Africa, *Report of the Commission of Enquiry on the General Distribution and Selling Prices of Liquor*, May 1960 [Malan Commission], unofficial translation prepared and issued by the Western Province Bottle Store Keepers Association.

Republic of South Africa, *Report of the Commission of Enquiry into the Cultivar Purity and Illegal Importation of Certain Vine Propagating Material* [Klopper Commission] (Pretoria: Government Printer, September 1986).

Republic of South Africa, "Land Distribution for Agricultural Development", www.nda.agric.za/docs/Policy/redistribution.htm, accessed 14 March 2022.

"Confidential Preliminary Report to the Registrar of Co-operatives: Assets of the KWV" (D. G. Steyn, Appointed Inspector), 31 January 1997.

"Investigation into the Affairs of the Ko-operatiewe Wynbouwersvereniging van Suid-Afrika Beperk in terms of Section 13 of the Co-operatives Act Number 91 of 1981", combined report of Inspectors, July 1997.

"Agreement Entered into between the Minister for Agriculture and KWV (Proprietary) Limited", document dated 17 December 1998.

Department of Agriculture, *Report of the Committee of Inquiry into the Marketing Act* (Pretoria: National Department of Agriculture, 1992).

Republic of South Africa, *Report of the Committee to Investigate Regulation of the Wine and Distillation Committee* [Kassier Committee], 1 February 1997 (Pretoria, 1997).

National Agricultural Marketing Council, *The Impact of Deregulation on the South African Wine Industry*, NAMC Section 7 Committee Report (NAMC, 2002).

Republic of South Africa, *Nomination of the Cape Floral Region for Inclusion on the World Heritage List* (Pretoria, 2003).

Department of Agriculture, *Forestry and Fisheries, A Profile of the South African Wine Market Value Chain* (Arcadia: Directorate Marketing, 2011).

SAWIS, *Wine Industry Statistics*, multiple years.

Archives

Western Cape Archives [CA]

CA A517 "Wine Commission: Evidence Given before the Commission", Vols. I and II, Farmers and Farmers' Organisation, A-K, 1935.

CA A1696 'Women's Christian Temperance Union', File 98: Correspondence A-C (1913–1941), "A Brief History of the Women's Christian Temperance Union in South Africa" (Cape Town, 1925).

CA AGR 498 C.65 "Grape Juice and Most Konfyt (1909–1911)", "Golden Vintage" (pamphlet, 1909).

CA AGR 498 C.67 "Cape Wine Commission and Lord Blyth's Report on Cape Wine Industry" (1909).

CA AMPT PUBS C/1/2/1/149 "Annexures to the Votes and Proceedings of the House of Assembly: Report of a Commission of Enquiry into the Economic Condition of the Wine Districts of the Cape Colony" [G-47, 1909].

CSC 2/1/1/760 ref 120 "Illiquid Case. Henry John Cyster versus Rhodes Fruit Farms Ltd. Action for a Declaration of Rights" (1915).

CSC 2/1/1/1430 ref 623 "Interdict and Damages, Stellenbosch Farmers Winery (PTY) Ltd. versus Henry C. Collinson Ltd." (1942).

CSC 2/1/1/1430 ref 624 "Interdict and Damages Stellenbosch" (1942).

CSC 2/1/1/1430 ref 625 "Interdict, Stellenbosch Farmers Winery (PTY) Ltd. Versus E.K. Green and Co. Ltd." (1942).

Pretoria Archives

TS 18/11 Vol. 1: "Wine Industry".

University of Stellenbosch Document Centre

"Echo from the Past – Extract from an Address by the Hon. D.F. Malan, Stellenbosch 1912", Stellenbosch University Document Centre.

Distell Archive, Stellenbosch

Boereboeke (SFW), various years.
"Bols Brandy Superstar Show (1980)".
"Brand Marketing Plan 1984/85: Chateau Libertas" (SFW).
"Brand Plans 1982" (SFW).
"Brand Plans 1984" (SFW).
"Distell: Report on Competition, January 2002" (unpublished).
"Distillers Corporation versus S.A. Breweries".
Distillers papers (various).
"Files of Phillip Myburgh".
Guard Books, various years.
"The House of Sedgwick" (unpublished typescript, 1951).
"Interview with Wally Sterry, Glencairn, 14 July 1982" (transcript).
"K.W.V. neem afskeid van Mnr. Frank Myburgh, vader van Witzenberg", 21 March 1944 newspaper clipping in Phillip Myburgh papers, Distell Archive.
"Market Research" (SFW).
"Martell 1971" (Green Book), "Lieberstein, 1970/71".
"Merger questions and answers: questions employees are likely to ask", Yellow file on Merger.
"Names and Label Designs".
"Paarl Perlé Litigation".
"Sales Letters, 1951–1962".
SFW publicity files.
"SFW sponsors NTA", *eSpontini* (official organ of the National Tavern Association).
"Stellenbosch Farmers' Winery Annual Review, 1987" (compiled by Dave Hughes).
Venter, Chris, *History of Die Bergkelder*, unpublished and undated manuscript.
"Pongracz", unpublished manuscript, 2008.
The Story of Zonnebloem Wines, unpublished manuscript, 2010.

Private Papers and Farm Records

Rev. A. J. Cooke: private papers in possession of A. T. McCutcheon.
Tim Hamilton Russell: private papers shared with author.
Joostenberg (Stellenbosch): farm records.
Rustenberg (Stellenbosch): Winemakers' diaries.

Unpublished Memoirs

Back, Phyllis (ed.) *Sydney Back, 70 Years of My Life, 1926–1996*, unpublished document (Klapmuts, 1996).

The Memoirs of "Spatz Sperling", 19 July 2005 (unpublished manuscript). Available online at www.delheim.com/wp-content/uploads/2019/05/The_Memoirs_of_Spatz_Sperling.pdf, accessed 24 July 2023.

Van Zyl, Diko, *Frans Malan Van Simonsig: Visionêre Baanbreker en Leier in die Moderne Suid-Afrikaanse Wynbedryf en Landbougemeenskap* (2002).

Newspapers and Magazines

Cape Argus
Cape Times
Platter's South African Wine Guide
White Ribbon
The Wine Press
Wine and Spirit
Wine, Spirit and Malt
Wynboer

Interviews

Wayne Gabb, Lomond Wines, Gansbaai, 24 August 2006
Anthony Hamilton Russell, Hamilton Russell Vineyards, Hemel-en-Aarde Valley, 25 August 2006
Tim Hamilton Russell, Hermanus, 29 August 2006
Simon Barlow, Rustenburg, Stellenbosch, 30 August 2006
Paul Cluver Jnr, Paul Cluver Wines, Elgin, 31 August 2006
Achim Von Arnim, Haute Cabrière, Franschhoek, 5 April 2007
Jan "Boland Coetzee", Vriesenhof, Stellenbosch, 12 April 2007
Peter Finlayson, Bouchard Finlayson Wines, Hemel-en-Aarde Valley, 13 April 2007
Charles Back, Fairview, Stellenbosch, 17 April 2007
Danie De Wet, KWV offices, Paarl, 17 April 2007
Johan Malan, Simonsig, Stellenbosch, 18 April 2007
Jan "Boland" Coetzee, Vriesenhof, Stellenbosch, 19 April 2007
Spatz Sperling, Delheim, Stellenbosch, 20 April 2007
Hannes Myburgh, Meerlust, Stellenbosch, 6 August 2007
Norma Ratcliffe, Warwick, Stellenbosch, 7 August 2007
Kallie Hickman, SAWIS offices, Paarl, 16 January 2009
Philip Van Zyl, editor of *Platter's South African Wine Guide*, Stellenbosch, 21 February 2009
Phillip Myburgh Snr., former Progressive Federal Party (PFP) Member of Parliament and wine farmer, Joostenberg, Stellenbosch, 26 February 2009
Lindsay Hunting, Slaley, Stellenbosch, 7 March 2009
Martin Hunting, Stellenboscch, 7 March 2009

Bennie Howard, Stellenbosch, 17 March 2009
Giorgo Dalla Cia, Stellenbosch, 17 March 2009
Lourens Jonker, Weltevrede, Bonnievale, 20 March 2009
Francis Naughton, Constantia, 24 March 2009
Dave Hughes, Stellenbosch, 25 March 2009
François Malan, Simonsig, Stellenbosch, 24 July 2009
Braam Van Velden, Overgauuw, Stellenbosch, 11 August 2009
Johann Krige, Kanonkop, Stellenbosch, 17 August 2009
Günther Brözel, Somerset West, 18 August 2009
Francois Naudé, Stellenbosch, 31 August 2009
Nicky Krone, Twee Jonge Gezellen, Tulbagh, 28 September 2009
Abrie Bruwer, Springfield, Robertson 16 October 2009
Danie de Wet, De Wetshof, Robertson, 16 October 2009
Freddie de Wet, Excelsior, Robertson, 17 October 2009
Pietman Retief, Stellenbosch, 20 October 2009
André "Kraai" Van Niekerk, former Minister of Agriculture under Nelson Mandela's Government of National Unity, Stellenbosch, 23 October 2009
Neil Ellis, Stellenbosch, 29 October 2009
Danie Malan, Allesverloren, Riebeek Kasteel, 2 November 2009
Mark Solms, Solms-Delta, Franschhoek, 14 November 2009
Hans Stroebel, former Managing Director of SFW, Stellenbosch, 17 November 2009
Abie Konstabel, retired farm worker, Rustenberg, Stellenbosch, 18 November 2009
Corné Grobler, Spar Retail Operations Manager, Simonsrust Shopping Centre, Stellenbosch, 2 December 2009
Riaan Kruger, former Executive Director of CWSI, Stellenbosch, 2 December 2009
Matthew Cyster, Pniël, 17 December 2009
Francis "Duimpie" Bayly, Stellenbosch, 17 February 2011
Farmworkers, Solms-Delta, Franschhoek, 9 December 2011
Riaan De Waal, Darling Cellars, Darling, 23 January 2015
Adi Badenhorst, Badenhorst Family Wines, Kalmoesfontein, 11 February 2015
Andrea Mullineux, Mullineux and Leeu Wines, Franschhoek, 23 February 2015
Johan Reyneke, Reyneke Wines, Stellenbosch, 14 August 2019
Charles Back, Fairview, Paarl 15 August 2019
Francis "Duimpie" Bayly, Stellenbosch, 15 August 2019
Kevin Grant, Ataraxia, Hemel-en-Aarde Valley, 19 August 2019
Phillip Retief, Van Loveren, Robertson, 19 August 2019
Bevan and Gordon Newton Johnson, Newton-Johnson Family Vineyards, Hemel-en-Aarde Valley, 20 August 2019
Paul Cluver Snr., Paul Cluver Wines, Elgin, 20 August 2019
David Sadie, David and Nadia Wines, Malmesbury, 21 August 2019
Eben Sadie, Sadie Family Wines, Malmesbury, 21 August 2019
Riandri Visser, Cape Point Vineyards, Noordhoek, 22 August 2019
Billy Hughes, Nativo wines, Cape Town, 23 August 2019

Secondary Literature

Books

Adendorff, Ruby, *Alkohol – Wat Dit is en Wat Dit Doen* (Paarl: WCTU, 1946).
Anderson, Kym and Pinilla, Vicente (eds.), *Wine Globalization: A New Comparative History* (Cambridge: Cambridge University Press, 2018).
Ashforth, Adam, *The Politics of Official Discourse in Twentieth-Century South Africa* (Oxford: Clarendon Press, 1990).
Atkin, Tim, *South Africa 2014: Special Report* (author, 2014).
Barrows, Susanna and Room, Robin (eds.), *Drinking Behavior and Belief in Modern History* (Berkeley, Los Angeles and Oxford: University of California Press, 1991).
Baumgartner, A., *The First 35 Years of Distillers Corporation (SA) Limited within the Oude Meester Group* (Stellenbosch: Distillers Corporation, undated).
BAWSI, *Farmworker Voices: Reflections of Worker Conditions on South African Farms* (Western Cape Sample Study) (Paarl: BAWSI, 2011).
Bickford-Smith, Vivian, *Ethnic Pride and Racial Prejudice in Victorian Cape Town: Group Identity and Social Practice, 1875–1902* (Cambridge: Cambridge University Press, 1995).
Biermann, Barrie, *Red Wine in South Africa* (Cape Town: Buren, 1971).
Bird, William, *State of the Cape of Good Hope in 1822* (London: John Murray, 1823).
Bittner, Steven, *Whites and Reds: A History of Wine in the Lands of Tsar and Commissar* (Oxford: Oxford University Press, 2021).
Blackwell, Leslie, *Blackwell Remembers: The Memoirs of the Hon. Leslie Blackwell Q.C., M.C.* (London: Howard Timmins, 1971).
Bohling, Joseph, *The Sober Revolution: Appellation Wine and the Transformation of France* (Ithaca, NY and London: Cornell University Press, 2018).
Bolsman, Eric H., *Bertrams Guide to South African Wines of Origin* (Cape Town: Bertrams, 1976).
Briggs, Asa, *Wine for Sale: Victoria Wines and the Liquor Trade, 1860–1984* (Chicago: University of Chicago Press, 1985).
Campbell, Gwynn and Guibert, Nathalie (eds.), *Wine, Society and Globalization: Multidisciplinary Perspectives on the Wine Industry* (New York: Palgrave, 2017).
Cloete, Bettie, *Die Lewe van Senator F.S. Malan (President van die Senaat)* (Johannesburg: Afrikaanse Pers-Boekhandel, 1946).
Conningarth Economists, Final Report – Macro-Economic Impact of the Wine Industry on the South African Economy (Also with Reference to the Impacts on the Western Cape) (Pretoria: Conningarth Economists, 2015).
Conrad, Sebastian, *What Is Global History?* (Princeton, NJ and Oxford: Princeton University Press, 2016).
Crosby, Alfred W., *Ecological Imperialism: The Biological Expansion of Europe, 900–1900* (Cambridge: Cambridge University Press, 2004).
Cyster, Lot, Cyster, Matthew, Damon, Eleanor and Simpson, Freddie, *Pniël en sy Mense* (Pniël: authors, 2008).

Demossier, Marion, *Wine Drinking Culture in France: A National Myth or a Modern Passion?* (Cardiff: University of Wales Press, 2010).

Burgundy: The Global Story of Terroir (New York: Berghahn Books, 2018).

Dommisse, Ebbe, *Anton Rupert: A Biography* (Cape Town: Tafelberg, 2013).

Dooling, Wayne, *Slavery, Emancipation and Colonial Rule in South Africa* (Scottsville: University of KwaZulu-Natal Press, 2007).

Dubow, Saul, *Apartheid, 1948–1994* (Oxford: Oxford University Press, 2014).

Evans, Ivan, *Bureaucracy and Race: Native Administration in South Africa* (Berkeley: University of California Press, 1997).

Fahey, David M., *Temperance and Racism: John Bull, Johnny Reb and the Good Templars* (Lexington: University of Kentucky Press, 1996).

Fridjhon, Michael, *The Penguin Book of South African Wine* (London: Penguin, 1992).

Fridjhon, Michael and Murray, Andy, *Conspiracy of Giants: The South African Liquor Industry* (Johannesburg: Divaris Stein Publishers, 1986).

Gale, George, *Dying on the Vine: How Phylloxera Transformed Wine* (Berkeley and Los Angeles: University of California Press, 2011).

Giliomee, Hermann, *The Afrikaners: Biography of a People* (London: C. Hurst, 2nd ed. 2011).

Gladstones, John, *Wine, Terroir and Climate Change* (Mile End: Wakefield Press, 2011).

Goldin, Ian, *Making Race: The Politics and Economics of Coloured Identity in South Africa* (London and New York: Longman, 1988).

Guy, Kolleen, *When Champagne Became French: Wine and the Making of a National Identity* (Baltimore: Johns Hopkins University Press, 2003).

Hancock, David, *Oceans of Wine: Madeira and the Emergence of American Trade and Taste* (New Haven, CT: Yale University Press, 2009).

Hannah, Lee, Roehrdanz, Patrick R., Ikegami, Makihiko, Shepard, Anderson V., Shaw, M. Rebecca, Tabor, Gary, Zhi, Lu, Marquet, Pablo A, and Hijmans, Robert J., "Climate change, wine and conservation", *PNAS* 110 (17) 2013.

Hannickel, Erica, *Empire of Vines: Wine Culture in America* (Philadelphia: University of Pennsylvania Press, 2013).

Harrison, Brian, *Drink and the Victorians: The Temperance Question in England* (London: Faber & Faber, 1971).

Heath, Elizabeth, *Wine, Sugar, and the Making of Modern France: Global Economic Crisis and the Racialization of French Citizenship, 1870–1910* (Cambridge: Cambridge University Press, 2014).

Herman, Agatha, *Practising Empowerment in Post-Apartheid South Africa: Wine, Ethics and Development* (London and New York: Routledge, 2018).

Hirson, Baruch, *Year of Fire, Year of Ash – The Soweto Revolt: Roots of a Revolution?* (London: Zed Press, 1979).

Human Rights Watch, *Ripe with Abuse: Human Rights Conditions in South Africa's Fruits and Wine Industries* (New York: Human Rights Watch, 2011).

Inglis, David and Almila, Anna-Mari (eds.), *The Globalization of Wine* (London: Bloomsbury Academic Press, 2019).

Itçaina, Xabier, Roger, Antoine and Smith, Andy, *Varietals of Capitalism: A Political Economy of the Changing Wine Industry* (Ithaca, NY and London: Cornell University Press, 2016).

James, Tim, *Wines of the New South Africa: Tradition and Revolution* (Berkeley, Los Angeles and London: University of California Press, 2013).

Joelson, Annette (ed.), *The Memoirs of Kohler of the K.W.V.: Politician, Traveller, Founder of the South African Wine Industry* (London: Hurst & Blackett, 1946).

Jones, Percy T. (ed.), *The Liquor Laws of the Colony of the Cape of Good Hope with Notes of Cases Decided Thereon* (Cape Town: Juta, 1907).

Jung, Courtney, *Then I Was Black: South African Political Identities in Transition* (New Haven, CT and London: Yale University Press, 2000).

Kenney, Henry, *Architect of Apartheid: H.F. Verwoerd, An Appraisal* (Johannesburg: Jonathan Ball Publishers, 1980).

Kenney, R. U., *Abraham Izak Perold: Wegwyser van ons Wingerdbou* (Cape Town Pretoria and Johannesburg: Human & Rousseau, 1981).

KWV, *Entertaining with Wine Course* (Paarl: KWV, September 1964).

Planning a Wine and Cheese Party (Paarl: KWV, 1967).

Some Aspects of the Functions of and Control Exercised by the K.W.V. (Paarl: KWV, 1969).

South African Wines of Origin (Paarl: KWV, undated).

Quota Control Survey (Paarl: KWV, 1988).

Wines of Origin (Paarl: KWV, undated).

Lachiver, Marcel, *Vins, vignes et vignerons: histoire du vignoble français* (Paris: Fayard, 1988).

Laferté, Gilles, *La Bourgogne et ses vins: imagine d'origine controlée* (Paris: Belin, 2006).

Latour, Bruno, *The Pasteurization of France* (Cambridge, MA and London: Harvard University Press, 1988).

Leipoldt, C. Louis, *300 Years of Cape Wine* (Cape Town: Stewart Publishers, 1952).

Common-Sense Dietetics (London: Williams & Norgate, 1911).

Lester, Alan, *Imperial Networks: Creating Identities in Nineteenth-Century South Africa and Britain* (London: Routledge, 2001).

Lilja, Fredrik, *Whip of the Vine: Labour Relations and the Role of Alcohol in Western Cape Wine Farming from the 1940s to the 2010s* (Malmö: Malmö University, 2019).

Loubère, Leo, *The Red and the White: A History of Wine in France and Italy in the Nineteenth Century* (Albany: SUNY Press, 1978).

The Wine Revolution in France: The Twentieth Century (Princeton, NJ: Princeton University Press, 1990).

Ludington, Charles, *The Politics of Wine in Britain: A New Cultural History* (Houndmills and London: Palgrave Macmillan, 2013).

Mager, Anne Kelk, *Beer, Sociability and Masculinity in South Africa* (Bloomington and Cape Town: Indiana University Press and University of Cape Town Press, 2010).

Matthews, Mark A., *Terroir and Other Myths of Winegrowing* (Oakland: University of California Press, 2015).

McCracken, J. L., *The Cape Parliament, 1854–1910* (Oxford: Oxford University Press, 1967).

McIntyre, Julie and Germov, John, *Hunter Wine: A History* (Sydney: NewSouth Publishing, 2018).

May, Peter F., *Pinotage: Behind the Legends of South Africa's Own Wine* (St. Albans: Inform and Enlighten, 2009).

(ed.) *A Year in Paarl with A.I. Perold: Vine and Experiments 1916* (St. Albans: Inform and Enlighten, 2011).

(ed.), *Perold's Papers, Vol. 1* (St. Albans: Inform and Enlighten, 2014).

Miles, J. D., *Die Drinkpatroon Van Die Bantoes in Suid-Afrika* (Pretoria: Departement van Onderwys en Wetenskap, 1964).

Murdock, Catherine Gilbert, *Domesticating Drink: Women, Men, and Alcohol in America, 1870–1940* (Baltimore and London: Johns Hopkins University Press, 1998).

Nugent, Paul, *Boundaries, Communities and State-Making in West Africa: The Centrality of the Margins* (Cambridge: Cambridge University Press, 2019).

Nye, John V. C., *War, Wine and Taxes: The Political Economy of Anglo-French Trade, 1689–1900* (Princeton, NJ and Oxford: Princeton University Press, 2007).

O'Meara, Dan, *Volkskapitalisme: Class, Capital and Ideology in the Development of Afrikaner Nationalism, 1934–1948* (Cambridge: Cambridge University Press, 1983).

Forty Lost Years: The Apartheid State and the Politics of the National Party, 1948–1994 (Johannesburg: Ravan Press, 1996).

Paul, Harry W., *Science, Vine and Wine in Modern France* (Cambridge: Cambridge University Press, 1996).

Parker, Thomas, *Tasting French Terroir: The History of an Idea* (Oakland: University of California Press, 2015).

Percival, Robert, *An Account of the Cape of Good Hope* (London: C. & R. Baldwin, 1804).

Perold, A. I., *Handboek oor Wynbou* (Stellenbosch: Pro-Ecclesia Drukkery, 1926).

A Treatise on Viticulture (St Albans: Inform and Enlighten, 2012 [London: Macmillan, 1927]).

Pinney, Thomas, *A History of Wine in America, Volume I: From the Beginnings to Prohibition* (Berkeley, Los Angeles and London: University of California, 1989).

Pinotage Association, *Guidelines for Pinotage Vineyards* (Stellenbosch: Pinotage Association, 2005).

Posel, Deborah, *The Making of Apartheid, 1948–1961: Conflict and Compromise* (Oxford: Oxford University Press, 1991).

Redding, Cyrus, *A History and Description of Modern Wines* (London: Henry G. Bohn, 3rd ed., 1851).

Regan-Lefebvre, Jennifer, *Imperial Wine: How the British Empire Made Wine's New World* (Oakland: University of California Press, 2022).

Robinson, Jancis, Harding, Julia and Vouillamoz, José, *Wine Grapes: A Complete Guide to 1,368 Wine Varieties, Including Their Origins and Flavours* (London: Allen Lane, 2012).

Ross, Robert, *Cape of Torments: Slavery and Resistance in South Africa* (London: Routledge & Kegan Paul, 1983).

Status and Respectability in the Cape Colony, 1750–1870: A Tragedy of Manners (Cambridge: Cambridge University Press, 1999).

Rushburne, J. L. and Hamman, H., *A Survey of the Liquor Industry in South Africa*, No. 7, July 1972 (Johannesburg: Statsinfom, 1972).

Schutte, G. J. (ed.), *Hendrik Cloete, Groot Constantia en die/and the VOC, 1778–1799* (Cape Town: Van Riebeeck Society, 2003).

Scott, James C., *Seeing Like a State: How Certain Schemes to Improve the Human Condition Have Failed* (New Haven, CT: Yale University Press, 1999).

Scully, Pamela, *The Bouquet of Freedom: Social and Economic Relations in the Stellenbosch District, South Africa, c1870–1900* (Cape Town: Centre of African Studies, University of Cape Town, Communications No. 17, 1990).

Liberating the Family? Gender and British Slave Emancipation in the Rural Western Cape, South Africa, 1823–1853 (Oxford: James Currey, 1998).

Shell, Robert, *Children of Bondage: A Social History of the Slave Society at the Cape of Good Hope, 1652–1838* (Hannover, NH and London: Wesleyan University Press, 1994).

Simon, André L., *In the Twilight* (London: Michael Joseph, 1969).

Simpson, James, *Creating Wine: The Emergence of a World Industry, 1840–1914* (Princeton, NJ and Oxford: Princeton University Press, 2011).

Smith, Andrew W. M., *Terror and Terroir: The Winegrowers of the Languedoc and Modern France* (Manchester: Manchester University Press, 2016).

South African Temperance Alliance, *Red die Kleurling Volk!* (Cape Town: SATA, 1937).

Stellenbosch Farmers Winery, *Die Natuurwyn-revolusie* (Stellenbosch: SFW, 1965).

Theron, C. J. and Niehaus, C. J. G., *Wine-Making*, Farmers' Bulletin, Series No. 130. Union of South Africa, Department of Agriculture [GPS 11337, 1947].

Thurmond, David L., *From Vines to Wines in Classical Rome: A Handbook of Viticulture and Oenology in Rome and the Roman West* (Leiden and Boston: Brill, 2017).

Torrès, Olivier, *The Wine Wars: The Mondavi Affair, Globalisation and "Terroir"* (Houndmills: Palgrave Macmillan, 2006).

Tyrrell, Ian R. *Woman's World/Womans Empire: The Woman Christian Temperance Union in International Perspective, 1880–1930* (Chapel Hill: University of North Carolina Press, 2006).

Reforming the World: The Creation of America's Moral Empire (Princeton, NJ and Oxford: Princeton University Press, 2010).

Van der Merwe, Romi, *A Magic Blend: SFW 1925–2000, Its People, Products and Places* (Stellenbosch: SFW, 2000).

Van Duin, Pieter and Ross, Robert, *The Economy of the Cape Colony in the Eighteenth Century* (Leiden: Centre for the History of European Expansion, 1987).

Van Zyl, D. J., *Kaapse Wyn en Brandewyn, 1795–1860: Die Geskiedenis van Wynbou en Wynhandel in die Kaapkolonie* (Kaapstad: Hollandsch Afrikaansche Uitgevers, 1975).

KWV 75 Jaar (Paarl: KWV, 1993).

Van Zyl, Dine, *Prof. C.J. Theron, Pionier van ons Wybou* (Kaapstad: SFW, 1982).

Venter, J. D. *Die Drinkpatroon van die Blankes in Suid-Afrika* (Pretoria: Departement van Onderwys en Wetenskap, 1964).

Die Drinkpatroon Van die Kleurlinge in Kaapland en Natal (Pretoria: Departement van Onderwys en Wetenskap, 1965).

Viall, Jeanne, James, Wilmot and Gerwel, Jakes, *Grape: Stories of the Vineyards in South Africa* (Cape Town: Tafelberg, 2011).

Wallace, Robert, *Farming Industries of Cape Colony* (London: P. S. King & Son, 1896).

Warner, Charles K., *The Winegrowers of France and the Government since 1875* (New York: Columbia University Press, 1960).

WCTU, *The Women's Christian Temperance Union in South Africa 1889–1989* (Cape Town: WCTU, undated).

White, Owen, *The Blood of the Colony: Wine and the Rise and Fall of French Algeria* (Cambridge, MA and London: Harvard University Press, 2021).

Witz, Leslie, *Apartheid's Festival: Contesting South Africa's National Pasts* (Bloomington: Indiana University Press, 2003).

Worden, Nigel, *Slavery in Dutch South Africa* (Cambridge: Cambridge University Press, 1985).

Articles and Book Chapters

Anderson, Kym, "Australia and New Zealand", in Kym Anderson and Vicente Pinilla (eds.), *Wine Globalization: A New Comparative History* (Cambridge: Cambridge University Press, 2018).

Anderson, Kym and Pinilla, Vicente, "Global overview", in Kym Anderson and Vicente Pinilla (eds.), *Wine Globalization: A New Comparative History* (Cambridge: Cambridge University Press, 2018).

[Anon.], "Phylloxera in South Africa", *Bulletin of Miscellaneous Information* (Royal Botanic Gardens Kew) 18 (33) 1889.

[Anon.], "Agricultural education in Cape Colony: The Elsenburg College, a visit and some impressions", *The Agricultural Journal of the Cape of Good Hope* 22 (1) 1903.

[Anon.], "The wine farmers: anti-temperance crusade", *Cape Argus*, 9 September 1907.

[Anon.], "Wine farmer's demonstration: a great gathering", *Cape Times*, 15 April 1909.

[Anon.], "Trade notes: Wine Committee", *Wine and Spirit*, 1 November 1931.

[Anon.], "Wine farmers' conference", *Wine and Spirit*, January 1932.

[Anon.], "Trade notes: the new French Law of Viticulture and the wine trade of the 4th July, 1931", *Wine and Spirit*, February 1932.

[Anon.], "Trophy for the best wine: Stellenbosch farmer's achievement", *Die Burger*, 3 June 1932.

[Anon.], "The value of shows" (information), *Wine and Spirit*, October 1932.

[Anon.], "Catalogue for 1932 Wine Show", *Wine and Spirit*, November 1932.

[Anon.], "'Essay no. 4 on how to overcome and prevent the wine surplus', by B. Burger, De Hoop, Robertson 'on behalf of a number of wine farmers'", *Wine and Spirit*, November 1932.

[Anon.], "Editorial: ourselves in the world picture", *Wine and Spirit*, January 1933.
[Anon.], "Troubles of the wine co-operative: a leader of the Cape Times", *Wine and Spirit*, April 1934.
[Anon.], "Wine growers' great victory: great confidence in Co-operative Wine Growers' Association", *Wine and Spirit*, April 1934.
[Anon.], "Groot vergadering in Paarl besluit om Mnr. Rial Kloppers as KWV direkteur te ontstel", *Wine and Spirit*, May 1934.
[Anon.], "What is advertising", *The Wine Press*, IV (7) July 1948.
[Anon.], "Goodwill and the group", *The Wine Press*, date unclear 1948/49.
[Anon.], "Gelukwense aan N.C. Krone", *Wynboer*, September 1959.
[Anon.], "Droë wyn en verkoeling", *Wynboer*, January 1960.
[Anon.], "Oom Fanie Malan: 'n leeftyd in diens van die wynboere", *Wynboer*, February 1960.
[Anon.], "Coloured bar on station opposed", *Cape Argus*, 19 August 1960.
[Anon.], "Big study tour starts today: 84 to go on Distillers Corpn trip", *Rand Daily Mail*, 9 March 1962.
[Anon.], "A bag of wine please: Australian innovation has advantages for both domestic and export trade", *Wine, Spirit and Malt*, February 1966.
[Anon.], "Apartheid in retailing not realistic", *Wine, Spirit and Malt*, November 1967.
[Anon.], "Rembrandt expands into liquor", *Wine, Spirit and Malt*, November 1969.
[Anon.], "S.F.W. – Sedgwick Tayler state policy", *Wine Spirit and Malt*, September 1970.
[Anon.], "K.W.V. se nuwe droë rooi wyne" (editorial), *Wynboer*, January 1972.
[Anon.], "Superstar Richard: He's an ad man's dream", *Sunday Times*, 26 August 1972.
[Anon.], "Produksiekoste van wyndruiwe in die produksiejaar 1972/73", *Wynboer*, May 1974.
[Anon.] "Shebeens", *Wynboer*, July 1974.
[Anon.], "Suid-Afrika se landswyne onder die soeklig: 'n ontleding in al sy komponente", *Wynboer*, February 1977.
[Anon.], "Wine and shebeens in Soweto", *Wynboer*, October 1978.
[Anon.], "Die Stellenbosse Wynroete", *Wynboer*, November 1978.
[Anon.], "Intolerable monopoly: allow wine sales in supermarkets pleads KWV chief", *Star*, 22 November 1978.
[Anon.], "Burgundy-on-sea: the most southerly vineyard in South Africa", *Finance Week*, 25 February–3 March 1982.
[Anon.], "Wine industry: paying for growth", *Financial Mail*, 25 January 1984.
[Anon.], "KWV's 1983 profit tops 12 million", *Farmer's Weekly*, 22 June 1984.
[Anon.], "Pietman Hugo: KWV gets an A-team' leader", *Management*, August 1984.
[Anon.] "Catching the curve-ball questions", *Management*, August 1984.
[Anon.], "The thoughts of Tim Hamilton-Russell", *The Wine Press*, 9 September 1984.
Anon.], "The wine wenches taste Harslevelu", *Wynboer*, July 1985, pp. 56–58.
[Anon.], "KWV Plantverbeteringskema: bekendstelling van materiaal beskikbaar 1986", *Wynboer*, March 1986.
[Anon.], "Cape Crusader", *Wine*, March 1990.

[Anon.], "KWV: sprong deur verlede… die toekoms in", *Wynboer*, Mei 1991.

[Anon.], "Stellenbosch Farmers' Winery: stating as they are?", *Financial Mail*, 11 October 1991.

[Anon.], "Minimumprys bly sê Hugo by sy lasste Algemene Jaarvergadering", *Wynboer*, June 1994.

[Anon.], "Farm workers union Csaawu should be saved", *Mail and Guardian*, 17 November 2014, https://mg.co.za/article/2014-11-17-farm-workers-union-csaawu-should-be-saved.

[Anon.], "House of Mandela Wines: Q&A with Tukwini Mandela!", 8 November 2018, https://thesophisticatedlife.com/blog/house-of-mandela-wines/, accessed 25 February 2002.

[Anon.], "SA Legend Johann Krige", www.wosa.co.za/WOSA-News/Blogs/Cape-Chatter/SA-Wine-Legend-Johann-Krige/, accessed 22 May 2022.

Ashton, Robert H., "Reliability and consensus of experience wine judges: expertise within and between?", *Journal of Wine Economics* 7 (1) 2012.

Atkin, Tim, "South African wines worth fighting for", *The Guardian*, 7 January 2007, www.theguardian.com/lifeandstyle/2007/jan/07/foodanddrink1, accessed 24 March 2022.

"The Swartland Revolution", dated 8 August 2013, https://timatkin.com/the-swartland-revolution/, accessed 8 March 2022.

Baro, Joylean M., "A colonial hangover: big profits, massive exploitation in the Cape winelands", *Equal Times*, 1 July 2015, www.equaltimes.org/colonial-hangover-big-profits?lang=en#.XOsGhtNKgdU, accessed 26 February 2022.

Barth, Lothar, "Problems persist", *Liquor Store Monthly* (possibly 1991).

"50 years in the SA liquor industry – 1940 to 1990", *Liquor Store Monthly* (possibly 1991).

Basson, Rico, "The SA Wine Industry Strategic Exercise (WISE)", Cellar Conference, 6 August 2014, https://vinpro.co.za/Media/Default/Downloads/06_RBasson_SA_wine_industry_strategic_exercise.pdf, accessed 14 March 2022.

Biodynamic Organic Wine South Africa, https://biodynamicorganicwine.co.za/biodynamic-producers/, accessed 22 May 2022.

Booysen, Eugene, "Die NIWW: vinger op die pols van ons wynbedryf (2)" *Wynboer*, September 1985.

Boshoff, Willem H. and Fourie, Johan, "The significance of the Cape trade route to economic activity in the Cape Colony: a medium-term business cycle analysis", *European Review of Economic History* 14, 2010.

Bruwer, Johan, "South African wine routes: some perspectives on the wine tourism industry's structural dimensions and wine tourism product", *Tourism Management* 24, 2003.

Burgoyne, Alan H. M.P., "Colonial vine culture", *Journal of the Royal Society of Arts* 60 (3105), 1912.

BWI, "Biodiversity and Wine Initiative (BWI): stewardship within an industry context", dated December 2009, www.sanbi.org/wp-content/uploads/2018/04/2-stewardship-wine-industry-bwi.pdf, accessed 17 February 2022.

Carey, Victoria A., Saayman, D., Archer, E., Barbeau, G. and Wallace, M., "Viticultural terroirs in Stellenbosch, South Africa, I: the identification of Natural Terroir Units", *Journal International des Sciences de la Vigne et du Vin* 42 (4), 2008.

Carte, David, "KWV give-aways in bid to drain the lake", *Sunday Times*, 15 July 1984.

Cook, Rev. A. J., "The American experiment and its meaning for South Africa", in *The Drink Problem in South Africa: Addresses and Papers Delivered at the Local Option Congress Held at Cradock on December 5th and 6th, 1923* (Cape Town: SATA, 1924).

Cox, Major Leslie, "The Western Province of the Cape and its wine industry", in *Wine and Drunkenness: The Social Problem of the Day* (Cape Town: SATA, 1924).

Currin, Tamlyn, "Liquidation looms for showcase Cape estate", dated 6 September 2018, www.jancisrobinson.com/articles/liquidation-looms-for-showcase-cape-estate, accessed 22 February 2022.

Davids, Tracy, Vink, Nick and Cloete, Kandas, "COVID-19 and the South African wine industry", *Agrekon* 61 (2) 2022.

Demhardt, Imre Joseph, "Wine tourism at the 'Fairest Cape': post-apartheid trends in the Western Cape Province and Stellenbosch (South Africa)", in C. Michael Hunt (ed.), *Wine, Food and Tourism Marketing* (New York, London and Victoria: Haworth Hospitality Press, 2004).

Dooling, Wayne, "The decline of the Cape gentry, 1838–1900", *Journal of African History* 40, 1999.

"The making of a colonial elite: property, family and landed stability in the Cape Colony, c.1750–1834", *Journal of Southern African Studies* 31 (1) 2005.

Du Plessis, Cassie, "Farm labourer rights furore", *Wineland*, 1 October 2011.

Du Plessis, Stan, "Pearls worth Rds 4000 or less: reinterpreting eighteenth-century sumptuary laws at the Cape", Economic Research Southern Africa (ERSA) Working Paper No. 336, 2013.

Du Toit, Andries, "The micro-politics of paternalism: the discourses of management and resistance on South African fruit and wine farms", *Journal of Southern African Studies* 19 (2) 1993.

Du Toit, Andries, Kruger, Sandra and Ponte, Stefano, "Deracializing exploitation? 'Black Economic Empowerment' in the South African wine industry", *Journal of Agrarian Change* 8 (1) 2008.

Duguid, M. E., "Chairman's Address at Cape Province Convention by Mrs M.E. Duguid", *White Ribbon* 64 (1), November/December 1957.

Durr, Benjamin, "A toast to South Africa's black middle class", *Africa Renewal*, December 2013, www.un.org/africarenewal/magazine/december-2013/toast-south-africas-black-middle-class, accessed 8 June 2022.

Dutton, Jacqueline, "Geographical turns and historical returns in narrating French wine culture", *Global Food History* 5 (1–2), 2019.

Eckard, Rev. A. W., "Local option and the wine farmer", in *The Drink Problem in South Africa: Addresses and Papers Delivered at the Local Option Congress Held at Cradock on December 5th and 6th, 1923* (Cape Town: SATA, 1924).

Eggington, Shanaaz, "Sexwale's prize farm for sale", *Sunday Times*, 21 July 2013, www.pressreader.com/south-africa/sunday-times-1107/20130721/281672547552710, accessed 26 February 2022.

Estreicher, Stefan K., "A brief history of wine in South Africa", *European Review* 22 (3) 2014, pp. 515–516.

Ewert, Joachim Winfried, "A force for good? Markets, cellars and labour in the South African wine industry after apartheid", *Review of African Political Economy* 39 (132), 2012.

Ewert, Joachim and Du Toit, Andries, "A deepening divide in the countryside: restructuring and rural livelihoods in the South African wine industry", *Journal of Southern African Studies* 31 (2) 2005.

Fourie, Johan and Von Fintel, Dieter, "The dynamics of inequality in a newly settled, pre-industrial society: the case of the Cape Colony", *Cliometrica* 4, 2010.

"Settler skills and colonial development: the Huguenot wine-makers in eighteenth-century Dutch South Africa", *Economic History Review* 67 (4) 2014.

Fridjhon, Michael, "Monopoly: a tired vintage", *Business Day*, 20 April 2000.

"Stellenbosch – in need of an urgent re-think?", Winemag.co.za, 28 August 2019, https://winemag.co.za/michael-fridjhon-stellenbosch-in-need-of-an-urgent-re-think/, accessed 8 June 2022.

Garrett, Peter, "The Nederburg wine auction", *International Journal of Wine Marketing* 6 (1) 1994.

Giliomee, Hermann, "Western Cape wine farmers and the beginnings of Afrikaner nationalism, 1870–1915", *Journal of Southern African Studies* 14 (1) 1987.

Gontsana, Mary-Anne "Sesfikile, the women's winery", 14 July 2015, www.groundup.org.za/article/sesfikile-womens-winery_3116/, accessed 25 February 2022.

Goode, Jamie, "Recalling the burnt rubber controversy – what was the cause?", 3 August 2021, https://winemag.co.za/wine/opinion/jamie-goode-recalling-the-burnt-rubber-controversy-what-was-the-cause/, accessed 12 March 2022.

Gorfinkel, L. and Skelton, G., "Wheels of wine", *The Wine Press*, IV (7) July 1948.

Grundlingh, Albert, "'Are we Afrikaners getting too rich?': Cornucopia and change in Afrikanerdom in the 1960s", *Journal of Historical Sociology* 21 (2/3), September 2008.

Guelke, Leonard and Shell, Robert, "An early colonial landed gentry: land and wealth in the Cape Colony 1682–1731", *Journal of Historical Geography* 9 (3) 1983.

Guy, Kolleen, "Wine, champagne and the making of French identity in the Belle Epoque", in Peter Scholliers (ed.), *Food Drink, and Identity: Eating and Drinking in Europe Since the Middle Ages* (Oxford: Berg, 2001).

"Selling the French past, selling wine and erasing labor from *terroir*", *Global Food History* 5 (1–2) 2019.

Helfet, Arnold, "Wine tasting the lighthearted way", *Wynboer*, February 1975 (reprinted from *Cape Times*).

Henning, C. B., "A guide to the various wines and spirits produced in South Africa", in *South African Wines, Spirits and Liqueurs: A Handbook on Their Composition, Preparation and Serving* (Stellenbosch: Wine, Spirit and Malt, 1958).

Hogdson, Robert J., "An examination of judge reliability at a major U.S. wine competition", *Journal of Wine Economics* 3 (2) 2008.

IPW, "Manual for Farms", dated June 2020, www.ipw.co.za/content/manuals/MANUAL%20Farm%20FINAL%20June%202020.pdf, accessed 11 March 2022.

"Manual for wineries and bottling facilities", dated June 2020, www.ipw.co.za/content/manuals/IPW%20Manual%20Cellar%20June%202020%20FINAL.pdf, accessed 11 March 2022.
Jacobs, D. J., "Plantverbeteringskema bereik groot hoogtes", *Wynboer*, January 1973.
Jones, Muriel, "Roos liquor bill", *White Ribbon* XXXVIII (9), June 1928.
Knott-Craig, J. F., "Quo vadis? The K.W.V. after a quarter of a century", *Wine and Spirit*, July 1943.
Kobokoane, Thabo, "Punch-drunk KWV could be forced to settle with Hanekom", *Sunday Times/Business Times*, undated.
KWV, "New Year's message from Andre du Toit (chairman of the K.W.V.)", *Wynboer*, January 1971.
"New Year's message from André J. du Toit (chairman of the K.W.V.)", *Wynboer*, January 1972.
"Address by the Chairman of the KWV, Dr. André du Toit, on the Occasion of the 56th Annual General Meeting of Members on Tuesday 4 June 1974", enclosure to *Wynboer*, June 1974.
"Address by André Du Toit to 57th AGM of KWV, 3 June 1975" (supplement), *Wynboer*, June 1975.
"Address by the Chairman of the KWV, Dr. André du Toit at the Fifty-Ninth Annual General Meeting of Members on Tuesday 7 June 1977 at Paarl", *Wynboer*, July 1977.
"Address by the Chairman at the Annual Conference of Wine Farmers 27 November 1979", *Wynboer*, June 1979.
Leipoldt, C. Louis, "The medical aspect of the moderate consumption of alcohol", in *Wine and Drunkenness: The Social Problem of the Day* (Cape Town, 1924).
Letsoalo, Matuma, "Malema raps ANC leaders on race", *Mail and Guardian*, 28 August 2009, https://mg.co.za/article/2009-08-28-malema-raps-anc-leaders-on-race/, accessed on 23 January 2022.
Lizamore, Graham, "Wine industry in ferment over Cape farmer's attack", *The Argus*, 10 November 1989, p. 8.
Mace, J. E., "Venture into wine country ... Walker Bay", *Wynboer*, June 1975.
MacQuitty, Jane, "South Africa is struggling", *Times*, 9 April 2008, www.thetimes.co.uk/article/south-africa-is-struggling-3djt8bcd0jb, accessed 24 March 2022.
Malan, Frans, "Jaarverslag van Vereniging van Kaapse Landgoedwynprodsente: rede van F.J. Malan op die Jaarvergadering, 20 Mei 1970", *Wynboer*, June 1970.
Martens, Jeremy Creighton, "Conflicting views of 'Coloured' people in the South African Liquor Bill debate of 1928", *Canadian Journal of African Studies* 35 (2) 2001.
Matthews, Charlotte, "Lower profit and static turnover from Distell", *Business Day*, 21 August 2001.
"Distell lays off employees", *Business Day*, 22 August 2001.
Meloni, Giulia and Swinnen, Johan, "The political and economic history of vineyard planting rights in Europe: from Montesquieu to the European Union", *Journal of Wine Economics* 11 (3) 2016.
"Algeria, Morocco and Tunisia", in Kym Anderson and Vicente Pinilla (eds.), *Wine Globalization: A New Comparative History* (Cambridge: Cambridge University Press, 2018).

Mileham, Arabella, "South Africa must 'wake up' and stop selling bulk wine cheaper than water, Vinpro boss says", *The Drinks Business*, 17 January 2019, www.thedrinksbusiness.com/2019/01/south-africa-must-wake-up-and-stop-selling-bulk-wine-cheaper-than-water-vinpro-says/, accessed 17 February 2022.

Mills, Wallace G., "The roots of African nationalism in the Cape Colony: temperance 1866–1898", *International Journal of African Historical Studies* 13 (2) 1980.

Moseley, William G., "Farm workers, agricultural transformation, and land reform in Western Cape Province, South Africa", *Focus on Geography*, Summer 2006.

"Fair trade wine: South Africa's post-apartheid vineyards and the global economy", *Globalizations* 5 (2) 2008.

Myburgh, Frank W., "Through the wine country of France and Germany", reprinted from *Cape Times* 30th December 1933 and 4th January 1934 [copy at Distell Archive].

Myburgh, Phillip, "Frank Myburgh: a tribute from his son", *Wine and Spirit*, November 1945.

Naude, Rev. W. J., "The Bible and alcohol", in *The Drink Problem in South Africa: Addresses and Papers Delivered at the Local Option Congress Held at Cradock on December 5th and 6th, 1923* (Cape Town: SATA, 1924).

Niehaus, C. J. G., "South African sherries", *Wine and Spirit*, February 1937.

Nugent, Paul, "Do nations have stomachs? Food, drink and imagined community in Africa", *Africa Spectrum* 3, 2010.

"The temperance movement and wine farmers at the Cape: collective action, racial discourse, and legislative reform, c.1890–1965", *Journal of African History* 52 (3) 2011.

O'Donoghue, Terence P., "Wine from the Empire's oldest vineyards", in *Wine Book of South Africa* (Stellenbosch: Wine and Spirit, 1936).

Olsson, Lars, "Capital, market and labour in the Western Cape winelands c.1900: agricultural capitalism?", *International Review of Social History* 63 (1), 2018.

Payi, Bulelwa, "Solms-Delta workers left hungry as land deal sours", *Weekend Argus*, 5 September 2021, www.pressreader.com/south-africa/weekend-argus-sunday-edition/20210905/281801402071277, accessed 26 February 2022.

Perold, A. I., "The social aspect of the liquor problem", in *Wine and Drunkenness: The Social Problem of the Day* (Cape Town, 1924).

"The South African wine industry and overproduction", *Wine and Spirit: A South African Review*, no. 2, November 1931.

"Cape wines and their origin", *Wine and Spirit*, August 1932.

"Historical notes on the Cape wine industry", in *Wine Book of South Africa* (Stellenbosch: Wine and Spirit, 1936).

"Di wijnbou in Frankrijk en hier", in Peter F. May (ed.), *Perold's Papers, Vol. 1* (St. Albans: Inform and Enlighten, 2014).

Pilcher, Jeffrey M., "The globalization of alcohol and temperance from the gin craze to prohibition", in Carol Helstosky (ed.), *The Routledge History of Food* (London: Routledge, 2014).

Platter, John, "A barrel of trouble", in "Liquor, a Survey", supplement to *Financial Mail*, 26 October 1984.

"The Chardonnay furore", *Platter's Wine Times*, July 1985.
Pongracz, Desiderius, "Invoer en uittoets van nuwe wyndruifvariëteite", *Wynboer*, November 1970.
Ponte, Stefano, "The hidden costs of environment upgrading in global value chains", *Review of International Political Economy*, September 2022.
Ponte, Stefano and Ewert, Joachim, "Which way is 'up' in upgrading? Trajectories of change in the value chain for South African Wine", *World Development* 37 (10) 2009.
Rappoport, Simon, "Swartland: land of bread and wine", *Wynboer*, July 1978.
Regan-Lefebvre, Jennifer, "John Bull's other vineyard: selling Australian wine in nineteenth-century Britain", *Journal of Imperial and Commonwealth History* 45 (2) 2017.
Richter, Johannes, "SWB-Wynplan herdenk na 40 jaar", *Wineland*, September 2019.
Robinson, Jancis, "Young guns of Cape need ammunition", 11 April 2015, www.jancisrobinson.com/articles/young-guns-of-cape-need-ammunition, accessed 8 March 2022.
Ross, Robert, "The Cape of Good Hope and the world economy, 1652–1835", in Richard Elphick and Hermann Giliomee (eds.), *The Shaping of South African Society, 1653–1840* (London: Longman, 1980).
"The rise of the Cape gentry", *Journal of Southern African Studies* 9 (2) 1983.
Rossouw, André, "Drostdy, Suid-Afrika se eerste kooperatiewe wynkelder: van 'palmietsop' tot puikwyn", *Wynboer*, December 1975.
Schweitzer, Erwin, "How black farm workers become land and business owners: actors, resources, contexts and outcomes of Black Empowerment projects in the South African wine industry", *Stichproben* 15, 2008.
Scott-Hayward, R. L., "Slow fermentation makes finer wine", Wine News, supplement to *Wine and Spirit*, June 1965.
Scully, Pamela, "Liquor and labor in the Western Cape, 1870–1900", in Jonathan Crush and Charles Ambler (eds.), *Liquor and Labor in Southern Africa* (Athens: Ohio University Press, 1992).
Shanahan, Chris, "Australia and South Africa wines go head to head in South African Airways Wine Shield", 26 November 1995, https://chrisshanahan.com/articles/1995/australia-and-south-african-wines-go-head-to-head-in-south-african-airways-wine-shield/, accessed 1 May 2022.
Smith, Harvey, "Agricultural workers and the French wine growers revolt of 1907", *Past and Present* 79, 1978.
Solomon, Miss E. "Alcohol and the home", in *The Drink Problem in South Africa: Addresses and Papers Delivered at the Local Option Congress Held at Cradock on December 5th and 6th, 1923* (Cape Town: SATA, 1924).
South African Wine and Brandy Company (SAWB), "A strategic plan for the South African wine industry" (draft 2, July 2003), no page given, http://pmg-assets.s3-website-eu-west-1.amazonaws.com/docs/2003/appendices/030610sawbdraft.htm, accessed 24 July 2023.
Stern, Anne, "The protection of geographical indications in South Africa", in *Symposium on the International Protection of Geographical Indications: Cape Province 1999* (Geneva: World Intellectual Property Organization, 1999).

Swartland Independent Producers, "The core elements of a regional wine", https://swartlandindependent.co.za/values/, accessed 22 July 2023.

Theron, Karin, "Changes on origin terrain: more freedom for use of estate names – but 'estate wine' is another matter", *Wineland*, 1 November 2003.

Tyrrell, Ian, "Women and temperance in international perspective: the World's WCTU, 1880s–1920s", in Susanna Barrows and Robin Room (eds.), *Drinking Behavior and Belief in Modern History* (Berkeley, Los Angeles and Oxford: University of California Press, 1991).

Van Schalkwyk, J. "The medical aspect of the drink problem", in *The Drink Problem in South Africa: Addresses and Papers Delivered at the Local Option Congress Held at Cradock on December 5th and 6th, 1923* (Cape Town: SATA, 1924).

Vink, Nick. "The long-term consequences of agricultural marketing legislation in South Africa", *South African Journal of Economics* 80 (4) 2012.

Vink, Nick, Boshoff, Willem H., Fourie, Johan and Van Jaarsveld, Rossouw, "Wine cycles in South Africa", *Journal of Wine Economics* 13 (2), 2018.

Vink, Nick, Boshoff, Willem H., Williams, Gavin, Fourie, Johan and McLean, Lewis S., "South Africa", in Kym Anderson and Vicente Pinilla (eds.), *Wine Globalization: A New Comparative History* (Cambridge: Cambridge University Press, 2018).

Vink, N., Deloire, A., Bonnardot, V. and Ewert, J., "Terroir, climate change, and the future of South Africa's wine industry", paper for the pre-AARES conference workshop on The World's Wine Markets by 2030: Terroir, Climate Change, R&D and Globalization, Adelaide, 9 February 2010.

Visser, Wessel, "White settlement and irrigation schemes: CF Rigg and the founding of Bonnievale in the Breede River Valley, 1900–c.1953", *New Contree* 68, 2013.

"Water as agent for social change, 1900–1939: two case studies of developmental state approaches in establishing irrigation schemes", *Historia* 63 (2) 2018.

Weiss, Reg, "Oude Libertas: a fresh adventure in wine", *Wynboer*, November 1973.

"Red wine'72: the greatest – if you can get it", *Wynboer*, April 1974.

"The truth on wine labels", *Wynboer*, June 1974.

Wesgro, *Wine Fact Sheet*, March 2017 (Cape Town: Wesgro, 2000).

The Wine Industry in the Western Cape (Cape Town: Wesgro, 2000).

"Sector: Wine", March 2017.

Whalen, Philip, "'A merciless source of happy memories': Gaston Roupnel and the folklore of Burgundian terroir", *Journal of Folklore Research* 44 (1) 2007.

"'Insofar as the ruby wine seduces them': cultural strategies for selling wine in inter-war Burgundy", *Contemporary European History* 18 (1) 2009.

Williams, Gavin, "Black economic empowerment in the South African wine industry", *Journal of Agrarian Change* 5 (4) 2005.

"Importing Chardonnay: A South African political farce", American Association of Wine Economists, Working Paper No. 141, September 2013.

"Who, where and when were the Cape gentry?" *Economic History of Developing Regions* 28 (2) 2013.

"Slaves, workers and wine: the 'dop system' in the history of the Cape wine industry, 1658–1894", *Journal of Southern African Studies* 42 (5), 2016.

Winshaw, W. C., "The effect of Prohibition in America", in *Wine and Drunkenness: The Social Problem of the Day* (Cape Town, 1924).

Theses, Dissertations and Unpublished Papers

Bajwa, Uttam, "Frontier enterprise: immigrant winemaking in Mendoza, Argentina (1884–1914)", unpublished PhD thesis, Johns Hopkins University, 2012.

Bezuidenhout, François Anton, "South African producer/co-operative wineries", submitted in partial fulfilment of the Diploma of Cape Wine Master, 2014.

Brown, S. P., "An evaluation of the marketing strategies of good wine from selected co-operatives", unpublished paper, Durban, 1991.

Davidson, Neil, Ouane, Fayelle, Phillpotts, Christine, Thelwell, Aduke and Tung, Eric, "The South African wine cluster: microeconomics of competitiveness", Harvard Business School, Cambridge, MA, 2009.

Foxcroft, Mary-Lyn, "Growing the consumption of wine amongst emerging market consumers in South Africa", in partial fulfilment of the Cape Wine Master Diploma, January 2009.

Howard, Bennie, "Vader en Seun, Wingerd en Wyn: 'n Studie oor Vyf Families in die Wynbedryf", Cape Masters of Wine project, June 1983.

James, Tim, "Terroir and law: estates and single vineyards in South Africa's Wine of Origin scheme", submitted in partial fulfilment of the Cape Wine Masters Diploma, October 2000.

Kruger, Sandra, "A case-study of Fairtrade labelling and worker empowerment on two wine and fruit farms in the Western Cape", unpublished MPhil thesis, University of the Western Cape, 2008.

Le Riche, Yvonne, "Revolutionising Cinsaut", dissertation submitted to the Cape Wine Academy in partial fulfilment of the Diploma of Cape Wine Master, 2015.

Le Roux, E. G., "n Klimaatstreekindeling van die suid-wes Kaaplandse wynbougebiede", unpublished Masters thesis, University of Stellenbosch, 1974.

Malan, Marius, "Is the Swartland the new South African Wine hub?", submitted in partial fulfilment of the Diploma of Cape Wine Master, 2014.

Melck, Harold, "Strategy, vision and business transformation in the South African wine industry", submitted to the Cape Wine Academy in partial fulfilment of the diploma of Cape Wine Master, 2017.

McIntyre, Julie A., "A 'civilised' drink and a 'civilising' industry: wine growing and cultural imagining on colonial New South Wales", unpublished PhD thesis, University of Sydney, 2008.

McKinnon, June, "Women's Christian Temperance Union: aspects of early feminism in the Cape, 1889–1930", unpublished MA thesis, UNISA, 1995.

Nordestgaard, Simon Jonathan, "Phenolic extraction and juice expression during white wine production", unpublished PhD thesis, University of Adelaide, 2011.

Pearce, Jennifer, "The origins of the temperance movement in Cape Town in the 1880s", BA Hons. Long Essay, History Department, University of Cape Town.

Rayner, Mary, "Wine and slaves: the failure of an export economy and the ending of slavery in the Cape Colony, South Africa, 1806–1835", unpublished PhD thesis, Duke University, 1986.

Van Stappen, David, "Simon van der Stel en die uitbreiding van de Kaapkolonie, 1679–1699", unpublished PhD thesis, University of Ghent, 2007.
Weaver, Meryl, "The emergence of vine cultivation in cooler-climate viticulture areas in South Africa with specific reference to Elgin and Elim", submitted to the Cape Wine Academy in partial fulfilment of the Diploma of Cape Wine Master, 2006.
White, C. W., "The creation and development of a South African wine estate, the wines produced and the positioning thereof in the market place", unpublished report, February 2000.

Film

Angel, Nick (dir.), *Wine: Disc 3, The Future* (Oxford Film and Television for BBC director, 2009).
Nash, David and Mark-Brown, Samuel (dirs.) *A Seat at the Table: New Zealand's Wine Story* (Republic Films and Studio Nash, 2019).
Nossiter, Jonathan (dir.), *Mondovino* (Pathé, 2004).

Index

NB. Page numbers in bold indicate information found in tables

www.ingramcontent.com/pod-product-compliance
Lightning Source LLC
LaVergne TN
LVHW052030200926
848481LV00005B/1631
* 9 7 8 1 0 0 9 1 8 4 2 5 0 *